HOW TO BUILD SALES WITH MANUFACTURERS' AGENCIES

The Insider's Guide to Recruitment, Management, Evaluation, Training, and Compensation

Compiled and edited by

James J. Gibbons, President
Manufacturers' Agents National Association

A James Peter Book
James Peter Associates, Inc.

PRENTICE HALL
Englewood Cliffs, New Jersey 07632

Prentice-Hall International (UK) Limited, *London*
Prentice-Hall of Australia Pty. Limited, *Sydney*
Prentice-Hall Canada, Inc., *Toronto*
Prentice-Hall Hispanoamericana, S.A., *Mexico*
Prentice-Hall of India Private Limited, *New Delhi*
Prentice-Hall of Japan, Inc., *Tokyo*
Simon & Schuster Asia Pte. Ltd., *Singapore*
Editora Prentice-Hall do Brasil, Ltda., *Rio de Janeiro*

© 1989 *by*

Manufacturers' Agents National Association

23016 Mill Creek Road
Laguna Hills, CA 92654

10 9 8 7 6 5 4 3 2 1

Library of Congress Cataloging-in-Publication Data

How to build sales with manufacturers' agencies : the insider's guide
  to recruitment, management, evaluation, training, and compensation /
compiled and edited by James J. Gibbons.
      p.   cm.
  "A James Peter book."
  Includes index.
  ISBN 0-13-403007-9
  1. Manufacturers' agents—Handbooks, manuals, etc. 2. Sales
management—Handbooks, manuals, etc. 3. Success in business—
Handbooks, manuals, etc. I. Gibbons, James J.
  HF5422.H68 1989   88-27253
  658.8'1—dc 19   CIP

ISBN 0-13-403007-9

PRENTICE HALL
BUSINESS & PROFESSIONAL DIVISION
A division of Simon & Schuster
Englewood Cliffs, New Jersey 07632

Printed in the United States of America

How This Book Will Help You Sell Effectively Through Manufacturers' Agencies

Whether you have extensive experience working with sales agencies or are turning to this practical way of selling for the first time, this book will help you benefit immediately in the following ways:

- *Penetrate special markets quickly and cost effectively.* The best way to meet the demands of the specialized markets that are growing dramatically today is through a force of independent agencies. This comprehensive guide is your key to finding and working with the agents who know and sell to these markets.

- *Open new territories with zero fixed sales overhead.* The most profitable way to open and keep new territories steadily productive is with manufacturers' agencies. How to accomplish this is outlined in the practical experience of the manufacturers whose success stories are told in detail.

- *Run a cost-effective salesforce.* There is no comparison—the cost of using manufacturers' agencies is lower by far than the cost of selling with salaried salespeople. In this book, you will not only learn how to manage a successful salesforce but will discover the secrets of hundreds of manufacturers that have made, and continue to make, fortunes selling through manufacturers' agencies.

- *Make more money with the smaller customers that salaried salespeople tend to ignore.* Because agents spread the cost of sales over the number of principals they represent, they can afford to call on accounts that your highly paid employees seldom reach. Case histories give you step-by-step instructions on how to do it.

- *Market new products more effectively and more economically.* Too many good products and ideas never make it simply because selling with salaried salespeople make it too expensive to bring them to market. By using manufacturers' representatives, rather than salaried salespeople, you can introduce these products without putting a strain on your finances.

- *Compensate directly and immediately for variations in your sales volume.* It's just not practical to remain fully staffed all of the time. However, you must maintain regular sales contact or lose business to more aggressive competitors. Since agents are paid only when they make a sale, they can hold your sales costs constant relative to volume.

The Trend to Sales Agencies Continues

During the 1970s, the use of sales agencies increased by a phenomenal 21 percent. At the same time, the use of salaried salespeople declined by 14 percent. Current indicators show that this trend has accelerated and that sales agencies are considered by many top marketing people to be the most cost-effective way to reach just about any market.

In the pages that follow, you will find everything you need to tap this force. You'll find it in easy-to-read reports. You'll find the experience of thousands of manufacturers, who have been successful selling through agents, distilled to the point where the answers you want are right at your finger tips.

Since 1976, sales and marketing executives have turned to one source every month for practical help to find, select, appoint, and manage manufacturers' agencies. That source is *RepLetter*. Now, in this all-inclusive guide, you have instant access to all of this information. One hundred and twenty issues of *RepLetter* have been reviewed, carefully edited and updated, organized, and indexed to provide you with the most practical tools you need to sell successfully with sales agencies.

Because this book is based on short reports published in *RepLetter*, it will not have the same continuity you'd find in standard book formats. The major advantage of this is that you can turn to the information you need right away—you don't have to wade through a lot of information that does not interest you. Keep in mind that many of the subjects covered have been written from several different perspectives and you may notice some minor overlap. The important thing, however, is that each report is complete—you'll get everything you need in each one.

Practical, Real-World Guidance on Every Page

RepLetter is not a rehash of the marketing theory you learned in college but is practical, authoritative, and to the point. It is the only publication in the field backed by the full resources of the oldest, largest, and most respected organization devoted entirely to selling through agents—the Manufacturers' Agents National Association (MANA). It's the only newsletter that publishes monthly case histories, how-to articles, interviews, and research reports in every issue.

With this book, you have all the information you'll need to help you sell successfully and economically.

Jim Gibbons

Contents

Testing: A word of caution
How many agencies should you have?
How to impress an agent you want on your team

5 MANAGING AGENCY TERRITORIES EFFECTIVELY / 140

Use the agencies in your own backyard
More agencies are selling for foreign companies—good or bad?
Competitive pricing must be universal
Why call reports are not appropriate for manufacturers' agents
How to discover if your company is in a "minor" classification
Kind words bring more in sales than threats
Use teamwork to seal a deal
Handling changes in lead time
New on the job? Tread carefully
Sign up major metro areas first for quick results
Can you have two agents in the same territory?
Select management people carefully
Holiday time? Notify your agencies
Demand plans for continuity from your agencies
Getting product knowledge into the field
Whose lines do your agents sell when traveling with you?
How to help your agents be familiar with your policies
Help new sales agents
Assign each agent an inside contact
How exit interviews with agents can be revealing
Planning your territory visits
Alert your agents when shortages occur
Why territorial visits are productive
Plan for the summer
Use agents to cover all territories, including home base
Sales quotas—Looking at a controversial question from both sides of the fence
A territory management system helps your sales agencies make the best use of their time
How to make winning buddy calls with your agents
Notify your customers immediately when you change agents
Encourage your agents to talk with each other
Selling through overseas agents
When you're tempted to shake up the team
Switching to agents? Make sure everybody is ready
What's wrong with unannounced visits to agents?
How to send non-salespeople into the field with your agents
It's time to review your second-in-command
How to help your successor take over the agency team
Think twice about splitting a territory
Expanding territory coverage
Two agents in the same territory?
A checklist for manufacturers who make trips with their agencies
Watch product mix when your agencies call on distributors
Pitfalls to avoid in the product path from agent to distributor to customer
Questions distributors ask agencies
How to deal with shifting markets
Setting sales goals for agencies
Territory management that helps agencies grow
Let your agents know where to reach you when you're away
How to help regional managers get their sales agencies' best efforts
How to handle the switch from direct sales to agency sales
How to handle unprofitable accounts
Sales agencies help you gain market penetration for a new business venture
Limit competition among your agencies
How to balance your control over your agencies
How to be an effective area sales manager

12 BUILDING BUSINESS WITH TRADE SHOWS / 295

13 CREATING EFFECTIVE ADVERTISING, PUBLICITY, AND CONTESTS / 304

14 PROVIDING SPECIAL HELP TO SALES AGENCIES / 339

15 BUILDING BUSINESS WITH PRACTICAL RESEARCH / 354

1

Strengthening Manufacturer/Agency Relations

Whether you're reading this book as a guide to setting up a new sales agency network or your goal is to strengthen a network you have, you'll find that the key ingredient in the manufacturer/agency relationship is understanding that it's a *partnership*. That is, your agents are fellow business people. You both have the same goal—to build sales and maximize profits.

The best agent, the best product, the best contract will not make the effort successful unless everyone in your firm understands and appreciates the agency method of selling. This means that not just your marketing, sales, and advertising people must be well versed in agency selling. It means that your technical, financial, management, and operational people must understand and work closely with your agencies, too.

In this first chapter, we have collected material from *RepLetter* that can help you strengthen this relationship from virtually every perspective. This is a sourcebook—the kind you turn to for fast answers. However, we strongly advise that you read everything in this first chapter, even if you have been working with sales agencies for years.

A GOOD REASON FOR USING
MANUFACTURERS' REPRESENTATIVES

A private study, recently released, showed employed salespeople to be distinctly unhappy with their role in the company. Too often, because of the lack of attention received, they move from company to company trying to gain recognition for what they consider to be an entrepreneurial effort.

Salespeople are convinced they use originality and considerable innovation to accomplish their objectives. They feel their managements don't appreciate their ingenuity and would like to be more involved in sales planning and strategy.

One offshoot of this dissatisfaction is a trend toward unionization of salespeople in some larger companies. This disturbing possibility could have negative effects on sales results, with seniority and all the other typical union demands undermining effectiveness.

> **➤ OBSERVATION** An agent is an entrepreneur, with no such concerns about receiving recognition. Commission checks are his recognition, and he can use them to satisfy whatever psychological satisfactions are important to him.

It was also pointed out in the study that the salespeople interviewed were less than enthusiastic about extra paper work, sales contests, quotas, and the cutting of sales territories. Again, smart sales managers need not resort to these stratagems to motivate their agent salesforce.

COMPULSORY RETIREMENT FOR AGENTS?

A leading manufacturer of fastener products has a mandatory retirement age for company personnel and has extended this to its agents.

Is this good business sense? Yes and no, depending upon the circumstances involved in each individual case.

> **➤ OBSERVATION** It stands to reason that past a certain age we all slow up a bit. However, a salesperson in his later years can slow up and still show more effectiveness in the marketplace than a bright newcomer. His years of experience and resultant relationships can bring him more business in 10 calls than a new salesperson can garner in 30 calls, but not forever. The new salesperson will learn from his mistakes, and over a period of time will also establish profitable relationships. In setting a retirement policy for manufacturers' agents, there is a solution that will allow a company to retain the irreplaceable value of a seasoned pro and gain the longevity and continuity a younger salesperson will provide.

A policy that appears to work to the benefit of the company and the agent is one that allows an individual to continue his representation beyond retirement age if, by that time, he has shown solid evidence of establishing his own program for agency continuity. There are many ways to accomplish this, and they all involve bringing in younger people. A son or daughter may be brought into the business, a younger employee hired, or a partnership formed with a younger partner.

Being young should not be the only criteria, however. The new person must be acceptable to the principals and must be allowed to service a substantial number of customers. This prevents the agent from making a token acceptance of the company's condition for the continuance of the agent's contract by hiring a short-term or weak employee.

It doesn't matter whether or not the new salesperson has a share of the business as long as he or she is learning the products, the business, and the territory.

However, for his own protection the agent should welcome a new partner. He can bind him to a no-compete clause—more effective in some states than others—and arrange for the gradual sale of the agency to the new person. If he is not fore-sighted enough to begin sharing his business with the younger person, he runs the risk of his business having no value when he fully retires, as the younger person can easily take over all the lines at no cost.

A retirement policy of this nature may even be the vehicle for forcing short-sighted agents to take steps to establish an estate that they might not have created if left to their own devices. Some people believe they're going to work and live forever.

STAR PERFORMERS SOMETIMES STRIKE OUT

As a sales manager, it's tempting to make a good impression on those field trips with your agents. One midwestern fastener sales manager would preside at agent-arranged seminars for engineers and toss out lowball figures on custom fasteners for interested engineers.

When inquiries were received and the quotes sent out, prices were always 30 to 40 percent higher than those quoted at the seminars, completely destroying the company's credibility (and the agent's, too).

Agents for this company complained loud and long about such practices, and after one or two seminars with the same results they resigned the account. Consequently, that company can no longer attract capable agents in many territories.

>>>→ *OBSERVATION* It pays to be honest when quoting prices or promising short deliveries of needed components. Not only does your company benefit from a better rapport with prospective customers, but you strengthen your agents' confidence in your firm. As the word gets around, you'll find more professional agents bidding for your line.

AGENT-CHANGERS ARE RUNNING INTO TROUBLE

An irritated purchasing agent of a large school furniture manufacturer says he can no longer keep track of which agents represent which companies, particularly in the particle board and hardware lines. His tendency is to try to stay with vendors who employ direct salespeople so that he is assured of continuity in communications and service.

Warning: Unfortunately, some industries seem to change agents indiscriminately and consequently find their new agents lacking in professionalism and sales ability—primarily because the word gets around in agent circles and top agents shy away from companies with known agency-changing habits.

It's hard to stay with agents who don't produce or show an interest in your company and its products. The safest strategy is to avoid this complication by conducting a thorough and exhaustive search when seeking new agents, regard-less of the expense. Contracting top agencies and staying with them will repay you many times over.

Once your company develops a reputation for changing agents, not only will you find it harder to get good ones, but you'll find your customers looking at you with a jaundiced eye and looking closer at your competition.

COMPOUNDING THE BENEFITS OF YOUR AGENCY SALES GROUP

Companies that are tied into one product or one product line have found a new strategy to lessen the dependence upon their line and add to their sales income (and that of their agents).

Sales managers of these firms seek out complementary products being marketed on a local basis and add them to their line. These are then presented to the rep salesforce as additional products to sell and earn commissions on.

The end result is more sales for the principal and more commissions for the agents. Occasionally, however, these lines will conflict with lines already being sold by the agents, so a careful analysis is required before plunging headlong into such a program.

It takes a bit of investigative work to ferret out a likely prospect for handling by your agency group. Normally such a company is making a product for a small select group of customers and isn't interested in administering responsibilities, yet if you help increase its sales, you'll have a willing listener to your proposition.

CONTINUITY IMPORTANT FOR GOOD AGENCY RELATIONS

A concern for the agent and the principal?

We all know the story. The founder retires and the son, son-in-law, or grandson is now ready to take over the reins and steer the corporate fortunes to new heights, or . . .

The veteran agent has labored long and hard for his respective principals and his son, son-in-law, or grandson is on board and prepared to modernize the old sales agency by using modern advertising and selling techniques. Sometimes things turn out well in both cases, and quite often they don't.

Warning: The basic problem stems from the second generation's not having gone through the struggle that is always a part of starting a business, whether it is a manufacturing company or a sales agency. They start with the company or agency long after the survival battle has been won and, not knowing the traps that can spring up and engulf the unwary and take him to ruin, they often use the organization's working capital as a plaything to try out theoretical innovations their business professor suggested in Marketing II.

One of the first things a second-generation manager is prone to do is to examine the commissions that agents are receiving. He usually decides it will be much less expensive to put a direct person in Georgia or Oklahoma and terminates an agent or two who have been responsible for establishing countless customers in those areas. The agent loses immediate income and has to rebuild his commissions with another competitive firm, which may take a long time. The company eventually loses sales to the former agent, but by that time it's too late to do anything about it.

A second-generation agent often commits similar errors but in another way. He doesn't realize how much hard work, door-knocking, and travel it took his predecessor to pioneer the territory and build up a flourishing business. His reaction may be to ignore the obvious need to continue calling and selling, and instead becomes an order-taker. Of course, by the time he finds that he can't survive by taking this route he's lost most of his good customers, good principals, and his agency.

One of the solutions that many firms and agencies have utilized is to make a prospective second-generation manager get out and make it on his own in another job before bringing him into the business. This experience usually goes a long way toward eliminating the untold number of failures in businesses and sales agencies. By the time the heir-apparent comes into the business he has a better appreciation of the sacrifices and common sense management it takes to survive in today's competitive marketplace.

TODAY YOUR AGENT, TOMORROW YOUR COMPETITOR

Example: A chemical company specializing in ingredients for the dairy industry utilized agencies across the country to sell its products. The line was an attractive one and had a fine reputation for quality and service; however, it could be easily duplicated without any danger of patent or licensing infringement.

One of the larger agencies representing this company figured out a way to increase their earnings—they went into the chemical business and started making some products identical to those made by their principal.

The agency concentrated only on the high-profit chemicals and continued selling the balance of the company's line in the usual manner, receiving their normal commissions.

Naturally, the company eventually wondered why some products continued to move rather well while the profitable products lagged badly. It didn't take them long to discover their new competitor. But although they terminated them promptly, it was not until considerable damage had been done.

Caution: If you have a line that is easy to manufacture or duplicate, a discussion of the legal steps that can be taken should be discussed with your attorney. It may be possible that a clause can be added to your contract protecting you from this type of encroachment. But since laws vary so from state to state, only your attorney can properly advise you.

ARROGANCE—WHO NEEDS IT!

During the luncheon break at an agency seminar, a number of us were grouped at a table with a particularly loquacious member of our profession. He was monopolizing the conversation and instructing us all on the proper attitude to project toward our principals. "You gotta show 'em who's boss right from the start," he argued. "They come into our territory," he continued, "and ask us to take on their line and we give them our guidelines for handling their products. First, we tell them how to price their product for our market, and then we tell them to stay away. We do the selling, and they do the making, and they're lucky to have us rep them."

Warning: He said his firm has been in business 35 years and that's how he operates. And he insisted he had principals standing in line waiting for his agency to sign them up. And he was probably right; firms were eager to have his agency sell their products because the agency was unusually successful in its selling area.

What we didn't learn till later was that the pugnacious speaker was the son of the agency's founder and had little or nothing to do with the success of the agency, but it was obvious to all of us that he would have a lot to do with its ultimate demise.

>>>→ *OBSERVATION* Arrogance works for only a short time, whether it is a characteristic of a sales agency or a principal. It is a doubtful luxury that can be practiced only at the peak of success, while everything is going exactly right; but it is a precursor of a decline that it initiates by its unpleasantness and the desire it creates in others to see the perpetrator fail.

It's not unusual to see some companies practice it also, but perhaps in not so obvious a manner. An example is the case of a firm that doesn't bother to keep its agencies informed by sending them copies of orders, quotes, and other vital communications. This is tantamount to saying the agent really isn't very important to the overall success of the company and his role is about at the level of a raw trainee.

A good agent feels he's important to your company, and he also feels that his contribution should be recognized by a constant flow of communications indicating his worth; that is, copies of important correspondence to your customers.

The type of agent mentioned previously may do you some good over the short term, but think twice before you sign him up. It's the long term you're interested in. Mutual respect in rep/principal relationships is essential for long-lasting successful results. Arrogance went out with the robber barons.

REP SELLING COSTS VARY BY REGION

Some agents consistently complain about their operating costs and others seem relatively unconcerned. The reason may well have to do with their geographical locations. For instance, a business lunch in New York City can cost quadruple that of a similar lunch in Billings, Montana.

Caution: Be aware of these differences. They can account for some of the strange antics of your agents—reluctance to pick up a dinner check or to fly at their expense to a company sales meeting.

Many agents are close with the dollar—just plain tight. But others are experiencing much higher operating expenses. If you pay attention to the costs in the territories you visit and take them into consideration when traveling with your agents (pick up an extra check or two), you'll find them much more receptive to your visits.

INCLUDE REPRESENTATIVES IN YOUR PRODUCT LIABILITY INSURANCE COVERAGE

Whenever a suit is brought against a company involving product liability, inevitably the suit also includes the company's sales agency who sold the product originally. The courts have consistently dismissed the case against the agent, but he has still incurred the expense of legal fees.

However, although the rep rarely suffers (other than financially), it's not unusual for the company to suffer from his testimony.

The reason for this is the necessity of two separate defenses if the agency is forced to employ its own attorney. His lawyer can look at things differently from your lawyer, and varying testimony can weaken your case.

It's best to present a united front, to have only one defense and one attorney or legal firm handling the defense. Many insurance companies even favor this arrangement because they have the most to lose if the case goes against you.

You'll be doing yourself a favor if you check with your insurance company and make sure your manufacturers' agents are included in this vital coverage. Product liability cases are not going to go away—they're a fact of life today and will probably even increase.

HOW HONEST ARE YOUR AGENTS' EMPLOYEES?

A southeastern sales manager recently complained about the dishonesty practiced in one of his agencies. The owner had improved his business to a point where he needed a new salesperson to cover part of the territory. The new salesperson did quite well and it soon became necessary to hire a second person.

For over a year these two made calls and also made notes. The first two activities were commendable. The salespeople made calls and they made sales, but they did an even better job of making notes. They listed all of their agency-employer's customers, what products they purchased, and the going price. The sales manager's firm was the agent's major principal, and most of his customers were apparently on the list.

The rest of the story is pretty obvious. With their list complete, they approached a competitor of the sales manager's firm who promptly hired them as his new representatives in the territory. Armed with the old company's confidential price list, they were able to quote lower prices to its customers and lure away a good portion of the business.

Naturally this was upsetting to the sales manager and his company and they were unhappy with the agent who had hired the two culprits. The agent wasn't too happy either, as he saw much of his business slip away rather rapidly.

Every manufacturer faces the same danger, and there are several precautions that can be taken before the barn door is closed, as follows:

• Don't rush your successful agent into taking on another salesperson to cover his territory. Let him take his time, and if he'll accept your help in evaluating prospective personnel, give him that help. He may be inexperienced in knowing how and whom to hire.

• Don't be upset if he tends toward an older, semiretired, experienced salesperson. This type of person is less likely to run off with accounts.

• Do encourage him if he takes on a younger man to arrange for the new salesperson to have a piece of the action. This is also a deterrent to an early departure and can be legally more binding.

• Recommend that the agency owner enter into written agreements with his/her employees. Those agreements can offer some protection if a noncompetition clause is in effect.

A little caution mixed with some common sense can go a long way toward preserving the safety of your customer list and pricing secrets.

BEFORE TERMINATION, TALK IT OVER

A small parts manufacturer hadn't had any action from his agency in the Kansas–Colorado area for several months, although the agent had performed admirably up to that point. The manufacturer, figuring the agent was concentrating on other lines and not on his, fired off a letter of termination.

The manufacturers' agent, who was responsible for some good business in the principal's shop, phoned immediately and asked for a conference to discuss the problem, and the manufacturer agreed.

Since both parties were interested in the same goal—increased sales—and both were responsible businessmen, the meeting went well. The agent pointed out that inquiries forwarded to the plant were being "no quoted," and he also said that orders that had been shipped were plagued with quality problems. For this reason, he had slowed up considerably in soliciting new business.

The manufacturer agreed that quality had been a problem but announced that his quality control group had been successful in upgrading the product. He also pointed out that the agent was sending in a lot of inquiries for parts that simply weren't in the range of the manufacturers' facilities.

Both men agreed that these misunderstandings didn't constitute insurmountable barriers, and their agreement was quickly reinstated. The agent and his salesforce are back beating the bushes for new business, and the manufacturer is committed to making good parts.

>>> *OBSERVATION* There are often good reasons on both sides for the decline of business, so before terminating a promising sales agency, take time for a personal discussion to see if some insignificant problem is causing the slowdown. Usually the basic problem can be solved by improved communications. It pays to keep an agent who is familiar with you

and your products, if he can be restored. This is preferable to starting all over again with a new agency.

WHY DO AGENTS BECOME MANUFACTURERS?

Some agents have a strong wish to operate a manufacturing plant and go into business for that reason. The majority who take the plunge, however, do so for an entirely different reason.

Most of the agents starting up their own operation or buying an existing one do so because they haven't been able to find a company to represent that can capably supply products for their customers.

In many cases, noncompetitive prices or poor quality from one of their principals convince them that they can do a better job by starting their own plant.

There's a simple moral here: If you can keep your customers happy with your pricing, quality, and delivery, you probably won't have one of your agents as a competitor.

DON'T INVOLVE YOUR AGENTS WHEN YOU HAVE TROUBLE WITH YOUR BOSS

If you do, try not to involve your representatives, but try to keep them informed of any conflicts that they might stir up by unintentionally saying the wrong thing at the wrong time.

Since they're not able to visit your offices too often, your representatives won't be too aware of any interdepartmental squabbles or political intrigues, and they'll appreciate your aid in helping them keep their foot out of their mouth.

PLANT BACKUP: A VITAL PART OF EVERY SALES TEAM

An increasing number of manufacturers have established branches and factories in more far-flung areas of our country. Thus, a sophisticated method of selling is more in demand than ever. Most of the time your representatives will be able to handle your product sales easily in their territory. But from time to time an agent might send out a cry for help. It is essential that you respond.

Many companies are accustomed to group buying, and this dictates group selling. It means that you may need to spend more time in the field with your agents in order to garner your share of the available business.

In areas where you employ direct salespeople who are specialists in your product, you often have to back them up with good technical aid from the factory. This is even more important when team selling is necessary in one of your representative's areas.

Make sure you let your agents know they can count on you. They'll need this assistance to combat group selling teams from competitive firms. Emphasize that you can't be there to help close every order, but also make them aware that when a really important opportunity comes up, you'll be there to help get the order.

CROSSBREEDING: THE AGENT'S ACE IN THE HOLE

Every once in a while when volume increases significantly, sales managers get to pondering the merits of a sales agent program versus a direct-employee sales program. In analyzing the differences, they usually decide that the two main advantages of the independent sales agent outweigh advantages to be had with a direct-employee program. These two advantages are (1) a fixed sales cost and (2) professional in-place salespeople. This latter feature refers to the fact that the independent sales agent will always remain in his territory.

Although these are important assets of a representative sales program, there is still another that veteran observers say should be considered ahead of the other two, and that's crossbreeding.

>>→ *IDEA IN ACTION*   Very simply, crossbreeding means the selling of several compatible but not competitive products. For instance, one company may make toys for children, another toys for adults, and still another computer-type toys. If a store buyer decides he doesn't want to purchase computer-type toys, the manufacturer has nothing more to sell him, and his salespeople will try more fertile fields. On the other hand, an agent can carry all three lines, and if he can't sell computer-type toys, he may be able to sell the second or third line. But the real advantage comes about because of his continuing relationship with the toy store buyer. And through repeated visits he may be able to convince the buyer that computer-type toys are worth a try.

The advantages of crossbreeding are even more evident in industrial sales. Sometimes a direct salesperson or an agent cannot easily determine if a company is a potential user of his product. He may sell rubber molded products, castings, and other components that appear to be logical for the customer to use, yet the buyer is uninterested in pursuing the point because he has a fine supplier for that particular component. The direct man can make repeated calls, but after a while the buyer may refuse to see him. The agent, on the other hand, may already be selling the buyer one or more of his other lines and can eventually have an opportunity to bid on the component simply because he's there or the current supplier has started to cause problems.

This happens often in the agency business, much more often than you would think. There are other instances where, for example, a buyer may want to buy a certain part such as a precision casting. Perhaps the best way to make the part is by machining it out of a piece of steel. Here the agent, if he's carrying several compatible lines, can direct the buyer to the proper manufacturer and save him money in the process. Again, the direct man usually has one commodity to sell and can't offer the choice of several competing manufacturing processes to the buyer.

Caution: To take real advantage of crossbreeding you, of course, must have agents with good product knowledge. When negotiating with prospective agents for your company, it's important to determine if they have the capability for understanding the fine points of your products. A good look at their other lines will tell you a lot. The more compatible they are with your products, the better the chance for success.

INDUSTRIAL SALESPEOPLE ARE DIFFERENT

A successful representative—one who was formerly a direct salesperson—doesn't fit the typical sales' image. His strongest suit is endurance; he gets low marks on ego and empathy.

A recent study reported that industrial salespeople have good work habits and are willing to work longer and harder than most other types of salespeople.

The empathy needed in retail sales and what is termed *direct selling* isn't an important characteristic of the industrial salesperson. He spends his time filling the needs of an engineer or buyer, and this type of customer is more interested in solving a problem than he is in selling strategies or ego-massaging.

If your firm makes industrial products, take a good look at your prospective agent's background in selling. If his previous experience was in selling intangible products, you may want to probe a little further to make certain he possesses the needed traits of an industrial salesperson. He should have endurance, be physically able and persevering, and smart but not overly intellectual.

THE SALES MANAGER IS THE MIDDLE MAN

As manufacturing companies grow, the top executive officers must grow away from the hour-by-hour and day-by-day function of most of their departments. The department heads are concerned with the workings of their own vital areas. They too lose touch with the working machinery of the sales department even though their operations must mesh.

Everyone philosophically should recognize that the sales department and the people in the field perform the vital function of keeping the orders moving in so that the product can move out.

Too frequently we hear that the president of the company makes the statement, "We paid that guy more last year than I made." It might well just be so.

Every dollar that was paid to the agent, however, was tied to an invoice of goods shipped. Just as the check in payment to a steel supplier is not net income to the president of the steel company, that money was far from being net income to that agency. It paid for miles and miles on the road, hotels, salaries, and expenses of employees.

In short, it appears to be the duty of the sales manager to inform the operational heads of his company just where the advantages lie and why they are using a manufacturers' agency team to market their products. So here, once again, are the five advantages your company has by using manufacturers' agents:

1. Manufacturers' representatives can give a manufacturer a predetermined fixed sales cost tied directly to the goods shipped.

2.   Representatives are self-motivated. Since they work solely on commission, they have the most powerful incentive of all to do well for themselves and their principals: the profit motive.

3.   Sales representatives give local management to the manufacturer no matter where he is located. Experienced, competent agents know the territory, where the business is, and how to get it. Today, competition demands no less.

4.   The sales agency, working in partnership with the manufacturer's people, becomes a trained salesforce in the field. The years of experience that the agent has in his territory is of inestimable value.

5.   The manufacturer enjoys the benefit of immediate access to his market. Market information can be a matter of hours, most frequently, rather than months and years.

Of course, principal/agency cooperation is the key to success. The president of the company who recognizes the potent force he has available to him and the sales manager who keeps him informed of that strength turn out to be the winners.

HOW TO AVOID FIRST-ORDER MISHAPS

Most problems occur when something is being done for the first time. Examples: Running a business meeting in a new location, making a presentation to a new boss or customer.

Nowhere is this more true than in the case of the first order for a new customer. What makes this particularly annoying, not only to you but to your agents, is the fact that a new customer has been developed because he's been convinced that your company can do a better job than your competition. A lot of time and energy has been expended in bringing the customer to this point. You don't want to lose him because of a poor performance on the very first order.

Why does this happen? Well, naturally, part of it's due to Murphy's law. But far too much is blamed on poor old Murphy. The main reason a new order is fouled up is because your personnel are unfamiliar with the customer and treat the new order just as they would any other routine order. They may misspell the new company's name, get the wrong address on the shipping details, or forget that part of the deal was to include the freight in the price instead of billing the customer for shipping charges.

How can first-order mishaps be avoided? It's really very simple. Here are several steps you can take:

• Red-flag the order. Advise your agents that whenever a new customer is obtained, they're to notify you in a separate letter. You may be out of town and that new customer's order may sneak through without your knowing it.

• Write a welcoming letter. Let that new customer know he's a happy addition to your customer list. Tell him about your firm and mention your agent's name in the copy. Then give copies of that letter to everybody: the president, production manager, order department, and shipping department.

• Give that order your personal attention. Every time you return to the office, check on the progress of the order. By doing this you put all departments on notice about the importance of filling the order properly and on time.

>>>→ *OBSERVATION* The main emphasis, of course, is to get the entire company in on the act. Make your people new-customer conscious. Make them realize that the lifeblood of any company is the number of new customers it can develop. With this kind of emphasis, regularly practiced, you'll soon find new interest by all groups within your company on how successfully you perform on that "first order."

MAKE SURE YOUR AGENCIES UNDERSTAND YOUR CREDIT POLICIES

There are widely varying opinions on who is responsible for determining the credit rating of a customer.

Caution: Under the average contractual agreement between agent and principal it is acknowledged that the agent is an independent contractor and his primary responsibility is to solicit and obtain orders for the companies he represents. However, he has no authority to set prices, to accept orders, or to do anything else that is the express right and responsibility of the principal—and that includes setting credit terms for individual customers.

It has always been the responsibility of the principal to determine if he wants to accept an order from a new customer under the same terms of credit he extends to his established customers. To do this requires sophisticated capabilities such as good banking connections, a Dun and Bradstreet service, and other credit-rating bureaus whose services are exclusively offered for the purpose of establishing the credit rating of a prospective customer.

The agent has none of these services at his command, nor does he normally expect to subscribe to their services. He expects his principal to set credit terms, and many contracts specify this responsibility.

However, the agent is just as interested in the credit rating of a new customer as is the principal. He knows that if he goes to a great deal of work in wooing a prospective user of his principal's wares and the new customer doesn't pay for the commodities, he, the agent, won't get his commission.

>>>→ *HOW TO DO IT* Enlist your agent's aid when a new firm is about to be put on your books. Ask him if he's done any business with the company before, through any of his other principals. If so, were invoices paid on time? Ask him to check with other agents and possibly other local vendors who may have done business with the company. Any feedback of this type can aid your credit department in setting the proper terms.

Also, keep your agents informed when a customer becomes delinquent. Let him know immediately when a customer is slightly overdue. He can then pick up the phone or drop in on the customer with a big smile on his face and say, "Hey, we haven't gotten your check yet." This usually prompts the buyer to check into the matter and have a voucher sent off within the next few days.

On the other hand, if he asks him to get the money after ninety days have passed and the customer has received two nasty letters and a veiled threat, he's going to be in trouble with the buyer.

So keep your agents informed when things get tardy, but don't hold them responsible for bad debts.

AFTER-SALE SERVICE IS CRITICAL FOR CONTINUED SUCCESS

In many companies, customer service deserves more attention. Remember, it costs five times as much to acquire a new customer as to maintain an old one. Dissatisfied customers' complaints should go as high in the organization as possible. It provides checks against organizational weaknesses, and the response by higher-ups is good public relations. This further points up possible problems the management may be unaware of.

Caution: One of the main complaints voiced by agents is the lack of service offered by their principals after the sale. After conscientiously promising prompt and effective service to the customer, they often find that the home office appears to be somewhat disinterested in the processing and servicing of the order that resulted from the agent's vigorous efforts.

Almost any department within a company can be afflicted with the poor-service syndrome. The sales department may sit on the order for a few days waiting for an update on pricing, thus delaying its entry. The production control manager may insert the order in the production schedule in routine fashion even though special precautions have to be taken for some secondary operations provided by an outside source. The production manager may look upon the order as a headache because of previous problems associated with that particular customer and may change the schedule to suit his own purposes. The inspection department may have previously waived some quality standard in order to get out a rush order for the same customer and may assume that it can be waived again.

Service is a total company commitment, but some company managements act only when a situation reaches crisis proportions. Up to that point one department can negate all the good work of the other departments in the company by not performing as required.

Optimistically, all departments of a company should be service departments. The sales department should promptly enter the order and make certain that all conditions stipulated by the customer on his purchase order are properly recorded, such as shipment by air freight or a change in the product's dimensions.

The production control department should carefully assess the delivery promised by the agent (with factory approval) and make certain the order is entered accordingly.

The production department should take every precaution to assure quality commensurate with what the customer was sold and should adhere to the scheduling assigned by the production control department.

The inspection department has the final word on the quality of the product the customer ordered and should conscientiously carry out this substantial responsibility.

Caution: Many service problems occur with repeat customers. A part or product that has been sold over and over to the same customer may lose its importance and the customer is taken for granted. Late deliveries and poor quality, which perhaps were accepted by the customer in times of great demand, become the norm. One day your agent may walk in to find the latest order went to a competitor.

It's much easier to provide dependable service on every order than to attempt to regain a lost customer. Good service makes it harder for a competitor to woo away a customer.

THE PITFALLS OF CHANGING AGENTS FREQUENTLY

With all we've said in the past about being careful during agent interviews, there are still some manufacturers who take on the first warm body that walks through the door. But more often than not, that warm body ends up a dead duck in short order, only to be replaced by the next unsuspecting agent.

Warning: Apart from the management problems of the manufacturer that hires and fires with the speed of a western gunslinger, the problems with customers are far worse. Customers faced with new agents every few months feel that they have no continuity with the manufacturer. Let's look at this problem closely.

Some purchasing people told us that they often turn to companies represented by factory people when they face frequent agent changes with some vendors. What they are saying is that they value stability.

When you change agents frequently, the word gets around and your chances of attracting top agents drop dramatically. This, of course, reflects itself in the quality of the agents who will be willing to work for you. We're sure that you can imagine how this looks to those people to whom you want to sell.

»»→ *HOW TO DO IT* One answer to the problem is to screen your agent candidates carefully and not make snap decisions. Your judgment is important, but it must be tempered with a careful evaluation of the agent's qualifications and your view of how well they will mesh with your organization.

The other answer is patience. Too often agents are bounced before they get a chance to do the job for which they were hired. If you feel that a new agency isn't performing according to expectations, don't fire him—dig into the problem and find out why. As we've said many times before, the first few months are critical to the manufacturer/agent relationship, and each party must take the time to get to know the other and to understand each other's expectations.

WHAT TO DO WHEN YOU GET MINOR LINE TREATMENT
FROM AN AGENT

Everyone tends to organize things and events in their lives depending on their personal criteria and the force of the world in which they live. When you have two phone calls to make, why do you call Charlie before you call Tom? You have your reasons, and they are usually logical. Agents are no different from the rest of us. If they have more than one line, there will be a hierarchy.

Caution: An agent is an independent businessperson and, as such, must arrange all sorts of priorities, including the ranking of principals. But what does this mean to you?

1. It could mean that the agent knows the market and the potential for your products and treats them accordingly.

2. It could mean that he has a "mad on" for you for some reason and is intentionally giving you second-class service.

3. It could mean that you have not supported him properly and he is responding to the effort put forth by the other principals.

4. It could mean that he is working to capacity, based on the territory potential for your product, and your interpretation and his of this potential are in conflict.

5. Or it could mean a lot of other things. The point of this section is not to give you a laundry list of possible problems but to try to put the minor line problem in perspective.

How do you handle minor line treatment? Head-on, but not like a bull in a china shop. The best way to solve the problem is to talk about your feelings face to face with the agent and to present your analysis of why the problem exists. If your agent is worth keeping, he will be just as forthright with you. It could be that your prices are out of line, making it difficult for the agent to meet competition. He might also be facing excessive competitive selling and simply decide that his efforts are better spent on other lines. And the fault may lie with you. Perhaps you have been sending poor or too few sales leads or not providing adequate follow-up on inquiries and quotation requests. There may be problems with product quality and delivery.

The reasons for minor line status are usually quite real. And they seldom go away until both you and your agent discuss the problem. Unfortunately, many manufacturers assume that all agents should treat their products as the only product being sold. Anything that smacks of second-class treatment is taken as a personal affront. When you and your agents face the problem squarely, you're more than halfway to a solution.

Minor line treatment may not be all that bad. Not everyone can be first. But if you've got the best agent in the territory and he can give you good reasons for what you perceive to be minor line treatment, you may be a lot better off than with a poor agent who promises you the moon.

Caution: Don't make a relative evaluation. If you are getting everything you can from a territory but your agent is spending more time with someone else's product, you have no reason to kick. What we are saying is this: Don't judge an agent's performance by where you perceive your product to be in his hierarchy of importance. But do judge him by the volume he produces relative to your estimate of the territory potential.

GET TO KNOW EVERYONE ON YOUR AGENT'S STAFF

"Everyone" may turn out to be just the agent and his answering service, or it could include a very large staff. But the point is this: You should know and be known to everyone who works with and for your agents.

Example: We once knew a sales manager who refused to talk with anyone at his various agency's offices except the owners themselves. After a while, this man found that his sales were dwindling and that he had virtually no contact with any of the agents who represented him. He soon changed his approach.

The national average size of an agency is 4.8 people. However, many agencies are one- or two-person firms, using wives or part-time people to back them up in the office while they're out selling. Sure, you may have an important point to make that can only be considered by the agent himself. But if you look carefully at it, you'll find that much of your agent contact is routine. Get to know each person at every agency on a first-name basis. Get to know something about each so that you have more than business to talk about when you call.

You will never know how much influence other people in an agency have on the owner unless you get to know them. If you deal with people other than the owner offhandedly, you may find yourself getting the short end of the stick and not knowing why. Apart from being just good business, it's also a good way to treat people.

AVOID THE DANGERS OF RANKING YOUR AGENCIES

If you have two or more agents, one of them has to be Number One. Anyone who manages a team of agents is forever concerned with getting more out of them, especially those at the bottom.

It's a mistake to look at rank order and assume that Number One is doing the best job and that the guy in the rear should be bounced. Number One may be turning in the highest sales, but he may be only skimming the territory. "I found that my big producer was only hitting the high spots in the best territory and that the guy I was ready to can was getting every nickel he could from a rotten territory." That's how one sales manager put it recently. However, when you know that you have poor sales in a territory that should be stronger, you have to find out why and try to help the agent. Here are a few ways to pinpoint the problem.

1.   Yours is not the only product the agent is selling. The fault may lie at the factory. You may not be giving the agent the help and materials he needs. And you may find that one or more of his other principals keeps the heat on him. Before you broach the subject, investigate the situation carefully.

2.   Your agent may be facing serious local competition. Remember that many companies gain dominance by applying pressure on one territory at a time. Your agent may be a victim of such a campaign.

3.   You just may find that the agent took on your line to round out his other lines. Or worse, he might be very happy with the commissions he is getting for very little effort.

4.   You might find that you and he have overestimated the market. This is especially easy to do when you have no experience or little information on a new territory and an agent anxious to get your line becomes overly enthusiastic.

These are just a few of the reasons why you might be having problems. Now let's look at some of the steps you can take to correct them.

1.   The first step is to reassess the territory potential to determine whether the agent's production is in or out of line.

2.   Try to find out what kind of heat the agent's other principals apply. The squeaky wheel does get the oil.

3.   Compare your line with others carried by the agent. Try to determine why the agent took it and what its profit potential for him is compared with the other lines he carries.

4.   Look at your own expectations. We all get carried away with something we really want to succeed, and appointing an agent is a good example of such a situation. Did you let your enthusiasm color your perception of the reality of the situation?

5.   You may have oversold the agent. Telling a new agent that he is going to make a fortune with your line sets up a situation where a lesser performance can be shattering for both of you. Even if the agent's results are on target based on a realistic estimate of the territory potential, anything less than super success can set up a failure chain. It's really a matter of defining success and failure realistically.

6.   Make a visit to the field with the agent. When you do, be very clear that your goal is fact finding, not criticism. Even if you find much to criticize, hold off until the field trip is over and then discuss the points in a positive way. You may, of course, find that the agent just isn't going to work out. If this is the case and you feel that no amount of factory support will solve the problem, it's best to end the relationship. But remember that you must honor your contractual obligations and that you do owe the agent a detailed explanation of why it isn't working out.

7.   Encourage your agents to push for more business with old and familiar customers. These people are usually easier to sell than new prospects, and quick results can fire up enthusiasm for the more difficult new business efforts.

8. Watch your timing. Jumping on an agent for a slump can be quite destructive when the problem is only transient, but waiting too long to take action on an obvious problem can also cause problems. Base your determination on elements that have historical perspective for the situation: dollar volume, number of calls made, units sold, territory inquiries, and even customer complaints.

PRODUCT COMPATIBILITY: A LITTLE OVERLAP MAY BE BETTER THAN NONE AT ALL

Think about it: The agents you would like to sign up are probably doing a great job for your competitors. They have the market and application knowledge you want; they have the contacts; and they are making money for their principals. But if you wait for a falling out, you will probably never get the agent force you need. Many of the agents who could do a bang-up job for you are probably carrying lines that are only marginally competitive.

One manufacturer of flowmeters sees no problem with his agents carrying other lines. "As long as the flow ranges of the other products are not in our range, we think it's a definite advantage for agents to carry other flowmeter lines. After all, these agents are in business to stay in the territories, and we might as well all benefit."

When an agent can offer a broad range of products to a buyer, sacrificing a little product overlap may gain you an agent who will be much more productive than one who is completely noncompetitive. Of course, negotiations can become sticky because the other manufacturers may take a hard line. But we think it's definitely worth checking out.

WHAT TO DO WHEN YOU THINK AN AGENT IS IN TROUBLE

Sales were off. RFQs weren't coming in at the usual rate. And the agent seemed discouraged when Bill called. Bill is the owner of a firm that has sold through agents for many years. "I can usually tell when something is wrong," Bill said. "When you work with guys for ten or fifteen years, you know a lot about them. You know much more than they say in their memos."

Manufacturers who use agents usually form close relationships, and it becomes harder to recognize and handle problems. There is always a tendency to put off action in the hope that the problem will go away. And if it doesn't, there is often a bitter parting of business and personal friends. However, in many cases the situation may not be what you think it is. Let's look at the reasons for some territory problems and see why it's so important to dig below the orders, memos, and balance sheets.

• When an agent hires a new person, it usually takes quite a bit of his energy to get the new person off to a good start. If your agency is a one-man band and he has just increased his staff 100 percent by adding another person, he's going to be spread pretty thin until the new person is comfortable in the territory. Remember, in the long run you're going to be a lot better off with the additional coverage.

• Your agency may have lost a line. First of all, the emotional reaction associated with the loss of a line will have a strong but temporary effect. Then, as your agent attempts to replace the line some of his attention will be diverted. If you know that this problem exists, you can do him and yourself a lot of good by helping to find a replacement for the lost line.

• Your competitor may have launched a tough-to-match campaign in your agent's territory. When this happens, for whatever reason, your sales are in for trouble. Rather than land on the agent, you'd better get your heads together for a practical strategy session.

As you can see, there can be a number of reasons for slack business. And unless you take the time to find out what the problem is, you and your agents are in for trouble that neither of you needs. Here are a few ways to stay ahead of these problems.

1. Make regular visits to each agency. Discuss the operation as well as your needs in the territory. You don't have to pry, but you can have an open discussion with any agent when he or she knows that you are interested in making the partnership work and grow.

2. You can train your agents' new salespeople to make them effective more quickly.

3. You can encourage your agencies to come to you when they have problems. When they know that you won't be judgmental and that you sincerely want to help them, the partnership will be most productive.

"MY DOOR IS ALWAYS OPEN." BUT IS THERE SOMEONE GUARDING IT?

If ever there were a cliché, it's the open door bit. Sure, your door may be open, but have you put boulders on the threshold? Are people who want or need to see you intimidated? Obviously, we're concerned with the access your agents have to you. You may have rep councils and you may have a reputation for being fair and open-minded, but is the path clear for agents who must have your ear occasionally?

>>>→ *OBSERVATION* Whether you're the president of a small firm and you handle the agent salesforce along with other details or you're the VP of sales for a large company, there is almost always someone between you and those who would like to talk with you. Without your knowing it, your secretary or assistant may have set up his or her own rules for access to you. These people have good intentions, of course. Such screens, however, are seldom obvious to those they are designed to protect, and they can be extremely troublesome for those agents who need to talk with you.

• It's a good idea to check your staff to make sure just how they handle agents who need to talk with you. Subordinates can be very protective at times without intentionally trying to do any harm. Often it's their way of "helping" when they see how busy you are. You can solve this problem without causing bad feelings by simply setting up your own screening guidelines or by setting aside specific times each day for agents' phone calls. When your agents and those in your office know your schedule, the lines will be open and there should be no problems.

• When an agent bypasses the normal communication channel, it could be a sign that you have become difficult to reach. Before you take the agent to task, it's a good idea to see just how well protected you are, by whom, and for what reasons.

• Don't take it out on an agent who makes an end run to get your attention. Remember that you are working with entrepreneurs, not employees, when you sell through manufacturers' agencies. Employees must follow the prescribed communication chain, but your business partner—the agency—should not have to stand in line.

HOW TO HELP YOUR AGENTS SOLVE A MAJOR PROBLEM—PAPER WORK

We've discussed before the problems you can cause your agents—and the loss of selling time to you—when you request a lot of paper work. Experts in the field claim that the easier you make it for people to respond, the better their cooperation and the better the quality of the finished work.

One way to do this is to design forms that require little more than checking off boxes and/or filling in lines. If an agent has to spend time composing a report, time and money are wasted.

This system will also help you to standardize on input from the field, making the job of interpretation much easier. Remember, though, don't push your agent's ship out of the safe harbor into a tricky tax problem. Regular reporting can do this. Frequently an IRS adjuster will claim that regular call reports indicate that the agent is an employee rather than an independent contractor. This could mean a strong backlash on you regarding withholding and worker's compensation taxes, and so on, plus penalties. Irregular requests for reports should cause you and them no problems.

DO YOUR AGENTS RESPECT YOU?

An agent we talked with recently said this about one of his principals: "He's one of the brightest guys I know, and he's built one hell of a business. But I really don't respect him." Consider the old saying: "I can respect a man I don't like, but I could never like a man I don't respect." This is an important distinction in the agent/principal relationship.

⟫⟩→ *OBSERVATION*   Most agents want to respect the person to whom they report at their principal's headquarters. It may sound basic and not especially important in these tight economic times, but when you must be sure that you and your agents have everything going at the same time, why not take a look at the characteristics most agents look for in a sales manager they feel they can respect.

• *Trust*—It's critical that all your agents know that you will never take advantage of them. Trust is most often violated when one person tries to manipulate another. If you ever persuade an agent to do something without revealing the real reason, you will lose trust instantly. If you can't level with an agent right from the start, don't try to get something done by manipulation.

• *Fairness*—Your agents are driven by the same goals that motivate you. If you understand that they have the same need for achievement and that together you can accomplish a lot more than you can individually, you're on the right track. When you recognize an agent's accomplishments and reward him, you have established yourself as a fair person. And when this occurs, you have taken a giant step toward building the respect you need to be successful with agents.

• *Confidence*—Your agents must believe that you are leading them in the right direction and that you are creating a climate in which they can work productively and openly. You really don't need the polish of a leadership course to do this—you just have to be open and positive with all your agents. They know that you, too, are human. And they have much more respect for a manager who tries and goofs occasionally than for a manager who never tries but cloaks himself in personal charisma.

The way agents feel about you is, in large measure, the way you feel about yourself. That is, if you don't have a high regard for yourself, the chances are that your agents will share that perception. However, self-respect must be real—not a front. If you feel that you must maintain a front as a barrier against your agents, there is a very good chance that your real self-perception is quite in line with the way your agents feel about you.

WHO ARE YOUR KEY AGENTS? DO THEY KNOW WHO THEY ARE?

"Harry can make me believe that I am the mainstay of the organization," an agency owner told us in describing his relationship with his principal. When we talked with Harry, the principal, he said that the agent was, indeed, a key figure in the success of his company. He also said that most of his other agencies fit the same description, but under different circumstances. And he made absolutely certain that each agency knew about it and knew that he appreciated their efforts.

    ➤➤➤ *WATCH THIS* How do your agencies feel about their importance —about their relationship with you, your company, and the other agencies on the team? Of course, much of their feelings depend on their value as you see it. And this brings up the key question: Who are the mainstays —those to whom you can turn for ideas, support, and flat-out effort? We're not saying that you should play favorites; that is bad policy no matter how you look at it. But you should know who your strong agencies are, why they are strong, and how you and the other agencies can benefit from this strength.

To help you with this task, we have developed a practical review system. Its purpose is to identify the strengths you can count on and to help you pass on the secrets of their success to your other agencies.

1. What does one agency do better than all the others? For example, if one is an ace prospector, he's very important to you, and his techniques can help the other agencies on the team. Sure, the others are prospectors, but perhaps one does the job much better than all the others. The point is this: Make an effort to discover the strengths of each agency, let them know that these skills are valued by you, and then pass on the techniques to all the others.

2. What does one agency do that none of the others do? This, of course, is an extension of the first point. However, it does deserve separate attention. In any group, regardless of how successful each individual is, there are always people who do something that all the others just don't do. It's not that the others are incapable, it's just that one has discovered the winning technique, sharpened it, and uses it effectively. For example, one agent we met has become the unchallenged master of qualifying that mass of unqualified advertising leads that most manufacturers send to their agencies by the pound each month. His technique simply evolved from hard practice on the telephone. He found that a few hours a week on the phone were well worth the effort. Of course, most wouldn't touch an unqualified lead unless they had absolutely nothing else to do—and with good reason. But what works for one agency can work for others if the successful agent is willing to pass on his secrets. These are key agencies. They represent deep resources for you and the team. Identify them quickly.

3. Suppose a key agency stopped doing its unique job. Suppose the owner of that key agency who was your ace prospector decided to close up shop and rent beach chairs during the summer on Cape Cod. You would have a problem. If you have identified this person, tapped his skill for the benefit of your other agencies, you have no problem. And if he does decide to call it quits, you or he can train the successor in the unique skill he possesses. He's a cornerstone. Treat him accordingly.

4. Does one agency's success depend on another? Theoretically, each agency operates independently and in a tightly specified territory. But suppose for a moment that you have one agency in a territory loaded with consulting engineers. They never buy anything but pencils, but they do design projects worth millions of dollars that are built using your components in a territory covered by another agency. This agency is probably on a split commission arrangement; part of the commission being paid to the engineer/specifier territory agency and the balance paid to the agency that services the contractor in the territory in which the products are used. As you can see, other agencies are dependent on a single agency. You'd better be sure that this key agency is treated accordingly and is appreciated. Don't go overboard, just be honest and sincere.

When an agent is made to feel like a cornerstone, he feels motivated. This is not a plea to praise everyone indiscriminately. It's a plan to make the most of your agency team by identifying specific strengths and making sure that the people in each agency know that you are aware of them and that you appreciate them. It's a well-known psychological fact: Recognition is a powerful motivator.

AN EARLY WARNING SYSTEM FOR AGENT PROBLEMS

A manufacturer we know used to be a Navy destroyer skipper. "When the crew griped openly—when they expressed their feelings—I knew I could handle it," he said. "But when they stopped showing their feelings and talked only in terms of the facts of the issue, I knew I had personnel problems." This skipper's intuitive response has helped him deal with problems of his new crew—his team of manufacturers' agents.

       ⟫→ *OBSERVATION*   There are a number of indicators that can signal the deterioration of a group and of the work of the group. In the example just cited, the expression or lack of expression of feelings can be an important indicator. For example, a new system you have instituted with your agencies may be more efficient. However, if your agencies don't share your enthusiasm and don't express their misgivings, you have no way of dealing with a potentially crippling problem.

To help you spot some of these early warnings, we have developed the following checklist.

• Be on the lookout for less risk taking. By their very nature, agents are risk takers. Who else would go into business and expect to prosper on commissions alone? In other words, risk taking is not only a criteria for success, but the lack of it is an indicator of potential trouble. It could be your fault for not encouraging innovation, or it could be a sign that the agent has lost interest for other reasons.

• When you notice a drop-off in personal contact, you might be having a problem. Even in the best agency/principal relationship, personal contact is somewhat limited. After all, the agency doing its job is on the road, and the principal doing his job is managing a company or an entire agency sales team. However, once you have a base line of experience with each agency, it's not too difficult to spot a drop-off in personal contact—and a drop in the quality of the contact.

• When there is less give and take than there was in the past, you probably have problems. We touched on this concept earlier, but let's look at the situation critically. If you think that total agreement is the ideal state, you're in for a jolt. When everyone starts agreeing with you, either they have given up trying to convince you of something or they have gone to fry bigger fish. Either way, you lose. Nonconformity is *not* insubordination—it's usually a very healthy way for people to express feelings and ideas.

• When your agents stop complimenting you when compliments are truly deserved, they have lost interest. We're not talking about the person who takes every opportunity to make points. We're talking about those who have taken the time in the past to say something nice but who are now silent.

All of these elements can serve as indicators of problems. However, you should remember that the problems some agencies may be experiencing may not necessarily be the result of problems they are having with you, your company, or your products. Their problems may be personal, with the family, or with other principals. However, any problem can be a problem for you in terms of agency effectiveness. If it's appropriate and you feel you're not treading on personal ground, you can often be a good friend by letting the agent know that you can be counted on for personal counsel.

A LOOK AT AGENTS WHO BECOME MANUFACTURERS

Some of the agents we know are both agents and manufacturers. And a number of successful manufacturers started out as agents. Most of the manufacturing agents we talked with didn't get into manufacturing mainly to make a fortune, although the lure of building a business that could be sold more easily than a sales agency was important. Many agents who now manufacture do so out of frustration. Often they discovered customer needs that couldn't be filled anywhere—there just was no one who made products that would solve the problems. Those agents who could do it often created the products on a part-time basis and gradually slid into manufacturing. Others claimed that they could make better products than those made by others.

》》→ OBSERVATION Whatever the reason, there is a moral to the story of many agents-turned-manufacturer. They saw weaknesses, either in poor products or in the complete lack of products, and filled the gap. These entrepreneurs were really living the marketing concept: They found a need and filled it. Have you talked with your agents about their customers' needs recently? It might be a good time to do it. It is the agency's responsibility to find out about its customers' needs. Once they pass that information on to you, the ball is in your court.

HOW TO COLLABORATE WITH YOUR AGENTS

The agency/manufacturer relationship is a collaborative effort—independent businesspeople working together for a common goal. Sounds nice on paper, but there are times when the going can be pretty rough. The mistake that most people make when they work together in a relationship such as this is thinking that the partners are equal in all situations. This just isn't so. Depending on the situation and the experience of the individuals involved, the strength shifts from person to person.

>>>→ ***OBSERVATION*** Successful manufacturers and agencies know their own strengths and weaknesses. They know when they should play the dominant role in a working situation and when they should play the subordinate. And they know that individual success depends heavily on productive collaboration.

The following points will help you make the most of your collaborative efforts with your agencies:

• *Recognize that your ideas and methods may not be the same as those of your agencies.* And recognize that in very few cases are positive answers possible. For example, you may want to dig into a problem immediately but your agency may prefer to think it through for a while before taking action. The chances are that in most cases you will both come up with workable solutions and that the job will be done in the same amount of time. You can have a clash of styles, however, that will prevent anything from happening. When you face a problem such as this, make sure that your agency knows exactly what you plan to do and how you plan to do it. And make sure that you know just what the agency's plans are. You will probably find your collaboration will work a lot more smoothly and effectively when you discuss your methods and come to an agreement that is acceptable to both parties.

• *Be prepared to tinker.* For many problems that require agency and manufacturer collaboration, there just may be no ready-cut answers, or even directions to take. In a collaborative situation, both you and your agency will have to try new approaches together. This, incidentally, is one of the best ways agencies and manufacturers can learn about each other and how to work together productively.

• *Take your time at first.* You may be in a big hurry to get something done, but collaborating with another person requires getting used to the other party's ways of working. The time spent in adjusting to each other early on will be picked up later when you're working together to solve the problems you have in common.

• *Deal with interpersonal stress immediately.* If you or your agencies let an unresolved personal problem smolder, you're in for a bad time under any circumstances. However, don't be too concerned when such stress appears. The important thing is to recognize it and deal with it quickly and effectively.

• *Keep reviewing the work that has been done during the collaboration.* Be sure to praise the agency for accomplishments, and let them know if you feel the work isn't up to snuff. However, be prepared for the same straightforward treatment from your agency. Remember, a collaborative effort is *not* a contest. Many collaborations turn into contests, but they shouldn't.

The process of collaboration can be very rewarding. More often than not, the results will be better than either of you could have produced alone. And the experience of bouncing ideas off each other cements the agency/manufacturer bond.

What kinds of projects can an agency and manufacturer collaborate on together? Apart from the basic collaboration of selling together, you can work with your agencies to create new products, develop new ways to reach markets, and find alternative selling strategies for those that no longer work. You might also consider collaborating with your agencies in the development of a training program, one aimed at getting new agencies and new employees of your current agencies off the ground quickly and effectively.

"MY PRODUCTS SELL THEMSELVES. WHO NEEDS AGENTS?"

We don't hear this comment often, but when we do it always sparks the same response: What is the person really saying? The only products we know of that sell themselves—to a certain extent—are commodities bought on a repetitive basis. However, someone had to make the first sale. And someone has to keep the customer sold.

Agencies serve many sales functions. One is to open accounts. Another is to service them. In truth, no product ever really sells itself. Let's look at the facts:

1.   When an agency opens an account for you, it's business that you didn't have. Effort and cost went into the pioneering, and that effort should be rewarded with commissions.

2.   Even if the product is ordered repetitively, the agency is paid for the work that went into landing the account.

3.   If you think that you really have a product that sells itself and that you don't need agencies to continue servicing the customer, just imagine your competitor's agent sitting across the desk from that customer. Try to imagine what he's saying and what could be said by someone on your behalf—if he or she were there. Sure, the orders may be phoned in once a week, and you send checks to your agencies once a month for what appears to be automatic business. But if no one calls on these "automatic" accounts, your competitors will, and they're going to get the business sooner or later. Do your products really sell themselves? Think about it.

ANNOYED BY SEEMINGLY TRIVIAL QUESTIONS FROM YOUR AGENCIES? LOOK BENEATH THE SURFACE FOR THEIR MEANING

It's easy to get steamed when an agent bugs you with trivial questions. "When do you send commission checks?" "Do you want these cards back?" "What's the date of the sales meeting?" The list is endless, but your patience may not be. However, let's look at what's really being said.

⟫→ *WATCH THIS*   Agency people may be turning to you for a number of reasons. Sure your time is valuable, and answering questions that should be answered by your staff may not be your idea of high productivity. But the questions must be answered, and you should find out what has happened to the lines of communication between your agencies and your staff.

Agency personnel often assume that you do know everything that is going on in the company as it relates to them. This may be true, but they should be made aware of others in your organization who also know what's going on and who should be communicating with your agencies. Solve the problem by identifying the people and getting the lines of communication open and flowing.

Some agency personnel, not unlike corporate employees, and even some astute politicians, recognize the need for regular visibility. They use routine questions to maintain contact and to maintain visibility. Nothing wrong with this—unless it takes up too much of your time. When it does, you can solve the problem by keeping the line open from your end—by making sure that the agency person knows that you are keeping in touch. Such a disguised plea from an agent may be telling you that you really haven't been accessible and that you should be.

An agent might be seeking reassurance. A seemingly routine question may be a disguised request for help in making a difficult decision. This is more the case when an agency is relatively new with your company. The agency people haven't been through enough campaigns to be sure of themselves. When you suspect such a decision, don't jump in and make the decision, but supply all the help you can. It's the team effort that counts.

> ⇉→ *OBSERVATION* Keep an eye out for patterns—for questions that are repeated by different agents and by the same agents over again. The questions being asked may not be as important as the messages that are being sent unconsciously to you. In short, keep your eyes and your mind open.

WHAT TO DO WHEN AN AGENT SAYS, "THIS IS CONFIDENTIAL"

A top agent has just called you out of the blue. He says, "I'm turning the business over to my son. Last week the doctor told me I have to go into the hospital for exploratory surgery. Don't tell anyone else at the factory." What do you do? You know the implications of exploratory surgery, and you know that the son still needs a few years of his father's tutelage before he'd be ready to take over. And the request was to keep the secret.

This is a problem that most executives face from time to time. Agents must make major decisions, often in less than optimum time, and their decisions have serious effects on the company. Agency people often confide in people they have come to trust at the factory. But this trust may put you in a position that will be difficult to handle. What is your obligation to an agent who confides in you information that could have serious implications for your firm? What is your obligation to the agents who have come to trust you? Let's look at this thorny problem from several points of view.

Warning: This may seem unreasonable, but by definition a manager is not strictly a personal friend. And an agency owner who thinks of you as a personal friend—regardless of how friendly you may be—can put a severe strain on the relationship. From this point of view, it's often best to stop an agent from divulging a secret to you. Or you can set the ground rules for divulging the secret. When you do, you and the agent understand that business secrets told to you in your capacity as an employee of the company place a serious burden on both of you.

    ⋙→ *WHAT TO DO* In most cases, you will get a chance to prevent someone from telling you something in confidence that could breach your relationship with the company. However, when a secret is told before you have a chance to set the ground rules, you still have a heavy responsibility to the company. One manager we talked with said this, "I am up front about my responsibility to the company with all my agents. I have told them that I'm on their side all the way and will help them whenever I can. But when they tell me something that will adversely affect the company, I am bound to my employer." He told them this when he signed them up. He didn't wait until there was a problem and the relationship had to be put on the line. As a result, this manager has the full respect of every one of his agencies. They know that he has ordered his priorities and that he has not set himself up to be a spy and a rumor monger.

It's important for sales managers and agency people to understand each other's position from the outset of the relationship. Many managers and agency owners become close friends, but they still respect the binds that tie each to their business. These binds should not become boundaries but just respect for the role that each individual must play in business. This doesn't mean that you shouldn't become friends with your agents; it means that you should build the relationship on solid ground and the understanding that each of you has personal responsibilities that must be considered in times of personal stress. Be up front with your agents on this point and they will respect you for it, and the chances are that you will never be put in that bind that begins when someone says, "This is confidential."

WHAT TO DO WHEN AN AGENT CALLS ON YOU TO SOLVE A CUSTOMER PROBLEM

"He missed delivery schedules and never told me about it. Then, to make matters worse, when I got him (a manufacturer) to have a meeting with me and the customer, he took over and made it even worse."

The agent telling this went on with the horror story, but the point he was trying to make was that the help he sought from the manufacturer in a face-to-face meeting with the customer turned into a nightmare.

The fault may not be yours, but there will be times when you will be called on by your agents to smooth out problems with customers. Sure, most of them can be solved on the telephone, but when a meeting becomes necessary, we have a set of guidelines that should help you handle the situation without putting your company and your agency on the spot. Here's how to do it:

1.   Decide in advance whether you or your agent will be in control of the meeting. In most cases, it doesn't make any difference which of you does the job. However, for purposes of control, you should both agree on who will take the lead and what the ground rules will be.

2.   The person who runs the meeting should not hog the show but only provide the central focus and direction for the meeting.

3.   The leader should be a role model for the others. If a shouting match erupts, the leader shouldn't play the game. It usually takes a lot of self-control to sit still while people shout at each other. But you'd be surprised at how quickly such a display grinds to a halt when the leader sits back and says, "Whenever you're finished, gentlemen."

4.   Help others in the meeting to understand both sides by paraphrasing what has been said that could be misinterpreted. This will not only help you to confirm your understanding of what has been said, it will give others in the meeting a fresh view of the point. "You didn't ship on time" paraphrased could lead to the conclusion that the order was, indeed, shipped on time but delayed by the carrier.

5.   You can often solve head-to-head conflict by asking the combatants to paraphrase what the other has said. You will find that in many cases the shouting is a result of a misunderstanding and that the paraphrasing technique helps each person get a focus on the other's points.

6.   When members of the group express feelings in very emotional terms, you can help defuse the emotion and reduce its impact on the other members of the group by asking for a restatement. When people have to rethink an explosive statement and say it again, they often see the harm they are doing with explosive behavior.

7.   If the meeting goes off in inappropriate directions, ask the group if the current direction is going to arrive at the answer. Such meetings frequently get bogged down in charges and countercharges that become emotional and seldom have any bearing on the outcome.

8.   Put everything on the table. If you notice personal attacks taking place that have nothing to do with the problem, it's best to deal with them immediately. The two parties may be embarrassed, but in a meeting such as we are describing, each individual should be aware that problems are to be solved.

9.   Try to show every participant that your goal is to solve the problem and that the meeting is not just a whitewash. You can do this by placing yourself physically away from those who might be considered as your allies. When you encourage fresh input from both sides, you show that you want to solve the problem and not to railroad your goals.

It isn't easy to take part in meetings with your agents and their customers when bad feelings run high. But a calm third party can often do more to cement cracked relations than either party could do on their own. But keep your cool, even though you will probably have a lot at stake.

HOW TO WORK WITH AN AGENT YOU DON'T ESPECIALLY CARE FOR

"Marty's my best representative. I can't remember when he hasn't been on top of the pile, despite the fact that he has a lousy territory. But I really don't like him. He's loud and just plain difficult." Not an unfamiliar story. In fact, it's a story that is frequently told in business as well as in everyone's personal life. The fact of life is this: There are people with whom we must associate but who are not the kind of people we like to be with socially.

>>>→ *OBSERVATION* According to industrial psychologists, most business relationships are built on successes, rather than personal likes. And the most successful businesspeople are those who are able to see the strengths in their associates and work productively with them, regardless of whether or not they get along personally. This is a problem that manufacturers often encounter with their agencies. The traditional manufacturer came up through engineering or finance, disciplines that don't stress sociability. Those who run agencies, however, made their way up through the sales ranks, where being outgoing and dominant can mean the difference between success and failure.

It does, of course, make a big difference when you can get along personally with your agencies, but when you find yourself dealing with personalities that clash with yours, we have some suggestions to make the relationship work.

Don't dodge the situation by using an intermediary. Whether you're the president of the company or the marketing manager running the agency team, the chances are that you can find someone to deal with the agent. But, this is a serious mistake. First of all, you will cut yourself off from an important channel of information. You know what happens to information when it's passed from person to person. Second, your action is a signal to the agent that all is not right. You surely don't want this. However, you can use a third party, but not as a go-between. Whenever you schedule meetings with your unpopular agent, make sure that you take along another person. But make sure that the other person fits. Take someone from marketing or sales who has direct responsibility in the department. Don't take an engineer or the shipping manager just to have a third-party buffer. The third person can often serve to interpret situations that you find difficult to handle because of the personality problems. And that third person, without doing a thing, will tend to keep animosities from arising.

Make your meetings coincide with your moods. It's a lot easier to deal with irksome people when you're up than when you're down. It's hard to predict when you're going to be up and will feel like dealing with your problem person, but when you know your mood is good, seize the opportunity. Even if it's just a phone call made on the spur of a good moment, do it right away.

Make sure that you control the meeting. We don't mean that you should dominate and dictate, but you should be able to control the timing. Most people can deal with a difficult person for a short period of time. It's often easier to handle these meetings when you are the visitor and not the one being visited. Just plan your time with the agent so that you cover what you want to discuss, but don't leave enough time to become annoyed.

Keep your cool. You may never say anything to the agent directly, but everyone knows when friendships are strained. For this reason observe the common rules—try to be friendly, smile when it's appropriate, and try to keep the hard edge out of your expression and your voice. Observing the amenities will keep the meeting on course, and it may even open the door to friendship. Animosity usually produces the same response in the other person. Friendliness has the opposite effect.

»»→ OBSERVATION The chances are that the agent you're not too fond of is liked by most other people in your organization. And others on your staff may have similar feelings for other agents. The psychological fact is that this is just personal chemistry. Good businesspeople learn to work productively with everyone, regardless of personal likes and dislikes. However, it's important for you to make sure that any problems you have with an agent aren't generalized to others. View each relationship individually and learn to work with people with whom you might not be especially fond, and you should be two thirds of the way to running a top agency team.

AVOIDING THE MYTHS ABOUT AGENTS THAT HINDER YOUR RELATIONSHIPS

"My agents want as little interference from me as possible, and the only thing that keeps them producing is the money." So said a sales manager who also admitted he has had serious agency turnover problems for a number of years. Like most bold statements in business, and just about every other human endeavor, these are half-truths. They are feelings that represent the facts but represent them from the point of view of personal bias.

The truth of the matter is that agents today are a lot different from the way they were ten years ago; so are sales managers. Traditional motivation techniques that used to do the job are thought to be archaic by many. The expectations of manufacturers and their agencies are a lot different. Manufacturers' agents have stronger academic, business, and personal backgrounds than they had in the past. In fact, they are probably among the most achievement-oriented, well-educated groups in the business world today. This is not soap box stuff—it's fact. But, you the manufacturer, the sales manager, are in similar circumstances. It's these modified profiles that mean it's imperative for you to reevaluate some of the myths you may have inherited concerning agencies.

The first myth is that money is the only thing that motivates a manufacturers' agent. It's true that most agents do make considerably more money than they did the salaried jobs they left, and money still is and always will be a powerful agency motivator. However, most of the agents today are in the field for another reason—they thrive on competition and achievement. They are seeking self-satisfaction that, for them, can be found nowhere else. Research has shown that in organizations that reward their agencies well but deny them any self-satisfaction, the turnover is as high as it is with companies with lesser compensation programs. Everyone knows you go only so far with financial rewards, but the strokes, the praise and recognition possibilities, are virtually endless. When was the last time you called an agency owner out of the blue and told him or her how good a job that person was doing?

The next myth centers on the idea that good agents are loners, people who want to have as little interaction with anyone as possible. Again, this is a half-truth that has caused a lot of unhappiness for manufacturers and agencies. Agents aren't loners, but they do like to do it their way. Those in the corporate world frequently think that anyone who leaves the embrace of the corporation must be a loner. The truth is that most agents can tolerate being alone in order to do the job they want to do, but they are not loners as most people use the term. The complaint we hear frequently from agents is that their principals don't spend enough productive time in the field with them. They do say that the unannounced or protracted and pointless visits make life difficult. Most agents welcome productive help from their principals, but don't tell them how to sell. Don't grab their act when you make a buddy call on a customer; do get in there with the help that each agent says will be beneficial. Just because agency owners dislike paper work and reporting doesn't mean they want to be left alone. They do want positive, practical help—and no backslapping.

Again, input indicates that agency people who feel least able to handle certain lines are those who have been poorly prepared by their principals. When a poorly prepared agent doesn't do as well as he feels he should with a line, the feelings of failure are reinforced by less attention to the line. Do you make support calls, do field coaching, go out of your way to include every agency person in your corporate family?

This myth often has some visible evidence for it, but as you will see, the myth has grown from irrelevant ideas. The image of an agent in the eyes of many manufacturers is that of a one-man band working out of an office knee-deep in paper. In short, most manufacturers tend to think agent activity is almost random—that very little planning goes into their work. When more agencies have computers than don't, you have to assume organization is a major part of their activity. It's true most agencies run lean, and the result can be a messy office. It is, however, a mistake to judge an agency by such irrelevant criteria.

The last myth may hit close to home. Most sales managers feel that after a few years they can spot "good" and "bad" agencies when they are recruiting. Incidentally, agents have the same problem, too. The fact is that there are really no good or bad agencies. There are just agencies that are better qualified to do the job you want done than others. Feelings do count, but there is no substitute for time and a careful evaluation when you are planning to appoint an agency to a territory.

⋙→ ***OBSERVATION*** It's a different ball game today, but the goals are the same. By understanding your needs in detail and the unusual challenges and opportunities that exist with agencies today, you can have the best marketing system available—with very little effort.

DON'T HIDE BEHIND YOUR COMPANY WHEN YOU HAVE AGENCY PROBLEMS

An agent we spoke with recently related a scene that took place at a sales meeting. "After the meeting, I spoke with Charlie (the sales manager) and wanted clarification on their new policy of credit qualification. Frankly, I thought the idea was a bad one, and one that would put a lot of restrictions on us. No sooner did I bring this up—in a friendly way—than Charlie got defensive and began passing the buck. All he would say was something about new company policy."

Caution: Whether you're the president, the sales manager, or whatever, you are the company when dealing with your agents. You can't take the position of being one of the boys when the heat is on, and you can't go the other way as a hard-nose. This doesn't mean you can't maintain friendships and still represent your company properly. You can and should. Here are a few tips that will help you in this touchy situation:

⋙→ ***IDEA IN ACTION*** When you are faced with an agency problem, address it directly and rationally. Make sure the agent involved knows that despite any personal relationships, you are speaking for the company. When you speak "excathedra," you will always be in a strong position to handle the problem. When you take the one-of-the-boys approach, you lose status with the agency, with your boss, or others in the company.

In any dispute, you must always give the agent the full opportunity to state his or her case. If you're handling the problem face to face, this means being a good listener and not interrupting—even when you are upset about something that may have been said. If the problem is being handled by mail, urge the agent to make a complete case in writing.

Problems occur in all aspects of personal and business life. When you are trying to resolve them, stick to the facts; don't drag extraneous elements into the discussion. Above all, don't raise the question of the other person's motives. Most agent/manufacturer problems hinge on specific points: a manufacturer fails to deliver on time or an agent fails to follow up on an inquiry. If these are the problems, stick to them. Don't accuse the manufacturer of sloppy production control or the agent of poor planning. Stick to the issue at hand.

Avoid being defensive. This isn't easy most of the time, whether you're an agent or a manufacturer. You take your business seriously, and you probably take it personally. However, just as soon as you let personal feelings creep into the discussion it will fall apart.

Make sure that the agent knows exactly what can and cannot be done about the problem. Don't be vague—be up front when you present the alternatives.

Agents, like anyone else, appreciate straight answers. You can ensure the respect of your agencies and the management of your company by facing problems squarely, not by hiding behind a corporate smoke screen.

HOW TO DEAL WITH AN OVERDEPENDENT AGENT

"Ed came well recommended. I talked with a few of his principals and they all told me the same thing—Ed's a good agent. He's been on board now for almost six months and he still comes to me with questions I think he should handle himself." The manufacturer speaking was having mixed feelings about a new agent. On the one hand, he had positive feedback from several of the agent's principals whom he respected. On the other hand, he knew that he was spending more time with the new agent than he thought he should.

Any new agency takes time to get the lay of the land and to get on the move with a minimal tie to the principal. Assuming that the agent is experienced and has a successful track record with his or her principals, there are a few questions you should ask of the agent—and of yourself.

>>>→ *IDEA IN ACTION* Review your possible contribution to the problem first. Assume that your new agent has brought you some quotes that are a little offbeat—that don't quite measure up to the business you and he discussed during the interview. Ask yourself just how vital the difference might be. You want to make sure that the agent is on the right track. More often than not, new agencies are anxious to bring in as much business as possible early in the relationship, and their relative inexperience with your line will lead them to depend more heavily on you to decide on the acceptable orders.

Too often a sales manager is overanxious about the success of his new agencies. When this happens, the sales manager usually spends a lot of time looking over the new agent's shoulder. This is seldom done because the manufacturer is concerned about the choice. It's done because the manufacturer wants the agent to succeed. When too many questions are asked, agents frequently get the impression that you may not have as much confidence in them as you should. This, in turn, leads the new agent to run a little nervous and to be more dependent than he or she should be. As you can see, the whole thing becomes circular. If you find yourself in such a situation, back off and let the agent fly. Remember, one of the reasons you have agents is to free yourself from managing a salaried salesforce. Agents are entrepreneurs and should require very little supervision. If after you back off the dependency cycle doesn't change, then you should try to get directly at the problem. Ask the agent if there are any problems and what you can do to help solve them.

Make sure that you are giving the new agents all the information they need. Are you keeping them up to date on product development, modifications, shipping schedules, sales aids, and everything an agency needs from you to be successful? Without good and sufficient information, a conscientious agent will be at you for help. This will probably appear to be dependence, but it really is your agent/ business partner pleading for information in order to do the best job.

If you have an open relationship with all of the staff in the agency, make sure that every contact you make with a staff person is reported one way or another to the owner. An apparently dependent agency owner may just be looking to close the information loop.

Are you too critical of early mistakes? Every new agency, not unlike every new employee, makes mistakes early in the game. If you treat mistakes as learning experiences and are not overly critical of them, your new agents will be less likely to make the same mistake again. However, if you are especially critical of early mistakes, the chances are very good that the agents whom you have criticized will come to you with similar problems in the future, rather than try to solve them themselves. You can avoid this kind of dependence by not being too critical of mistakes and by helping the agent to solve the problem himself.

The overdependent agent is not a common problem. But when it occurs, the roots can usually be traced to the early days of the agent/manufacturer relationship. Early impressions are strong and frequently difficult to change. Here are a few approaches you can use to solve the problem. Remember, though, that agents are by nature independent, and you can make the most of this important characteristic by not putting a tight rein on in the early days.

The next time a new agent comes to you with a question or a problem, try not to provide the answer directly. Say something like this, "I'm not too sure about that. What do you think we should do about it?" Then when the agent supplies the solution, lay on a few strong but not obvious compliments. This technique will soon undo the problem that may have been created in the early stages of the relationship.

The next time an agent presents a plan that may have a few minor problems, don't point them out immediately. Rather, ask the kind of questions that will lead the agent to spot them and to come up with corrective action. Once an agent is given the impression that he must turn to you more frequently than he does with his other principals, the chances are that he will be less likely to take risks. This is a risk-taking business; don't squash this important agent characteristic by doing things that make him or her feel more dependent on you than is really necessary.

>>>→ *OBSERVATION* To let the agent know that his views are valued and that his independent ideas are welcomed, it's often a good idea to seek his or her advice on a problem that isn't directly related to the relationship. One manufacturer said this: "After I realized that I had held the reins too closely, I helped make the break by asking my new agency to offer suggestions for the expansion of the market. I made sure that I used their suggestions and also made sure that I told them that we did what we did because of them. From then on, they were on their own."

WHO'S IN CHARGE WHEN YOU'RE NOT THERE?

In many smaller companies, the person responsible for managing the agency team has many other jobs to do. When one of these jobs, or even a sudden illness, prevents you from taking charge, you should make sure that someone can step in and hold the fort. Even if you're on the top of the sales organization chart and have a strong group of departmental people reporting to you, you should write down all the jobs that have to be done in your absence. Oddly enough, when you write down all of these jobs, you will probably find some tasks that waste your time and that can effectively be delegated to someone else on a permanent basis.

HOW TO TURN A SALESPERSON INTO A SALES MANAGER WHO CAN WORK WITH AGENCIES

In too many cases, successful salespeople are "rewarded" for their effort by being put in charge of a salesforce. When the salesforce consists of a team of manufacturers' agencies, the newly appointed sales manager has a lot to learn about management.

In too many cases the new sales managers feel they can motivate by example. They hit the territory like a whirlwind with the agency and "show" them how it's done. But this isn't the way to do it. The new sales manager knows how to sell—but so does the agency team. What the agencies are looking for is someone to represent them fairly with principal management. We talked with some agency people about this and thought their comments would be of interest.

Example: "The new guy was a real hotshot. No doubt about it, his sales record was first class. However, he was so self-sufficient that he never learned how to tap the strengths of others. He always took the bull by the horns, even when there were people to whom he could turn for faster and less turbulent answers."

The new manager with this outlook usually feels that all his agencies should behave the same way. But this just isn't a good use of human resources. However, it's important to know when to offer help and when not. When the offer of help will look like meddling, it's best to back off.

"The new manager really didn't pay any attention to what we said. He looked as though he was listening, but I guess he was just being polite."

Frequently the person who behaves this way has his or her own agenda and is just going through the motions with an agent. This is a waste of time for both people. Sure, it's not easy to take over the top sales job without some preconceived notions, but success will depend heavily on what is sold—and heard—by the new manager.

"He only knew one way to sell. Yeah, he was very successful at it, but so are we with the way we sell."

Caution: New sales managers may have to help direct people get started with the basics, but they should avoid telling agency people how to sell. Their selling styles may be just the opposite, but as long as they work without creating any problems, this should be a hands-off territory.

HOW GOOD AGENCIES BUILD CUSTOMER LOYALTY

When you think of customer loyalty, chances are you think mainly in terms of consumer brand loyalty—people who seldom switch brands. However, good agencies build loyalty to their operations by providing a combination of good service and good products. But the picture is a little more complex than this.

People who buy regularly from favored agencies do so because the agencies have solved problems for them and made it easy for them to get the products and services they want. However, even though many buyers are intensely loyal to some agencies, they still talk with representatives of other manufacturers. Why? According to business psychologists, they want to make sure that they are still making the right decision. They are usually not talking to other agencies to keep them honest or to keep them under the gun. The implications of this are significant. The agency that works at confirming the fact that a customer has made a wise choice will continue to have the edge.

Even though a buyer may have established strong loyalty to one agency and the products it sells, that buyer will probably still buy some competitive products. This is simply self-protecting behavior. It would be a mistake to push your agency to get all the business. Being the favored agency is to get the lion's share of the business. Even though the competitor and his or her agency may be in there getting some business and pushing hard for more, let it be. Concentrate on keeping the customer happy. As a manufacturer, you can do this more by strong factory backup of your agencies than anything else.

AGENCY CONTINUITY IS AN IMPORTANT FACTOR
FOR YOUR GROWTH

"I can remember that in the past when an agent called it quits, the territory went uncovered until a replacement could be found," a sales manager said. He continued, "With the trend to multi-person agencies today, however, this just isn't a problem." Agencies and manufacturers are doing things differently, and agency continuity is a subject of importance to both.

The manufacturer/agency relationship is a working partnership and bears little resemblance to the relationship that existed twenty years or so ago when most agencies were agents—one-man bands. And each has a vested interest in the long-term relationship. It is not appropriate for each to level with the other on plans for the future.

When you work with larger agencies, it's important to get to know everyone in the agency—and to make sure that they know you, your company, and your products. Individuals in the agency may leave or retire, but the agency goes on. However, to make sure that the same interest is taken in your products, you should take an active interest in the agency.

Your company, from an agency's point of view, is more than just the products you make and the commission checks you send. It's an ongoing organization with a history. That history can be very important to an agency in building a long-term relationship. When an agency can view the direction your company has taken against a background of what has happened in the past, it can work more closely for long pull. There should be no surprises. And you should expect the same openness from your agencies.

Even multi-person agencies can encounter occasional problems with the loss of a key person. "A man who had worked closely with our people and represented us very well in the territory and who owned half of the agency died suddenly," a marketing VP told us. "However," he continued, "we were able to solve our problem and help the agency at the same time. One of our bright salesmen was leaving—we just couldn't move him up fast enough. The agency hired him and we both reaped a lot of benefit."

WHY AGENTS ARE RELUCTANT TO REPRESENT CLOSELY HELD FIRMS

The closely held firm is frequently in the hands of a family, an individual, or a few individuals who bring to the business needed skills. But they frequently also bring to the business a set of blinders that makes it difficult for agencies to do the best job they can for them. When a firm is publicly held, the management team has to answer to stockholders—those who have put up their money to make money.

"I represent a firm that has one of the best lines on the market," an agency owner said. "Their personal goals are being met very well. However, they won't invest in more equipment to increase output. When I sell more than they can make, they simply say that the orders will take a little longer. I can appreciate their personal position, but I'm not sure that I want to continue handling the line under these circumstances." There are, of course, many elements in the decision to expand capacity, but it's easy to lose a good agency team when you play it safe.

Another agent said, "They (a closely held principal) react to situations when they occur and never plan far enough ahead to prevent problems or to take advantage of potentially good situations." Again, publicly held companies must answer to stockholders, and even relatively unsophisticated stockholders demand planning of corporate management.

Perhaps the most common problem for the closely held corporation is that of raising capital. Expansion requires capital, and owners are seldom excited about giving up any equity for a capital infusion.

There are plenty of problems with publicly owned companies, too. However, we bring up these points because of recent comments we have had from agencies who wanted to grow but were limited by the growth limits set by their principals. Not all closely held corporations are limited by these problems. However, we feel it's important for all concerned to recognize their goals and to level with each other when problems occur. An agent helped one of his principals with a delivery problem by locating a subcontractor who took up the slack when orders exceeded capacity.

HOW TO LEAD YOUR AGENCY TEAM THROUGH A TOUGH TRANSITION

"One of my principals sold out—literally," an agency owner complained recently. "He sold the business to a large conglomerate, and he also sold out the team of sales agencies that helped build his business for almost twenty years. The new owners took over almost immediately and no one knows yet where we stand." Take-overs occur every day. When they do, enlightened managers usually plan for such dislocating experiences well in advance.

Your agencies need special support from you and your corporate management team in order to cope with the emotional stress that sweeping changes can often bring. When your company undergoes a major change that directly affects your agencies, you as a company executive must exercise the best qualities of leadership in dealing with the anxieties and fears that people typically feel in such situations. Unless you give them support before, during, and after the change, the resulting stress can destroy your agencies' identity with and loyalty to the company. Here are some suggestions for handling a tough transition with your agency team.

    »»→ *IDEA IN ACTION* These are the basic principles that will help you lead your sales agency team through a turmoil: Understand an agency owner's complexity as a human being and be prepared to deal with the psychological needs of that person in adapting to change. When you plan and carry out change, be sure to protect the huge investment you have in the human assets of your agencies—their loyalty and their commitment. Be sure to avoid a course of action that will offend an agency owner's cherished values and thus evoke negative reactions. Above all, don't revert to the primitive carrot-and-stick theories of motivation that rely all too heavily on material rewards and punishments. Make sure that you allow more than enough lead and lag time for everyone to adjust to the changes.

Be sure to provide information. The more information your agencies have about the need for the change that is taking place and the criteria that guide it, the less threatened they will feel. If you don't provide information, the rumor mill will work overtime—to your detriment.

Get your agencies involved. Get as many people in each agency involved as is possible. When individuals feel that they are taking an active, rather than a passive, part in the change, they are more apt to respond positively.

Provide plenty of reassurance. During any change, agents depend on their contacts within the firm for morale boosting, feedback, and direction. They need authoritative assurance that only those in close contact with the management of the firm can provide. They need to know that corporate officials care—that they still recognize their contributions and understand their needs.

Provide active guidance. A new routine means that old responses are no longer acceptable and that new ones must be learned. When you leave enough time for a smooth transition, your agency people will be able to learn what will be expected of them in the future and you will give them an opportunity to rehearse their new roles.

Provide closer supervision. Everyone, including sales managers and agencies, tend to groove in success-tested routines. When the rules change, you can help your agency people make the change by staying closer to them during the transition.

Encourage open conversation about the changes. Invite them to state their concerns or vent their anger. Internalized anger just quietly boils until it finally erupts when you least expect it. When people are encouraged to talk about it, they can express and acknowledge their feelings, and the chances are they won't turn into scapegoats.

Continue to restate and clarify the situation. Uncertainty and confusion can be greatly relieved as individuals come to understand the exact nature of the change and how it will affect them. This understanding is frequently blocked by the emotional content of the situation. However, restatement and regular clarification can help penetrate the emotional feelings that often lead to misunderstanding and even open hostility.

Don't deny the real implications of the transition. If you hide the truth, your agents will not be prepared to face the truth when it is finally revealed. If this happens, you will go down many notches in their esteem.

Don't oversimplify the problem. It's tempting to reduce difficult situations to simpler, more palatable problems with simplistic solutions. It's a mistake and does far more harm than good.

>>>→ *OBSERVATION* Always remember that fairly treated people in the sales territories will speak well of you. You won't have to deal with the acrimony that so often accompanies unfair treatment.

Whenever anyone undergoes change, they inevitably have a genuine sense of loss. Giving up familiar places, people, habits, and routines is jarring. It should be noted that even changes for the good produce similar problems. Giving an agency a bigger territory may mean change in the fortunes of the agency, but it also means personal changes that require adaptation. If you follow the thoughts we have presented, you will do a lot to minimize the problems.

HOW TO GET MORE TIME FROM YOUR AGENCIES AND MAKE THE MOST OF THE TIME YOU GET

"I know that I'm sharing time with other manufacturers," a sales manager said, "but how can I get more of the agent's time or make the best use of the time that I do get?" Even those sales managers who are fully pleased with their agencies still want more of the agency's time. Let's look at a few ways to solve the problem.

>>>→ *OBSERVATION* The agency method of selling is not unlike computer time sharing; the computer user and the sales manager are getting cost-effective service that could be too expensive if others weren't involved. However, there are a number of ways a sales manager can boost sales through agencies without making demands that the agency might not be able to meet. In order to maximize the results of your agency team, it's first necessary to envision how an agent's day is spent. Based on input from a number of agents, this is the average day of an average agent:

Face-to-face selling—40%

Preparing for sales calls—25%

Handling paper work and making phone calls—15%
Time between calls—20%

These figures will vary from agency to agency, from territory to territory, and from market to market. But, in general, this is the way a typical agent spends a working day.

Face-to-face selling. This is the time that most manufacturers are seeking to maximize when they say that they want more of an agent's time. "It's not the amount of time we spend with a customer," an agent told us when we discussed this problem with him, "it's how effectively we make use of that time. When I have to take time to explain how one of my principal's products is going to do a job for the prospect—without the best backup materials—time is being wasted. But when a principal gives me everything I need to make the most of my face-to-face meetings, I can be much more effective, without spending a lot of time." The agent went on to say that it's "not the amount of time, but the quality of the time" that really counts. He said that his best efforts can be enhanced by input at other points in his day.

Preparing for sales calls. Agency sales calls require preparation, even if they are only lead follow-up calls. The well-prepared agent takes time to know something about the prospect's business, his requirements, and any problems that might exist with previous suppliers. "One of my principals subscribes to a reporting service that gives me a pretty good profile of the prospect before I ever make a call," an agent said. "I don't spend anymore time in face-to-face selling for this principal," he continued, "but with the information he gives me, I can make every minute with a prospect work like two or three." Other agents whose principals do tight lead qualification on inquiries feel that their principals are getting more effective time during face-to-face selling.

Handling paper work and making phone calls. Whether the agency is one person or more than one, paper work is always a big problem. As you know, agencies should not be asked for daily call reports or the independent contractor status will be violated. You know what that means in terms of federal tax regulations. However, reporting is critical for agencies and manufacturers. One sales manager we talked with told us about a project-reporting sheet he developed for his agencies to use. "The reports are not call reports. They are only to be used to save time and to keep us informed when another step in the negotiation of sales has been reached," he said. The form is a multi-element checklist. All the agency people have to do is identify the project, check off a few boxes, and drop the form in the mail. The form is used only when a major step—forward or backward—takes place. "This information lets us know how we might be able to help the agent," the manufacturer said. "It's definitely not a call report. But it does let us get more effective use of the time of each of our agencies."

Time between calls. This is about the only time of the day that is not productive for agency people. Whether it's time driving between calls or riding trains or planes, it's 20 percent of the day that can be put to better use—as many enterprising sales managers have done. "We send out tapes every month to each of our agents," a sales manager for an instrument company told us. "I do the first part of the tape—it's sort of a report of what the company is doing and what is happening in terms of sales. The rest of the tape is narrated by a moonlighting local radio announcer. Our ad agency writes the material. This gives the tape a professional sound. In fact, we encourage our agents to send us short tapes. We sometimes incorporate their material with the tapes that we do. The whole thing takes some time, but it's worth it. We feel that we are getting attention from our agencies when they are in the best position to benefit from it," the sales manager said.

⋙→ *WATCH THIS*   As many agents have told us, getting more of their time is most productively done in other than the face-to-face selling situations. Helping them to be most effective during the other parts of their day will allow them to make the most of the time they spend with prospects and customers on your behalf.

HOW TO BUILD AGENCY LOYALTY

"All agency operators are lone wolves," said a sales manager with a nationwide team of agents. But another sales manager wouldn't let it pass. "That just isn't so," he said. "But you have to work hard to earn their loyalty. When you do, there's no better way to sell." As you might imagine, a controversy such as this set us to thinking—and to talking with other sales managers.

One of the sales managers we talked with made this insightful comment: "If management takes the time to recognize the needs of the agencies and to see that they coincide with the interests of the principal, the only result can be agency loyalty." Developing company-minded agencies has a lot of advantages for you and for your agencies. Here are just a few that were mentioned by some of the people we talked with: "It strengthens loyalty to the principal and makes the agency people more willing to follow policies. It increases pride in the principal and in the agency. It motivates them to represent your company as you want it represented. It makes them more interested in responding to emergency situations. It reduces agency turnover." How do you build agency loyalty? Here are some thoughts:

Building Firm Foundations

If an agency is to be loyal to a principal, there are three needs that must be met:

1. *Personal recognition.* Telling the agency owner or his or her employees that a job was well done not only builds morale, it builds sales. Here are a few ways to do it. Write a personal letter of congratulations for a job well done, a big order, or an idea. Make every face-to-face encounter an opportunity to recognize personal accomplishment, especially when others can share in the experience. Give recognition in printed bulletins circulated to all the agencies and be sure to show appreciation for unusual accomplishments such as training a new salesperson, handling a difficult service problem, or for contribution during a sales meeting.

2. *Self-expression.* Everyone needs to be able to express himself or herself on important matters, and the manufacturer that encourages agents to express themselves will build loyalty. Agency selling is much more than 9 to 5 work—it's dedication. Even though agency owners and salespeople have wide latitude in calling their own shots on a day-to-day basis, they still need to be able to express themselves to their principals. Here are a few tips to help you build agency loyalty by encouraging self-expression: Make sure that your agents know that they can speak frankly at meetings; seek ideas from your agents in formal and informal conversations; be sure that they know you are sincerely interested in what they are saying by acknowledging the good ideas—and doing something about them.

3. *A sense of status.* Times have changed, and the concept of professional selling is such that even major universities grant degrees and certificates in the field. However, you, the principal, can make the most important contribution to your agency team's sense of status. You are the one who sets the tone in your organization for how your agents are regarded. Because you are the person to whom people in your company look for leadership, here are some of the things you can do to enhance the status of your agencies: Show your agencies the respect you want others to show to them; make sure that you take every opportunity to sell your agencies to everyone in your firm; encourage your agencies to take part in professional groups and associations that will benefit from their participation.

So far, we have touched on the elements that satisfy your agents' personal needs as members of your sales team. Now, let's look at the professional relationships the agent has with his own business and with your business. You will see that the elements that are important here are much the same as those that are important to those who are on your payroll. Agents don't get paychecks from you, but they should get the same personal treatment as you would give to valued company employees.

1. *Compensation.* There is probably no one more motivated to make money in the selling field than the agent. Compensation is set by the commission rate that applies to all agencies. However, no one is ever locked into one commission system forever. If you take every opportunity to check their attitudes on the plan and discuss the plans of other companies in the field, you will go a long way toward building loyalty. And, of course, you can enhance any fixed commission plan with special bonuses for specific performance. In short, keep an open mind on compensation and make sure that your agencies are aware of your interest.

2. *Security.* Agents are no different from employees when it comes to matters of security. They worry when a new sales manager comes on board. They wonder if the agency team will be replaced with factory-direct people when the conglomerate buys out their principal. And they wonder if the sales manager gets nervous writing commission checks for amounts that exceed his annual salary. These are real problems. However, you can do a lot to alleviate them and to build loyalty by taking the time to be open and straight with them, respect their opinions and

ideas, build them up every chance you get, see them on an informal basis as well as on company business.

3. *Opportunity for advancement.* Wait, don't skip on; we are talking about agencies, not salaried salespeople. However, the advancement that counts with agencies is a bit different from that which rings bells for salaried salespeople. For instance, when opportunities for new territories open up, talk to your agencies before you go looking to add another agency to the team. You just might find a few agencies that would like to expand with your line. If you have a manufacturer colleague who is looking for an agency, recommend yours. This is the kind of advancement that has meaning for independent agencies.

4. *Factory backup.* The company-minded agency knows that the factory is ready to provide backup when it's needed. Whether it's sales tools, advertising, sales leads, fast service, or just some counseling on a tough project, let your agencies know that you are ready to help—and then be sure to follow through on that promise.

>>>→ *OBSERVATION* By providing all the help you can in satisfying both the personal and business needs of your agencies, you will be doing everything possible to strengthen the effectiveness of your agency team. You will be building the kind of loyalty that everyone dreams of—manufacturers and agencies working together for mutual profit!

HOW TO GET A FRANK OPINION FROM AN AGENT

Most marketing people agree that it's good management to encourage discussion when an important proposal is placed before the agencies. A bunch of yes men isn't what the company needs. Yet some people who tell you that they can handle it have a lot of trouble putting their words into practice. An agent who was encouraged to be forthright by a principal's sales manager, told how the man bristled and finally pounded the table saying, "I'm the boss, and this is how it's going to be done."

If you really want an honest opinion from your agencies, you can get it. But if you find that you do bristle more than a little when people tell you things that make you uncomfortable, here are a few ways to handle the problem. You'll get the opinions you need and your agencies will have helped.

• *Ask for suggestions but don't invite an attack.* When you ask someone, "What do you think of this?" they might tell you and they might attack you. But by asking, "Can this be improved?" you have phrased your request in a way that invites positive suggestions.

• *Take the opinions in small doses.* It's a lot easier to handle contrary opinion in small doses than it is all at once. Rather than asking for a broad reaction to a proposal, seek input on each element separately.

• *Take your opinions one at a time.* Asking everyone at a rep council for an opinion might be more than you can handle. But talking to each member individually can make it easier to handle contrary opinion.

- *Desensitize yourself before the encounter.* If it's difficult for you to handle adverse opinions and you expect to get them during an agency meeting, take a few minutes just before the meeting to mentally conjure up an image of the encounter with you handling the flack with ease. This may sound like a simple-minded exercise, but it's the basic concept behind an effective psychological technique called behavior modification.

- *Get your input in writing,* if you really have difficulty handling contrary opinions. This way, you'll save yourself the possibility of a damaging blowup.

Agency input is important for every manufacturer. But you must remember that no one will agree with you on every topic you bring up. You will end up the loser if your agencies are afraid to express their disagreement. Don't risk cutting yourself off from the vital information you can get from your agencies just because you get some negative opinions.

FOURTEEN WAYS TO SET PRACTICAL GOALS WITH YOUR AGENCIES

When manufacturers and their agencies set goals together, it's a forward-looking process that sets activity in motion and keeps it on track.

You may have some general goals in mind for all of your agencies, but to be most effective, goal setting should be done individually—and with the full input and cooperation of the individual agencies. These are the points that agents and manufacturers agree on as being most helpful:

1. *State goals in terms of some specific output.* This doesn't mean that the agency goals should be set in terms of dollar volume or units of sales but in terms of activity that is understood by both parties. For example, opening new accounts, getting specified on a new power plant, being included on specific bidders' lists. These are specific goals. But they must be agreeable to you and your agencies.

2. *Include a time element.* Getting on a bidder's list may be a fine goal, but it should be stated within a specific time frame that is agreeable to you and to your agencies.

3. *Include long- and short-range goals.* Long-range goals are generally strategic goals, and short-range goals are often called operating goals. Both are important. Long and short range is quite different for different industries. But you'll find it easier to plan your operating goals once you have defined your long-range goals. When your agencies participate in planning, you will not only get direct market information, but you will get ideas to help you plan other aspects of your marketing program, such as advertising and trade show development.

4. *Set ranges, rather than finite goals.* Sales and marketing is really the management of uncertainty. You never know what's going to happen to upset your apple cart. Since the business world has a way of upsetting apple carts, most marketing managers feel that setting ranges is the better way to go. However, within

the ranges, you might consider alternative courses to take when a competitor upsets your apple cart.

5. *Know what happened in the past before you set goals for the future.* Trends frequently tell you which way to go—and which way not to go. Setting goals without looking at history usually results in reliving a lot of mistakes.

6. *Set goals face to face.* Goal setting needs input from both sides—some bargaining and personal commitment from both parties—if it's to succeed. Since you and your agencies will be making commitments to each other, it's best to do it face to face.

7. *Make sure everyone is aware of the goals.* Don't set yourself up for surprises; include everyone. When everyone agrees to the goals being set, it becomes a lot easier to achieve those goals.

8. *Don't make a goal out of an ego trip.* Everyone's under the gun one way or another. This doesn't mean that the goals should be set to make anyone a hero. Practical goals that are achieved make everyone a hero.

9. *Make your goals written and verbal.* When you and your agencies agree verbally to specific goals during a face-to-face meeting, it's always best to summarize in writing those things on which you agreed and disagreed. This gives both parties an opportunity to check performance along the way.

10. *Be prepared to adjust goals if necessary.* Even the best planning is based on some uncertainty. When you and your agencies discover that some goals must be revised, do it right away and with the cooperation and approval of all.

11. *Set conditional goals when it's appropriate.* It's fine to say that you want to establish a beachhead at such-and-such company. But that beachhead may not be important if the company doesn't get a big contract it's after. When there are contingencies, be sure to include them in the specified goals.

12. *Be prepared to deal with side effects.* No matter how carefully you plan, goal setting and goal attainment will produce positive and negative side effects. Be ready to neutralize the problem effects and to take advantage of the positive effects.

13. *A solid customer request should become everyone's goal.* Planning is a big help, but between planning and execution, a lot of interesting things can happen. When these interesting things happen, and when they can become practical and profitable, make them goals to be included with your plans-in-action.

14. *The people who set the goals are as important as the goals.* Some people are very good at setting high goals but fall short of total performance. Others set reasonable goals that they meet. Make sure you really know the people with whom you set your goals.

Example: "Until we started setting goals with our agencies, it was like pulling teeth to get project funding from management," a sales manager said. "When the brass saw what we and the agencies felt we could do together, the money appeared. This was a backward way to do things, but now we get top attention when we ask for funds." This is just one of the fallout effects of good goal setting with agencies.

Others have told us how they get better at goal setting every time they do it. "It's almost routine now," a marketing VP reported. A word of caution, though. If you make a mistake in setting a goal, you will set a lot of mistakes into action as the goal activity gets in motion. One way to minimize this is to plan very carefully with your agencies every step of the way.

Caution: Don't use goal setting as a measuring device for agency termination. If a goal is not obtained, all aspects should be carefully studied to determine why the goal was not reached, rather than just assuming that the agency did not do its job.

HOW TO SOLVE AGENCY PROBLEMS BEFORE THEY GET STARTED

More than a few sales managers are proud of their open door policy with their agencies. This is fine, but by the time an agent comes storming through the open door with a problem it may be too late. Sales managers who have the respect of their agencies usually claim that they try to deal with difficult situations before they appear in the open door. Here's how they do it.

1. Stay in touch with your agents regularly—in writing and either on the phone or face to face.
2. Don't rely on one agent passing information to another. Make sure that each agency gets the message directly.
3. Tell your agencies that they can send you complaints anonymously. It's not easy for an agency to unload when you hold some pretty high cards. However, early anonymous communication can shortstop a lot of difficulty.

HOW DO YOUR AGENTS LIKE BEING PART OF YOUR TEAM?

Time changes everything, including an agency's feelings about you and your company. More than a few manufacturers send questionnaires to their agencies regularly (once or twice a year) to take the pulse of the team. Here are a few questions that seem to get at important issues:

1. When you became our agent were you given everything you needed to do the best job you could?
2. Do you feel that you can get to the people within our company who are in a position to help you make sales?
3. When you get to these people, are they helpful?
4. What are your feelings about our business relationship (commissions, advertising, field sales support, and so on)?
5. What are your feelings about our line (quality, delivery, relationship to competitors)?
6. What can we do to help strengthen our agency relationship?

⋙→ *OBSERVATION* Manufacturers who take this approach usually tell their agencies that they can either identify themselves or return the questionnaires without signing them. Most agencies, these people claim, identify themselves. It seems that only the manufacturers with a lot of problems, as far as their agencies are concerned, get a lot of unsigned questionnaires. Another tip: Send questionnaires to those agencies who are no longer on your team—whether you terminated them or they left of their own accord. You can get some very insightful information from this group.

IS YOUR LINE REALLY ATTRACTIVE TO MANUFACTURERS' AGENCIES?

"Manufacturers' agencies always show a keen interest in selling our products," a sales manager said the other day. "The ads I run turn up a lot of agencies, but when we get down to the short strokes, there have been no takers." This sales manager had been looking for agencies in prime territories, and on the surface he seemed to be doing a lot of things right. Yet he was unable to sign on the agencies he wanted.

⋙→ *OBSERVATION* The best agencies for you may well be agencies that are already successful in the territory. And when it comes time to sign up a new principal, they ask a lot of searching questions. They want to know everything they can find out about your products, your sales policies, how much you advertise, how you screen your inquiries, and many other things.

After talking with many manufacturers who sell through agencies, we have compiled a list of some of the questions that agencies most frequently want answered when talking with a prospective principal.

- *What is the history of the company?* Agencies want to know not only how long you have been in business but how long it took to get to your present condition. They want to know how your company stands in the field. They are concerned with the reception they will get when they make calls for you. Let's face it, they want to make sure that your line has the same reputation that their other lines have.

- *Is there a strong story behind the product?* Agencies are looking for products to sell today, but they are also looking for principals who are actively engaged in developing new products. They also want to know if you're a leader in new product development or if you follow a leader. It isn't always necessary to be first with a new product. Frequently those who add new twists to products gather the largest share of the market.

- *What about production?* Agents want to know whether you can keep up with the demand they create for your products. This, incidentally, is one of the reasons most agents want to visit your plant before they agree to take on your line.

- *How is the product sold?* To end users? To distributors? Good agents know that it takes a much different kind of selling to move products to distributors than it does to sell those same products to end users. There may be a product line match, but there also has to be a customer match.

• *What kind of backup do you provide?* The first thing most agencies want to know is how you advertise and how you qualify the leads generated by your advertising. They also want to know about your other promotional activities such as trade show participation.

• *What about sales policies?* This, of course, translates into the question of commissions—how much and how they are paid. With the number of manufacturers turning to agency selling these days, it's critical that you know the standards of your industry and meet or better them.

• *Is the product line complex and does it require considerable experience to master it?* A complex line means considerable agency involvement, and sharp agencies want to make sure that you are going to spend the time with them that they need to master the line and to take it to market effectively.

• *Is competition a serious question?* There is hardly a product that doesn't have a competitor, but agencies want to know every detail of your story and the competitor's product. If they are to represent you successfully they have to know everything —including the warts.

• *What are the major markets you serve?* Agents want to know exactly how you perceive your markets; they will use this information to play against their own experience in the marketplace. Most agencies are especially interested in neglected markets, assuming that your product has been on the market for some time.

• *What is the potential for your company and for your products?* This is the age of acquisitions and mergers. You can't blame an agency for being a little nervous when it takes on a line that might be a takeover candidate. New brooms like to sweep. That might include a marketing strategy shift that could affect the agencies.

• Here are a few other questions that agencies frequently ask of principals: What are your gross sales? What were your sales in the territory last year? What is your share of the market? What sales volume do you feel we should be able to produce from the territory? What is your policy on sales literature and other sales aids? What kind of product training do you provide for new agencies? Do you provide periodic product training updates? Do you make field calls with your agencies? Who was the previous agent in the territory? May we talk with four of your present representatives? Who are your major customers in the territory? What is your policy concerning house accounts?

You have to make as much of a commitment to an agency salesforce as you would to a salaried sales team. In the case of agencies, you are dealing with other businesspeople, not employees. The questions they will ask—and should have answered— are more searching than those asked by prospective employees. It's important to keep this distinction in mind during agency interviews.

WHAT DO MOST MANUFACTURERS EXPECT FROM THEIR AGENCIES?

The first thing a manufacturer expects from an agency—or from anyone who takes on the sales role—is sales. However, because the manufacturer/agency relationship is a working partnership, manufacturers expect more than just sales. They expect that they and their agencies will interact on any number of things and that a solid relationship will be established over the years. Here are the points manufacturers consider to be important in the relationship.

- *They should grow with their principals.* Most manufacturers who talked on this point said their agencies should be willing to invest in expansion if they (the principals) do the same. The manufacturer/agency relationship is a working partnership, but both sides must be up front when it comes to investment for expansion. It's unfair to expect agencies to invest in growth to get order levels up before you invest in expanded production facilities.

- *Feedback is necessary.* "We want to know what's going on in the field." And you have a right to be kept up to date on all matters relating to the sale of your line. Feedback is a two-way street. The lack of manufacturer feedback is a key criticism most agents level at their principals. Remember that feedback cannot take the form of formal call reports or you will violate the independent contractor status of your agencies and put yourself and your agencies in a bad position with the IRS.

- *Honest views are valued.* If you're a heavy-handed pusher, the chances are that you will be told only what you want to hear by your agencies. However, if you make sure that your agencies know that you value their honest opinions, no matter how difficult they may be to take, you will get them. Open relationships survive and thrive.

- *Strong follow-up is rewarded.* Most manufacturers that sell with sales agencies spend considerable sums on advertising and promotion. And the more sophisticated of these know that it's the follow-up that counts in making the most of this effort. If follow-up requires specific customer service, such as installation of a product, you should make certain that your agencies are compensated for this work in addition to commissions paid for sales.

- *Attendance at sales meetings is critical.* Most of the manufacturers who mentioned this feel that it's critical for at least one person from each agency on the team to attend sales meetings. It has become more and more of a pattern for manufacturers to pay the expenses of the agents who attend sales meetings. Even though your costs may be high, remember that the day or two that the agent is out of the field is costing him money. The point is this: Make sure that you have a real reason for having a sales meeting.

- *Fast response to queries is important.* It seems that one of the things that sticks in the craw of most sales managers today is the notion that they don't get fast response to letters and calls to their agencies. We hear this from both sides of the team. Agents claim that one of their pet peeves is that their principals don't respond to them as quickly as they would like. We don't have an answer for either.

- *Handle the line as though it were the only line in the bag.* This can be roughly translated to the age-old question of trying to get more of your agency's time. Everyone would like to have their agencies devote more time to their line. The only way an agency can work on a commission basis is by selling a number of lines. But you can get more attention if you give your agencies more attention. It's the manufacturers who put on agencies and then proceed to neglect them who seem to complain the most.

- *Stand booth duty at national trade shows.* More than a few manufacturers that sell nationally expect some of their agencies to stand booth duty at trade shows, even when the show is out of their territory. As we mentioned earlier when we discussed sales meetings, even if you pay all expenses, time out of the territory is money out of the pocket of your agents. We know that manning a national trade show booth can be a difficult problem when you don't have a salaried salesforce that does exactly as it's told. But it's unfair to lay that burden on out-of-territory agencies. Some manufacturers have solved this problem by not only paying all expenses but by paying their agencies a per diem rate based on what the agent feels his time is worth in terms of average commissions earned.

- *Nonselling services are important.* Some types of selling require nothing more than making the sale. However, in some fields, particularly those that require engineering and installation, nonsales services may be important. Factory salespeople do whatever their job specification calls for. But when the work is to be done by agents, the duties should be spelled out in the contract, as should be the compensation arrangement. Agents in fields that require duties other than selling seldom have any problems doing the nonselling work. However, they most frequently complain that the amount of the work was misrepresented to them initially. Our advice is to be up front about this aspect of your agency relations. Don't wait until there's a blowup. If you expect your agencies to do market estimates, sales forecasting, and similar sales-related work, discuss this, too, well in advance of making the request. Many agencies do this work as a matter of routine for their own use and can simply pass on the information to you. But if it has to be done from scratch, you should expect to compensate the agency for the work.

As you can see, many of the manufacturers' expectations are reasonable once they are looked at from the perspective of both the manufacturer and the agency. There are other points that are frequently mentioned when we open this topic at seminars, but these are the points that seem to generate the most interest. Most of the other subjects that are mentioned really don't require discussion. They are things that most agents agree on anyway. For example, some manufacturers say that they expect their agencies to keep their trade secrets and not to sell competitive products. We suspect that the manufacturers who mention these and several other obvious points are usually inexperienced in the use of sales agencies.

WHAT DO MOST AGENCIES LOOK FOR IN THEIR PRINCIPALS?

As you might imagine, agencies are asking some tough questions today before they take on a new line. "We weren't too selective in the early days," an agent told us, referring to the days after World War II. "But now that the agency method of selling is accepted by everyone, including some of the Fortune 500, most agencies are very careful about the lines they take on."

Most agencies today are multi-person operations, and their owners are capable of some sophisticated management—as well as some pretty aggressive selling. The agent we talked with claimed that it is a mistake to take on a line if the agency can't make a big success of the effort. As one agent put it, "Nobody takes on a line these days just to fill out a line or to add a name to a line card. Any new line must fit very carefully, not only with the products being handled but with the agency personality and with the long-range plans." This same agent explained that he still actively seeks new lines but the lines he looks for meet rigid requirements that he has established for the growth of his agency. Here are some of the major points that agents use when they evaluate a new line and the manufacturer that makes it:

Does the product line fit? This, of course, is basic. Agents not only want to know if your line fits with the lines they already have, but they also want to know how your line will help move the other products in the agency.

What is your history in terms of product delivery and commissions? Today, more than ever, agents are asking for clear statements about deliveries and shipments. Since agencies are paid only when they sell something, they want to make absolutely certain that they can get repeat business for your line. If there is even a hint of delivery problems, most agents will think twice about taking on a line.

What is your financial status? You don't have to expose sensitive financial information, but good agents will want to get a handle on your general financial health. After all, they are going to invest their own time and money selling your products, and they want to make sure that you have the resources to deliver when they sell.

Why are you signing on an agency? If there is already another agency in the territory, the agencies you interview will want to know why you're making the change. Or if you're switching from direct sales to agencies, they'll want to know why. And even if this is your first stab at the market, most agencies would like to know why you decided to sell through agencies. Your reasons are reflected in your goals, and when an agency understands your goals, it can do a better job for you.

What about sales volume? Most agencies won't work on a sales quota system, but they do want to know how you read the volume for their territory. This can help them set internal goals that relate to your expectations.

Who are the current customers? If you've been doing business in the territory, the agency will want a list of the current customers and an estimate of the volume you are doing with them.

What about the growth of the company? Be prepared to tell the company story to prospective agencies. They will want to know just where you are in terms of the industry, your competitors, and the technology that makes your company and your products competitive.

Do you promote your products? Sales leads are critical for success in many fields, and the agencies in these fields will want to know where and how you promote and how carefully you qualify the leads your promotion generates.

Do you provide the support that's needed? Most agencies take for granted the samples and catalogs that are needed to do the job. However, today they are concerned with the speed and quality of responses to their requests for price, delivery, and technical specifications.

Do you keep your agencies informed regularly? It's lonesome in the field, especially when you're spending a lot of time, effort, and money selling a product for a manufacturer that doesn't communicate. Agents will ask you about your field visits, newsletters, memos, and phone calls. In fact, more than a few we've talked with said that they tell their principals in advance that they are going to call them regularly.

Are your commissions fair? Because of the intense competition for agents, it's the rare manufacturer that doesn't pay at least the industry rate or better. Agents will want to know the exact rate. Although a higher than average rate is important, it's just as important for the agent to know that you pay commissions on time.

Do you really understand an agent's motivation? Unfortunately, there still are some sales managers who feel that their agencies should behave much the same as salaried employees. The agents of today will want to make sure that you understand that the manufacturer/agency relationship is a partnership of two businesses.

Will you provide early training? Agencies don't need to be told how to sell, but they do need help with the specifics of your product line. A popular question centers on how soon after the ink is dry on the contract will you make the time to help the agency understand your product and your markets.

What are the territorial boundaries? This may seem to be very obvious, but more than a few manufacturers that haven't worked with agencies in the past fail to look carefully at this point. You actually could lose an agency candidate by offering more territory than he wants. Even though good agencies are always looking to expand, your offer may be beyond their projections and capabilities at the moment. Discuss territories before you make any pronouncements.

Will your agencies be included in the decision process? As we mentioned earlier, your agencies are your business partners, not your employees. They expect to be consulted when decisions are to be made that affect them in any way.

What are your realistic expectations for the territory? We heard of a manufacturer that dropped its regional factory salespeople in favor of agencies. This manufacturer reasoned that an agency with ten men in the territory is going to be a lot more effective than a single salaried salesperson. So far, the reasoning holds water. But this manufacturer multiplied his expectations by the number of men in each agency and was deeply disappointed when a ten-person agency didn't bring in ten times the business. Agency owners will want to know just how much you know about agency selling and what you expect them to do.

How flexible are you? The first year or two is a test for agents and manufacturers. As time goes on, conditions change, and both should be willing to make adjustments when necessary.

Agents are asking some tough questions today. Recently, a manufacturer told us that he "wasn't going to answer all of those questions. It's my product and my business," he continued. This same manufacturer spent about a year talking to agencies and not answering their questions. He wasted an awful lot of time before he realized that he wasn't hiring salespeople, he was entering partnerships with other businesspeople.

AGENTS TALK ABOUT EXPEDITING

Why should the average agent care when the products he sells for a principal aren't shipped on time? After all, the commission has already been paid and the agent is busy generating other orders. As an agent told us recently, "The customer refused to place another order until the previous order was shipped. When I tried to expedite the order with the factory, they told me that I had to get in line." There was more to the story, but this snippet makes the point.

It's too easy to think of internal matters such as a production slowdown only in familiar terms. However, as many agents have pointed out, a slowdown in delivery frequently results in a slowdown in future orders. There are, of course, times when nothing in the world is going to get a production line moving fast enough to catch up with a backlog. However, it's just as important to keep the question of future sales in mind, as well as the details of speeding up production. We asked a number of agents for their views on this subject, and their opinions follow:

• If you know that delivery is falling behind, don't hope that the lack of shipments will go unnoticed. Take the initiative. Contact your agencies first. If they feel that a late shipment will be a problem for the customer, get on the phone or write as soon as possible. It's tempting to ask your agencies to handle this chore because they have the face-to-face contact. But it's also possible to pass on your problems to the agency that has spent considerable time, money, and effort to establish a solid selling rapport.

• Most delivery problems are a long time in the making. That is, it's rare for production problems to develop overnight, unless of course there are unforeseen difficulties such as machinery failure and labor disputes. When you know that a slowdown is in the making, let your agencies know in advance. They aren't going to quit selling; they still make their money on commissions. But they are going to sell honestly, relating the problems to the customer. Nobody likes surprises. Good customers will pull with you when you are honest with them. But deceived customers go to competitors.

• Make firm commitments. Let your agencies relay the dates you will deliver products. The commitments are not only helpful internally to keep things on track but they show your agencies and their customers that you are serious about business.

- If it's a serious enough problem, it might be wise for someone from the factory to make a visit with key customers with the agencies involved. It's surprising how effective such a visit can be, especially if it's made early in the game. Last-ditch visits made to placate irate agencies and customers are usually doomed to failure.

- It isn't over when you deliver. It's tempting to forget about the hassle after you finally deliver. But the chances are that your customers are still living with the problem, especially if you sell OEM products that have held up an assembly line. A note, a phone call, or even a visit if the problem was serious enough might be called for.

MANAGEMENT BY WANDERING AROUND, AGENCY STYLE

One of the current theories of good management is based on what its proponents call wandering around. The notion is based on greater personal contact between managers and those whom they manage. However, more than a few management experts warn those who haven't taken to wandering around that a sudden and unexplained interest in those being managed is usually taken as prying. But there is real validity to direct regular personal contact, and it's as valid for a manager working with a team of agents as it is for any other manager. Here are some thoughts to help you make the most of the concept with your agencies.

- Don't wander around your agencies' territories without letting them know you're coming. Most agents welcome a visit from the factory, especially if it's aimed at accomplishing a specific goal. They like to plan for these visits—to set up meetings, to have information ready. But they really have difficulty juggling tight schedules when someone wanders in unannounced.

- Be prepared for direct communication. If there is a layer of management between you and your agencies, direct communication is especially practical in working with agencies that have a difficult time getting to you through a chain of command.

- Set up a system that provides a constant flow of information. The notion of wandering around has a positive psychological effect when you show that your intentions are to strengthen the bonds between your company and your agencies. However, most field visits are short, and the time between them is usually long. You can use the visits to set up regular communication and to discuss issues that relate to specific agencies.

- Ask for ideas. One of the reasons why the Japanese style of management is so effective is that managers are encouraged to offer imaginative ideas, and they are not penalized when they don't work. Unfortunately, quite the opposite exists in many domestic companies. Agents are sources of ideas because they face the customers on a daily basis. But most are reluctant to share them for the reason just mentioned. When you "wander around," encourage your agencies to blue-sky their ideas with you—and make sure they know that they will be rewarded for those that work and not blasted for those that don't.

• Build your image with your agencies. Direct interaction with your agencies demonstrates your concern for their success. And it has been shown time and again that increased visibility stimulates productivity.

STAYING IN COMMAND—A MANAGEMENT MAXIM THAT SHOULD BE EXAMINED CLOSELY

Any good manager will tell you that staying in command is basic to successful management. However, slavish adherence to this notion can reduce a manager's effectiveness, whether he's managing employees or a team of manufacturers' sales representatives. When you are constantly "in control," people tend to offer less help when you're not around. This is mainly because tight control usually means that you don't give people, or agencies, the opportunity to grow. This is a vicious cycle that reflects back on the manager, who usually becomes less confident and less willing to discuss problems openly. The maxim should be lead, not rule.

AN INTERN PROGRAM HELPS BUILD AGENCY RELATIONS

Most manufacturers employ summer help, and that help is usually related to company executives. Why not offer summer intern programs for the children of your agency owners. It will not only strengthen relations, it will give those you employ an opportunity to see your side of the business clearly.

WHAT TO DO WHEN YOU'RE ASKED TO PROVIDE A REFERENCE FOR AN AGENCY

It's a litigious world—people sue each other at the drop of a hat—or the drop of a name. In fact, we've heard of a few manufacturers that really wanted to give their agencies a good recommendation but were reluctant to do so because of just plain fear. Not that they had anything bad to say, but local lawyers kept pointing out how they could get in trouble no matter what they said.

Caution: Since one of the best ways you or any other manufacturer can get a handle on a specific agency is by way of recommendations, we urge you to continue to be helpful but to handle the requests for recommendations carefully. The first step is to positively identify the person who wants the information. If you get a letter asking for a recommendation, call that person on the phone to verify his or her identity. Then it's always a good idea to get written consent from the agent whose references are being checked. And, of course, make certain that the person requesting the information agrees that everything you say is confidential and to be used for business purposes only. You should only respond to specific questions and avoid volunteering any information that could be misinterpreted. This may be difficult to do if you face a person skilled in nondirective questioning. Keep the information business related and don't disclose any personal information such as the amounts of commissions—unless you have specific permission in writing from the agent.

⫸→ *IDEA IN ACTION*   The best way to give an agent a recommendation is to be specific. Don't say merely that Jim is a great closer. Say something like this: "We send Jim about 30 leads a month and he's usually able to close on most of them within 90 days." Be helpful. Be careful. But don't fall into the trap that some lawyers lay: They try to scare you into saying nothing at all. It is their job to point out pitfalls, but where would anyone be if they didn't take positive steps.

HOW TO RUN AN EFFECTIVE PLANT TOUR

Sure, you know where the screw machines are and you know where the assembly is done. You could walk to these departments blindfolded. And if you've been working for the company for any time, you really do walk around with a blindfold. On the way to the secondary department, did you notice the degreaser that had spilled last month and left an ugly stain on the floor? And how about all the cutting oil and chips near the millers? It may not mean anything to you because you just want to make sure that the products get into the field. However, a call from a very upset agent pointed up a fact that is worth reviewing. The agent had brought a big customer for a plant visit. Everyone at the plant was notified well in advance of the visit, and the executive veep had even set up lunch at his club for the agent. First-class treatment? It would appear so, but when the group walked through the plant the agent's customer was horrified to see more than a few signs of sloppiness. He saw a box of rejected parts that looked as though it could have been an entire week's output. No one says you have to put curtains in the machine shop to impress visitors. But you should make sure that the place is at the very least clean and up to speed. And you should make absolutely certain that there will be no surprises—no boxes of rejects for the visitors to see and wonder about.

An agent who lost some good business because he took a customer on a disastrous plant tour had a few suggestions: "I always give the plant at least a month's notice of the visit," he said, "and I follow up at least twice before the visit to remind everyone." This particular agent claims that he prefers to have the "real" people handle the tour. By this he means that he would prefer to have his customers be able to talk directly with the manufacturing manager, no matter how untrained he is as a presenter, than to be in the hands of a P/R type who doesn't know what the turret lathe does. "I also ask them to have their trade show exhibit set up in the plant if possible."

As a side note he commented that one of his principals agreed with this and left the exhibit standing in the plant a year—just in case! A good thought, but by the end of the year, the exhibit was so grimy from the plant environment that the agent avoided taking his customers to see it.

In addition to having front line people available on the tour, the agent pushes very hard to have someone from upper levels of management along for at least part of the tour. "Even if it's just the comptroller who never will understand manufacturing, it shows that there is top management involvement," he explained.

The agent tries to get a few questions from the customer before he brings him to the plant. "If the factory people are primed and ready, it's not only very impressive, but it makes the trip worthwhile early in the game."

Follow-up plays a critical role in the success of a plant tour. This should be, at the very minimum, a thank you letter to the agent's customer who made the visit. But if more than a casual view of the works was involved, the follow-up answers and specifications should be sent out immediately.

HOW TO MAKE THE MOST OF YOUR PEAK PERFORMING AGENCIES

Peak performing agencies are, in many ways, like peak performing individuals. They often respond to the same motivations and the same challenges. As one astute sales manager told us: "I use my peak performing agencies to train those I feel should be doing better." When this man talked about training, he was referring to presentations his star agencies made during his annual sales meeting and to reports they prepared for him during the year. "I asked a few of the top agencies to give me outlines of the presentations they made and how they handled objections in the face of competition. This was passed on to the other agencies, and it made a difference in sales." This sales manager didn't ask for favors. "I paid these agencies for their help," he explained. "I would have paid an outside consultant to do the job and wouldn't have gotten anything as close to the mark as the material I got from my agencies."

WHAT DO AGENTS AND MANAGERS HAVE IN COMMON?

Those managers who say that they really get a big kick out of their work claim that they have a clear and unobstructed channel to senior people in the company. For the agent, this means that he or she doesn't have to fight through layers of management to get to top people. And this is true even though there may be some heavy duty problems in the relationship. Keep the channels open!

RESOLVING AGENCY GRIEVANCES QUICKLY AND EFFECTIVELY

Agency grievances are, unfortunately, a fact of business life. However, they are seldom a matter of life and death, even though they do seem to be at times. Left unresolved, agency grievances can build into major conflicts that tear down morale, productivity, and, in some cases, longstanding relationships. "One of my oldest and most productive agencies taught me a lesson," a sales manager told us the other day. "We hadn't responded to what we thought were minor complaints from him on late shipments until he made a special trip to the plant to talk about it. If I had realized the significance of the problem, I would have handled it immediately."

⟫→ *OBSERVATION* A formal grievance procedure provides your agencies with a path for protesting practices and procedures in an acceptable and dignified way. Even agencies that have never had a complaint against a principal feel more comfortable when they know that a procedure is in place. And for you sales managers, the grievance system can provide an early warning alarm to monitor virtually every problem that can arise in the manufacturer/agency relationship. Any grievance procedure should be viewed as a fact-finding procedure—a search for solutions to problems—not for personal attack. However, for the system to work, it must protect the agency's right to fair treatment.

Here are a few tips to help you run a successful grievance procedure:

• *Listen to complaints.* Any grievances are best handled immediately. To agents, grievances can be highly urgent matters that they want someone to listen to right away. Agents should be instructed to take their problems directly to the person within the manufacturing firm to whom they report. If the problem has to go higher, the path should follow the chain of command.

• *Try for a fast resolution.* If you're the person to whom an agent would come with a grievance, do everything you can to resolve it as quickly as possible. When the resolution is found, it's best to put the solution in writing so that there are no misunderstandings later on. And if any follow-up action is required, the facts should be stated in the document. If an immediate solution can't be found, you and the agent should set a specific date for the next meeting or phone call. The problem shouldn't be left hanging.

• *Search for facts.* Statements on both sides are important, of course, but you should make every attempt to look for underlying problems. Also, you should make yourself aware of precedents that may have been set in earlier grievances with other agencies. Remember that you and the agency involved should search for facts. If your discussions remain at the level of the initial complaint, there will be nothing but emotion in the discussions.

• *When you must, take the grievance to a higher level.* It isn't always the noisy and acrimonious discussions that have to be referred to a higher level, but the little problems that need executive decisions frequently require either input or a decision from someone higher up. When you must do this, it's important that the person to whom you take the grievance be fully aware of every aspect of the problem—and that this person be aware of exactly why a settlement couldn't be reached. You should also give the agency the opportunity to state its case in person or in writing. There is going to be some obvious bias, no matter how fair you try to be. Giving the agency the opportunity to plead its case is critical to success.

Not every agency/manufacturer complaint is serious enough to warrant using a formal grievance procedure. Frequently, less formal channels such as an ordinary phone call can solve the problem. However, when routine approaches fail to provide a solution, the grievance procedures we have outlined here will probably do the job.

HOW TO GET YOURSELF OUT OF A RUT

An agent told us recently about the sales manager of one of the firms he represents who found himself in a rut and did something about it. "His memos started to sound alike, and he was doing the same thing he did last year," the agent related. "But when he realized what was happening he started making more field trips with his agents, and he sought more interaction with customers through the agencies. In fact, he even decided to hold the sales meeting at another location." It's easy to fall into a rut, and some ruts can be very comfortable. But we've never seen a rut that was terribly productive.

ARE YOUR AGENCIES SECURITY CONSCIOUS?

You probably lock the plant tightly at night, and you might even have a burglar alarm. But have you thought about sharing your security feelings with your agencies? If you feel that any of the papers they have—quotes, drawings, marketing plans—might be of benefit to the competitor, you might want to establish some form of security. It's not a matter of trust, it's a matter of being practical. We heard of one agent who left an open briefcase momentarily in a sales meeting room to attend to something else. His competitor wandered in, saw the figures he was quoting, and the cat was out of the bag. Explain your concerns and what you are doing to protect information to your agencies, and they will share your level of interest.

THE FOUR PHASES OF A SUCCESSFUL MANUFACTURER/AGENCY RELATIONSHIP

Manufacturers that see their agency relationships in a long-term perspective take different steps in the building of the relationship from those who appoint agents on the fly and then treat them offhandedly. "We're team oriented," a successful user of agencies explained recently. "Even though the agencies we appoint may have been in business for many years, we try to establish a mentor relationship for at least the first year." This company spends both time and money to cement the bond as early as possible. And it is also very careful in its screening of agencies.

>>>➔ *OBSERVATION* Mentoring is nothing more than a way to describe a good relationship between people, or in this case between principals and agencies. Both are interested in succeeding, and both work closely to achieve goals they have in common. But there are a few things to keep in mind. A close relationship should be voluntary on the part of both parties. There should be coherent goals, and the relationship should be structured so that both parties know where they want it to go.

Let's look at the four phases of a good manufacturer/agency initial relationship:

• During the initial phase, which usually lasts three or four months, the relationship often takes on added value to both parties. The manufacturer sees the agency in action and the agency gets to know and appreciate the product, the applications, and the potential.

• During the next few months the interpersonal bond strengthens considerably. The agency people and the individuals in the principal's plant get to know each other as people, not just as working partners.

• The third phase, which ordinarily occurs about six months into the relationship, is a sort of breaking away stage. The agency and the manufacturer both feel secure in the relationship. They are comfortable with each other personally and as business organizations.

• The fourth phase cuts in toward the end of the first year and lasts as long as the agency/manufacturer relationship survives. If the first three phases went well, there is every chance that the relationship will last a long time. But if the first three phases didn't go smoothly, there could be problems later on.

Delaying the fourth phase or pushing an agency out on its own too early can damage the relationship, many consultants caution. They also warn against being overprotective, and being overbearing. "Just treat your agencies as business partners and everything will be fine," they say.

A CLEAR PERSPECTIVE OF THE FAMILY BUSINESS

As you are probably aware, more than a few sales agencies are family operations. Just in case you tend to look down on such "mom and pop" operations, consider these statistics: More than 90 percent of the 15 million businesses in America are owned by members of a single family. These family businesses account for the majority of jobs in the country, and the sales from family businesses total approximately 40 percent of the U.S. gross national product. Although you might consider family agencies as small businesses, many employ more people than some of their principals. Of the Fortune 500, 175 firms are controlled by single families. Next time you question the strength of a family business, remember these numbers.

DEALING WITH TODAY'S PROFESSIONALS

Today's agent is an educated professional. But dealing with professionals today is more than a little different from the way it was only a few years ago. According to a study done at the University of Denver, today's professionals have a high degree of self-confidence. They have high career expectations and are willing to work hard to achieve their goals. Also, they perceive the ability to get along with others, formal education, and personal performance as top requirements for success. And they want regular feedback on their performance. Agents frequently claim that they are left in the dark about their performance by their principals.

When you give your salaried employees performance reviews once or twice a year, why not take the time to let your agencies know how well they are doing? Even if you don't have the time to do a formal report, an occasional phone call will be appreciated. And it will go a long way toward strengthening the agency/manufacturer relationship and motivating your agencies.

Remember, most agencies today do at least an annual evaluation of each of their principals. This kind of interplay is the fabric from which strong agency/manufacturer relationships are woven. Push both parties to strive for optimum productivity within the framework of the individual organizations and within the operational relationship of agency and manufacturer. Both parties should agree that the goals are achievable, and both should make certain that everyone involved in the agency relationship knows what is being sought. Here are some ideas on how to do it.

- *Obtain agency and manufacturer commitment.* Since we are discussing goals that are created by mutual consent, the executives of the agency and those of the manufacturer will, by acknowledging them, be committed to them. However, failure to achieve goals usually breaks down because others who must work to achieve them are unfamiliar with what is to be accomplished and how it is to be done. When all concerned are informed of the plans and asked to agree to support them, this is a form of management by objectives. It works well when everyone not only nods in agreement but signs off on a printed set of goals.

- *Monitor progress.* Goal achievement requires rather careful monitoring. Too often the plan is forgotten after the goals have been set. Then when the end of the goal period approaches, there is a flurry of activity. This isn't the way to do it. Nor is it practical to set up controls that are so tight that everyone spends all of their time writing reports to each other. The point is this: Set up some system of communication so that you and your agencies are aware of the progress of the goal achievement program.

⟫→ ***OBSERVATION*** A systematic and cooperative system of setting and achieving goals clarifies the agencies' role in contributing to your sales success. It can be a time-consuming process if it is allowed to get out of hand. But when it's well planned and effectively monitored, a goal-oriented program gives both participants a clearer picture of their roles in the sales program. Clearly understood goals also lead to greater motivation and more efficient selling.

HOW AGENTS CAN HELP YOU SAVE MONEY IN MANUFACTURING

"We'd been making our connectors the same way for about ten years," a manufacturer told us recently. "But," he continued, "when one of our agents came to us with a redesign idea, we found that not only could we make a better product, but we could also cut some of the manufacturing costs." This manufacturer said that he was not inclined to listen to this agent at first simply because he felt that their ten-year history meant that all the bugs were out of the operation. Since our conversation with this man, we have spoken with others who have told of agency-inspired manufacturing changes that have enhanced product quality, raised the state of the art, and resulted in new and time-saving production systems. More often than not, redesign costs can be paid with profits from current sales. Customers seldom pay much attention to minor design changes that can cut manufacturing costs.

AN AGENT RESPONDS TO THE CRITICISM
THAT HE HAS PLATEAUED

By definition, a plateau in sales is a leveling off. Recently we talked with an agent who told of some rather severe criticism he received from a principal when his sales remained relatively constant for a two-year period. "First it was a written report, and then it was a verbal barrage," the agent related. "It's true that the sales figures were level for about two years, but that was only one side of the picture." The agent related how the principal, without resorting to any market and territory statistics, was very unhappy because the agent hadn't shown the 14 percent average gain his agents in other territories had posted. However, this manufacturer didn't do any of his homework before he shot from the hip. The agent's territory had lost two major customers who had relocated to the Sun Belt. When the customers moved, the agent notified the principal, complete with revised sales projections. The existing customers were all buying only the products of the manufacturer. And there were no other prospects to sell to. Add to this fact that the manufacturer's advertising had done little to attract new interest in terms of new applications and you have both sides of the picture. The sad part of the story is that the agent, who was really doing a top job despite the plateaued sales figures, had to work hard to defend himself against the attack—time that should have been spent in the field. And the agent had already kept the principal informed of all changes. It pays to know what you're talking about before you sound off.

WHY CORPORATE SALESPEOPLE SEEM TO BE ATTRACTED
TO AGENCY SELLING

More and more manufacturers are either cutting back on their pension and benefit plans or dropping them altogether. And this seems to be one of the reasons some of the newer agents decided to take the plunge. People who start agencies and succeed have always been risk takers. But many of the pension plans in larger companies were once attractive. Of course, these new agents all have an entrepreneur spirit in common. The changes in corporate circumstances seem just to have gotten them started earlier.

WHY SOME SALES MANAGERS DON'T WIN
POPULARITY CONTESTS WITH THEIR AGENCIES

According to an informal poll of agents taken over the past few years, these are the reasons that some sales managers fail to make the top ten, as follows:

Insensitivity. It appears that a disregard for the feelings of agents and an apparent lack of interest in their opinions is the main reason some sales managers don't get raves.

Unreliability. This characteristic runs a close second, with many agents claiming that their sales managers fail to back them up, even after they have committed to doing so.

Inflexibility. According to some agents, sales managers who go by the book and who aren't willing or capable of flexibility cause more than a few problems.

Overmanagement. Agents are independent businesspeople. The overmanaging sales manager treats his agencies as he would a team of inexperienced employees. Agents resent this behavior.

Lack of firm strategies. There are often many miles and several hours between sales managers and their agencies. When an agent acts on what was presented as firm company strategy only to find that the sales manager has changed his mind, positive points just aren't racked up.

Of course, manufacturers have their pet peeves about agents, but the one that seems to be mentioned most and is most irrational is the fact that some sales managers are uncomfortable when an agency is paid more than the sales manager makes as a salary. Remember, this is a gross figure. Out of this the agent has to take care of all his expenses.

BEWARE OF THE PRICE YOU MIGHT PAY
FOR RAPID GROWTH

Reading in *Fortune, Forbes,* or *Business Week* about the phenomenal growth some companies have posted is exciting, motivating, and envy producing. However, there can be some challenging side effects.

According to recent research, the drives that push owners and managers to seek rapid growth are expansion, diversification, and changes in competition. The firms that are most successful in managing the transitions in these areas required by rapid growth are most able to delegate and improve the flow of information. Agencies who work for these dynamic firms tend to confirm this. They usually report that their rapidly growing principals seldom second-guess them on the sales front and that these firms give them the kind and quantity of information that helps directly in the selling effort.

ARE YOU A COMPUTER-FRIENDLY SALES MANAGER?

More than half of all agencies are actively using computers in one or more phases of their day-to-day operations. And many of these agencies have invested heavily in terms of hardware, software, and employee computer training. However, some agents report that they have not been getting the kind of support they need from their principals in order to make the most effective use of their computers. As one agent said recently, "About one third of our principals have computers. From these computers we get almost instant stock information by way of phone lines and our computer. And we can get quick answers to important questions by using our portables in customer's offices. If only the other two thirds had computers." Are you computer friendly? If not, you should be.

HOW TO REDUCE AGENT TURNOVER

"If I keep half of my agents for more than three years, I'm lucky," a corporate marketing manager commented at a recent seminar. "The trouble is," he continued, "we just spend too little time in the interview and selection process." Whether agents leave on their own or are terminated makes little difference on the bottom line because time and money are lost forever. And people are hurt.

   ⇛→ *OBSERVATION* Many manufacturers spend too little time on the recruiting, screening, and interviewing process. When they discover that the agents they have appointed are not quite what they expected, a lot of effort is usually needed to straighten out the situation. If this time were spent up front, rather than trying to make the best of a less-than-successful situation, the relationship would be much more productive for all concerned.

These are the factors that lead to problems:

1. *Corporate strategy.* If, for example, you're planning to cut your ad budget and you know that a number of leads will be reduced, tell your agents. If your shipping is slow, be honest about it. Don't let a new agent find out after he has started.

2. *Growth potential.* A good agent should be able to determine the potential of his own territory, but be sure that he knows what the corporate growth plans are.

3. *Commission systems.* The details should be put in writing for the agent to review prior to offering a contract. State the terms clearly and make sure that the agent understands the language as well as the figures.

Use this checklist to help you conduct more productive agent interviews:

1. Outline the characteristics you know will be important for agent success. When you conduct an interview, cover every point. Gut feelings are important, especially when they correlate with known success factors.

2. If more than one corporate executive is to interview prospective agents, be sure that each is acquainted with the success characteristics that have been outlined. After the interviews have been completed, each point should be rated by each executive.

3. Don't play psychologist. You may know what motivates you, but unless you have professional training, stick with the facts. And the facts that will most likely predict success are past successes.

4. Don't let your biases get in the way. Maybe you like conservative clothes. Don't rule out a candidate just because he or she dresses in a different style.

5. Watch out for the halo effect. That is, don't assume a person rates well on all scores just because he or she impresses you on one point. Most people think those with good verbal skills are skilled in other areas too. Be careful.

6. Look for winners. This may seem a blinding glimpse of the obvious, but many people tend to look for characteristics that will prevent them from making a blunder, rather than looking for the top choice.

7. Don't jump to conclusions too early. If you do, you will find yourself looking for ways to confirm your judgment, rather than gathering more information.

8. Don't be pressured into hiring someone. Even if you have only two choices and both are bummers, don't take the lesser of two evils. It's best to cover the territory from the factory until the right agent can be found.

9. Maintain control of the interview. Unstructured interviews work only in the hands of professionals. Unless you know what you are doing, a rambling, nondirective interview rarely produces enough solid information to make a sound decision.

10. Watch the agent sell himself. If the agent is interested, he will try to sell you on his or her services during the interview. This will be your first chance to observe selling skills in action.

WHAT TO DO WHEN YOU HAVE A PRODUCT THAT IS AHEAD OF ITS TIME

There is hardly a manufacturer that hasn't been ahead of its time with a product or service at one time or another. In some cases, the company that created the product had a good idea but might have lacked either the money to create a market or the sales network to do the job. Over the years, we have heard of manufacturers that have had products in this category, but at the time that they developed them their sales effort wasn't sufficiently focused to do the job.

One R & D manager told us recently, "The product we developed was ahead of its time by about five years. We probably could have shortened that time if we had had the marketing muscle back then, but we didn't. Now, however, we have a very strong agency network and we are reintroducing the product through them with considerable success." This R & D man went on to explain that there can be as much success potential in some shelved products as there might be in brand new ideas. He claims that R & D must go on to develop new products, but a regular review of product ideas that had been put on hold should be examined from time to time. This particular executive finds it productive to seek input from his sales agencies when it comes to reviewing old ideas.

HOW TO HANDLE A BUSINESS CRISIS THAT THREATENS YOUR AGENCY AND CUSTOMER RELATIONS

A successful agent in the Southwest recently complained that one of his best principals had been hit by a wildcat strike. "It had happened once before, a long time ago," the agent related, "and the strike was over before it had any effect on us and on our customers. But this strike has been going on long enough for our customers to begin seeking new sources. No matter how much I explain to this principal, they seem to think that everything will be back to normal just as soon as they settle the strike. I know it won't." Although we don't hear of problems of this magnitude too often, we thought it would be a good idea to take a look at crisis management from the point of view of your agency relationships.

>>>→ *OBSERVATION* Any crisis that affects you will have some effect on your agencies. Although there is seldom much that your agencies can do directly to help solve the problem, in most cases when you include them in your planning they can operate with their customers much more productively. Keeping your agencies in the dark is the worst thing you can do. It may seem like a waste of time for a company that seldom faces a crisis to plan for one now. But a little advance planning can save you major headaches when a crisis strikes. And you will find that your agencies can be a major bulwark in your public relations to prevent customer defection.

Here are some suggestions that will help:

• Set up a crisis management team within your company that includes members of departments that would be most affected by a crisis or who could have a major impact on the resolution of a crisis. Be sure your agencies know the individuals who are on this team and that they have ready access to them when it's needed.

• Designate one person in your company to be the spokesperson for your agency team. This may be the same person who is to be responsible for general public relations or it could even be a top corporate officer. However, that person should know that it is his or her responsibility to keep your agencies informed on the progress in resolving the crisis.

• Establish a file within your company that contains facts and figures that can be accessed quickly and easily. It's impossible to tell you exactly what should be in that file because each company is different from the others. However, knowing the type of business you are in, you should have a relatively good idea where the pressure points exist, and you should know what kind of information will be helpful in a crisis situation. You should include legal statistics on your company, sales records, background on your board of directors, production specifications, safety records, distribution statistics, insurance data, key contacts in the publications that serve your industry, and the names of key individuals in the unions that represent your employees.

• It's best to maintain media contacts, even though you have nothing to say to the press under ordinary circumstances. With a crisis on your hands, it's much better to be on a first-name basis with the reporters who cover your industry.

PROPERLY HANDLED COMPLAINTS SAVE BUSINESS

According to a report published in *Small Business Report,* attention to complaints is critical for business success. According to a survey of people who have complained about poor service, nearly 85 percent again purchased the products made by the companies to whom they complained when the complaints are handled promptly. More than half bought again when their complaints were handled later on. This is powerful evidence for fast attention to customer complaints. However, there is another side of the picture as far as manufacturers' agents are concerned. Far too many manufacturers let their agents flounder when complaints have been lodged. We're not talking about complaints that have anything to do with the agents; we're talking about product quality and delivery problems. Most agents will correct their own mistakes, but they shouldn't be put on the line for a manufacturer's mistake.

SUGGESTION SYSTEMS CAN BRING VALUABLE IDEAS FROM YOUR AGENCIES

The old company suggestion box is enjoying a well-deserved revival. Recent reports that Japanese workers regularly contribute ideas to their company suggestion system resulting in many new product ideas as well as in time and money-saving suggestions have caused more than a few companies to recruit ideas from their agencies. According to those who have tried the idea, you should reward those who contribute ideas that are used and you should make sure that everyone on the team knows who contributes the accepted ideas. This is not the same as a rep council. It's an ongoing program for all agents to take part in.

WHEN YOU HAVE TO REPRIMAND AN AGENCY

Although we don't like to think about it, there are times when it can be necessary to reprimand a sales agency. Any reprimand should be done just as soon as the problem is noticed. Waiting for a "better" time is always a mistake. And once the reprimand is over, don't dredge it up all over again at a later date. Your reprimand should be done seriously and it should include all the particulars that have led you to the point of having to take action. It's important not to use the occasion to lean on the agent for other matters. And unless you feel that the problem is not reconcilable, make sure that the agent knows that you have continued faith in him after the reprimand is over.

HOW TO HANDLE THE RUMOR MILL

Example: "My assistant asked me when we were going to cut agency commissions," a marketing manager told us. "When he saw the surprise on my face, he didn't know whether he should read it as a faux pas he had committed or dismay that some super secret had been exposed. The truth of the matter is that it was news to me, and I'm the guy who would make such a decision." The manager recognized the rumor mill at work. But it took him a while to discover that it all started with a factory salesman from a major competitor innocently, or not so innocently, chatting it up with one of the manager's agency people in a customer's waiting room.

The rumor mill, the grapevine, the gossip chain exist in every company. Sure, they run overtime in poorly managed companies where everyone is kept in the dark intentionally. But even in well-managed companies the word gets around. However, the word can be the good word or the bad word, depending on how you handle this primitive but effective system of communication.

"We had our share of rumors chipping away at our agency network," the president of a small manufacturing firm said. "So we decided we would go directly to our agencies by publishing our own newsletter to them. Additionally, we swapped 'gossip' about new sales applications, new customers, and lots of other information we wanted to pass on. It was well received, but it certainly didn't shut down the rumor mill. It was then that our public relations consultant said that rather than fight it, we should use it to our benefit." Here are some of the ways this manufacturer and others have made the rumor mill work positively for them and for their agencies.

Caution: The rumor system is a two-way communications network—it sends and it receives. It's sad but true: Strong rumors are frequently perceived as more believable than directly sent messages. Many people who have learned to make use of the rumor mill will first "leak" their story to the grapevine and then later confirm it directly. When there is a question of believability, this simple technique can be a very practical way to make an important point—a point that may be doubted if first stated openly and directly. This says something about the state of civilization, but let's stick to the practical use of the system.

During times of uncertainty, rumor mills work overtime. Uncertainty is always characterized by a state of limited information, and the information that is available is always subjected to several interpretations by those plugged into the rumor mill. When you find yourself facing such a problem, you can turn the mill to your use as a positive force by seeing to it that the information that would counter the destructive rumors gets into the pipeline. Again, you could step in and make a bold statement. But this step is frequently viewed not only as a way of heading off "true" rumors but of squashing the mill that circulates them. Before we leave this topic, it's important for you to understand that false rumors almost always begin with uninformed and anxious people. They are seldom the work of malicious individuals.

The information that is fed into the rumor mill never emerges in the same form. Those who teach freshmen psychology courses usually demonstrate this by whispering a statement to a student at one end of the class and having the message passed verbally from student to student. The last student usually hears a story that is grossly distorted from the original. Keep this in mind when you listen to the grapevine and when you plan to use it to pass along positive messages. If you keep your message simple, limited to one or two major thoughts, there is little chance that it will be grossly distorted. However, if you have a complex idea to get across, it may be best to be direct and do it immediately.

Getting in on the receiving end of the grapevine isn't easy. Those to whom others tell the stories you want to hear would, more than likely, consider your interest less than honorable. And those who hear and tell are frequently called finks. However, if you go to everyone on your staff and explain that this isn't a spy mission but that you are genuinely interested in building the relationships, you should get cooperation. This is a matter of serious trust and not a matter of setting people against people. However, the best way to find out just what is happening is to talk with your agencies face to face and to do it regularly. Rumors start when time intervenes between personal contact.

Let's spend a moment talking about the information the rumor mill may have that will be of value to you. You should look for information that is really misinformation. "They're going to cut commissions." "There's no more second shift, but they aren't telling anyone." "They're going to sack the agencies and go direct." Notice that these are rumors that produce personal anxiety, and understandably so. Agency people are out on a long string—frequently thousands of miles and many hours from the factory. That's why misinformation-type rumors can and should be corrected immediately. When the rumor mill produces personal garbage that every office produces by the clackers who hang around the water cooler, it's best to put an end to it immediately.

> **»»→ *IDEA IN ACTION*** You can put the rumor mill to productive use in a number of ways. However, it's important that you view the grapevine as a valid communications network and that you don't use it to mislead anyone. At this point, the term *informal serial communications* better describes the process. You are simply telling one person something that you would like passed along to the others in the organization. When your people understand that you are not putting out smoke and that there is no attempt to manipulate them or the information on the grapevine, it will work positively for all involved. Never exploit people on the grapevine.

You can use the grapevine to send and receive information, and it frequently works best when you have information that must reach everyone when a formal personal statement may not be appropriate. For example, one of your grapevines may have brought you the news that your competitor just lost a big order. You certainly don't want to go on record with this information in a letter or a memo. You could hurt the person in the system who passed the information. However, the grapevine is the ideal way to send the news. Communications theorists have recognized the power and adaptability of the grapevine, but they caution that it should be used positively or it's sure to backfire.

2

Building Legal Protection into Your Agency Relationships

The agency relationship is a legal one. In simple legal terms, an agent is one who acts for another party or who is empowered to act for another. Unfortunately, too many manufacturers interpret this definition in the simplest terms and don't negotiate written contracts with their agencies. "A handshake will do," seems to be the way many look at the agency relationship. A person's word is, of course, important and you may want to seal an agency appointment with a handshake, but you should always have a written agreement. Far too many things can take place in the agent/manufacturer relationship that will strain the handshake relationship.

In this chapter, you will find the major comments made in *RepLetter* on this subject—from a simple discussion of why contracts are important to insight into the touchy question of contract termination. Although the major points you should consider in a contractual relationship have been included, there is no substitute for professional legal advice. You'll be on a lot safer ground if you use the MANA contractual guidelines and have your attorney draw up an agreement than if you depend only on a handshake.

HOW TO AVOID PROBLEMS WHEN AGENCIES MERGE

The contract with your agencies should include a clause that requires notification of merger plans of your agents. Often the first time you hear of agencies merging is when you receive a letter asking you to amend the contract to include the new partners or shareholders. There's nothing wrong with agencies merging. As a matter of fact, most mergers strengthen firms, as young partners are brought in or when parts of the territory are covered more thoroughly.

Unfortunately, however, most agents are novices at mergers and are unaware of the pitfalls that can occur when previously unrelated agencies join forces. Agents are independent thinkers and are successful in the business for that very reason. If

72

they've never experienced partnerships before, they're in for a rude shock. Disagreements can boil up over a number of differences—split commissions, remuneration plans, fringe benefits, and buy and sell agreements.

>>>→ *IDEA IN ACTION*   If you require notification of your agents' plans to merge prior to the actual merger or buy out, you may be able to counsel them and meet the new additions to your salesforce. This is important, as you may discover such things as a new salesman who has a poor reputation in the industry or a contractual deficiency designed to squeeze out your original successful rep. Of course, you have to leave running the business to the agent. Nevertheless, it pays to be informed.

WHY WRITTEN CONTRACTS ARE IMPORTANT

It's a popular theory among some manufacturers that if they can get along without an agency contract, they're in a dominant legal position if they wish to end the relationship. However, their agents are in fact in the dominant position.

>>>→ *WATCH THIS*   Certain courts have held that if there is some evidence of a business relationship, such as paying a commission, it constitutes a binding business agreement, and it's subject to all sorts of interpretations regarding rates of commissions, termination conditions, and the extent of the territory.

This comes as a surprise to many principals and an even greater surprise to their agents when they successfully collect commissions they've been pessimistic about receiving. If you currently don't have a good solid contract with all of your agencies, get one in the mail right away to help protect you and your company from future expense and embarrassment.

Apart from the legal aspects, putting everything in writing just makes good business sense, the most important of which to prevent future misunderstandings. This is especially important considering that other parties may be involved with either business in the future.

How to Make Contract Changes

From time to time it may become necessary to make revisions in your agents' contract; perhaps commission rates will vary on a new product or termination conditions will be enhanced. Remember, changes should be mutually discussed and agreed upon, and put in writing as a contract addendum.

In case of a contract change, do not notify agents by any other means than an addendum to the original contract.

>>>→ *WATCH THIS*   By writing a letter or covering the changes in a phone conversation, you run the risk of not having them considered as part of the contract in the event of future litigation with your agents.

If your present contract is short and to the point—which it should be—it's best to draw up an entirely new contract and submit it to the agents for their signatures. The cardinal rule, however, is to get in touch with your attorney whenever any change is necessary in your contracts. It may mean a few legal bills now, but perhaps a large saving in time and money later.

DIFFERENT CONTRACTS WITH DIFFERENT AGENTS SOLVE PROBLEMS

Fewer complications will arise if all agent contracts are kept identical, but sometimes favoring one agency over others may have its advantages.

>>>→ *IDEA IN ACTION*   If you're trying to woo a particularly effective agency and there are some real pros out there, you may be able to seal the deal by offering a percentage point or more in commission.

It's best, of course, to keep your agency contracts as uniform as possible. This cuts down on complications that can arise within your company as your inside personnel attempt to adjust records and pay varying commissions depending upon which agent is involved. But from a legal point of view there's no need to keep all contracts identical.

PROTECT YOURSELF BY COVERING COMPETITIVE LINES IN YOUR AGENCY CONTRACTS

A simple but often overlooked necessity in every agency contract is the clause that prohibits your agents from taking on a competitive line. You certainly don't want your agents out selling for your competitors or choosing which inquiry to send to you and which one to send to them.

There's often a very thin line between a company that may have complementary products and competitive products, and your contract should insist that if there is any question, you have the right to say yes or no on the agent's agreement with the other company.

One sales manager we know puts a clause in his contract that calls for his agents to obtain his permission before taking on any other line. This type of restrictive agreement is really not necessary and most agents wouldn't agree to it. However, be sure to protect your rights whenever signing up a new sales agency.

SHORT CONTRACTS ARE BEST FOR EVERYONE

A west-coast agency was signed up by an east-coast firm that hadn't worked with agents before. The company's legal counsel (who also hadn't worked with agents before) came up with a twenty-five-page document that covered just about every eventuality that could have come up between the two parties. But because of its complexity, it was unworkable. The agent incurred considerable expense having his attorney go over the contract and wound up having to fly east to renegotiate the terms.

If you haven't had a lot of experience with agents or you find it difficult to convince representatives to sign your present contract, ask your successful agents for their help. Chances are they have a number of different contracts in their files that have proven effective for their principals and themselves. They could be of great assistance in helping you draw up a contract that would be readily acceptable to most agencies. Naturally, you shouldn't abdicate the responsibility for the completed agreement, but expenses can be reduced and time saved by following this route.

Caution: Another problem with longer contracts is they may stipulate several conditions that represent a form of control. Uncle Sam takes a very dim view of your issuing conditions that dictate certain obligations the agent must perform regularly, such as sending in call reports on a given day, if you want to consider that agent an independent contractor.

MANA has two contract specimen forms, a short form and a long form, that you can use. These are free to its members. They are well written and are the result of years of experience in the agent/principal field. These can be very useful as guidelines when developing your contracts.

WATCH OUT FOR THE RISKS IN ONE-YEAR RENEWABLE CONTRACTS

Some firms issue agreements to their agents that have to be renewed yearly. Most of these companies would like to establish long-term relationships; however, their legal counsel has advised them that a contract for twelve months is best in the event of a sellout or take-over.

This sounds interesting and feasible on paper, but what about the agencies contracted under these conditions? How secure do you think they feel with only a one-year contract? How enthusiastic can they be about trying to make long-term customer relationships for a firm that imparts a short-term trust?

The normal termination agreement gives you as much protection as the one-year renewable contract . . . even more, so it would appear that this type of agreement works against your best interests. If you want an agency group that will go all out for you, don't stifle their enthusiasm by making them wonder whether or not they're long-term partners—your results will be much better.

THINK CAREFULLY BEFORE YOU TERMINATE AN AGENCY

"Covenants with agents may not hold up in court—check with your attorney."

There's a mistaken impression on the part of some companies that they can prevent their agents from competing with them upon termination by having an agent sign a "covenant not to compete." This is usually signed when the original contract is negotiated.

A covenant is a very real legal document when used correctly and where some equitable consideration is paid, as in the case of the purchase of a business. The buyer can prevent the seller from competing with him for a stipulated number of years providing payment is made for this covenant and included in the contract.

Warning: You cannot, however, restrict an agent from making a living. If you terminate him, the courts have agreed that he is free to go out the day after the termination date and compete with you. If you have a covenant agreement or are considering one with your agents, check with your attorney for clarification of this advice.

WHY, WHEN, AND HOW TO TERMINATE AN AGENCY CONTRACT

"Why terminate an agent's contract? Because he isn't doing himself and you any good." That may seem an oversimplification, but it's the nuts and bolts of the problem according to one sales manager we talked with. The same sales manager went on to say: "Who cares if he wears sneakers or oxfords; if he brings in the business that I know exists in the territory, he stays on the team." This fellow's views are shared by most people who use agents today.

When to terminate an agent's contract is a question that is not as easily answered. However, most of the people we discussed this point with felt that this decision should be made only after all the facts have been carefully reviewed—by both parties!

> ⇛⟶ *OBSERVATION* Companies that will bend over backwards to accommodate a faltering staff salesperson will often drop an agency at the first sign of weakness. Some principals think of salaried salespeople as more of an investment to be nurtured, perhaps because they are in closer contact with management than is the average agent. However, this apparent distance on the part of the agent should have nothing to do with the decision to terminate.
>
> Over the years we have heard many complaints from both agents and manufacturers. We feel that most of the problems could have been solved without ever getting to the end of the line if both sides had admitted that problems existed and agreed to do something about them instead of pushing each other to the wall.

How to terminate an agent is another problem. Assuming that both parties feel that the relationship has nowhere to go, the act of termination should be one that both parties can learn from. The loss of an agent for a manufacturer and the loss of a principal for an agent is seldom a pleasant experience. But if both parties are mature enough to look at the situation clearly, a lot can be learned.

It may be easier to write your to-be-terminated agent a Dear John letter, but it's absolutely the wrong way to do it. A face-to-face meeting is the only way to handle the situation. The chances are that your agent will have anticipated the reason for your visit and will be prepared for a session of rebuttal and defense. If your goal is to build sales and not to act as a hatchet man, you will learn a lot from the situation. Make no mistake, it will be tense. But you will either learn how not to get into the same bind again when you appoint your next agent or you may find that the person-to-person session was long overdue and that you really didn't want to lose the agent anyway.

Caution: It is essential that you abide by the terms of your contract when concluding your relationship with the agency. Give proper notice and include an accounting of commission payments due. If you are completely fair in your evaluation of whether to terminate an agency, if you talk openly to the agency owner, if you follow the terms of your contract with the agency, and if payment of earned commissions is prompt—you can terminate your agency and still end up wearing the good guy "white hat."

RESPONDING TO AN AGENT WHO TERMINATES A CONTRACT

Manufacturers' agencies represent several manufacturers and concentrate their selling efforts in a complementary grouping of products. As a result, they become captive within a territory and a product line.

Because of this, a manufacturer can usually depend on the agent for a long-term relationship. But, if the agent does cancel the contract, the effect on the manufacturer can be devastating, both emotionally and economically.

When this happens, be sure to talk with the agent and carefully consider the causes, the effects, and what can be done to pick up the pieces.

There was a time when a defecting agency or company employee was thought of as a traitor. And the thought of trying to convince the defector to stay or to return in the future was absolutely out of the question. But times have changed.

Today, manufacturers on the receiving end of an agency resignation may smart a little or a lot, but they do accept the fact that the entrepreneurial spirit that motivated the agency owners to start their business must be satisfied. Apart from violating any specific contractual agreements, agencies that terminate their contract with a principal should be viewed as businesspeople who are doing their best to maximize their potential. We must point out that we are talking about pure business decisions in the context of this issue. Agencies that bounce from one competitive principal to another, playing one against the other, are no different than principals who exploit their agencies in the same manner.

How Best to Handle the Announcement of Departure

Your first reaction to the announcement will probably be one of surprise and resentment, but after you cool down, you should view the problem from a purely practical point of view. You've probably become friendly with people at the agency, so don't let this action destroy that friendship. There are really only two things you can do:

1. Try to convince the agency to stay. This is not always a good plan when a salaried employee leaves, but you should try to see what it would take to keep the agency on board. More often than not, the agency is resigning in order to take on another line, and that line may not necessarily be competitive. Seldom will an

agency resign for the same reasons that motivate employees. Therefore, do a careful analysis of the situation, have an open talk with the agency people, and see what can be done to keep them on board. After all, even if it costs you more money, you have a known quantity, and you won't have to go through the agony and expense of finding and establishing another agency in the territory.

2.   If there is no way of changing the script, you should part friends and be sure to leave the door open for future relations. Remember, your departing agency could come back to you or could be calling on your customers in his territory. In other words, don't burn your bridges.

What do you do in the mean time? You and your former agency have parted on friendly terms. You're either looking for or have found and are training a new agency. While you're at it, there are several things you should do concerning your previous agency.

- *Review your loss.* Look at it in terms of sales and the overall contribution the agency has made. This is a good time to sit back and take a long look at the relationship. It's a point at which the emotion of daily selling and the feelings of the parting won't cloud your judgment. The insight you get from this exercise will not only help you get your new agency off to a good start, but it should help you in your dealings with your other agencies.

- *Stay in touch.* You'll probably stay in touch as friends, but do make it a point to keep up on the progress of your former agency's new activities. Don't pry and spy—just let them know that you're interested and concerned.

The loss of an agency is jarring. But it can often help you to put things into perspective. If you can take the time to review all of the circumstances that led up to the parting, the insight you gain from the experience will more than likely help you strengthen your present agency force. However, it's especially important to remember that whatever the reasons for the parting, hostility does nothing for you. It's time to move on, to build a stronger agency team.

PUT THE OFFER IN WRITING WHEN YOU FIND AN AGENCY YOU LIKE

You will, of course, use a formal contract when you appoint an agency, but it is far more professional to make the offer in writing than to do it over the phone. According to agents we talked with who have had offers in writing and over the phone, the company that takes the time to write makes a much better impression. And impressions do count, as you probably know.

When writing the offer, include the date you'd like the agency to take over the territory, outline the arrangements that you have agreed on in your meetings, and specify that the actual agreement will be in the form of a contract. You may work with your contract or with one created by the agency. In either case, the MANA contractual guidelines will probably be of considerable help.

3

Setting Commissions and Managing Effective Agency Compensation Programs

Agents are paid commissions when they sell something. Depending on the industries, locations, and individual companies, the commission picture can vary quite widely. For example, some manufacturers pay commissions when orders are placed; others pay when orders are shipped. And some even pay their agents when they receive payment from the customer.

Since there are virtually no hard-and-fast rules, commission agreements and rates must be mutually agreed upon between manufacturers and agents. How to go about this task is the subject of this chapter. In the pages that follow, you will find solutions to such thorny problems as how to handle split commissions, whether or not to pay commissions on tooling, handling sales that come in "over the transom," and paying commissions on repeat orders.

Specific commission rate data have not been included because it can change from year to year. However, this information can be gotten from the biennial survey done by the Manufacturers' Agents National Association and published in *Agency Sales* magazine.

IF YOU CAN'T FIND A GOOD AGENT—WAIT

George Essig, executive vice president of Federal Drop Forge, once flew to Atlanta from Chicago to interview seven candidates who answered his advertisements for a manufacturers' representative appointment. After two days and seven disappointing interviews, he flew back to Chicago without entering into an agreement with any of the seven. Smart move.

It seems absurd to spend your company's money to fly to a distant city, spend several days conducting exhaustive interviews, and come home empty-handed. But it may be the wisest course of action.

Timing has a lot to do with your success, or lack of it. Your best prospect in the area may have just taken on a competitive line or may be about to resign a line and in several months will be ripe for your proposal.

>>>→ *HOW TO DO IT*   Your best bet is to go home and try again another day. Avoid the mistake of signing up an agent who you're not convinced can do the job for you. This eliminates later complications. Allow three months to a year before making a second attempt in the same area.

PAY COMMISSION ON TOOLING? WHY NOT?

Historically, those firms selling products requiring an expenditure by the customer for dies or tooling before parts or products can be manufactured have never paid commissions on this tooling—only on the parts that have been produced from the tooling. Their rationale is based on the philosophy that they don't make money on tooling charges. They try to keep them as low as possible in order to be competitive.

A particularly aggressive small company owner disputes this theory. "My agents work harder on getting the tooling order," he argues, "and this is required before I can receive an order for parts. So I feel they should be rewarded for their efforts."

Caution: Many agents consider this reluctance to pay commissions on tooling as a poor excuse for not paying any more commissions than necessary.

Needless to say, the small company owner quoted above has a good motivator going for him and finds his agents working just a little bit harder for him than for their other principals—and that's his aim.

There's more than one way to skin a cat if you can't pay full commissions on tooling. You can pay half commissions, for instance, or pay an established amount regardless of the value of the tooling. Many sales managers will find their managements resisting paying commissions or other rewards, but motivation is the name of the game and good strong arguments can be made for such a policy.

HOW TO KEEP YOUR COMMISSIONS COMPETITIVE

Commissions vary widely from industry to industry. Be certain your company's rate is within your industry's parameters. How do you find out what the going rate is? Ask agents in your industry . . . they'll know. Don't bother asking competitors, you could receive a misleading answer.

Paying lower than average rates will discourage professional agents from taking on your line. If you go to the other extreme and pay higher than average commissions you may find yourself pricing your product out of the market.

RETAINERS ARE "IN"

A new Southwestern agent is breaking even after nine months on his own, thanks to retainers from two of his principals. This places him well ahead of schedule. Normally, break even is reached only after two or three years of hard work.

Two hundred dollars a month from one company, an attractive compensation package from another, and established business from a third principal give the new agent a good financial base from which to expand.

More and more established agents are seeking out firms who will provide a retainer or subsidy in order to pay for the increasing costs of pioneering a line in their territory. Without such an incentive, many agents are showing little interest in taking on new lines with no existing business in the area.

> ⫸ *OBSERVATION* Firms using this approach say it pays off. With a direct-employee salesperson demanding $25,000 to $35,000 a year in salary plus fringes, a minimum expenditure of $2,000 to $5,000 for a retainer or subsidy seems like a bargain. It allows a company to enter a productive territory without a large investment and still attract professional agents.

SHOULD YOU PAY COMMISSIONS FOREVER?

One of the attorney speakers at a MANA seminar startled attending sales managers with news that many of their current contracts might not give them the protection they think they have. He cited a theoretical case where an agency was terminated by the principal. The agent ceased soliciting business, returned the brochures, and informed the company he expected to continue receiving commissions on all business from customers he originated for the principal. Needless to say, this sparked quite a bit of interest and discussion, since the attorney told the group the courts have upheld agents' rights to continued commissions under certain conditions.

Unfortunately, not all attorneys are familiar with the ins and outs of the agency/principal relationship and may not be acquainted with the results of current litigation in the field.

> ⫸ *WATCH THIS* It may pay to have your legal counsel review your contracts in light of recent events.

HOW TO HANDLE ORDERS THAT COME IN "OVER THE TRANSOM"

Advertising, sales promotion, and a good reputation for quality and service will bring in unsolicited business. And every so often you'll receive an order or obtain a new customer without your agent's help; he may not even know the company or purchasing agent who sent in the order. Do you resent paying commissions when this occurs?

It's a natural reaction to feel this way. But do keep in mind the countless calls your agent has made on your behalf without bringing in an order—that's the way it is in selling.

An Evanston, Illinois, manufacturer told us he's delighted to award agents commissions on orders that are received unsolicited. He figures that it all evens out. If you can adopt a similar philosophy, you'll find it a great motivator in getting your agents to work harder for you in the field.

MAKE YOUR COMMISSIONS UNDERSTANDABLE
PRIOR TO NEGOTIATIONS

While most companies in the same industry have similar commission rates, often there is a variation in some aspect of the commission structure, such as higher commissions for obtaining new accounts.

If your company has such a variation from the norm, make certain this is explained before you get into serious negotiations with an agency—not after. Make sure you have both interpreted the amount of commission, what is commissionable, and when the commission will be paid in the same way; otherwise there can be serious misunderstandings in the future.

USE INCENTIVES TO BOOST BUSINESS WITH
EXISTING CUSTOMERS

The major emphasis in most incentive programs is to develop new accounts. Sometimes this is to the detriment of good follow up on current customers, with a resultant slowdown in overall sales. A large automotive parts company, while still vitally interested in opening new accounts, has come up with a different angle that is so simple it almost appears too obvious.

>>→ *IDEA IN ACTION* This year, instead of offering incentives for new customers, the company is planning its incentive program around new business from current customers.

This is a smart move. Where is a better place to look for more volume than a customer who knows your capabilities and is already buying from you?

This same philosophy can work with your agency salesforce. Pay an added commission or devise some other type of monetary reward for increased business from regular customers. Don't go overboard, however. Keep the program to a year or less. New customers are still the lifeblood of every manufacturer.

SOLVING SPLIT COMMISSION PROBLEMS

A request for questions MANA member agents would like asked of other sales managers pointed up some very important questions we hadn't thought of. One question which seems to plague many members, is the age-old question of split commissions. No doubt this problem causes sales managers more headaches than any one other topic, and with good reason.

>>→ *OBSERVATION* No matter what policy you set for your troops, it's inevitable that someone will be unhappy with it. For instance, if engineering is done by a customer in one area and your agent there initiates

the customer's interest, and the order is placed in another territory, the first agent is going to feel entitled to the lion's share of the commission. On the other hand, once the business is placed, the second agent may be able to fend off potential competitors by offering good reliable service, and then feel he should receive most of the commission because the first agent's work is completed.

This is only one of a thousand different situations that can take place when you have a customer with plants and buying and engineering offices in different parts of the country. Another is the case of a good customer who moves his plant from Territory A to Territory B. Does the agent who originated the business in Territory A lose all his commissions, or does he continue to receive them for a year, or ten years? And does the rep in Territory B inherit all or a portion of the commissions now that the customer is in his territory?

There are no textbook answers to the split commission dilemma and it's almost impossible to establish a policy in writing that will cover all eventualities. As soon as you attempt to create a policy that appears to cover all possible situations, a new one crops up that makes interpretation difficult and even your most conscientious effort to be fair may be greeted with considerable skepticism.

However, here are general guidelines to some of the approaches that have worked in the more commonly encountered situations.

• If your products and markets are such that split commission problems are likely to occur, it's best to establish a firm policy in advance and make sure your agents understand it and agree with it. In some cases, the problems can be so complex that it becomes impossible to specify every condition in advance. Under these circumstances, the best approach is to establish the machinery that will be used to mediate the dispute. When you and your agents can at least agree on how the problems will be solved, you will have taken a very big step.

• Most manufacturers feel that the best way to allocate split commissions is to weigh the amounts based on the efforts involved. For example, when a product is sold by an agent in one territory but delivered in the territory of another agent, the bulk of the commission should go to the agent who concluded the sale. However, if the agent in the territory where the product is shipped is required to handle installation, training, or some other phase of the sale, he should receive a larger portion of the commission.

• When products are sold by an agent in an assigned territory but are shipped into a territory not covered by any agent, there is no question that the agent who made the sale should get the entire commission.

• Since the numbers vary so much from industry to industry and the problems within each industry are so diverse, it's impossible to give you figures. However, as with any form of negotiation, you want both parties to "win." That is, when each is satisfied, the figure is right. And when you're dealing with professional agents, you will rarely find them to be unreasonable. As we said before, be up front—before any problems arise. When you're prepared and the agents know the procedure that will be used to determine the split, the job of playing Solomon will be a lot easier.

- The MANA Contractual Guideline Booklet can be helpful. If you don't have a copy and you're not a MANA member, send $35.00 for a copy. MANA members can get a copy free of charge. While you're at it, you should also send for a copy of MANA Report Number 1015 "Split Commissions." MANA members get the report for $1.50; nonmembers, $3.50.

USING OVERRIDE COMMISSIONS TO BUILD BUSINESS

If you're on the west coast and you're trying to sell through agents on the east coast, it can be a difficult task. It takes time and money to work with agencies that far away, and other principals that are closer may get more of their time. A different approach is practiced by some firms that appoint a particularly good representative in the general area to be, in effect, a regional sales manager.

> **》》➔ *IDEA IN ACTION*** In addition to selling in his own territory, the appointed agent makes trips into your other agents' territories and works closely with them. By doing this, he refines their techniques and gives that personal touch you can't, because of distance and expense. The appointed agency receives an override from all sales in the other agents' areas and will naturally work harder in order to increase his income.

Obviously, this isn't for everyone. First the agent must be extremely knowledgeable about your product and company to do a good job. Second, he can't afford to neglect his own territory or personnel too much or the added sales in the other territories will be offset by loss of sales in his own territory. It's a fine line, but if you have all the ingredients and just the right agent, it may pay to think about it.

Another possibility would be to take that direct-employee salesman you have who's been wanting to get out on his own, and appoint him as an agent. The override will help him get started and you'll have a man in the field who knows the current reps, the company, the product, and how to sell it.

WHEN TO CUT COMMISSIONS ON COMPETITIVE JOBS

This is a touchy subject, both from the point of view of the principal and his agent . . . but let's bring it out in the open and discuss it.

Some agent/principal contracts include a clause allowing the manufacturer to adjust commissions on orders when competition is severe, forcing the profit margin to a very low point. But a survey of *RepLetter* subscribers found that even though the manufacturer may have the commission reduction clause available to him, he will still discuss the situation and negotiate the commission with the agent involved in almost every instance.

This can be a difficult negotiation, since there are so many factors involved. The order may mean a lot to the principal. Even at a low profit, it may help with the overall plant burden and overhead. The agent has put forth a great amount of effort in getting the order and has probably incurred extra cost to do so. Both parties want to salvage as much as possible from the dollar value of the order.

The basic reasoning may be sound. You want the job and the agent wants his commission. You're both willing to sacrifice to bring in the business; so why not share in this sacrifice, rather than put the entire burden on either the company or the agency. However, most agents feel things get out of hand when the principal asks them to absorb half of the price reduction, which is a typical request. Let's look at a hypothetical case.

»»→ EXAMPLE You have a product that sells for $1.00 and you've been getting your price and making about a 15% profit. This means it cost you about 85 cents to cover all your costs including the agent's commission. You run up against Mr. Smart Buyer, who matches you against a new competitor and it turns out that you can no longer get $1.00 for the product. But an order is yours if you can cut the price to 95 cents.

If you agree to this, you'll have to cut a nickel out of your profit, leaving only 10 cents profit on the dollar item, which hurts a bit. Well, how about asking the agent to share part of the loss, let's split it 50–50. If you each give up 2½% (or 2½ cents each), you can get the order.

Strangely your agent doesn't jump for joy when you suggest this arrangement; but he may grudgingly agree to it. After all, 2½ cents per item on $100,000 worth of business is better than nothing. And you're happy. Sure you make only 12½ cents profit instead of 15 cents, but it takes care of the burden and overhead and makes management happy because the job is being brought in at a profit.

But let's get back to your agent's restrained enthusiasm about sharing this sacrifice and take a look at exactly what you're asking him to do. While you reduce your gross income on this job by 2½%, you're reducing your agent's gross income by 50%, that's right 50%. "Yes," says management, "but the agent only had to sell the job; we make it, ship it, and take the blame if it isn't right." Agreed, but 2½% compared to 50% is not quite an even sacrifice. And your sales agency also has overhead.

In the meantime, you've taken care of all your expenses on that job, made a profit, and contributed considerably to the cost of running your business. The representative may or may not feel it was worth it, but nevertheless he has sacrificed a lot more in percentage of gross income than you have.

The next time you think about cutting commissions to get a nice big job, work out an equitable arrangement for everyone. If it's equitable enough, you may have your agents suggesting the next commission cut rather than you.

USE HIGHER COMMISSIONS TO SELL SLOW-MOVING PRODUCTS

At a recent **MANA** seminar for manufacturers, a frustrated sales manager complained that his agents weren't pushing the company's new products. Instead, they kept bringing in sales for old products that were rapidly becoming obsolete. What to do?

The suggestion was that he increase commissions on the new products and, after a reasonable period of time, consider reducing commissions on the products that would soon be obsolete.

Agents are just like other people; they'll take the least line of resistance. If the old tried and true products are easier to sell, that's what they'll sell. This approach, however, takes a bit of planning. Springing it unexpectedly on the representative salesforce can have a detrimental effect on morale and produce poor results.

>>>→ *HOW TO DO IT*   The best time to announce such a move is during the gathering of the clan, either at a sales meeting or a trade show—and then set the deadline several months down the road. This will give you an opportunity to ease into the program without the shockwaves that result when a plan is put immediately into effect.

Better still, consider a graduated commission arrangement. Start out with a modest commission increase and decrease on the respective products and change these slowly over the period of a year. Everyone should settle into the new routine in fine fashion as long as there aren't drastic decreases in their commission volume—and a gradual program can accomplish this.

"WHY DO WE HAVE TO PAY COMMISSION ON REPEAT ORDERS?"

At almost every MANA seminar for manufacturers the panel is asked, either from the floor or in coffee break conversations, why it is necessary to continue paying the manufacturers' agent's commission after the initial order. This is a very real concern to the questioner who is usually a new sales manager or one who has not had much experience selling through agents.

The concern of sales executives who ask this question centers around their belief that the agent is appointed primarily to find new customers for the principal and, they reason, after the first order most of the work is performed by the company, not the agent.

>>>→ *HOW TO DO IT*   There is really only one answer to this question: Just as the manufacturer needs repeat orders to stay in business, so does the agent. This point can be justified by exploring the goals and sacrifices that are common to both parties, the manufacturer and the agent.

The manufacturer is usually an entrepreneur inspired to enter his own business and assume the sizeable risks that are a part of this venture, in order to create his own independence, make a larger than normal income, and perhaps eventually sell his business so he can enjoy a comfortable retirement. He may mortgage his house, ask his wife to work in the business, and incur large debit obligation which, if not paid on time, can force him into bankruptcy. His risks are large but the payoff can be worth it.

The manufacturers' agent has exactly the same goals as the manufacturer. He desires independence, assumes a proportionate risk to make a handsome income, and hopes to sell his agency in later years and enjoy the comforts of a good retirement.

»»»➞ ***EXAMPLE*** Let us suppose that after the initial struggle the manufacturer attains the goal of establishing a group of customers (usually through a manufacturers' agent at no cost to the manufacturer), and each customer arbitrarily decides to place only one order with the manufacturer and no more. The manufacturer would soon go out of business. His whole profit structure is based on repeat orders from his customers and the investment per customer—in equipment, salaries, etc.—is tremendous. He often needs an order or two just to obtain an experience factor that will allow him to make a profit on future orders.

The agent is no different. If he spends all his reserve on building customers for his principals and then receives a commission on the first orders only, he will not sufficiently be reimbursed to allow him to continue in business and will join the manufacturer in bankruptcy court.

In addition, with no commission accruing on repeat orders, the agent cannot afford to service the customer, which allows other competitors to take advantage of this void.

Repeat orders are an essential element to both the manufacturer and the agent if they are to remain in business—and the agent plays a vital role in making those repeat orders possible to obtain.

HOW TO GET NEW BUSINESS—PAY HIGHER COMMISSIONS FOR NEW CUSTOMERS

Any good salesperson knows that it's a lot easier to sell something to a person who has already bought from him. And, of course, exploiting this fact usually accounts for increased business. But there comes a time when the expense, effort, and commission curves cross and the territory flattens out—for the agent and the manufacturer—unless new fields are plowed.

»»»➞ ***HOW TO DO IT*** It's getting harder and harder to get new business, and for a number of good reasons. Increased competition, the general economic malaise, and the raw cost of getting that first sale have made life tough for all of us. However, the idea of higher initial commissions has a lot going for it. Consider a boosted commission structure for new business in the same way you look at a capital investment in the plant. You can always limit the period of time you would use this special commission rate.

Many manufacturers have tried this plan with considerable success. Since the cost to develop new business is high, why not make it worth your agent's while by establishing a higher commission on first-year sales? It's not uncommon for those manufacturers who use this technique to pay as much as 50 percent more than the standard base commission. Of course, the exact amount that will be best for you, yet provide a strong enough incentive, must be determined by you and your agents.

Everyone knows that first-year orders are usually smaller than orders from existing customers. The customer is really testing you, your product, and the services provided by your agents. This fact, combined with the effort required to get new business these days, makes it quite clear that unless the prospect's really hot many agents aren't too excited about digging up new business when they could be tending to those who are providing the bread and butter.

Essentially what you are doing is investing in the future, not subsidizing your agents. Since most sales start out low and then build to a higher level, you should be able to predict from past sales and financial records just what your individual curve should look like. And from this, you should be able to develop the added percent of increase for first-year sales that will be practical for you as well as a good incentive for your agents.

A NEW WRINKLE IN INCENTIVES—BASED ON A VERY OLD IDEA

In most industries, it's often easier to build volume by working present customers a little harder than it is to get new customers. Sure, no business can survive without continuing new business development, but today short-range goals are often very important. And because of this, you might want to take an oblique look at incentives.

With good reason, most incentives are paid for new accounts. Once an account is opened and business begins to develop from it, sales efforts are often diverted to getting new accounts. A maintenance sales program keeps business coming, but there are times when a little additional effort with present customers can turn up a lot more volume. So why not try offering incentives for increases in existing business? Of course, you should have a good history of the level of sales from your customers so that you can plan and run the program properly.

This is an unusual approach, but these are unusual times. Worth thinking about, isn't it?

HOW TO ESTABLISH A COMMISSION RATE

"I set my rate at 5 percent ten years ago, and it's still there," a manufacturer told us the other day. We weren't talking about commissions specifically, and this statement was made in the context of another point. However, we later quizzed this manufacturer on how he set the rate originally and whether or not he thought the rate was adequate.

Asking how rates are established is much like asking how high is up? The answer depends on so many things that no one number is likely to be appropriate for everyone. Obviously, every agency would like to have the highest rate and every manufacturer would like to keep it to rock bottom. However, most agencies and manufacturers do recognize the practical limitations of the situation. To make it easier for you to solve this problem, we have developed the following checklist:

• Try to determine what your agents' other principals are paying. Frequently this information isn't secret, but when it is, be sure to respect confidences.

• Make sure you know the current practices of your industry. When you determine what commissions your agents' other principals are paying, you know one part of the competitive prices. No, you're not competing in terms of products with the other principals, but you're competing for attention—and the right commission rate gets a lot of attention.

• What's involved in selling your line? If your agencies are expected to do a lot of pioneering and the commission isn't the greatest, you're in for some trouble. You might consider one rate for pioneering work and another for maintaining the business that exists in the territory.

• Are there good reasons for having varying commission rates in different territories? If there are, make sure every agency knows what you are doing and exactly why you are doing it. There is nothing worse than having this thrown in your face by a disgruntled agency. An agency expected to do a lot of service should receive payment for it. An agency in another territory that is maintaining long-term business is another thing. In general, differing commission rates should be avoided. But when they are absolutely necessary, be open about them to everyone.

>>>→ *WATCH THIS* When trying to establish a commission rate, be sure to take into consideration everything your agencies will be expected to do. Very few manufacturer-agency relationships are simple and clear-cut. Do you expect your agencies to deliver market intelligence, for example? Do you expect them to do extensive training of distributors? Are they to install and calibrate equipment? Just make sure the rate reflects everything your agencies will be expected to do.

Are you absolutely certain your agencies will be able to make a profit on your line? The only way to make sure is to be open about the rates you can afford to pay and the commitment the agency will be expected to make. Many a hotshot manufacturer has negotiated a low rate with a new agency and felt good about his skill. But when the sales don't materialize because the line is not profitable for the agency, all the negotiating skills in the world will not save the day.

Your rep council will be one of the best sources of direct input on the subject if you're already up and running. Remember, rep councils are not bargaining units. They are individual agents who want to see you succeed as much as you do.

HELPING YOUR AGENTS SPOT COLLECTION PROBLEMS BEFORE THEY BECOME REAL PROBLEMS

It's not a new story. An agency turns up a new customer who buys furiously and promises the moon. Come collection day, it's another story. Apart from the legal questions and problems, there's a lot you and your agencies can do to prevent these problems.

Let's face it, every once in a while we run into a company that does not pay its bills. As we've said before, the question of credit approval rests with you, the manufacturer. However, you and your agencies can work closely to detect credit problems before they haunt you. Here are a few tips:

• If the customer has been discounting its bills and begins to slip out of the discount period, this can be a sign of trouble. It's especially significant when you notice this happening to a customer who has a strong history of paying within the discount period.

• Watch for sudden shifts of business. When a customer you have been trying to get for a long period of time suddenly shifts to you, look for reasons other than your quality products, fast service, and superb agency sales work. This may sound cynical, but such sudden shifts of business are frequently the result of credit problems with other suppliers. It's often possible for your agencies to get a handle on this from his or her local contacts.

• Watch for sudden cancellations of advertising programs. If you sell to companies that have a strong tradition of space advertising and you suddenly notice that the advertising campaign has been stopped or drastically cut back, it could be a sign of liquidity problems. Unfortunately, the first cost to be cut by many companies when cash is short is advertising. Agents bear the brunt by the reduction of sales leads, but you can frequently spot credit problems in the making.

GET NEW AGENTS OFF TO A FAST START WITH
SPECIAL COMMISSIONS

You may choose to pay the same commission percentage to all your agents, but to help a new agency in a new territory get up to speed as quickly as possible, you might want to consider an introductory commission rate. Since the agency will be doing missionary work for you in a new territory, there will be more money and effort expended by the agency. It's not uncommon to offer additional commissions for the first few months of the relationship. If the agency does some stocking of your products, additional discounts will have the same effect.

HOW TO MAKE SURE YOUR COMMISSIONS
ARE COMPETITIVE

If your commission is no longer competitive with the rest of your industry, you could at best lose agency enthusiasm or at worst lose some of your best agencies.

Every two years MANA conducts a survey of commissions paid to manufacturers' agencies in a wide range of fields. In general, commission rates have stabilized. In some fields, however, commission rates have risen dramatically. In others there have been some declines. Our view of the overall picture is one of general health of the economy and of vitality in individual industries.

HOW TO ESTABLISH A FAIR COMMISSION RATE

Because competitors seldom talk with each other about commissions, it's often difficult for someone entering the field to know just how much to pay an agency in commissions. MANA does a commission survey every other year, but the information developed relates to product categories, not to specific products. However, the survey chart does show the range from the lowest to the highest. Before you make any attempt at establishing a commission rate, you should first consult this material. Keep in mind that these numbers are not "cast in concrete" and should only be viewed as a starting point.

After you have an idea of the commission ranges in your industry, here are a few tips that will help you to establish an effective commission rate:

• Understand all of the practices within your industry. Knowing only the commission rates is not enough. You should also know what kind of special incentives might be involved and you should be aware of trends. Look at the MANA commission surveys published over the last ten years and you'll see decided increases in most of the categories. Remember, these figures are rates, and therefore are not immediately related to an inflationary spiral. They are mainly the result of the increased interest in agency selling and the competition to work with good agencies.

• Understand just what it takes to sell your product. A tough sell calls for a more competitive commission.

• Understand what it takes to get the attention your product needs within the agency. One of the ways to answer the question, "How do I get more of my agents' time?" is to be just a little more competitive in terms of commissions. It's also important to pay those commissions in a timely manner.

• Understand that you can pay too high a commission. This may be a strange thing to point out, but the most effective commission is usually higher than average, but it isn't a giveaway.

• Understand exactly what you want your agencies to do for their money. If it's a pure commission selling job that's to be done, the job of establishing commission rates is relatively easy. But is there any service involved? Research? Customer service? These and other nonselling chores should be planned for when setting up an agency commission program.

4

Recruiting the Best Agencies for Your Line

Although there are more than thirty thousand active sales agencies in the United States, many manufacturers list recruitment as one of their most difficult problems. They often claim that the agents they want are now representing competitors or that other well-qualified agents are often too busy to look at their lines.

Recruiting agents is not much different than recruiting a top executive. Before you start looking, you have to profile the "best" agent for the territory. Then you have to gather information on the agencies in the area that serve your markets. But these two steps can be more than intimidating and time consuming for an active manufacturer.

In this chapter, we have identified the techniques that have proven successful for a number of major manufacturers. In addition to the many specific suggestions, you will find several checklists that will make the job a lot easier and more productive. In particular, the checklist, *Important Points to Cover with a Prospective Agency*, will be especially helpful.

Although there are a number of good recruiters in the country who specialize in the location and selection of agencies, most manufacturers prefer to do the job themselves. The techniques in the next section should prove most helpful to those manufacturers.

WHY TOP AGENTS ARE SOMETIMES HARD TO RECRUIT

Because of abuses practiced in the past by a small group of firms selling via agencies (unfair terminations, nonpayment of commissions due, etc.), established agents have become wary of relations with any but the most reputable manufacturers. Further, many of the top professionals are reluctant to represent companies without doing a thorough investigation.

➤➤➤ *WATCH THIS* Of particular concern to these agents are companies with captive shops—operations that make products for their own consumption. This is because of a fear that a temporary diversification to outside work will dry up once the company's own product needs grow.

How to combat this growing wariness? In the case of the captive shop, it's hard. You'll have to convince agents that your firm means what it says about outside work . . . a policy statement by the top brass or a testimonial from a satisfied customer you've serviced for many years. Companies without the captive-shop syndrome can rely on references from current agencies and customers to attract top agencies to their firms.

ASK YOUR AGENTS TO HELP YOU RECRUIT FOR OTHER TERRITORIES

Don't rely exclusively on directories or advertisements to attract new agents. Those methods are good and useful, but you have another excellent tool at hand— your present agents.

Agents are getting to know each other through sales meetings and seminars. They often know how well other agents are doing for their principals and can be a reliable source for potential representatives for your company.

>>>→ *IDEA IN ACTION*   Next time you have an opening in an area, try your current agents first. Write or phone them individually and ask if they are familiar with responsible agencies in the targeted area.

An additional plus occurs when your agent recommends another agent. The recommended agent can rely on your current agent's appraisal of your organization, and you may well snag a top agent that might otherwise be hesitant to take on your line because he is unfamiliar with your company and its products and policies.

You must still go through the entire procedure, however. Simply because one agent knows another doesn't mean that the new prospect is good for your company. Check him out thoroughly just as you would one who responded to your other recruiting efforts.

TWO AGENTS IN ONE TERRITORY SOLVE A PROBLEM

One of the most frustrating decisions a sales manager faces is what to do with a tried-and-true agent who is effective at only a limited number of customer firms and who probably does little, if any, missionary work. Adding to the overall problem is the fact that even some very good agents are unable to crack a certain number of firms in their territory. Usually this is due to the different personalities of the agent and the buyers at these potential customers' plants. In other words, we can't sell everybody.

>>>→ *IDEA IN ACTION*   There's a new trend, somewhat disturbing to professional agents, that seems to be slowly gaining some acceptance with sales managers, and it bears some discussion.

When faced with the realization that they have an agent or two who have "peaked out" in their territory, these sales managers are appointing a "second agent" in the same territory with the knowledge, but not necessarily wholehearted acceptance, of the original agent.

Under this arrangement the first agent's accounts are frozen and, while he may solicit more business from these accounts, he is requested to limit his activities on the principal's behalf to only these customers. The second agent is encouraged to call on all other accounts in the area.

Warning: While this can often open more doors to the principal's product line, it can do more harm than good. If the original agent is an effective performer he can take on a competing line, negating the advantage of the second agent, or he may lose enthusiasm and fail to go after additional business at his remaining accounts.

Also, the second agent may eventually become unhappy with this less-than-exclusive arrangement and badger the sales manager for the original agent's accounts. Overall it appears that the risks outweigh the advantages sought from this type of dual representation.

There is one circumstance, however, that comes up in many territories, and in this instance the dual representation may be a practical route to follow. This occurs when an agent who has done a good job over the years feels the need, because of age or health factors, to physically reduce his activities. An agent in this situation may welcome a new agent who will do much of the calling necessary to develop new accounts. The older agent is then able to handle his favorite accounts without the fear of being replaced until he no longer wishes to carry on.

AGENTS GET THE NOD OVER
DIRECT-EMPLOYEE SALESPEOPLE

In a recent article in one of the country's leading publications for purchasing executives, respondents to a survey were quoted as saying they found that manufacturers' agents and salespeople working for distributors excelled in their craft.

This comes as no great surprise to most sales managers who work through agents. A large majority of agents are graduates of the corporate sales group and have had numerous chances to observe what's wrong with a direct salesforce, but have had little opportunity to do anything about it. Now, in their own independent agency, they are able to sell in the fashion that suits them best—and to achieve success and prosper their methods must work.

If you have both a direct and an agency salesforce, it might be a good idea to ask one or two of your better agents for an unbiased critique on the sales management philosophy of your company.

RETIRED SALESPEOPLE—A GOOD BET FOR YOUR AGENTS

A St. Louis representative firm hired a telephone company employee who had taken an early retirement at 55. He works three days a week and has proved to be a boon to the firm which didn't need, or couldn't afford, another full-time person. This suggestion, passed along to your agents in the same position, could stimulate hiring of additional personnel and mean more coverage for you.

Also, in areas where you have difficulty finding capable agents to take on your line, it may be possible to aim your recruiting efforts at early retirees who may be looking for something productive to do. By working out of their homes on straight commission, they may be able to bring in surprising results.

WRITING POWERFUL LETTERS TO PROSPECTIVE AGENTS

About seven out of ten of the letters that professional agents receive inquiring about their availability start out with a phrase similar to, "We have now expanded our facilities and are ready to accept business in your area." This is not inclined to generate much enthusiasm in the recipient of the letter, for several reasons:

He knows the company has no existing business in his area.

He doesn't know whether or not the company can be competitive in his area.

He knows it will take six months to a year to find out if the company can be competitive and if it has good quality and service.

He knows it's going to cost him a fair amount of money to pioneer the line.

While most companies don't wish to give this impression, they make it appear that now that their facilities have been enlarged and they're able to handle more volume, agents in the chosen area should run to the nearest phone in an attempt to be appointed as the company's representative. Many of the letters are made even more unappetizing because they're printed with a fill-in heading and address . . . in other words a form letter.

Pioneering new lines is a costly endeavor, and only if the line fills an important gap in the agent's line or if he is new and is trying to garner all the lines he can, will he seriously consider representing a company which has not sold in the area before.

≫→ *HOW TO DO IT* If you're in this position, try a personal letter to professional agents in the new territory and put the "you" back in your letter writing. For instance:

"A real opportunity exists for you in the Greater Atlanta area! Through expanded facilities, our company has been able to lower its overall cost structure by 10 percent, and this savings is being passed on to our customers. We've not sold in your area before, but with our new pricing philosophy we expect to penetrate your market easily and would like to count on you to help us make record sales in our first year. With our excellent advertising and promotion program, together with helpful field visits, we feel that the rep we sign up will soon consider us his No. 1 principal."

Wouldn't you like to receive such an invitation?

WANT INSTANT CREDIBILITY? SELL THROUGH AGENTS

As companies grow, they expand their marketing areas—and also increase their selling expenses as they pioneer new areas. Direct-employee salespeople are often sent out to open these new territories, but despite their talents they're often recalled in six months to a year because of the excessive expense of supporting them in the field until their sales become high enough to warrant the expenditure.

>>>→ *WATCH THIS*   Unless a company is well known through its advertising and promotional programs, purchasing agents are slow to accept the company's promises of good quality and service. It's safer to deal with known sources, and a new company's salesperson often becomes discouraged because of the time required to convince buyers to give his firm a try.

After one or two such occurrences, many companies have resorted to selling through agencies in these new territories, mainly to save additional expense. Much to their surprise, some of their new agents began to show results almost immediately.

For example, a Chicago firm that abandoned the direct route appointed an agency in Denver. A representative of the agency happened to be in Chicago the following week to sign the agreement. Before he left Chicago, his partner forwarded an inquiry from a Denver company. And when the agent returned home, an order acknowledgment had already been received.

This was, of course, an unusual bonus and most principals have to wait somewhat longer for their first taste of business. A good agent, however, can usually generate some immediate interest. This is because the barriers that were so difficult for the direct salesperson to penetrate are not quite the same for the agent. The agent is operating on familiar ground—he's made many a friend over the years and has developed a following among buyers and other important executives in companies in his territory.

As a result of his reputation, the agent can provide "instant credibility" for his new principals. When a trusted agent introduces a new line to the buyer, the buyer knows that the agent has researched the firm's capabilities and the buyer is less reluctant to take a chance on the new company.

>>>→ *OBSERVATION*   The basic problem for a company seeking to enter a new area is how to appoint an agent with the necessary qualifications . . . for not all agents have this rapport with their customers. And those agents who do may well have all the lines they desire.

Again, we emphasize the importance of a thorough recruiting effort when entering a new area. By spending time and money on your search, you'll have a better opportunity to attract those agents who can give you "instant credibility" and successful selling results.

THE AGENCY BUSINESS—A SECOND CAREER

If you're at or near retirement age, you may want to consider the agency business as a way to continue using your skills and also make a little extra money—or maybe even a lot.

Company presidents, sales managers, or any executives experienced in meeting the public or other industry people can easily enter this field by following a few simple rules, as follows:

- Don't bank on making a lot of money to start.

- Tread cautiously and don't take on any lines that require a lot of pioneering; leave that job to the pros, at least for the present.

- When seeking lines, point out your background and experience to potential principals and, by all means, try to stick with products that you're familiar with.

Many a former executive has launched a successful agency . . . it may be worth a try.

DON'T BE COY ABOUT EXISTING BUSINESS IN A NEW AGENCY AREA

When writing agents asking about their availability, many sales managers don't refer to existing business in that territory. Often they'll refer to "our customers across the country," leaving the agent wondering if the company can sell successfully in their area.

This is a mistake. Neglecting to point out that you're now doing business in his area may mean you'll miss out on the very agent who can perform best for you.

Caution: By mentioning the existing business, you run the risk of receiving replies from agents interested only in the current commissions—but that's a nuisance you'll have to face if you want to find the real professional.

We've said it before and it bears repeating: The professional agent can be recruited much more successfully if you can convince him you'll be competitive—in price and quality—in his area. Naturally, he won't object to commissions he'll receive from present customers, but he may ignore your recruiting efforts completely if you don't give him the facts the first time 'round.

ASK MORE QUESTIONS WHEN INTERVIEWING AGENTS

Sales managers are prone to ignore the real nitty-gritty when they find a sales agency that appears to be well suited to their needs . . . and they often sign up the wrong firm.

Pry, pry, pry. Agents are great at name dropping and are particularly adept at providing vague answers to your questions. But if you have a good line with existing business in the territory, you can demand straight answers to your questions.

If you're entering a territory where you have no existing business you can't be quite so stringent, but you can still try to obtain important factual data. Here's a sampling of a few questions that are not asked nearly often enough:

1. *How long have you been in business?*

The agent may give the impression of being in business for years, but may have just started up.

2. *Do you presently sell to our potential customers?*

He may do very well in his area, racking up hundreds of thousands of dollars worth of sales . . . but not necessarily to firms representing your best potential.

3. *Why do you think you should have our line?*

This is a key question and the agent should have a good answer. He should possess a good knowledge of your product and have several pertinent ideas as to why he's sure he can sell it effectively in his area.

4. *Have you ever handled a line like ours before?*

You may find he handled an identical line before, which would be ideal. If he hasn't, find out if he's worked a line that is closely compatible. This could be a plus.

5. *What happens when you decide to retire?*

We've stressed continuity in rep organizations, and it's essential your reps have definite plans to bring in younger personnel well in advance of retirement.

It's natural, during agent interviews, to get carried away with details of your company and its products. The agent may sit there and take it all in, and in some cases not volunteer any more information than is necessary. It's up to you to dig for this information, finding out how effective you think he can be in selling your product. Tell him more about your company after you think he's the person for you. Don't be surprised when he asks very similar questions about you and your company's products, capabilities, and future plans.

SHOULD YOU VISIT WITH CUSTOMERS OF A
PROSPECTIVE AGENT?

A local agent called the editor the other day telling of a company that had phoned him regarding representation . . . and also asked him to fly to their plant for an interview, at his expense. He politely declined, figuring that if the company was really interested in his agency, the sales manager should come to see him.

In this case the agent was right. The sales manager should have come into the area and visited the agency, as well as several potential customers, to see if the marriage would have been a good one—the plant visit can come later.

HIRE ESTABLISHED AGENTS WHEN YOU FEEL
A RECESSION COMING ON

This advice may not be fair to the newer agents, but your obligation is to hire the best agents available and to make sure they have "staying power." Hiring established agents is always a good idea, but it pays to take a chance on a new agency from time to time, particularly if the owner or owners show enthusiasm, promise, and knowledge of your product line.

A new agency often has the initiative to spend more time in the field and can generally open new accounts at a rapid rate. The time to become cautious is when sales appear to be slowing down in your industry and it looks like you're in for a period of reduced demand. At this point, if you have to open up a new territory or replace an inefficient agent, it is wise to investigate your prospective sales firms very carefully.

> ⟫⟶ *OBSERVATION* Most old-line agencies have survived because they've been able to weather the financial storms that occur every 3 to 4 years. In the good years, they put enough aside to carry them through. Younger firms may not have had enough good years to build up a reserve to carry them through these crises and simply may not have sufficient capital to last until the economy picks up again. Just because a firm is new, however, doesn't mean it can't survive. If the owners have other resources and reserves, they'll be in as good a position as the established firms.

The trick, as often mentioned, is to ask questions and investigate thoroughly whenever appointing a new agency. This is doubly true when the economic picture turns bleak.

DON'T LET THAT FIRST IMPRESSION FOOL YOU

Too many sales representatives are contracted on the basis of one interview; and this practice can be disastrous for both the agent and the principal. First impressions are important, but they are often misleading.

There are smooth operators in every field, and the manufacturers' representative business is no exception. In fact, they're the ones most likely to make the best initial impression.

> ⟫⟶ *IDEA IN ACTION* Two interviews, sometimes three, are best even if it means that you have to make an extra trip into the territory. And if you do, take along an associate for a good alternative appraisal.

SPEND EXTRA TIME AND EFFORT IN SELECTING A NEW AGENCY

Never conclude an agreement with an agency until you are virtually certain of the basic compatibility of your organization and his. The changing of agencies in a territory is an expensive proposition, not only for the agency but for you too. Consequently, extra time and effort spent in assuring that you have the best possible working relationship with an agency should make your profitability more positive.

Actually, it's a good idea to meet for a second or even a third time in the offices of the prospective agency. Observe not only the attitude of his employees but their activities as well. Check with your customers (or potential customers) in his territory regarding their opinion of the prospective agency and, of course, check on some of his incumbent principals.

Regard this phase of exploration to be one of "getting to know you" rather than a "checking up on" procedure. The more you know about the personalities and philosophies of the agency, the better you will be able to understand the operation and to keep the lines of communication open. And, certainly don't forget that "getting to know you" is a two-way street. People like the things best which they know the most about. Consequently, the more informative you can be about your company and its policies and personnel, the more productive your agency will be for you. Make every effort possible to dispel the old canards of suspicion between your company and the agency. Demand professionalism in your sales agency, but be sure to give them the same professionalism in return.

RELOCATION EXPENSES ARE NIL WITH AN AGENT SALESFORCE

Is your boss wondering if you should appoint direct people in some areas now covered by sales agencies? There are plenty of reasons why this isn't a good idea, but one major reason often overlooked is the cost of relocation of direct salesforce personnel.

Often you can't find the right person in the general area, so you'll have to move one from another territory, perhaps from across the country. Moving costs have increased tremendously, and the extra $4,000 to $5,000 this move costs can really dent the sales budget.

Agents, of course, don't involve moving costs of any type. They're already in the area and know the customers and their buying habits, and sales costs are directly commensurate with their ability to bring in orders.

USE YOUR TOP AGENTS WHEN RECRUITING IN OTHER AREAS

The Research Institute of America, in their "Marketing for Sales Executives" feature, advises sales managers to utilize their top salespeople in attracting good potential salespeople for their companies. You can do the same with your top agent.

➤➤➤➤ *IDEA IN ACTION* If there's a real pro out there that you'd like to have on your agent salesforce but he's somewhat hesitant to join up for some reason, set up a meeting with him and bring your top agent along.

Give your agent plenty of notice since he's representing several principals, not you alone. He may need a couple of weeks to fit you into his schedule.

Naturally, you'll pick up all the expenses and, if he owes you a favor, it may not be necessary to pay him a consulting fee. On the other hand, you may want him for a repeat performance, so the payment of an agreed-upon figure will make it easier for you to ask him again.

By relating the successes he's had with your company, a good agent can often coax a reluctant agent to join your group. If the prospective agent is really a professional, the money spent on recruiting him can be a drop in the bucket compared to the increased sales he can ring up in his territory.

>>>→ *OBSERVATION*   Another plus: A good agent may be able to ask a few pertinent questions that you haven't thought of and can probe in areas with which you're not familiar. For example, your agent may be familiar with the prospective agent's other principals which will be a tip-off as to the quality of principals the agent has on his line sheet—a valuable thing to know.

WHO ARE MANUFACTURERS' AGENTS?

"80% of them are former salespeople."

In polling attendees at seminars for its agent members, MANA discovered that most of the men and women entering this field formerly worked in the sales field in some capacity.

Perhaps the most obvious reason for this overabundance of former sales personnel is their proximity to the field of action. In other words, they were working with agencies in some capacity prior to becoming one.

Strangely enough, relatively few of those in attendance were formerly connected with purchasing functions—contrary to popular opinion. And the reason may be that while many former purchasing agents enter the agency business upon retirement, their tenure is short due to age and lack of a real desire to build an agency business.

ARE YOU CONTACTING THE BEST AGENTS FOR YOUR NEEDS?

"Be sure to check references."

When it comes down to decision-making time, often the deciding factor will be the references that prospective agents have laid upon you with the hope of becoming your new agent in a major territory. But many sales managers still don't check references. They tend to appoint agents who are most appealing to them, but this doesn't necessarily make for a good agent. Remember, empathy and ego—normally assumed to be necessary characteristics—are not mandatory traits for an agent. The painstaking chore of checking references is often overlooked or eliminated and a very valuable source of agent analysis is not even used.

>>>→ *WATCH THIS*   Sure, most agents will give you references that they're certain will work out to their best advantage, but you can insist on references of your choice. Ask for the name of every sales manager they have, and call each one. You may find one or two who are negative, so give the agent the benefit of the doubt. However, if you detect an unenthusiastic trend setting in, you'd better have another interview or two before appointing that alter ego.

A PROSPECTIVE AGENT MUST FIRST CONVINCE YOU

When visiting with prospective agents for your line in new areas, what criteria do you use for choosing the best representative—size of office, age of the agent, his customer list, or the type of car he drives?

None of these are good reasons for signing up an agent; they have little to do with his selling ability, yet sales managers often make their decisions on an equally irrational basis.

>>>→ *IDEA IN ACTION*   The real proof of the pudding is how he sells you! If he can't sell you, how can he sell your product? He may have a nice house, a ready and willing sales staff, and a list of fine principals. Of course, these things are important . . . but they still don't sell the product. All of these apparent advantages may be due to one big customer or one big principal, so look behind the man.

If he convinces you he can sell your product in his territory, then you have some real basis for appointing him. Sure, he may only have a small office, no staff, and just one or two other principals, but he may possess that tremendous desire and drive to carve out a better life for himself. This type of incentive could make him the ideal agent for you in his area—and your company may be the one that provides the catalyst for his success.

CONDUCTING FINAL NEGOTIATIONS WITH AGENTS AT YOUR OFFICE CAN BE PRODUCTIVE

Before you contract with an agency to market your product, it is essential that you (1) establish standards for selection, (2) plan the marketing functions you expect the agency to perform, and (3) qualify and screen the agency thoroughly. A great deal can be learned about an agency's operation, office efficiency, etc., by interviewing him in his own territory. After this has been done and an interest has been established by both you and the prospective agency, you may find that having him visit your plant at your expense can have several positive effects on your negotiations. By picking up the tab you indicate you are running a professional agent's sales program.

>>>→ *HOW TO DO IT*   You can bring in one or more of your fellow executives to help in the appraisal of the agent and to aid you in negotiations.

As said, normally we recommend field visits when appointing new representatives. But if you're talking to the agency you feel is best suited to your needs and there's no question about his capabilities, following, and effectiveness, then it may pay to bring him to your office and give him the red-carpet treatment. Since this is seldom done by manufacturers, he'll be impressed and you may land yourself an agency that can increase your sales volume dramatically.

Important Points to Cover with a Prospective Agency

Name: _____ Date: _____

Address: _____ Phone: _____

Person Interviewed: _____ Position: _____

1. Is the agency a corporation, partnership, or sole proprietorship? _____

2. How long has the agency been established? _____

3. Describe your agency's growth pattern (i.e., present sales volume): _____

4. Number of field sales personnel: _____ office personnel: _____

5. Is the principal agency owner actively involved as a salesperson? _____

6. Describe the territory you cover: _____
_____

Can you provide a map of your territory? _____

7. Describe the kinds of customers you currently are contacting: _____
_____

8. Would you be willing to deviate from your present territory or product market? _____

If so, how would you handle the new product line or increased territory? _____

9. How many offices do you have? _____

Locations: _____ Do you have any plans for opening any new office facilities and/or expanding your coverage?

Please describe: _____

10. What kind of communication facilities do you have? (i.e., TWX, Telex, Watts) _____

11. Do you use the facilities of any data processing equipment? _____
If so, please describe use: _____

12. Do you have warehouse facilities? _____ If so, what size? _____
_____ What is your method of stock control:

13. How many principals are you currently representing? _____ Do you have a line card? _____ Would you be willing to furnish us with a copy? _____

14. Are your present product lines compatible with ours? _____ Do you feel there would be a conflict with your other principals? _____

15. Would you be willing to assist us in compiling market research information for use in making forecasts? _____ Are you presently doing this with your other principals? _____

16. How do you monitor your agency's sales performance? _____ _____

17. Do you have a direct mail program? _____ If so, how many people are on your mailing list? _____ What types of mailings do you make to them? _____

18. Do you have a brochure describing your agency? _____ Would you be willing to provide us with a copy? _____

19. Do you participate in trade shows? _____ Do you require financial support from your principals for this? _____

20. What is your policy regarding field visitation by factory personnel? _____

21. Would you and/or your sales staff attend factory seminars? _____ If so, what expenses would you expect the manufacturer to pay? _____ _____

22. Who are your key accounts and how do you service them? _____ _____

23. Can you provide references from some of your key accounts? _____

24. Describe your agency's program for sales staff compensation, benefit programs, and training: _____

25. Does your agency offer services such as writing quotes, making proposals, minor service or customer education? Please detail: _____ _____

26. Have you established a long-range growth plan for your agency? _____ If so, please describe: _____

27. References:

Key customers: _____

Principals: _____

Banks: _____

28. Additional information required for your particular needs: _____ _____

HOW INNOVATIVE ADS ATTRACT PROFESSIONAL AGENTS

Companies that create some of the most interesting and effective ads for their products do just the opposite when trying to find agents in a new area. This deficiency can be partially attributed to the fact that professional ad agencies usually dream up the product ads but have nothing to do with the advertisements for representatives.

It's really not necessary to call in an ad agency when writing up an ad for agents, but they can help when you get to the final draft. In the meantime, there's a lot you can do to prepare an ad that will draw results. A Chicago firm drew 77 replies from a simple classified advertisement and a Philadelphia firm drew almost as many from a similar ad, neither of which were prepared by professional ad men.

The next time you're ready to prepare an ad for *Agency Sales* magazine, *The Wall Street Journal,* or your industry trade journal, consider including the following information:

1.   Who you are and what you make (no ". . . leading manufacturer of quality components," type stuff). If you make nuts and bolts, say so. And don't use a box number, identify yourself.

2.   Whether or not you are doing business in the area now. This is important to good professional agents—they want to know if they have to pioneer the line or can build on existing business.

3.   Why your products or services are better than the competition's. You should have some good reasons for being able to sell your products in competition with local suppliers.

4.   How long you have been working with agents. If you're new at it, be honest, but be prepared to offer some special incentives or veteran agents will be somewhat disinterested.

5.   Any special incentives or anything else that makes your sales program stand out from your competition.

Too many ads tell very little about the company but make it very plain as to the type of agent desired. Naturally, it's important to describe the desired agents' qualifications, but unless you tell more about your company and why it should be a plum for any professional, your replies will be minimal.

The biggest mistake most companies make is placing a small ad. Amazingly, good-sized companies take out very small ads . . . and get very small responses in return. Considering the volume of business a good agent can produce, a large ad is an excellent investment. Try it the next time and watch the replies roll in.

WHY PRODUCT-LINE OVERLAP CAN CAUSE AGENT SCARCITY

Most industries working through agents have little trouble finding a supply of agents anxious to represent them. The quality may vary widely however, since many of these agents are just starting in business.

Warning: The opposite is true in several prominent industries, particularly in the consumer product field. Some of the companies in these industries constantly complain about the lack of available agents and are also highly critical of the actions of those who do represent them. Their complaints are primarily aimed at the agents who secretly (or openly) represent companies making competitive products.

This is a very real problem for these companies, not an imagined one. The affected industries have a few agents serving them and the remaining professionals—those who have stuck it out—are besieged with offers to take on additional lines.

A good deal of the cause for this dilemma is self-generated by the very companies that complain the loudest. These firms are naturally aggressive and interested in developing as large a market penetration as possible. Consequently, after the success of their major product they cast about for another product to piggyback the successful product, and usually come up with a new one that is in direct competition with another company in the industry.

There's nothing illegal or immoral about bringing out a competitive product, particularly if it's an improvement over whatever is presently in the marketplace, but it can create havoc with a company's marketing strategy.

>>>→ *EXAMPLE*   Let's take a company that specializes in adult games. The firm may have a first-class agency representing it on the west coast that makes $20,000 a year in commissions from this line. That same agency may also represent another fine firm making children's games and earn $20,000 a year from this firm, for a total commission of $40,000 from two noncompeting firms.

The first company now decides it wants to expand at a faster rate and, since its manufacturing facilities can easily produce children's games as well as adult games, it plans to enter the children's market . . . and does so. The company brass suddenly realizes that its west-coast agency already represents a good children's games company and recognizes that a conflict has arisen.

Usually an ultimatum is issued to the agency, such as "Stop representing the other firm or lose our line." This comes as a shock to the agent who now stands to lose half of his income; however, there is little he can do but make a decision which costs him money.

The solution to this problem isn't easy and it will require the industries involved to reach some compromises, within the law, that will prevent the debilitating effect product overlap has on their agents. Without a satisfactory solution these industries will continue to watch existing agents gradually defect to greener fields where product overlap isn't a major threat.

BLIND ADS

Are you looking for a new agent in an area but are afraid to alert the present agent that he's fallen from favor? Sure, it happens all the time, for one reason or another. So, how do you find a new agent? You place a blind ad.

Warning: This is the best possible way to throw recruitment dollars down the drain. By placing a blind ad and not informing the prospective agent who you are, it's probable that you'll miss the top five agents in the territory.

Why? Most professional agents want information up front, just as you do, and they're not about to reveal their availability to an unknown company. They may also represent a company with compatible products, which could be a real plus for you, but because of the fear that you're currently one of their principals, they'll simply not reply to the ad.

If you're going to make a change in a territory, go ahead and reach an amicable termination arrangement with your present agent. This gives you free reign to go out and try and attract the most capable rep for your line.

BE CAREFUL OF AGENTS WHO BRAG, "WE SELL FORTUNE 500 COMPANIES EXCLUSIVELY"

While you won't find too many agents making the above statement, you will run into agents who are proud of the fact that most of their business comes from several large companies . . . and in some cases this is a good sign.

Warning: Be careful, however, if your product is sold to a variety of customers— an agent with a lot going for him with just a few customers is not necessarily your best bet.

Most agents diversify their customer list as much as possible. This gives them protection against that one big customer who may decide to do business elsewhere. Nevertheless, if your products are sold in large quantities to few companies or chains, you'll want to seek out an agency that concentrates on that type of business to the exclusion of many smaller customers.

RANKING YOUR AGENCY CANDIDATES

The forty-four top-ranking sales executives of the nation's leading corporations were interviewed by *Sales & Marketing Management* magazine recently as to how they evaluated candidates for the selection of an agency. They rated the most desirable traits for the agent interviewed in the following order: enthusiasm, well-organized, obvious ambition, high persuasiveness, general sales experience, high verbal skill, specific sales experiences, highly recommended, apparent sociability, and general overall aspect of office, personnel, and management characteristics.

DO ENGINEERS MAKE GOOD AGENTS?

If you have an engineered product don't ever hesitate to consider appointing an agent who appears a little short on "sales personality" and long on "engineering talent." You may be appointing the best person in the area.

Too few professional engineers enter the agency business, primarily because they feel uncomfortable selling and are certain that they'll never make the grade. However, a few do plunge into their own business, and if they pass the point of survival, they're usually very successful.

    »»→ *IDEA IN ACTION* A good argument for engineers is in the sales made by Al Forbes, Marketing Manager for Riverside Steel of Santa Fe Springs, CA. In an issue of "Sales Manager's Bulletin," Bureau of Business Practice, Waterford, CT, Mr. Forbes, whose company is both a seller and fabricator of steel products for architects, general contractors, and developers, says of his customers, "They are not the type of people who are impressed with a slick sales talk; they're involved in projects that cost millions and they want facts explained in understandable terms."

He states that an engineer is the only person who can easily accommodate himself or herself to the technical requirement of selling steel. "A good salesman," says Mr. Forbes, "who has had some success in a less technical field can learn the engineer's language, but he will always lack the background that will enable him to answer technical questions in a manner that inspires confidence."

Most successful agencies whose owners are engineers have a full complement of lines and it is often difficult to find one to take on your products. However, through a comprehensive search you may be able to find an engineer who is just beginning his agency. If you locate one and offer a little extra in the way of encouragement and financial assistance, you may have found yourself a gem.

THREE TYPES OF AGENT MARKETING . . . WHICH IS THE BEST ONE FOR YOU?

At a MANA seminar for manufacturers, participants were treated to a unique explanation of several different types of marketing needs required by companies using the agency method of selling their goods.

One of the seminar leaders explained to the group that his agency analyzes each prospective principal from one of three viewpoints. In his opinion, the average firm seeking to contract for services of a manufacturers' agent is in one of three stages:

The Market Survey Stage

Here the principal has a definite interest in expanding into a new marketplace or territory, but has little or no knowledge about the potential for his product in the new area. He will be relying completely upon the agency he appoints to make this initial study.

The Market Development Stage

Either after the market survey stage or through past experience in the territory, the principal knows his product has a potential in the area and also knows where this potential is located (which firms are prospective users of his product). This information is imparted to his new agency with the goal of developing the market to its greatest potential.

The Market Maintenance Stage

There is existing business in the territory at present and this must be expertly maintained. In addition, this business must serve as a base from which additional business can be obtained.

The speaker's reason for identifying which stage a prospective principal is in is to enable his agent to determine its strategy in meeting the principal's goals.

If merely a market survey is required with neither party knowing whether the territory holds any potential, then a considerable investment in time and energy will be required by the agency. How this investment is to be funded is a matter of negotiation between the principal and the agent.

The market development stage can be a result of the information obtained during the market survey stage and also requires a substantial investment, but at this point the rewards are apparent. Either the agency or the principal, or both, have forecasted the potential for business and arrangements can be made for the funding of this stage.

At the market maintenance stage, the cost of maintaining current business and seeking out new business can usually be sustained by the commissions the territory is producing.

In this seminar leader's agency, the result of their analysis of the stage the principal is in determines the commission arrangement that is negotiated with the new principal.

This is not a common approach to negotiations that normally precede the signing of a contract between a principal and an agent. Usually the agent tries to decide if the prospective principal has a potential that will make it worthwhile to invest his time in promoting the sale of the principal's goods, and he is looking at the long-term results. Often, however, for one reason or another, the long term turns out to be a short term because of changing sales philosophy at the principal's headquarters or new ownership.

On the other hand, he does not shy away from strictly using the market survey stage, where no commissions will ever ensue and the principal merely wants to determine if there is a market for goods. How the principal exploits this potential— if there is such a potential—can be the subject of further negotiation with his agency or a completely different agency. Common sense, however, would dictate new negotiations. If only a market survey is required, then a fee might be negotiated for this service. Naturally, the principal's product must be one that the agent can identify with in order to make his survey meaningful.

    ≫→ *OBSERVATION* A principal in the market development stage will stimulate a different proposition from our seminar leader's agency. Here the potential is known and, all other things being equal (good pricing, delivery, and service), the cost of such a program will cost the agency less out-of-pocket expense and the suggested financial arrangement will be less than the market survey stage.

    A principal in the market maintenance stage will probably be offered representation at the going commission rate for obvious reasons.

Caution: While the approach taken by this agent may be somewhat controversial, particularly when viewed by prospective principals, it represents a realistic view of the problems an agency faces with various principals that approach it for representation.

Too often a company with no existing business in an area contacts an established agency and is abruptly turned down with the excuse that the agency has enough lines or the line is not compatible with other lines carried by the agency. In most cases, this is a tactful way of telling the principal that the agency is not in a position to invest the $25,000 to $30,000 it may take to explore the territory effectively to determine if a potential exists and, just as importantly, to also determine if the principal can compete in that area.

The agent's policy of identifying the marketing stage a prospective principal is in, aids the principal in facing that same fact himself and allows him to assess realistically the possibilities of signing up a truly professional agency in the area in which he wishes representation.

SCREEN AGENT CANDIDATES CAREFULLY

From time to time MANA has emphasized that the interview phase, when selecting new agents, is perhaps the most important part of the search. There are a number of good reasons for asking questions that reveal the stability and reputation of the prospective agents under consideration.

There is also another reason for investigating these agents and their modes of operations: the variety of differences in agency makeup and operational philosophies.

If you are seeking a new agent in the Southeast, you may receive legitimate inquiries from reputable agencies with the following characteristics:

A one-man firm operating out of his home covering Atlanta only.

A three-person organization with offices in three different cities—Atlanta, Mobile, and Lynchburg, for instance.

A three-person organization consisting of separate agencies that have joined together for better coverage of the area, each retaining its own financial independence and freedom of action.

A father–son agency covering the area.

A multi-person agency with as many as 20 salespeople and 10 or 12 offices representing 15 or 20 principals.

We tend to classify agents as one group, but as you can see from the above descriptions—and these are just a few of the possibilities—there is a wide variety of agency operations in every industry. Each has its own advantages and can be a real asset to a company that can take advantage of the strong points of these firms.

If you have a small organization that offers a limited potential to a prospective agency, then you will profit by selecting the smaller agency to represent you. The potential you represent may be very interesting and motivational to a small agency, but would not be of interest to a large multi-person organization.

On the other hand, if you have a product that must be sold to hundreds or even thousands of firms, then perhaps a larger agency with more salespeople would be a much wiser choice than a small father–son agency.

In between these two extremes are all types of individual needs, and the choice is often difficult. By recognizing exactly what type of agency can do the best job for you—and this can often be determined by examining the successful agencies among your agency group—you can make a wiser decision after a thorough investigation of the agents who reply to your solicitations.

COST ADVANTAGES OF MARKETING THROUGH MANUFACTURERS' AGENTS

During the past several years, MANA has developed a program designed to bring the sales manager and his manufacturers' agents closer together. Seminars for manufacturers and articles in *Agency Sales* magazine are a few ways that have led to a rewarding increase in the cooperation between these two groups, and the results speak for themselves; companies taking advantage of these opportunities have witnessed increased sales by sophisticated marketing through agents.

While increased cooperation and the resulting sales increases have been emphasized, we've neglected to point out that these same companies are also increasing their profits through the use of agents. The increased profits that are being realized take two forms: (1) tangible and (2) intangible. Let's take a look at each.

Tangible Benefits

Right now a good salaried salesperson costs a company about $50,000 a year. His salary averages $35,000 and maintenance (travel expenses, insurance, social security, pensions) about $15,000: a very hefty figure. In a good established territory, this expenditure may not be excessive. It may even represent a savings over the cost of an agent, at least for a year or two. But let's say that this good territory is producing approximately $1 million in sales a year and is growing. Your $50,000 a year salesperson is going to need help, so you'll have to hire another salesperson, adding another $50,000 to your sales cost. The cost of sales ratio will be thrown completely out of line until the new person can improve sales to the point where the ratio approximates the veteran salesperson's figure—a process that could take years. In the meantime, your company is pouring an excessive amount of sales costs into that territory. This may still be acceptable provided sales continue apace; but nothing is certain in sales. Let's take a look at what can happen:

1. Your top salesperson in that territory leaves and joins a competitor, taking along a nice chunk of your business. This means hiring a replacement, which results in additional hiring and training expense, perhaps as much as $12,000. Add this to the $50,000 in salary and expenses and you're paying $62,000 for the new person in a territory which now has to be built back up. But you still need both people and your cost is again out of line because of reduced income and increased costs.

In a comparable situation, it would be extremely unlikely for an agent to drop your company and take on a competitor. He's spent too much time developing your line in his territory. His cost to you in this million-dollar territory is $50,000 (based on a 5% commission) or even $75,000 (based on a 7½% commission). But the addition of another person to cover increased potential is the agent's responsibility and his cost. You don't pay for the new person until he produces, and then only on a gradual basis, which maintains a level percentage of cost of sales.

2. Things slow down and business drops off. Despite the best efforts of your salespeople, sales are off 25%; but the salespeople's salaries and expenses remain the same. You may even spend more in expenses since a greater effort is needed to bring in business. This automatically increases the ratio of selling costs to sales.

With agents, your selling costs drop commensurate with the amount of business they're doing for you—a very real savings just when it's needed the most.

3. So far we've talked only about established territories. The expense of opening up a new territory is terrific. With little or no business, you have to invest $50,000 a year in a salesperson who you hope can bring in sales fast enough to justify his upkeep within a year or two—almost an impossibility.

Again, an agent will open that territory for you with a minimal investment on your part (product training, commissions on existing business) and your sales costs will rise only as your business increases, and then on a predictable percentage of cost of goods sold.

So much for the tangible benefits. Let's consider some of the intangibles that have a real impact on selling cost.

Intangible Benefits

1. Your sales manager is freed of many daily and weekly administrative chores when your salesforce consists of manufacturers' agents. He no longer has to worry about setting salespeople's schedules, checking expense accounts, holding weekly sales meetings to motivate his salespeople, time-consuming hiring and firing, or overseeing the leasing and upkeep of company cars.

2. Other than product training, an agent needs no additional help in learning how to sell. This saves training costs.

3. Through his contacts with established customers, the agent finds potential users of your products that wouldn't be apparent to a salaried salesperson selling only one line. The agent is working with many people in each customer location on behalf of several of his lines. This helps him discover practically all products that are sold to that company. One of them could be yours.

4. Through familiarity with his territory, an agent is able to establish immediate credibility and a very fast penetration of his market for a new line.

A salaried salesperson may take months or years to establish his credibility with potential customers before he can even begin to sell your products. Agents mean faster sales at less cost.

5. Good professional agencies offer a continuity in the territory not available from salaried salespeople. The agent stays in the area and increases the size of his agency as the business grows. The longer you're associated with him, the more familiar and trusted your company becomes with your customers.

6. You can count on your agent to provide you with better feedback. Since he knows many people at each customer location, he's able to better determine what's happening there. Through his acquaintances in engineering, research and development, production, inspection and, of course, purchasing, he will notice any unusual changes in a company's health, philosophies, and direction. He can see inventories building, which may herald a slowdown in ordering; or he may see a competitor's product showing up in increasing numbers on the storage rack. He may be in on the development of a new product line and be able to get your designs in at the prototype level.

As he makes these observations he will alert your organization in the early stages, enabling you to anticipate actions needed to benefit from whatever is happening.

7. In a territory where it simply would never pay to put on a salaried salesperson because of the modest customer potential, an agent can explore and exploit whatever business is there for you. He will be making calls for his other lines and can easily promote your line with little added expense to him. Multiply this by ten or fifteen similar territories and you can realize a goodly amount of business for your firm that would otherwise be unobtainable.

Of course properly utilizing the advantages recounted here takes a commitment from you and your top management. Sales through manufacturers' agents are successful only with the cooperation of everyone in your organization. Sales managers are often faulted for unsuccessful agency sales programs when in reality events beyond their control doom the program to failure. However, enlightened management can make a fair program good, and a good program excellent.

Here are some things corporate management can do to make your sales manager's job effective:

1. Commit your company to a policy of selling through agents—and don't change it. Policy variations, where companies vacillate between salaried salespeople and agents, hurt your sales manager's efforts to recruit professional agents, makes prospective agents gun shy, and results in a mediocre sales group.

2. Through your actions make sure that everyone in the organization is committed to the agency style of selling. The controller should pay commissions on time, just as he does salaries. The production department shouldn't favor house account customers' deliveries over those sold by agents.

3. Don't terminate agents for making too much money, and then replace them with salaried salespeople. This makes your sales manager's job more difficult, since he'll find it harder to locate agents to represent your company. It also penalizes the company because the more successful an agent was in building your business in his area, the more successful he'll be in taking it away.

4. Insist that all departments communicate promptly and effectively with your agents, keeping them well-informed. An uninformed agent is a poor one, and

his attention will turn to those principals who allow him to be effective in the marketplace.

> ⋙→ **WATCH THIS** Whenever agents are polled about incentives, they're quite outspoken about what motivates them the most. While a high rate of commission is important, it trails several other factors that are obvious but which are extremely basic to their financial health. The reputation of your company, the service and backup your people provide, the quality of your products, and on-time delivery, all outdistance higher commissions as motivators. Unfortunately, one or more of these vital motivators are often ignored. And when this happens, your agents become discouraged and quickly turn to selling the products of their principals who provide these qualities in abundance.
>
> By insisting that your personnel back up your agent sales program in these important areas, you need not offer special commissions or incentives, thereby again saving your money (or increasing your profit).

One more intangible benefit of using manufacturers' agents was outlined to *RepLetter* by Mike Brunner, President of Simmons Juvenile Products, an operating unit of Simmons Universal. "Agents give us the advantage of having sales executives in the field," explained Mike. "Many companies," he continued, "have a sales manager at the home office and he attempts to administrate the selling activities of the salesmen in the field. In Simmons' case, we appoint agents very carefully and search for men who have managerial talent as well as selling ability, and who know their territory better than we do. Then, with few exceptions, they act as district sales managers and our administration obligations are practically nil. This gives us executive talent that can't be matched by a direct-employee salesforce."

HOW TO MAKE SURE YOU CHOOSE THE RIGHT AGENT

Forget your pet peeves, your image of the ideal agency, and all those industry stereotypes. In other words, keep an open mind. In addition to the specific answers you get from the following questions, analyze how they hang together. Consistency is the key word. Judge the answers you get relative to each other and you will see a profile of the agency emerge.

Questions to Ask

1.   Will your line be compatible with those already in the bag? Obviously, the lines should be related, yet not competitive. More important, though, the lines should relate to each other in terms of price and quality. A significant difference could foreshadow problems.

2.   Will all the territory you want covered be included? Seldom does an agent cover exactly the same territory for each principal. Make sure that your prospect covers the geography and the market you want.

3. Is the agent calling on the right people? He or she may be selling the companies you want to reach, but if calls are being made on purchasing and your product is sold to engineers, there may be a problem. However, most agents selling to specific industries can shift gears to suit the individuals they see.

4. How about service? If your agents are required to install equipment, perform calibrations, run seminars, or handle jobber training, be sure that you get a chance to see them in action. And be sure that these conditions are spelled out.

5. What about drive? An agent taking on a new line must be prepared to push hard to build the territory as well as supply the sustained effort needed to keep it productive. This could mean future expansion, discussed in the next point.

6. Is the agent willing to expand? Being highly motivated people, most agents try to run their own show close to the vest. When the time comes, will your prospective agent be willing to add salespeople, take on partners, or do whatever else is necessary to accommodate your growing business? Most want to grow, and it's their business; but it's best to determine now how they plan to handle it.

7. How long has the agency been in business? Longevity is seldom a critical factor. A good agency could be a year new and be extremely productive, yet a veteran may have always been a marginal producer. Look at time-in-service relative to productivity.

8. What facilities are available? This question has probably been responsible for more manufacturers rejecting good agents than you can imagine. For example, an agent working from his home is a red flag to many. This is just plain poor judgment. Rather than ask the "home" question, ask whether the agent can provide the services you need, wherever he is. Many agents, at that critical growth point between two or three people and a larger staff, find themselves running an office and not selling or motivating others to sell.

9. What does the agent think of you? Remember, the agents you interview are also interviewing you. Whether they have thought about it formally or not, most agents are giving prospective principals the once-over with these thoughts in mind: Is the line compatible with the lines now handled? Does the product fill a "hole" in the present product mix? How about profitability? Can the agent make use of the extensive list of contacts he or she already has? If the agent comes up with go answers, he will try to sell you.

Forewarned is forearmed. You must get the answers to the first eight questions. But while doing your probing, you should be planting the answers to the questions the agent will ask—those outlined in point 9. Be up front! There's no sense wasting your time and the time of the new agent just to fill out an organization chart. MANA has a list of agent-manufacturer interview discussion topics available. Review it.

WHERE ARE ALL THOSE GOOD AGENTS HIDING?

They're not hiding, they're just working very hard for their principals and don't have the time to let you know who they are.

Personnel specialists say that the working executive is usually the best candidate for a top job. That is, they are working and not actively looking. However, few are unwilling to listen to a pitch, regardless of how happy they are. The same holds true for agents. Most of them are busy and growing, yet seldom show disinterest in a sound proposition. But how and where do you find these people? Here's how many manufacturers handle the problem.

1. *The MANA Directory of Manufacturers' Sales Agencies*. This may seem like an obvious commercial, but this is the most complete guide to agents in this country.

2. *Purchasing agents*. If you can get a purchasing agent for one of your customers to recommend an agent, you know he will be welcomed at the plant. And if the same agent is recommended by several PA's, you know you're on to a winner.

3. *Magazine editors*. Trade magazine editors are often good sources. Over the years, they get to know the top agents in their field and seldom hesitate to recommend them. You will probably find that these editors will give you the names of several agents to choose from, rather than recommending one agency. This is just a matter of personal and editorial integrity.

4. *Other agents*. Good agents usually know and associate with other good agents. Ask the agents in whom you have confidence. If they know, they'll help; if they don't, they can often produce contacts that will know other agents.

5. *Advertising*. Try the publications that cover your field as well as those devoted to selling, such as *Agency Sales* magazine. *The Wall Street Journal* and *The New York Times* also provide good national coverage.

6. *Trade associations*. Many trade associations maintain lists of contacts for their members. If you belong to any associations, check with the executive secretary.

7. *Rep search firms*. There are several firms that provide search services for manufacturers. The services range from expensive, in which the consultant may take a year or more to cover a territory, to those who simply make mailings for you.

8. *The guest register*. Those who sign in at your company and the companies to whom you sell are usually worth contacting. At the very least, they know you and your market. Often the receptionist can give you some insight into the personality of the agents she sees. Are they friendly? Too friendly? On time for appointments? Neatly dressed? Well liked by the people they call on?

9. *Agent advertising*. It's not just the new and hungry agents who place ads looking for principals. Often you'll find a well established agent who just lost a line and is looking to pick up the slack. And those who just want to grow show the initiative by spending their money on advertising.

WHAT SIZE AGENCY IS BEST FOR YOU?

"I like 'em small and hungry," one sales manager told us. Another, selling exactly the same products to the same market, said that he would have nothing but large, multi-person agencies on his team. Who is right?

Small or big, like beauty, exists only in the eyes of the beholder. Neither of the two gentlemen just mentioned could give good, sound reasons for their decisions. However, both were running successful agent networks. What it boils down to is this: It's less the size than the ability of the agency to do the job. Of course, some products and territories require big outfits and others need nothing more than one man covering ten states. The following are some guidelines to help you make the choice:

1.   Define the market and territory first. Can one person handle it? Will it take many? Would it be better to break up a big territory and assign each segment to a smaller agent than to have one multi-person agency handle the entire area?

2.   Estimate the growth potential of the territory as well as the agencies you are considering. Are both growing? Is the smaller agency capable of expanding to meet the demands of the territory?

3.   You must be able to determine just how much attention you will get from the agency that you select. Even though conventional wisdom says that small agencies are more inclined to pay closer attention, the big agency may need you as much as you need it. Make sure you know the score before you make the decision.

4.   Size may not be the most important factor. Don't be stampeded into selecting a big agency just because it's big. Look at the background and accomplishments of the principals as well as the staff.

BE UP FRONT ABOUT CURRENT BUSINESS WHEN RECRUITING NEW AGENTS

The agent/manufacturer relationship must be built on trust. However, with many manufacturers and agents, this trust is a long time in coming.

Warning: There seems to be an almost universal feeling that telling prospective agents the size of the business you are now doing in the territory you want to cover will influence them. That is, if you've got a lot of sales, the skimmers will push for the account just for the current commissions. If your sales are skimpy, none but the desperate will be attracted by your offer. You should always tell your prospects the truth about current territory sales.

It's difficult to get a true picture of any agent unless you talk with several in the territory. The skimmers will stand out and so will those who want your account for more than current commissions. The best agent will want to join your team because you have good products, are competitive, offer solid services, and appear to represent a long-term relationship. Of course, agents are in business to make money and none will turn down the commissions. But the agents you want to work with will ask you about future plans for new products, corporate growth, and the strength of your R & D department. So, don't hide anything, but listen carefully to the reasons why your candidate agents want the territory.

HOW TO PRE-SCREEN AN AGENT BY TELEPHONE

When you open a new territory or find it necessary to replace an agent in a distant location, it's often wise to begin the process with telephone interviews. It's impossible to get all the information you need to make the best possible decision, but when you plan your telephone calls carefully, you can save a lot of time on the field trips that will be necessary for the final evaluation.

An interview is not the place to make a decision; it's strictly a method of collecting information. It's not easy to avoid making judgments during a phone interview. One person's voice may be pleasant and he may say everything you want to hear; another's voice may be grating and he may fumble most of the questions. Whatever you do, don't prejudge your candidates during the interview. Use the time on the phone to gather facts. Make judgments later when you have the answers you want and when you have talked with the candidates face to face. Here are some tips to help you with telephone interviews.

1.   Tell every agent you interview by phone that the information they give you will be held in strict confidence—and be sure that you do just that!

2.   Treat all interviewees equally. Ask each the same questions. There is often a tendency to anticipate the way a person might answer a question from his previous responses. When you feel strongly enough about your impression, you might be led to skip a question because you "know" how it will be answered. Don't do it. No matter how redundant it may sound, ask every question of every agent you interview and be sure that you ask all the questions in the same order. Answers to questions trigger different responses in different individuals. If you change the order, you change the conditions and may bias some responses.

3.   Tell each agent that you will get back to him, whether or not he is selected for a personal interview. Be sure to do it.

4.   Try to be as natural as possible during the interview. By this, we don't mean that you must be secretive, but that you should avoid leading the agents into areas that go beyond factual information. Save this kind of probing for your face-to-face interview.

5.   Summarize the responses the agents make to your questions by restating them before you move on to another. Interpretive errors can be difficult to rectify once you hang up the phone.

6.   If you tape-record the interviews, be sure to ask permission first.

AGENT RECRUITMENT: A DO-IT-YOURSELF APPROACH

Many of the requests we get from our manufacturer members are for help in finding qualified agents. It seems that most of those who are seeking qualified agents find it difficult to locate agents who serve their markets, who are qualified to do the selling job, and who are not now selling competitive products—not an uncommon dilemma. For those of you who must have good agents selling your products, this is a deadly serious situation.

As an organization of agents, we simply cannot recommend one agent over another. We can, however, see that you get the names of *all* our members (in the annual membership directory), give you some guidelines to help you sharpen your search tactics, and help you make the best decision.

    »»→ ***IDEA IN ACTION***   Begin by putting your own objectives in focus. Perhaps the biggest mistake made by manufacturers seeking agents is that of not defining their markets sharply and then not relating that definition to the markets served by prospective agents.

The sales manager of a company that makes valves told us: "When I first started looking for agents, I contacted every agent I could in the open territories who said they handled valves. Many of them sounded great until I got to the markets they served. I make needle valves, and anyone selling faucets to hardware dealers is definitely not for me."

We've found that one of the easiest ways to help yourself define the market and to help the prospective agent put his market in perspective for you is to use a carefully worded questionnaire. When you talk with prospective agents you should not only describe the products you make but go into considerable detail about the people who specify, buy, and use them. When you and prospective agents are speaking the same language, there will be fewer chances for problems of market interpretation.

Where to Look for Qualified Agents

If you organize and plan for your agent search with essentially the same approach you would use to recruit a top executive, you're off on the right foot. You're going to appoint someone who will contribute to profits as well as bear the image of your company to the marketplace. The following sources will be most helpful:

- *Directories.* The MANA directory of members is a good first choice. It's revised annually, and the price includes a one-year subscription to *Agency Sales* magazine.

- *Customers.* Talk to customers you have been selling directly to and ask them for the names of agents they would recommend who have been selling them related products.

- *Other manufacturers.* Talk with those who make related but noncompetitive products. Ask them to recommend the agents who have been most productive for them.

- *Advertise. Agency Sales* magazine is one of the most productive places to attract competent agents. You can also try advertising in the business section of the newspapers that serve the territories you want to cover. Further, see if there are any chamber of commerce publications or specialized business magazines serving the area. For example, the Instrument Society of America has many local journals that can be used to locate agents serving this field.

- *Local Yellow Pages.* Unless the agent buys a larger space than just the conventional line listing, you probably won't be able to tell very much about him, the products he sells, and the markets he serves. But the Yellow Pages can be a place to start. However, learn to use headhunter tactics—ask those who don't qualify to recommend someone who does. This branching and twigging can be quite productive.

Conducting Your Search

Assuming that you have picked up the names of several agents in the territories you want covered by one or several of the methods just described, you are now ready to qualify each. A phone call won't tell you who is the best candidate, but it will tell you in broad strokes who doesn't meet your specifications. Whatever you do, make sure that you allow yourself plenty of time to make a proper evaluation and choice. Don't make snap decisions—they're not good for you or for the agents you appoint.

Here are some major points you should check.

1. Will your line be compatible with those the agent already represents?
2. Does the agent cover all the territory you have in mind?
3. Is the agent calling on the right people?
4. If your products require service and installation, can the agent supply this?
5. Is the agent motivated and willing to grow as you grow?
6. How long has the agent been in business? How long has he worked in the field, either for himself or someone else?
7. Are the facilities appropriate for your needs? Don't rule out an agent just because he works out of his house. Many of the most successful agents work from one room in their homes.
8. How does the agent feel about your line? Is he enthusiastic about the product and its prospects with his customers?
9. Does he have sufficient personnel to cover the territory—if it's large or complex?
10. What about his qualifications and those of his salespeople?
11. How does he pay his salespeople? Incentive payments usually signal strong motivation.
12. Does he maintain and use a current mailing list of customers as well as prospects?

TECHNICAL QUALIFICATIONS ARE BECOMING MORE IMPORTANT FOR AGENTS

As the cost of a sales call goes higher and higher, it's imperative for manufacturers to do everything they can to help their agents be as effective as possible. Agents who have built their business with a combination of strong selling skills and product or technical knowledge are going to find the need for in-depth product knowledge becoming more important.

Agents are, first and foremost, salespeople. But to make it through these tight economic times, you're going to have to provide them with better product and applications training. This is especially critical for manufacturers who are selling high-ticket products through agents. Repeat business of inexpensive products will still depend heavily on selling and service skills. But to be cost effective, your agents are going to need to be able to solve more problems on the spot.

• Problem solving starts with good product knowledge, but it must go farther than this. The most effective way to achieve this without taking your agents off the road for formal training is by way of regular self-teaching programs. These need not be formally prepared. Tapes, newsletters, and documented case histories on the applications you consider important can be quite effective. However, be sure you show in detail how a problem was solved and how the same problem can be applied to other situations involving your products.

• Encourage agents who have faced and solved tough application problems to share their secrets with you so that you can pass them on to your other agents.

• Larger agencies can afford the luxury of training specialty salespeople to handle specific products or markets. However, such organizations are the exception, not the rule. You are going to be faced with the problem of fighting for time along with the other manufacturers the agency represents. It's a lot easier than you think, though, if you remember that your agents are looking for ways to make the sale easier, too. One of the best ways to do this seems to lie in helping your agents become consultive sales experts. That is, they must be able to solve problems for their customers quickly. If they have to consult the factory every time they have a tough problem, the door will be open to a more aggressive competitor. Of course, the sale of highly complex equipment will always require a lot of factory support.

WHAT TO DO WHEN AN AGENT TURNS DOWN YOUR LINE

"I couldn't believe it," the sales manager said. "I offered my line to one of the best agents in the territory, and he said no." And the sales manager went on to explain that he has one of the best lines in the industry and has to fight off agents in other territories. The funny part is that the sales manager is telling the truth. He's not deluding himself into thinking there's no other line but his. He does have first-rate products and yet the agent did turn him down.

It's always been true that the better agents can be very selective of the lines they take on. But today with more and more manufacturers turning to agency selling, the competition is heating up. We talked with a number of agents and asked them why they had turned down lines. These are the areas that seemed most important.

• *Sales history.* A good agent wants to know your sales volume nationally as well as in the territory he covers, and he wants to have the figures for at least the last four or five years. Cynical sales managers think that agents who want this information are only trying to estimate the commissions that will accrue to them immediately. Sure, there may be some agents who think this way. But the good ones—the agents who turn down more lines than they take on—are really concerned with knowing the growth picture of your company as well as the potential in the territory. They will also want to know what you expect from the territory and how you arrived at the figures.

• *Market mix.* If your products are used in more than one industry, agents will want to know the distribution. And they will want to know which markets are growing and which are contracting.

• *Capacity for growth.* Savvy agents today usually rise to top corporate jobs before they strike out on their own. Those with a good manufacturing background will often ask for such information as plant and personnel capacity. They then relate this information to your past and projected sales and will come up with a good idea of whether or not you're going to be able to deliver the product when they deliver the orders.

If you're asked these questions, be sure to add any qualifications that will help convince the good agent. If you are planning a plant expansion, be specific about the added capacity. Discuss new product development as well as any significant additions to staff.

• *Support personnel.* In addition to wanting to know who their routine contacts will be at the plant, good agents want to know who will be their advocate. In essence, they want to make sure that they have a voice at court—a person who knows, who understands, and who is committed to working with agents.

• *Support services.* Be prepared to document your promotional program. This means much more than show-and-tell with a few fancy catalogs and reprints of ads. It means that you should be able to show how effective the program has been—the cost per inquiry for space ads, the return on investment for trade show participation, and the amount of direct interest your direct mail has generated.

• *Other criteria.* Good agents will expect good reasons for your pricing policies, discounts, and commission levels. They will also expect you to provide sound product application training. And they will want to know the name of the previous agent in the territory and why he no longer represents you. Also, they will want to know the names of all of your other agents, and they will talk with more than a few of them.

Now, back to the question of what to do when an agent turns you down. If you just remember that you are not hiring an employee when you sign on an agent but that you are entering a joint venture with another businessperson, you will find it a lot easier to get the best agents on your side. When an agent turns you down, find out why. Tell him that you are concerned with getting the best coverage and would like to know just what the problem is. If you are direct and open and if you assure the agent that you are interested in finding a good agent, there are very few who will not offer to help. In fact, this kind of openness often results in the rejecting agent reversing his decision and taking on the line.

HOW TO WRITE CLASSIFIED ADS THAT ATTRACT THE AGENTS YOU WANT

Unhappy with the responses you get from your advertising for agents? If you're sure that no one out there wants to work anymore and that all the good agents are too busy to talk with you, it may be time to look closely at the copy you write for the classified and display columns.

Warning: There are a lot of manufacturers and agents who are looking to connect. In many cases, though, the ads they write just don't do the job of attracting attention and motivating individuals to write or call. Those with little or no experience writing advertising copy will usually try gimmicks to attract attention, and then fail to live up to the promise of the headline. Others will exaggerate the facts, only to disappoint and annoy those who respond. Still others, in an effort to avoid both sins, write their ads as though they were writing a laundry list—dull and uninteresting.

Let's look at a typical ad. We'll dissect it and then give you some pointers for writing strong classified ads that attract the attention of interested agents.

WANTED: Manufacturers' Representative

Leading manufacturer of high-quality valves for petrochemical processing industry seeks experienced representatives calling on all major installations. Territory open in major area. If you're selling OEM, we will not be compatible. Write to Sales Manager, Box 234, Dayton, Ohio.

First, let's look at the obvious problems in this ad. Then we'll get into the techniques you can use to create winning classified ads yourself.

1. The headline—there are thousands of agents in the country, and each of them has a specialty. This headline hasn't identified the type of agent being sought and it hasn't done anything to make the ad stand out from the crowd.

2. The copy starts with information that is important to the writer, "leading manufacturer," but not very exciting to the reader. In other words, there is no benefit to interest agents reading the lines available columns.

3. A major territory—where is it? An agent reading this ad in Dallas would probably assume that his territory is covered simply because it's one of the biggest for these products. But it may not be! Be specific.

4. Don't be negative. Rather than defining the exclusion, state just what it is that you want. Not compatible if you're selling OEM is a turnoff.

5. Write to sales manager of a no-name company—a definite mistake. Identify yourself and your company. You know the political problems in this business. No one but new, green, and hungry agents will respond to such a blind ad. You may find some good recruits among the inexperienced, but by writing the ad this way you will have ruled out a lot of good potential candidates.

Hints for Writing Successful Agent-Wanted Ads

1.   Even though you will probably not be competing directly with other manufacturers seeking the same type of agents, think of yourself as being in this competitive situation. The mind-set will help you put your company's features into perspective and help you write them as benefits for the prospective agents you want to attract.

2.   Make a list of all the advantages of working with your company, but do it from an agent's point of view. Be honest. Don't shade the truth, but do be enthusiastic when you have strong points to make. For example, if you advertise heavily in trade magazines, translate this into a benefit for agents by saying: National advertising develops hundreds of qualified leads every month.

3.   Write and rewrite the copy until it sells—until it tells your story in terms of benefits to the agents who will read it. There is a tendency on the part of people who don't write advertising for a living to dash off classified copy in a few minutes just because the ads are small. In truth, classified advertising is often the most difficult to write simply because you use few words and every one must count. Some of the best copywriters in the agency business came from agencies that specialized in recruitment advertising. They are trained to make every word sell.

4.   Be specific and upbeat. You've got to get all the facts into the copy, but you still have to attract attention. Just a straight description of your offer is seldom enough to excite people. Tell your story in positive terms that will intrigue the agents you want to hear from. The best test of your success in this approach will be to read your copy with the eyes of the agents you want to attract. Or, better yet, send the copy to the agents you now have and ask them if they would respond to it if they weren't working for you now.

Now, let's see how the dull ad we started with can be given life.

> **We're expanding and looking for an agent selling the southwest petrochemical market**
>
> Sales are up 22% this year . . . and our agents have made it possible. Now we need an additional agent in the Dallas/Ft. Worth area to help us grow even more. If you sell to petrochem plants and oil field stores, know valves and fluid control components, this could be the line you are looking for. Write or call Jim Wilson, Sales Manager, Talbott Valves, Inc., Box 234, Dayton, Ohio. (513) 777-1111.

Since the ad is classified, it will be placed in the appropriate section of the newspaper or magazine, and there is no need to waste words by saying "Agents Wanted" in the headline.

This copy has presented facts, but they have been stated in an interesting and intriguing way. Now the copy has to be placed in a publication that is read by the best agents, and those who are interested in your products. The chances are that you can advertise in local specialty trade publications, but you should consider

Agency Sales magazine as the prime source. For details, including rates, write to, Advertising Coordinator, MANA, Box 23016, Laguna Hills, California 92654.

A TOP AGENT TURNED YOU DOWN? LET'S LOOK AT THE REASONS

Strange as it may seem, even the top agencies have—and actively seek—smaller principals. Seldom will they turn down a principal just because of its size. The two major reasons agencies give for turning down a line are:

1. History with previous agencies: Unfair termination, slow payment of commissions, lack of support.
2. Stagnation: This may be in terms of product line, corporate growth, or just a general lack of aggressiveness in the marketplace.

If you have any of these problems, it could be the reason for a top agency turn-down. Be sure to clean house before you talk with a top agency.

TALK WITH YOUR PRESENT AGENCIES BEFORE YOU LOOK ELSEWHERE

We have given tips on how to make the most of your agency search. The main sources we highlighted were the MANA directory, talking with customers and other manufacturers, and advertising in *Agency Sales* magazine. And, of course, you can always get a raw list from the Yellow Pages of your phone directory. But one of the growing sources of leads on agencies is your present sales team.

As you've probably gathered from reading marketing publications, manufacturers' agencies are a growth industry. With this growth has come more and more inter-agency contact. So much, in fact, that we think one of the better sources of contact can be with the agencies with whom you are now working. Because of the close nature of the field, your agencies should be able to point you in the right direction when you have open territories. Some helpful suggestions follow:

1. When you ask your agencies for leads on other agencies, look for the positive elements that will qualify an agency to handle your line. Sure, you will turn up some negatives. Make sure of the facts. Don't dwell on gossip.

2. Be sure to give your present agencies all the facts when you ask them for help. If a current agent feels strongly enough about you, your products, and your potential, his or her recommendation might get you a top agency—one that might be difficult to land through other channels.

3. Even though you get some good leads from your present agencies and you feel positively about them, be sure to go through your regular screening procedures. Don't take chances just because the recommendation came from someone who is already representing you.

BE REASONABLE WHEN DEFINING THE "IDEAL" AGENCY

A sales manager at a recent MANA seminar asked for help in locating agencies. Not an uncommon request, but this man said that he, "had gone through four agents in one territory alone in the last year and a half." Apart from suggesting that he use the MANA directory, we felt compelled to ask why there had been such a rapid turnover. Without going into the details, it turned out that he had set up some rather tough criteria and his schedule for accomplishing the goals was much too short. Agent after agent tried to do the job and never met his standards. When we learned this, the only suggestion that made sense was to allow more time to get the job done.

Sure, agents do represent a way of having an instant salesforce in the field, but some jobs require time-on-the-job. Longevity counts as agencies become more familiar with you, your products, and your markets. When changing agencies seems like a way out of a problem, first ask yourself if the incumbent has had sufficient time in rank. Has he been given enough time to do just what you want to be done? With short-term goals dominating the long view these days, the same attitude can find its way into the agency relationship. Don't fall victim to the short view. Make sure that your agencies have had the time they need to do the job.

HOW TO GET LEADS ON AGENCIES FROM OTHER MANUFACTURERS

An agency recruitment program should draw on a number of sources, including input from manufacturers of compatible but noncompetitive products. When you have a territory to cover, one of the first things to do is to identify these manufacturers and to contact them for their views on the agencies they are using. Keep the following points in mind:

1.   Every manufacturer wants to get more of his agencies' time, and giving your name to an agency implies that the agency might have even less time available. However, manufacturers who make the most of agency selling know that their agencies must grow with them. They are interested in seeing their agencies get the kinds of lines that will enhance the exposure of their lines. When you contact manufacturers, be sure to show how the addition of your line will be of benefit to them and to their agencies.

2.   The views that will probably impress you most will be the extremes—the great and the awful will stand out. However, you should never reject an agency when either of these evaluations surface—but you should proceed with your own investigations with these points in mind. They are clues, not reasons, for immediate appointment or rejection.

3.   Don't allow yourself to be pushed into an agreement because you want to cover the territory right away. Take time to get all the facts and opinions sorted out.

GETTING ACQUAINTED WITH AGENCY CANDIDATES

More than a few savvy sales managers have hit the road for a day or two with agency candidates to see how they handle calls and to meet some of their customers. It's the situational test that is used in many other fields to identify strong people. However, it's just as important for you to make the arrangement reciprocal; invite the agency to spend some time with you. A sales manager who appoints agencies in airport terminals is asking for trouble and is probably a dying breed.

"One agent was very candid," a sales manager said. "He thought our products were great, but when he saw the plant and realized that our capacity would limit delivery of the orders he thought he could produce, he declined very gracefully."

PERSONAL CHEMISTRY IS IMPORTANT WHEN SELECTING AGENCIES

It's important for a personal chemistry to exist between the agency owner and the sales manager. "I have always felt that the manufacturer/agency relationship is made up of 50% personal chemistry and 50% what the agency is able to do specifically for my company," a marketing manager told us. Without the chemistry, even the most qualified agency has a very slim chance for success.

Caution: Personal chemistry is a very subjective thing. It involves emotion and has nothing to do with logic or the fact that the agency candidate sold your competitor's products very successfully in the territory for which you are considering him. It's something intuitive; it's something you feel. If it isn't there, the lack of that comfortable feeling is going to cause problems sooner or later.

Far too often sales executives recognize the need for this chemistry, but when a highly qualified candidate comes along, they allow themselves to be overwhelmed by the real-world events. Mind you, the real world is just as important, but the personal chemistry is the other keystone to a successful venture.

> **»»→ *EXAMPLE*** A sales manager who has built a team of successful agencies said that he tries to stress his company's environment in terms of the agency candidate's background. His company is fairly aggressive and the agencies that have succeeded have had similar characteristics. "My agencies live by their wits," he said. "And when we open a new territory we look for agencies that are less concerned with following a procedure than reaction to situations with imaginative and creative responses."

You may recognize the need for good chemistry between yourself and the agencies you appoint, but don't forget that the others in your company must find the chemistry compatible too. "I hit it off very well with Joe," a sales manager said of an agent he had appointed. "But the first meeting with the president was a disaster. Everyone tried to make a go of it, and it finally did work. But not without a lot of effort on everyone's part."

HOW TO NEGOTIATE SUCCESSFULLY WITH
MANUFACTURERS' AGENCIES

"He met me at the airport—between planes—showed me his product catalog, told me the commission he was willing to pay, looked me up and down and offered me the line." The agent who related this story claimed that the line was just what he was looking for, but the manufacturer's abrupt approach turned him off right away. On the other hand, it can also be just as difficult when negotiations go on forever. Another agent said: "We are ready to go. In fact, we had started scouting business right after the first meeting. But the negotiations dragged on and on. We never did get anywhere."

⋙→ ***HOW TO DO IT*** Robert Otterbourgh, an Englewood Cliffs, NJ, public relations consultant whose clients are among the top on data processing, claims that . . . "Winning a negotiation doesn't necessarily have a competitive meaning. You really don't want to win in the business at the expense of someone else. You want to achieve a goal that is relative to your own needs. This is best done by bargaining, by giving and taking, and by avoiding any behavior that will damage you or the other party." The negotiation strategies that follow are just as important for you, the manufacturer, as they are for the agencies with whom you negotiate. You both want things that the other has to offer. If you are an authoritarian, you will win a lot of first rounds. But if you recognize the needs of agencies, you will both win for the long run.

The basics: Negotiate only with those who have the authority. Avoid serious negotiations with anyone who isn't in a position to make decisions. Have a careful plan. Without a plan you will flounder. With one, you can consider the impact of points and concessions made by the other party. Limit the number of participants. The more people at the table, the more time it will take. Be flexible. A minor compromise or two usually gets more in return than a hard-nosed attitude. Make an early concession. If you give on a minor point, the other side feels obligated and will frequently give on something that is important to you. Don't discuss key issues until you have all the facts. If you do get involved in a key issue discussion without having all the facts at your disposal, you may have to change strategy—and this definitely puts you at a disadvantage. Know exactly what the other side needs. The needs of the other side may not be apparent—there may be a hidden agenda to contend with. Don't make promises unless you stand ready to keep them. Further negotiations could make you wish you hadn't made the offer. Don't waste people's time. More than a few agents have reported lengthy negotiation sessions that turned out to be disguised learning experiences. The word spreads.

Strategies: Avoid interruptions. If the meeting is under your control, make absolutely certain that you and the people with whom you are negotiating are not interrupted. Don't respond with a completely nondirective "uhmmmmm." Take the lead in bringing up major terms. Don't rush to do it, but being the first gives you a bit of an edge. Don't be afraid to leave something on the table. Put off the discussion of sensitive points until there is major agreement. Try to get agreement on as many major points as possible before you get into sensitive areas, especially those that are personally sensitive. Agree on the next steps. If the negotiation is going to take more than one session, both parties should agree completely on the next steps. Make your disagreements positive acts. Don't point out where people are wrong, unless you are convinced that they are totally unaware of it. Rather, bring up the advantages to be gained from your point of view. Don't rush people. A person rushed to make a decision may protect himself or herself by making no decision at all. Don't discuss points that you and the other party have already agreed on. Even when an agreed-on small point is reopened, you run the real chance of scuttling the entire negotiation. Don't be a nitpicker. You will find that some people retreat into trivia when they don't want to face the main issues. It's exasperating. Don't do it yourself. Never say, I told you so. When you have been proven correct, you know it and so does the other party.

Techniques that work: Represent yourself. Unless you are a multi-national conglomerate with more to do than time to do it, handle your own negotiations. Discuss terms face to face. Watching the reaction of the person with whom you are negotiating can be a key to success. You can't do this on the phone or through the mail. Deal with the person who has the power. Today, more than ever, the person who seems most articulate and dynamic in a meeting may be a front—the warm-up person. Pick out the person with the real authority and direct your comments and attention to him or her. Watch very carefully for negative responses. Negative responses in negotiations are frequently trial balloons—the person may really be asking you for an answer rather than saying flat out "no." Verify the things you are told. This just makes good sense in any negotiation. The absence of key people and documents is a sign to watch. When one member of the team makes a seemingly lame excuse for the absence of a person who has to take part or for "forgetting" important papers, watch out.

The personal factors: Always be yourself. Acts are easily spotted during and after negotiations. Don't bad-mouth people. You may want to rip into your competitor's products and the agent in the territory you want to cover, but don't do it. Even though it may never get back to the objects of your scorn, you will come off with the agent with whom you are negotiating as having personal weakness. Keep unrelated opinions out of the discussion. Be aware of the moods of the people with whom you negotiate. Moods vary from day to day and from hour to hour. When you get to know the person with whom you are negotiating, you should be aware of their mood shifts—and your mood shifts. Don't push too hard and too far. In any negotiation, there are usually many points to be resolved. Take each one step at a time, relative to your capabilities and those of the people with whom you are negotiating. Be prepared for negative reactions. No matter what is offered, both sides will think some of the suggestions are unfair. Think before you respond to them, though. More on-target negotiations are destroyed by personal critical remarks. Acknowledge the contributions made by others. Everyone takes pride in their abilities and the things they do. Be sure that those you negotiate with know that you are aware of and appreciate their efforts.

The short strokes: Always be fully prepared. This may seem obvious, but more people than you can imagine enter a negotiation thinking they know everything and are ready to wheel and deal. Have your facts substantiated. You may have sales of ten million and pay commissions the moment the order is received. But you will have a hard time convincing most agents without some documentation. Choose your negotiating team carefully. If others from your company are going to meet with agency people, make sure that those you choose are really related to the issue. As you and the agency reach agreement on points, nail them down, put them in writing, and say them clearly in front of each other. In other words, take every step you can to build on successes. Delegate very carefully. Earlier we said that you should handle the negotiations yourself—and you should. But, if you're forced to turn a stage of the negotiation over to someone else for a short period, make sure that person has all the facts and knows just what his or her responsibility and authority are. Don't provoke. Beware of someone who finds it necessary to be provocative to be productive. How people behave during a negotiation often foreshadows how they will behave after the contracts have been signed. Read the agreements you make very carefully. MANA has available specimen contractual guidelines which can be very helpful when manufacturers and agents draw up their contracts—but be sure to consult your attorney regarding the laws of your state. Read the finished documents carefully before you sign.

> ⋙➤ *OBSERVATION* When agencies and manufacturers enter negotiations, they both want something—and they should both be willing to listen carefully to the reasons presented for these wants. If you remember that this is not an adversarial situation but is a situation where you both want the same thing, you're on the right track—even if you have different ideas about how to achieve your goals.

ELEVEN WAYS TO BLOW AN AGENCY INTERVIEW

"Ten years ago I turned down agencies," the president of an industrial firm that sells with agencies told us. "But now," he continued, "I get turned down once in a while by an agency. There are a lot of good agencies around and they are getting very choosy about the lines they take on."

The agency interview is an opportunity for you to showcase your company and its products and accomplishments. Today, you may be one of several firms talking to an agency about representing your line. If you really want the agency on your side, here are eleven points that if not handled properly could turn the tides against you.

1. Talk with people who know something about the agency. Other principals, customers, and even suppliers can provide insight to help you guide the interview. Being uninformed is being unprepared.

2. Once you have scheduled the interview, prepare for it very carefully. Know as much as you can about the agency and what it has been doing for a number

of years. Try to find out about the individuals with whom you will be dealing and what they will be looking for.

3.   Don't assume that the agency people are as familiar with your products as you are. They should be selling to the same people you sell to, but don't back off because there seems to be less knowledge about your product than you think they should have. Concentrate on the market and applications. An agency that is selling your market successfully can learn what it needs to know about your products to see them.

4.   Don't be a bore. You're not going to win a good agency with a song and dance. More agencies are turned off by a wimpy interview than you can imagine. Be enthusiastic about your company, your products, and the potential for the agency with whom you are talking.

5.   Don't think that past history alone is going to get you the best agency. A strong history is a great beginning, but good agencies want to know what you plan to do to grow.

6.   Don't miss an opportunity to differentiate your company from the others in the field. Don't knock your competitors, but make sure that you position your company and its products so that the agency can see it clearly as it relates to the lines they carry and the markets they serve.

7.   If your company has a narrow product line, show the agent that you have a broad knowledge of the market and the applications for your products. Agencies claim that many small companies with narrow lines also have a narrow view of the realities of the marketplace.

8.   Don't underestimate the successes your company has had. This may seem odd to say, but more than a few agents claim that prospective principals have been almost shy about telling them about their accomplishments. An agent we heard of was about to turn down the line of a small manufacturer until the sales manager just happened to mention that the company's connectors were used on all the space shuttles. Don't spend your time bragging, but don't underestimate the importance of your accomplishments in helping a new agency make headway in a new territory.

9.   If you are going to give the agency references, make sure those references know that you are using their name. It's just as common for agencies to ask for references today as it is for manufacturers to ask agencies for them. But if the people you have given for reference are unaware, they just might flounder when they are called. You will get a good reference, but that momentary lapse at the beginning of the call could be a turnoff.

10.   Don't leave out your expectations. Yes, it's getting more difficult to get the agents you want, but don't try to set the hook by avoiding talk of what you expect the agency to do.

11.   Don't forget to ask agents what they will expect from you. You may not agree with their expectations, but hear them out and wait for the appropriate time to discuss them.

DON'T OVEREMPHASIZE POTENTIAL WHEN
INTERVIEWING AGENCIES

A recent letter from an agent described a matter that led to an agency resignation and some pretty bad feelings. The manufacturer involved had recruited several agencies and had told each that there was much more potential than really existed for the product. Also, this manufacturer stressed agency qualifications that weren't really needed to sell the products. As you might imagine, there were considerable differences between stated and actual conditions. The agencies were frustrated, and the manufacturer was disappointed. We're still not sure that the manufacturer realizes he oversold his line to the agencies. But we are sure that a few agencies are listening more closely to manufacturer presentations.

A GOOD SOURCE OF REFERENCES FOR A
PROSPECTIVE AGENCY

A good manufacturer always asks a prospective agency for references . . . and a good agency always asks a prospective principal for references. The best references you can offer an agency are, of course, the other agencies on your team. However, the vendors you buy from can provide a secondary picture for the agency considering your line. Your vendors cannot only attest to your approach to handling financial matters, but they can also give prospective agencies the idea of buying history that should correlate with the growth history of your company. You won't expect these suppliers to divulge confidential financial dealings, of course, only their impressions of your company as a business ally.

ANOTHER REASON WHY AGENCIES ARE THE
BETTER WAY TO SELL

Recent research indicated that managers are most productive just before and just after the normal working hours. This seems to indicate that normal working hours are not the most productive times. Think about this in terms of companies with salaried salespeople. Even though they may work without supervision in the field, they tend to follow the working hours established by the company that employs them. Agents, on the other hand, adapt to their own best personal rhythms. In fact, most agents claim that they average a 70-hour week. They are not bound by the arbitrary 9 to 5 hours.

TO SUCCEED WITH AGENTS, UNDERSTAND HOW THEY
DIFFER FROM SALARIED SALESPEOPLE

A manufacturer who had switched from a direct salesforce to a nationwide team of agencies said: "Lucky I'm a fast learner. I tried to use the same approach with that team of agencies as I had used with my own field people. I guess enough of them had been through this before to be patient with me." At the time we talked with this man he was celebrating—and celebrating is the operative word—three years of selling through agencies.

We have always tried to point out that agents don't respond to the same things that salaried salespeople do. However, most of the calls we get from agents and manufacturers are really the result of manufacturers trying to manage their agency team with the same approach that was successful with a salaried staff. We recently saw the results of a study that ranked the elements of satisfaction of employees and thought it would be an interesting way to point up the very real difference—the difference that must be acknowledged if agencies are to be successful. It follows:

1. *Job security.* Employed individuals place job security on the top of the other nine elements. Agents, who bank on success with absolutely no assurance of job security, simply aren't motivated in this direction.

2. *Type of work.* The average person employed in sales in industry has worn a lot of different hats—and will probably continue to do so. The agent has been through the chairs, but research by MANA shows that once a person becomes an agent, it's usually a lifetime career.

3. *Career advancement.* More good salaried salespeople become independent sales managers because of striving for higher status on the corporate ladder. The agent knows his only goal is to sell more of his principals' products and to make the agency grow.

4. *Quality of employing company.* Companies, like individuals, have distinct personalities. A domineering company never gets the best out of people, but it can usually work well with agencies because of the independent relationship.

5. *Compensation.* Most salespeople move to other corporate sales jobs for more money. Agents know that all they have to do to make more money is sell more volume and sell more efficiently. There still are a few corporate people who bristle when they write those big commission checks, but most know that for every dollar of commission there's another dollar of corporate profit.

6. *Pleasant co-workers.* More than a few manufacturers we talked with complain about having to be the company social director. Agents usually want nothing to do with the infrastructure—they have their own company to run.

7. *Good supervisor.* This is number seven for employees, but it's frequently a lot higher on the list of characteristics agents feel are important for success. But the word supervisor should be read—contact. Good agencies always claim that they have good principals behind them.

8. *Benefits.* When was the last time you picked up the tab for an agent's life insurance and retirement benefits? Never. Employees tend to agonize over benefits, but agents know that the real benefits come only from doing a first-rate job of selling.

9. *Good working hours.* Flextime is a concept that's hard to sell to the average worker. But it's second nature to the average agent who is up in the morning at 5 to drive 150 miles to the first call. Drive another 200 miles in the same day and

return to the office in the evening to handle the paperwork. You don't have to bargain for this kind of effort with agents. It's either there, or the agency isn't going to make it.

10. *Working conditions.* The same manufacturer who complained about having to be a social director for his employees had some choice words about the faction who argued for hours over the color to paint the office. An agent may complain to his fellow agents about driving 250 miles in the rain to a no-show call, but will seldom make a big deal about his problems with a principal.

USE THIS TEST TO QUALIFY PROSPECTIVE AGENTS

It's not a small step to appoint an agency to sell your product. You could be making a mistake—and so could the agency. We recently heard of a manufacturer with a try-before-you-buy approach that was interesting. This manufacturer had a core of agencies in major industrial centers and was recruiting to fill other territories. "No matter how carefully I qualify a candidate agency," the manufacturer said, "there is always an element of doubt. Now, however, I make a six-month agreement with agencies. I pay 10 percent more for the six-month trial period, and any agencies that aren't appointed at the end of the six months are guaranteed to get commissions on the products they sold in the territory for a full year." The agencies are fully aware of the trial period and they all have the same contractual benefits inherent in the MANA agreement guidelines. The manufacturer has tried this with only a few agencies so far, but it has worked. Each agency that accepted the challenge was appointed at the end of the six months.

AGENTS CAN HELP SOLVE MORE THAN SALES PROBLEMS

An agent recently described to us a situation where one of his principals had all the earmarks of the "wind-down" of a formerly strong principal. "We had close to a million dollars in back-orders," he explained, referring to the delinquent principal. "The manufacturer kept telling us that he couldn't get the bar stock he needed, and we kept believing him. Then I suggested that he call an agent-friend who sells metals in his territory. Within weeks, orders were cancelled with the old suppliers, and the new suppliers—represented by a friend of one of the company's agents— had delivered the material. *The moral:* Talk to your agencies about everything. You never know when they can do a lot more than move your merchandise.

HOW TO TELL AN AGENT THAT HIS AGENCY WASN'T SELECTED

"Next to firing an employee, the most difficult job I have is that of telling agents that they weren't selected when we are filling territories," a regional sales manager explained. This manager works for a major American industrial manufacturer with a large network of agencies. The company has more than one agency in a territory, but the products each sells is highly specialized and there is no sales overlap.

⟫→ *EXAMPLE* "When I have to pass on the bad news," he said, "I call each agent and explain personally why another agency was selected. Then I always follow up these calls with detailed letters. These letters I open with a positive statement about the agency. For example, when I have to reject an especially good agency, I begin by complimenting them on their qualifications. When I have to notify an agency that isn't as well qualified, I say something like this: "I appreciate the extensive time and effort that you went to to tell us about your agency." Then, in a very straightforward way I explain why another agency was selected."

This man claimed that almost every agency he ever interviewed was qualified to handle his line. He feels that this is mainly the result of being very specific when advertising for agencies. "I run display ads in *Agency Sales* magazine, but I never lead off by saying: Agent wanted. My headlines identify the products we sell, the markets we serve, and the kind of company we are. Therefore, the people who contact us are already pre-qualified." His job, then, is not one of weeding out the unqualified agencies, but selecting the best agency for the job. He claimed that it was much harder to reject these agencies than it would be to tell an agency that was out in left field.

So far, the question of how to notify the unsuccessful agency candidate has been outlined. It's just common courtesy to let those who didn't make it know as soon as possible. We don't hear about it often, but occasionally we will get a report from an agent that he heard he failed to get a line only when he ran into the agent who was finally assigned the territory. That's just not the way to go!

SPOTTING THE QUALITIES OF A GOOD AGENT

We have put the question of what makes a good agent to a number of people over the past few years. Admittedly this has not been a scientific survey, but it has been done through formal and informal conversations with manufacturers. The manufacturers we talked with seemed to share five views of the ideal agency, as follows:

- Good agencies don't push products on customers, they exchange information and use open-ended questions to uncover customer needs.
- They don't push for a sale until the customer's complete needs have been identified and confirmed.
- They sell personally as an individual, not as a company person, even though they do stress the service offered by the agency.
- They are always available as a source of information—before and after a sale has been made.
- They are willing to share with their principals and other agencies representing the principals the information that has lead to a successful sale.

FACE TO FACE IS THE BEST WAY TO GATHER INFORMATION
ON AN AGENCY CANDIDATE

We started out asking a few manufacturers how much value they placed on reference letters when they were interviewing agencies, but the conversations turned quickly to the most practical tool of all—the face-to-face interview. "I ask for reference letters," a marketing VP explained, "but I don't think they are very valuable. However, when I phone the person who supplied the reference letter, I get a lot more insight. People don't seem to want to put anything—good or bad—in writing these days. But they are quite willing to talk when you call them on the phone."

This same marketing man explained that his interviews are always carefully scheduled and are done either at the agency or at his plant. He pays the fare when he brings an agent in for an interview. "And I never do interviews between planes at an airport," he said emphatically.

TIPS ON INTERVIEWING PROSPECTIVE SALES AGENTS

Locating good agencies isn't an easy job. Interviewing them is even more difficult. The following are a few tips that will not only make the job a little easier for you, they will also give you a stronger grasp on the agency and its skills and background:

• Set up a specific interview agenda. Be sure to let the agent know exactly what will be covered in the interview. It's best to discuss your company and the requirements you have set only after the agent's qualifications have been covered in some detail.

• Let the agent do a good share of the talking. Use open-ended questions such as those that begin with the words why and how.

• Make sure that the interview is thorough. Avoid generalities—both giving them and accepting them from the agent you are interviewing. Don't leave any gaps open in the information you get from the agent and in the information you present.

• Avoid any kind of a "test" situation. There are some sales managers who like to throw out simulated sales situations as sort of situational tests during an interview. This not only creates stress, but such tests seldom predict anything. If you are concerned with an agent's sales ability, arrange to make a few calls with him or her. Seeing a salesperson in action is about the only way to understand fully how he or she would handle a sales situation.

• Don't make the decision to sign up the agent during the interview. Use every minute of the interview to gather information. Even though you may be totally impressed, resist the temptation to make a snap decision. Gather the facts, mull them over, then make your decision.

TESTING: A WORD OF CAUTION

Recently we heard of a manufacturer who had asked a prospective agent to submit a sample of his handwriting as a precondition of appointment. Traditional psychological tests devised to measure sales ability have proven clinically valid. However, graphoanalytic (handwriting) techniques are generally regarded with considerable skepticism by those who have reviewed the techniques and the predictive validity of the results. If you are one of those people who feel that there might be something to handwriting analysis, we suggest that you first get a sales profile from an accredited testing service and then compare the results with the data you get from a handwriting analyst.

Caution: Handwriting reports are usually quite vague and can be interpreted in many ways. Ask the analyst for specifics. Incidentally, the agent who was asked for the handwriting sample declined. He had nothing to hide and claimed: "If they don't want to measure me by the sales successes I've had for the past 22 years, then I'm not sure that we would get along at all."

HOW MANY AGENCIES SHOULD YOU HAVE?

This query, from the president of a new company who wanted to sell his products through agencies, led to some basic research. Of course, what this man was asking was, how should he define territories and how should he determine agency capability to cover the territory? Implied, but not asked directly, was the question of whether or not territories could be reassigned.

The answer to, "How many agencies should I have?" depends on whether you are just starting out with agencies or already have a network in place. If you're just starting out, you have an excellent opportunity to create territory assignments with agencies that will be most efficient. But if you already have an agency network in place, you are really in the position of fine-tuning the team rather than making a major change.

Let's look at the question from the perspective of a manufacturer just starting out building an agency network.

• The first step is to determine the type of agency that will be best for you. The seemingly obvious answer of an agency selling similar products is only the first step. You will have to define the agency a little more precisely, and these are the types you will have to choose from: trade selling agencies, missionary sellers, technical sales specialists, new business experts, and the closers who work from your leads almost exclusively to close sales. Of course, some agencies will be a blend of several of these characteristics and will be just what you need.

• The next involves setting marketing targets. Marketing targets will include territory sales estimates, but marketing targets and sales goals are not synonymous. Traditionally, marketing goals include such elements as the number of new customers to be gained in a year and increases in sales if you are already selling in the territory. The amount of effort required to accomplish the marketing targets will directly affect the kind and number of agencies that you appoint.

• The next step, reviewing the territories, should be closely related to a review of the agencies you have to choose from. You will need to know whether the agency has the background and people to work the territory smoothly, and whether the territory has sufficient potential to make it worthwhile for the agency. It's seldom possible to set up territories so that each represents approximately the same potential. In fact, any attempt to do this cannot only distort your sales efforts but it will make it difficult to attract the best agencies.

• Since manufacturers' agencies are given exclusive territories for the principals' products they sell, you will want to make sure that the agency has the capability to service existing business. Then, you will want to know that the agency has the capability and desire to grow to maximize territory penetration.

More is not necessarily better when it comes to appointing sales agencies. Manufacturers who use direct salespeople are constantly reinventing the wheel in this regard. "Business is good, demand is strong, let's put on some more salespeople." Selling with manufacturers' agencies is selling with business partners. Even though selling with agencies costs you nothing until sales are made, increasing the number of agencies will probably not result in a proportional increase in sales. If an uncovered territory can be served well by an agency in the next territory, and that agent would like to expand, give him the chance. It's been a long time since the multi-person agency was the exception. To answer the question, "How many agencies should you have?"—enough to realize the potential in each territory.

HOW TO IMPRESS AN AGENT YOU WANT ON YOUR TEAM

Attracting good agents is like hiring top executives; you want to present the best possible picture. Recently we talked with a number of top agents who claim that they turn down three or four lines for every one they take on. Here are some of the things these agents look for when they are evaluating a line:

• Agents who are careful about the lines they take on look for motivated manufacturers. This may seem like a switch—it's the agent who is always supposed to be highly motivated. True, but here's the way one agent explained it: "The company that is generally considered to be engineering- or manufacturing-motivated is seldom the company that we will take on. They may make the best products, but they are seldom driven in the sales department. Of course, we want the best possible products for our customers, but we also want to work with a manufacturer with the same marketing fire in its belly that we have."

• Another agent told us that he is usually wary of companies that want him on their team, but represent their growth in terms of percentages—without revealing actual sales volume. "If the manufacturer is reluctant to discuss the dollar base, a 50 percent increase is next to meaningless," an agent selling to the OEM said.

• Another agent told us how he very carefully checks on the stated accomplishments of his prospective principals. "Too often these accomplishments turn out to be little more than ordinary responsibilities stated in inflated terms." This agent explained that he had recently turned down a line in which the principal had put a lot of verbal stress on his advertising and lead qualification program. Upon closer examination, it turned out that there was nothing out of the ordinary, but the manufacturer genuinely thought it was great. This difference in perception, the agent reasoned, would probably be reflected in other areas of the relationship. The best advice we can give you is to know what the standards are in your industry before you claim more than you should for your efforts.

• If there previously was another agent representing your line in the territory, be up front with the prospective agent about the reason for the parting. It's a small world. Most of the agents we talked with claimed that they were much more inclined to go with a manufacturer who was honest about a parting when it was his fault than when there was a whitewash.

• Agents who have some pretty large principals tell us that one of the things that impressed them when they were negotiating for the lines was the fact that the top corporate people were part of the selection process. "We were recruited by the marketing VP," a Midwestern agent said, "and we were also contacted personally by the president and the executive vice president. Both of these people explained to us just how important sales was in their scheme of things." This gave the agents assurance of corporate support in the use of agencies as a marketing team. As you might imagine, the relationships these manufacturers have with their agencies are top flight.

• Timing is a factor that many mentioned. "We have had several manufacturers in the past year who have either been dumped by their agencies or who have terminated the agent themselves. But in all cases, they wanted to sign up an agency immediately. As interested as we were in some of the lines, we were put off by the sense of urgency. In most cases, it seemed to mask something that the manufacturer might not have wanted us to know." This is a feeling shared by several agents with whom we discussed this situation. Even though you may be anxious to cover a territory, don't try to rush an agency into making a decision.

5

Managing Agency Territories Effectively

Supervising a team of manufacturers' agents is in some ways like managing a salaried salesforce, but in other ways, it is very different. Agents are your business partners, not your employees. Any attempt to treat them the same as employees will lead to difficulties.

In the sections that follow, guidance that is immediately usable to solve some of your most difficult problems is given. For example, it's common practice to assign quotas to salaried salespeople. However, a quota system is totally inappropriate when selling through agencies. The two checklists provided will help you deal with this difficult problem. Joint calls, or buddy calls, are an effective way to sell. The protocol outlined for working a territory with an agency will help make this approach much more effective. It's always difficult to split a territory. But when you follow the guidelines in this chapter, it will not only benefit you but the agencies involved.

In some cases, manufacturers use a hybrid system consisting of salaried salespeople and agencies. Using the suggested techniques, you will be able to get the best out of both approaches. Also included are several practical tips on how to help your agencies make the best use of their time, especially when they are showing your products.

USE THE AGENCIES IN YOUR OWN BACKYARD

There's increasing sentiment for the all-agency salesforce—even in manufacturers' home towns. It's common for a company to have a sales manager and one to three local salespeople handling accounts within a 100 to 300 mile radius of home base. But this is changing.

By going exclusively to agencies, company management, including the sales manager, can give more time to day-to-day administrative functions and eliminate time-consuming supervision of a direct salesforce. There is no need for monitoring expense accounts, checking call reports, or performing a host of other duties usually associated with direct-employee salespeople.

Caution: Choosing your local agents requires expert judgment, as they'll be identified more closely with your company by your customers. Take your time and check out prospective agents very carefully. Talk to customers, the agents' other principals, and anyone else familiar with their operation.

Sales managers find that under the all-agent system, they can spend more time in the field traveling with their agents and effectively administering one sales program instead of two. Don't overlook the possibility of converting direct salespeople to agent status; you'll have personnel familiar with your products and policies plus you'll be helping start their own business.

MORE AGENCIES SELLING FOR FOREIGN COMPANIES—GOOD OR BAD?

Agencies are going international these days at a rate that's surprising. Some offshore firms are even paying handsome retainers to snare top agencies in this country. What does this mean to you?

It depends upon the type of products that your agent chooses to handle for these firms. A closely allied line made by a foreign company can cause some confusion in a buyer's mind and could eliminate your product from further consideration if the buyer is instructed to "buy American." He may automatically assume that the agent is handling all foreign lines and won't take a chance on making a mistake.

It's more likely, however, that providing it doesn't get out of line, an agent's handling of a line or two from another country won't hinder his effectiveness. And if it improves his variety of compatible offerings to a buyer, it could even mean a definite advantage to your company.

>>> *OBSERVATION* Most agents know when and where to offer their products for sale and are sensitive to the whims and prejudices of their customers. Thus, show some interest when your agents take on a foreign line. Then a careful analysis can help you decide whether or not to voice an objection.

COMPETITIVE PRICING MUST BE UNIVERSAL

Keep your pricing philosophy the same nationwide. In some cases, try a thinner margin in outlying areas in order to break into a marketplace.

>>> *EXAMPLE* A Cleveland firm, very competitive in its own regional marketplace, embarked upon a national sales agent program. It decided on a higher markup in agent areas to make a little extra profit and cover the expense of field trips by the sales manager and technical personnel. However, the program backfired. The company's prices were always high in the new areas and the orders went to either local firms or more competitive out-of-state companies who realized the necessity of universal pricing. In addition to losing out on new business, the firm lost its new agents at a rapid rate. The agents couldn't afford to continue solicitation for the firm's noncompetitive products.

WHY CALL REPORTS ARE NOT APPROPRIATE FOR MANUFACTURERS' AGENTS

Call reports have always been a bone of contention between sales managers and agencies. Sales managers, accustomed to receiving call reports from direct-employee salespeople, are often irritated by their agents' reluctance to provide regular reports.

It's not that agents don't want to share information with their principals; they do and should be expected to do so. However, the typical call report used by employee salespeople, when used by an agent, can endanger his or her independent contractor status. And when the independent contractor status of an agent is questioned, the tax implications for you and the agency could change dramatically. To determine this status, the IRS looks very carefully at the amount of monitoring and control a manufacturer exercises over its agencies.

Since the 1960s, the IRS has closely monitored the collection of payroll taxes. Independent contractors require no payroll taxes to be paid by those who use their services. In fact, one of the major advantages of contracting with another for the performance of necessary business services is the relief from this tax burden.

Despite the strict regulations that must be adhered to, agents should be expected to provide feedback on their work for you. They should supply you with information on specific projects as well as their general efforts on your behalf. However, this reporting should be done at the agent's discretion. It should not be done on a periodical basis, such as is done with daily and weekly call reports often provided by salaried salespeople. And the format should originate with the agent, not with you. Any attempt to monitor and control this reporting by you automatically puts you and your agency in immediate danger of violating the tax requirements defining the legal status of an independent contractor.

Whether an agent is an independent contractor or an employee can be determined by applying these tests:

1. The extent of control which, by the agreement, the principal may exercise over the details of the work;
2. Whether or not the employee is engaged in a distinct occupation or business;
3. The kind of occupation and whether it is one traditionally done without supervision or direction by the principal;
4. The skills required for the work;
5. Whether the principal or worker supplies the tools needed to do the job;
6. The length of time the person is employed;
7. Method of payment—whether by time or by the job;
8. The intent of the parties in entering the relationship, i.e., if it's intended to be independent contractor/principal;
9. Whether the work performed is part of the regular business of the principal;
10. Whether the principal is an established entity.

The test is complex and a court determination would probably look at every one of these items. For a complete report on this subject, see MANA Bulletin 542, *The Agents, His Independent Contractor Status and the IRS.*

HOW TO DISCOVER IF YOUR COMPANY IS IN A "MINOR" CLASSIFICATION

Agents often put each of their principals in a "major" or "minor" category and allocate their selling efforts accordingly. How do you discover if your company is in a "minor" classification? It's not easy to determine, but if inquiries are meager, orders nonexistent, and communications (from the rep) spotty, you should be suspicious.

⊳→ *HOW TO DO IT*   The simple way to find out the truth is to confront your agent—in person—and review with him his selling efforts for your company over the past 6 to 12 months. The agent may have legitimate reasons for neglecting your line . . . your product may not be compatible with his other lines, your prices may not be competitive, or there may be too much local competition. On the other hand, if he can't come up with a good reason for the lack of results, a frank appraisal should be made of the market potential for your product in that territory. If it's greater than the agent admits, it may be time for a change.

KIND WORDS BRING MORE IN SALES THAN THREATS

Occasionally, you'll run into a sales manager who keeps up a steady barrage of harassment in the mistaken belief that a stream of communication, regardless of its content, will spur his agents on to bigger things.

Most agents have an average of nine sales managers talking and writing to them. This is powerful competition, and the tactics of any one sales manager, good or bad, stand out in vivid comparison.

⊳→ *IDEA IN ACTION*   A suburban Chicago sales manager answers each phone call from his agents with, "How can I help you today?" He finds his phone always busy and his order book full as this perceptive handling of his salesforce boosts morale and creates loyalty.

Good agents usually respond to the intelligent and helpful sales executive and are turned off by demanding techniques. Some are in the agency business because they formerly worked for a dictatorial manager.

Teamwork is still the most effective method of winning sales and influencing agents. And sales managers who utilize positive motivation won't have to worry about sales results.

USE TEAMWORK TO SEAL A DEAL

When traveling with your agents, keep a close eye on who the buyer directs his comments to. Buyers vary in their policies. Some want it understood they're working with you, and the agent is merely a representative. Others are quite firm about their feelings toward the agent and consider the agent the first and most important line of contact with the company.

Caution: If the buyer talks directly to you, respond in kind and let the agent fulfill the function of goodwill ambassador. However, if the buyer directs most of his comments to the agent, let the agent take the lead in replying. To do otherwise can be a poor reflection of your confidence in your agent. The good agent will turn to you often for assistance in the conversation. At that time you'll have ample opportunity to join in the discussion.

Teamwork in obtaining an order is important, so don't be upset if the buyer defers to your agent . . . go along with whatever lead the buyer takes and you'll probably wind up with the order.

HANDLING CHANGES IN LEAD TIME

With day-to-day contact almost impossible, companies find their agents are not always up-to-date on current lead times. Consequently, many agents are inadvertently making delivery promises their principals can't meet.

This causes friction on two fronts; the customers become irritated because products aren't delivered when promised by the agents, and the principals become upset because they're convinced the agents are making wild promises to obtain orders.

>>>→ *EXAMPLE* An Ohio company solved this dilemma by mailing a simple printed form to all customers and agents whenever lead times change. The form shows the new lead time and puts everyone on notice of the firm's delivery capabilities. This simple device guarantees a minimum of misunderstandings about deliveries and keeps customers and reps completely informed.

There's always an added advantage to any innovative idea, and in this case the principal is keeping his name in front of the customer and is also reminding him that it may be time to place another order.

NEW ON THE JOB? TREAD CAREFULLY

A new sales manager is on the spot. He's been hired or promoted for the purpose of increasing sales and he immediately seeks new ideas and programs to achieve the desired results. One of the easiest moves—and the most dangerous—is to give the agency group a cursory review and make a few terminations . . . at least it gives the impression of doing something.

>>>→ *EXAMPLE* An east Texas firm hired an inexperienced salesman to act as sales manager and direct salesman. This small firm had grown from one man to ten men because of sales made by a local agent who had excellent connections with metalworking buyers. When the new man came on board, he promptly terminated the agent with the excuse that he—the sales manager—could now handle all sales. The agent promptly bought a small competitive shop and the ten-man firm is now back to one man, since the agent was easily able to regain the business almost overnight.

This was an extreme case, but it points up the danger of acting too swiftly. In larger companies the danger is less, but the stakes can be high there too.

Caution: If you're new to the company, try not to make agent-changing decisions too quickly. This breathing space will allow you to make a more leisurely and effective appraisal of your group . . . and a field trip is necessary to each territory before you can even begin to judge the ultimate potential of your newly acquired agents.

Agents who may have worked well with you at another company would appear to be logical choices for appointment with your new company. But you may find them unwilling to leave the previous firm where commissions have been established, or you may discover they simply don't click with your new company.

If you've been promoted from within, you'll have a better knowledge of the effectiveness of the salesforce. However, you may find that some agents who appeared relatively ineffective under your predecessor will start working better with you—sometimes just the change of personalities and responsiveness will do the trick.

Patience will be well rewarded in the appointment and termination of a newly acquired agency group. So go slow and look out for the detours.

SIGN UP MAJOR METRO AREAS FIRST FOR QUICK RESULTS

Although it pays to go slow when starting up an agency sales program, occasionally it's necessary to blanket the country in a hurry because of excess capacity or major cancellations from current customers. There is a way to get fast coverage with a minimum of effort and expense.

>>>→ *IDEA IN ACTION* Concentrate your efforts on the six or seven major metropolitan areas across the country: New York, Chicago, Los Angeles, Philadelphia, Detroit, Houston, and Boston. By signing up agents in many of these markets, you've covered a large share of the country's consumer and manufacturing activity—fast. There are also more agencies to choose from in the major markets and, if your product is in demand, you may find more of the pros available, which gives you a better selection of capability.

If you're marketing nationwide but haven't established representation in one of these areas, it'll pay to start recruiting right now . . . don't miss a major metro area.

CAN YOU HAVE TWO AGENTS IN THE SAME TERRITORY?

Sure you can . . . if you're serving two different markets. It's common practice for firms to appoint different agencies for different industry groups served by their companies.

>>>→ *EXAMPLE* In Texas, a fastener company routinely supports two agents—one for regular industrial accounts and the other for the mobile home industry. The two agents specialize in their field and neither is interested in calling on the other's customers.

Take a close look at your customers in the field. Can they be broken down into two or three definite industry groups? Are your present agents not making much headway in one of these groups which may be served by a specialized group of reps? For instance, agents serving the mobile home industry sell almost exclusively to that industry.

If you find a good dividing line, think seriously about splitting your representation among two or more good specialized rep organizations.

SELECT MANAGEMENT PEOPLE CAREFULLY

Experts on sales management perpetually point out that someone will not necessarily succeed as a junior sales executive or even a sales manager simply because he was an excellent salesperson. They add that the qualities needed in sales management are the same as those needed in any managerial position. Among these are leadership, organization, ability to delegate, and the ability to motivate subordinates.

Aside from the ability to organize work, the average salesperson need not be endowed with these qualities in order to sell his company's products successfully. However, when successes begin to mount, he is often looked upon as a candidate for the position of local or regional sales manager.

Wise sales managers go cautiously when pondering the transfer of a good person in the field into a management slot, and will approach this decision even more cautiously when their prospective candidate will be heading up a group of the company's reps.

> ⟫➜ *EXAMPLE*   A bright young salesman had been covering the western market for a west-coast manufacturer, and through genuine sales ability he increased orders to the firm every year.
>
> The sales manager was overjoyed with the growing business the young salesman was bringing to the firm and surmised that this talent, if put to work in a sales management position, would benefit the company even further. So he promoted the salesman to the position of regional sales manager over a group of agents in the midwest.
>
> The new regional sales manager soon arranged for visits to the field and found his agents welcoming him with open arms. What's more, with his flair for salesmanship and his authority to make spot decisions regarding price and delivery, he returned to the office with a goodly amount of orders and quite a few additional inquiries. And there the good times stopped.
>
> Once back at the office his managerial deficiencies surfaced and, for some reason, he was incapable of following through on communications with either the customers or the agents. Sales started to decline and a fairly respectable agency program gradually disintegrated.

The end of this story is yet to be written as the sales manager persists in his faith in the young man's management capabilities. But results are predictable; some agents will soon be terminated and replaced—a process that will be repeated a time or two until the sales manager realizes that he lost a terrific salesman and created an ineffective regional sales manager.

HOLIDAY TIME? NOTIFY YOUR AGENCIES

Different companies schedule different holidays; a union can dictate seven paid days off or a company can be closed on the founder's birthday. An agency working for eight or nine principals can be thoroughly confused by these varying holidays. Often they'll phone for important information and find the plant is closed. This can cause havoc with their traveling schedule.

Make sure your agents know about company closings. It's particularly essential to keep them informed of any holidays that are not consistent with the working world, for example, special state celebrations.

If an agent is kept advised, he can avoid traveling the territory on days when his important principals are closed. Unnecessary visits often result in a phone call to the plant from the customer's office. And if the buyer finds the agent wasn't aware the plant was closed, he will sense that communications aren't what they should be between the principal and his representative.

The easiest way of handling this is to make up a holiday schedule for your agencies at the beginning of the year.

DEMAND PLANS FOR CONTINUITY FROM YOUR AGENCIES

It is very important to keep close tabs on the future plans of the sales agencies representing you in the field. Keep a special eye on the one-person firms. If the owners of several firms are getting on in years, you have an obligation to ask for a game plan . . . and they have an obligation to give you one.

> **»»→ *IDEA IN ACTION*** Be certain the agent makes definite commitments to you about the continuity of his firm. You should find out if he is going to retire soon and close his agency or if he has well-trained people coming along who will carry on the agency either through a buy-out or continued employment.

The deadline practice usually works best, but make it fair. Sit down with your representative, tell him you are concerned about the future and that you'd like to have a report on his plans for the continuity of his agency within three to six months. You can always grant him an extension, but at least you'll have him moving in the right direction.

GETTING PRODUCT KNOWLEDGE INTO THE FIELD

Product knowledge is one of the most important assets your representatives can possess. Unfortunately, unless the agent formerly worked in your industry, he may lack this important ingredient even though his technical background may ease the learning process.

⋙➔ *HOW TO DO IT*   There are four ways an agent can learn about your products: (1) he can study technical manuals or industry publications, (2) he can visit your plant and see the product made firsthand, (3) he can attend your sales meetings where you'll indoctrinate him to the best of your ability, and (4) he can watch you in action with your customers.

When you go out into the field and travel with your agents, you face real-life situations. The first three methods are theoretical to a degree and are structured to suit the purpose. Questions may be asked and information given freely, but seldom is there an opportunity to duplicate the firing-line experience of being in a customer's offices when a crucial question is asked. And in a case like this, only experience counts. Without experience you may get by the first question or two, but sooner or later something will come up that defies an answer unless you've been there before.

The agent, sitting at your side or peering over a machine that's malfunctioned, can observe the problems that arise and the manner in which you handle them. He may have questions of his own which, if he's straightforward and not afraid of admitting his ignorance, he can ask on the spot and learn from your replies. He also gets an excellent feel for the company's policies on many issues that he'd otherwise learn only by making a mistake. Further, you may never have covered the handling of rejections with him before or mentioned some discounts that are available if quantities on an order reach an outrageous volume.

Another part of the learning experience is gained as you leave the customer's office or plant and the agent can discuss other questions that come to his mind as you drive to your next appointment. Many agents say this close contact with you, Mr. Sales Manager, and your cooperation in explaining the various functions of your product is the most helpful avenue they have for improving their product knowledge.

If several days are spent together your representative will be less hesitant to ask "dumb" questions . . . the answers to which may seem obvious to you and may have been puzzling him for some time. And by the time he drops you off at the airport, you'll both have gained immensely from your visit. Not only will your customers in the area be pleased that you have called on them, but you will have contributed greatly to the product knowledge of your agent who can now go out on sales calls with greatly increased confidence—a characteristic that always improves sales.

WHOSE LINES DO YOUR AGENTS SELL WHEN TRAVELING WITH YOU?

This may seem like a frivolous question, but you'd be surprised at some of the reports we receive from sales managers. Over-eager agents often trot out their entire repertoire of principals even though a sales manager is along. This is bad business.

Fortunately, most pros devote their entire day to you and your products; you're their guest. It's much more impressive to your customers when your product, and only your product, is discussed on team visits.

But how do you calm down the eager beaver? Point out that your company is paying for this call and that you didn't fly to the west coast to listen to him tell prospective buyers about the merits of all of his principals' products. If the agent has had advance notice of your visit and unless you make it a habit to visit weekly, he will generally pre-schedule to devote his entire day to you and your company's products.

However, if the customer does bring up one of the agent's other product lines, don't expect him to refuse to take advantage of the sales opportunity. He will no doubt handle the matter tactfully by briefly responding to the inquiry and setting a follow-up appointment.

HOW TO HELP YOUR AGENTS BECOME FAMILIAR WITH YOUR POLICIES

Terms of payment and other conditions of sale are second nature to you and your sales staff, but how about your agents? These conditions are almost always spelled out on either your quotation or order acknowledgment form, but very often the copy your agent receives has none of this information. With eight or nine principals to represent, your agent can't keep all of these conditions in his head and should have a ready reference at hand for each principal . . . but usually he doesn't.

>>>→ *IDEA IN ACTION* If you're one of those enlightened companies that has already supplied the agent with a manual, give him a condensed form of your policies that he can carry on all of his calls. Armed with this abbreviated policy manual, he can easily answer most questions a buyer will ask him. Cover not only terms of payment but what to do on return of goods, faulty packaging, and late deliveries, among other things.

HELP NEW SALES AGENTS

A new representative is much like a new direct salesperson or any new employee. The difference is that he doesn't have the advantage of day-to-day personal contact with the home office. You may have given him the red carpet treatment, shown him through the plant, and taken him to dinner with the president, but he's still going to be rather naive about a lot of things until he's been with you for a while.

>>>→ *IDEA IN ACTION* For the first three or four months give the agent some special attention. Phone him regularly and ask if there's anything he needs in the way of technical aid or procedure briefing.

It's only natural to appoint a new agent, send him some brochures, and sit back and wait for orders to begin arriving. He'll go out and eventually will either make it or toss in the towel. You can prevent some early disappointments by keeping in close touch and helping him in every way you can.

Warning: Don't smother the agent with attention as he may interpret this as a move to overwhelm him and take up all of his time. Just make certain he knows that the basic reason for your attention is your interest in his early success.

ASSIGN EACH AGENT AN INSIDE CONTACT

The "Mr. Inside–Mr. Outside" technique is a winner. Customers like it, agents like it . . . and you'll like it. By making someone in your sales group responsible for one or more agents and agents' customers, you can offer a personal service that not many firms bother with.

With agents out of the office so much, the customer needs someone to hold his hand and answer his questions. Agency office personnel are often very helpful, but someone back at the plant can be of even greater aid.

After adopting a policy of this type, take it one step further and allow that inside person to go "outside" one or more times each year. Meeting the customer face to face doubles the effectiveness of this service, and your agents will really appreciate it.

HOW EXIT INTERVIEWS WITH AGENTS CAN BE REVEALING

These are the essential features of an exit interview to help you avoid making costly mistakes.

≫→ *HOW TO DO IT* Use a neutral third party. This is helpful since the agent may have had an ax to grind with you, the sales manager. So turn this chore over to another executive, preferably from another department.

Be prepared. Know the history of the agent who's been terminated (or who has terminated you) so that you can honestly appraise what he's telling you.

Focus on the reason for leaving. Naturally, this is most important if the agent resigned the account. Here you may discover some very important things that your company is doing wrong. Poor response from sales personnel, noncompetitive pricing, or shoddy quality can quickly disillusion an agent—but he may not level with you unless you interview him.

Be flexible and relaxed. The cord has been cut, so nothing can be gained by recriminations. Listen to what he says and don't set a time limit. Be prepared for some surprises if they arise.

End on an upbeat note. Thank the former agent for being frank about his opinion. If you think he has some very good points, make sure he knows that these will be related to management. If you're fair and straightforward, he'll carry a good image of your company with him and will be more likely not to disparage you to your customers.

In interviews of this nature, it's best not to try to defend the company even if the agent is taking unfair potshots. Of course, if he's been misinformed or is mistaken about certain facts, then a gentle correction may be necessary. Basically, however, your role is that of a listener. The whole idea behind the interview is to gain a different insight into the actions that may cause you to lose a valued agent and to prevent such a loss in the future.

PLANNING YOUR TERRITORY VISITS

In your battle to compete for your agents' selling time, one of the most effective weapons is the territory visit. By going into an agent's area, you avail yourself of his undivided attention for one or more days at a time. How well you plan for and utilize this visit will have a lot to do with the results you obtain.

Warning: Some agents will be happy to see you and others won't. Those who welcome you will be among your best producers. The ones who put you off with one excuse or another may be apprehensive about your visit or just plain inefficient and not anxious to have you see how they operate.

Leading sales managers don't just "visit the territory," they take the time to plan their trips and thus reap the rewards. Here's a few things they do that make them successful.

1.   Trips are always scheduled as far as possible in advance. This gives the sales manager and his agents time to prepare.

2.   The agent is asked to decide which customers and potential customers are to be visited, and arranges the itinerary. Special visits requested or suggested by the sales manager are included, but the scheduling is left to the agent.

3.   Agents are encouraged to bring as many prospects as possible to the selling point. Also, accounts that are difficult to sell or personnel that resist the agent's attempt to sell are put on the schedule. Often the sales manager's authority is just enough to turn a reluctant buyer into an enthusiastic one.

4.   Visits are just long enough to get the job done well and short enough to make him welcome the next time a trip is planned. Three days is a good average, but this can vary depending upon the type of industry involved.

5.   A quick, one-day visit to an agent's territory when something special is brewing is an excellent idea. It keeps those important customers aware that the company values them and also backs up the agent's efforts in the area. It shows the customer that the agent is important to you and thus increases his effectiveness in day-to-day negotiations.

6.   Expenses are split between the sales manager and agent. The agent provides local transportation and takes his turn in picking up the meal tabs. The sales manager, of course, pays for his own air fare and lodging. A sales manager who waits for the agent to pay all local expenses will not find the agent waiting with open arms for his next visit.

A good agent will look forward to your aid in the field, and if you notify him well in advance of your visit and are well-prepared upon arrival, he'll soon be asking you how quickly you can return.

ALERT YOUR AGENTS WHEN SHORTAGES OCCUR

Often the last to know when major shortages occur are your agents. In some cases, they find out when an irate customer phones to ask when an overdue shipment will be made. Keeping your agents informed is important. This was stressed in a past issue of *Sales Manager's Bulletin*, Bureau of Business Practice, Waterford, CT, which offered some additional timely advice in the event you anticipate a shortage.

If the shortage is a minor one, the following steps are suggested:

1. Seek a substitute product from your own line. In many companies, any number of products from the line can be substituted for others.

2. Seek generic substitutes. If you cannot substitute your own products to alleviate the shortage and the product is widely available, another manufacturer may allow you to substitute an unbranded product.

3. Reduce promotions. It doesn't make sense to promote a product that's not available. So don't forget to avoid including the shortage item in your sales promotion programs.

4. Brief the salesforce thoroughly. This is the single most important part of any program to deal with shortages. If your salespeople can answer customer questions frankly and objectively, you will stand a much greater chance of keeping your customers. Be certain your salesforce knows

    A. the products affected
    B. the duration of the shortage
    C. the reason for the shortage
    D. the likelihood of a recurrence
    E. your plans to deal with the problem.

If it looks like the shortage is going to be a major one, then the following steps should be taken:

1. Change your distribution policies. The most obvious move would be to limit purchases to small quantities. That way every customer shares in the burden and no one gets completely left out. But is a straight limitation the fairest policy? Should a major customer have to limit its purchases to the same extent as a small customer? The answer is to classify your accounts by size, just as you do for call frequency purposes.

2. Allocate products to the salesforce. It would be unfair to your salespeople and to their customers to allocate shortage products on a first-come-first-served basis. Those with unusually productive territories could quickly deplete the inventory in a mad scramble to "protect" their customers. Instead, allocate product reserves according to the amount of product available and the amount of product the salesperson normally moves.

3. Alter your commission or bonus system. Consider temporarily lowering the commission on shortage items. This is a harsh step, but one that may be your only insurance against overselling the product. Also, don't apply the sales of a shortage item to a system of bonuses.

4. Above all else, be open. No matter how severe or mild the shortage, your salesforce should be frank with customers.

When a shortage is imminent, the single most important thing to do is to brief your salesforce thoroughly. If you don't, their actions can ultimately harm them.

WHY TERRITORIAL VISITS ARE PRODUCTIVE

Have you questioned the value of your trips to the field? At one time or another most sales managers wonder if the results are worth the time and trouble.

In a special report entitled *Making Field Managers Managers* issued by *Sales and Marketing Management* magazine, two excellent reasons for visits to the territories are put forth by Bill Harmon, mid-region sales manager for Sankyo Seiki (America), a marketer of motion picture cameras and projectors, are given:

1. It's the only effective way to get a fair share of their time. "If I work with an agent for two or three days," Harmon says, "all he picks out of his book during that time is my line. He wouldn't do otherwise."

2. He can help the agent custom-tailor a sales presentation or promotion to the specific needs of the customer, whether it be a department store, mass merchandiser, or camera specialty store.

Just as a sales presentation is custom-tailored to a specific customer, so Harmon's managerial style is custom-tailored to his agents. Many of them have more experience in the field than Harmon does and he says that they are of a caliber he couldn't duplicate for any amount of money. Thus, he says, the key is to work with them on a respectful basis and "direct them without being obvious."

PLAN FOR THE SUMMER

Remember that most companies in an agent's territory will not schedule their vacations at the same time. Nothing is more annoying and embarrassing for an agent than to make a call from a customer's office with a quotation request only to get a summer vacation recording. Therefore, you can make things a lot easier for everyone if you plan your summer time-off periods early and let your agents know about it right away. In addition to your summer schedule, the following are other dates to keep your agents aware of:

1. Trips to be made by key people at the plant. If your chief engineer is going to be away and fields a lot of technical questions from your agents, be sure to announce his schedule well in advance.

2. Plant downtime. For example, when a new machine is installed, it may throw the rest of the plant into a temporary turmoil. If such a problem will interfere with production, let your agents know so they can quote delivery times accordingly.

3. Quiet days. In some businesses, management designates a few days a month as quiet days. That is, business as usual but with a minimum of outside influence. During these days, company personnel are urged to get their work done if they are behind, or to use the time to plan their future work if they are ahead. If this is your policy, keep your agents informed.

4. Regular meetings. Many companies schedule their management, production, product development, marketing, and other departmental meetings on specific days each month. If you don't want to be disturbed, let your agents know when these days are scheduled. Tell them they should only interrupt when special circumstances arise.

USE AGENTS TO COVER ALL TERRITORIES, INCLUDING HOME BASE

Smaller companies often think they can handle sales that are close to home while turning over the remote areas to agents. Those who use this system usually try to do everything themselves, even though they may not be qualified to handle the tasks. They write their own trade advertising, avoid getting professional legal advice, and feel that no one can do the jobs better than themselves. An agent who is in this situation seldom gets the support that is needed, and as a result, his or her sales may be poor. The manufacturer seldom understands the real causes of the problem.

This situation is now changing, mainly because of the obvious economic benefits provided by agents, as follows:

1. Even though there may be only one or a few direct salespeople in the home territory, the job of managing these people is distinctly different from the management of an all-agent salesforce. It's not that managing a force of agents is any easier than managing salaried salespeople; it's that it requires a different approach. This is compounded effort that must be expended by the home–office staff. Think, for example, of the different types of paperwork involved in call reports, expense vouchers, and the handling of employee benefits that are not part of an agent's agreement.

2. Sales managers running an all-agent team can concentrate on one system of marketing. And they don't have to spend a lot of time defending real or imagined inequities between their treatment of agents and factory salespeople.

3. Some manufacturers use direct salespeople in the home territory because they feel that the sales close to home must closely reflect the image of the company. Think this through and you'll see that it just doesn't hold water if agents are used elsewhere. Sales managers have said that they tried to recruit agents for the home territory, but couldn't find any who fit their requirements for a home–office territory. A good agent is a good agent, regardless of how close or far from the home–office he or she is located. If you're convinced that there simply are no agents good enough to handle the home territory, grow your own by offering support to a staff person with the drive to be in the agent business. Turn that in-house hotshot into your newest agent.

Considering the dramatic shift from factory salespeople to agents that has taken place in the last year, it's hard to understand why companies still insist on a salaried salesforce in the home territory, if all the other territories are covered by agents.

SALES QUOTAS—LOOKING AT A CONTROVERSIAL QUESTION FROM BOTH SIDES OF THE FENCE

Manufacturers often use quotas as a method of setting goals and putting into place the components for an effective relationship with an independent group of agents. The subject has always been controversial, but now more than ever it's time to take a very careful look at the good and the bad from both sides of the fence and to determine how the agency and the manufacturer's inside people must work together to make a quota program succeed.

You will find the word quota used from time to time throughout this book. It's a term that everyone uses. However, it's one that should be defined very carefully. For one thing, a manufacturer imposing a quota on an agent could possibly find itself in violation of the legal terms which spell out who is and who isn't an independent contractor. This, of course, can have enormous tax implications for you and for your agents. Also, agents, as self-motivated individuals, find it difficult to accept edicts in the form of quotas. Goals, yes. But quotas are not at all popular.

Warning: Quotas should never be used as a means of evaluating the termination of an agency. A quota performance evaluation only has value to the manufacturer and the agency when it is a statistical analysis for the basis of subjective judgment. Never lose sight of the fact that the people in the field are the last people on the totem pole and that their performance is a culmination of the performance of lots of other people—the principal's production department, shipping department, credit policy, literature quoting—in general, the total team play by manufacturer and agency in creating a profit-making situation.

The Problems with Quotas

The following are questions that sales managers and agency owners ask most frequently when quotas are discussed:

1. What is the most appropriate unit for the quota? Unit volume? Sales volume? Profit?

2. Is there really any way to arrive at fair quotas for each agent territory? Be realistic—an agency's quota should not be set at a figure higher than it can reasonably be expected to make in order to insure that a satisfying figure is reached. Don't play games!

3. Do sales quotas prevent agency personnel from performing other responsibilities, such as training, product service, and installation?

4. Should quotas and commissions be related to each other?

5. Will the agency be made to feel solely responsible for reaching the quota or will there be strong cooperation from the factory in terms of prompt delivery, competitive pricing, quality products, timely shipping?

6. How do you handle the problem of an agency that fails to meet the quota?

How to Solve the Problems

Let's look at the factors that most companies consider when establishing quotas.

1. Sales figures from the previous year. This is a good place to start—but it's only a start.
2. Individual territory trends for at least the last five years. With this information, you can put last year's sales figures into perspective, determine the direction of any trends, and begin to get the information you will need to make a differential analysis when setting individual agent quotas.
3. Customer activity, other than purchases. You will want to know who is moving in and out of the territory and all about their plans for expansion or contraction.
4. Competitors' activities in each territory. Active competitors suggest that you may want to offer stronger support in some territories, and you may want to encourage your agents to expand their operations.
5. General industry trends. You will need information on general trends in order to analyze the information you get on territorial segments.
6. Your own capabilities. Will you have the ability to service the increased demands you are asking the agent salesforce to create?

Getting Information From Internal Sources

Most of this information is relatively easy to come by. Your own sales records, based on orders placed, inquiries received, quotes rendered, and orders shipped will give you a running start. When you have this information in hand, share it with your agents before asking them to make any predictions of their territorial potential for the next year. Although most of them will have a good picture of the facts and figures, they will be in a much better position to help you if they are working from the same base as you.

Getting Information From Your Agents

If your agents are going to share in the responsibility of planning and setting quotas, they should be asked to supply some of the information that will be used to set the figures. However, don't burden them with endless tasks. Rather than tell them how to get the information, tell them what you would like to have and leave it up to them to do it their way. Asking agents and their salespeople to probe their customers for next year's plans is not the way to do it. In the first place, this is time not devoted to selling. In the second place, most agents are reluctant to ask these questions of their customers; they just don't want to antagonize them. Allow your agencies to gather the information you need from their own files and to use their gut feelings, based on the routine conversations they have with their customers.

Establishing Quotas

Quotas should not be arbitrary. They should be reasonable and based on an educated estimate of the territory. But most of all, they should serve as practical goals for you and your agencies. Here are the elements of quota planning that you should consider:

1. *The unit of measurement.* Most quotas are based on either the number of units sold or dollar volume. When the product line is extensive and the product-price differential is wide, it's often wise to establish your quota using a combination of both elements.

2. *The quota time period.* A quota must be established to cover a definite period of time. This can vary with the industry. Those selling merchandise such as clothing may have quarterly quotas for each line. Manufacturers of machine tools, on the other hand, usually base their quotas on a twelve-month period.

Regardless of the stated period, there should be a system of periodic evaluation and reporting on the progress towards the quota. Make sure that you share this information with your agents and their personnel, and use it as a planning tool, not a hammer.

3. *Quota management.* Your administration of a quota system should include a review of the actual as well as the planned goals. Show the information in numbers and in some graphic form—charts, graphs, and the like.

4. *Purpose of quota.* Apart from the use of quotas for long- and short-term planning, a quota properly used can serve as an incentive for your agencies. Quotas should be high enough to motivate, but not so high that they stifle initiative. Conversely, if they are set too low, your agencies will wonder about your understanding of their territory.

The Characteristics of a Good Quota System

1. A good quota is based on a careful analysis of all the conditions in each territory.

2. It will be a positive motivational tool, not an implied threat.

3. It can serve as a basis for added incentives for those who exceed the quota.

4. It will give you closer contact with your agencies and allow you to check your progress toward your goal.

5. It will be established with the help and blessing of all your agents.

6. It will provide a means of evaluation of your promotional activities and help you determine effective allocation.

7. Managing a quota system will give you a clear picture of customer activity. Design your system to include appropriate feedback systems.

8. It will help you to determine the relative strength of each territory.

9. It will not be used as a means of selecting scapegoats. Someone has to be number one and someone has to be last. Do not use the final evaluation of your quota each year as a means of punishing some agencies and rewarding others. Use quotas only to motivate your agencies and to determine your own goals, such as production scheduling, inventory control, and the development and administration of a promotional program.

Quotas can be instrumental in planning sales goals. However, the best salesperson in the world can only be effective if he or she has strong cooperation from the manufacturer's internal team. The sale is not complete until the goods have been shipped. More than just the salesperson is involved in this ultimate effort. The agency's ability to meet the goals that are set depend as much on the performance of your internal team as on its own actions.

A quota is never reached nor breached by the agency alone. The above mentioned team play is the most important factor of the quota system.

MANA has been encouraging use of the term goal rather than quota. Although this may seem to be only a cosmetic change, it isn't. Goals, as we have described quotas in this section are mutually agreed upon. An agent will have a more positive response to a mutually agreed goal rather than the setting of an arbitrary quota.

A TERRITORY MANAGEMENT SYSTEM HELPS YOUR SALES AGENCIES MAKE THE BEST USE OF THEIR TIME

A sales manager with a factory salesforce can run the ship just about any way he wants, but one using sales agencies must take a different view. You can't tell independent businesspeople how to run their businesses. But you can certainly give them all the help they need to be effective for themselves—and for you.

>>>→ *EXAMPLE*   Frank Sterne, an agent based in Wyckoff, New Jersey, has developed a system of territory management that has worked well for him and that is praised by his principals.

The system is based on sound planning. Frank's system is based on the development of projections for individual customer volume and the assignment of weighted time priorities. Although the system does give Frank a fairly rigid set of guidelines, he uses them only for general planning. "A system like this," Frank said, "can work only if you view it and use it loosely. There are times, such as when a principal introduces a new product, that you have to chuck the numbers and go with your gut feeling."

Let's take a look at how Frank does it. Follow these steps on the sample worksheet (Figure 5–1).

1. Begin by estimating the potential dollar volume for the year for each account. (Column 1)
2. Make realistic estimates of the chances of achieving this business with each account. Express this estimate as a percent. (Column 2)
3. Multiply potential dollar volume figures by the probability figure for each account to get the estimated value of the account. (Column 3)
4. Express each estimated account value figure as a percent of the total estimated account value. (Column 4)
5. Determine how much of the total agency business is represented by the account and come up with the total number of hours that should be allocated to the account. (Footnote under figure)

SAMPLE TERRITORY MANAGEMENT PLAN FOR ONE AGENCY PRINCIPAL

(1)	(2)	(3)	(4)	(5)
Potential $ Volume Per Account	Estimated Chance of Getting the Business	Estimated Value of the Account	% of Total Estimated Account Value	Hours Assigned to Account
200,000	40%	80,000	36%	187
100,000	90%	90,000	40%	208
75,000	50%	37,500	17%	89
20,000	70%	4,000	7%	36
395,000	—	211,500	100%	520*

* This principal represents one quarter of the agent's income; therefore one quarter of the normal annual working hours would be 520.

Figure 5-1

6. Determine the number of hours that should be assigned to each account by multiplying the total number of hours assigned to the principal by the percent of estimated account value for each customer. (Column 5)

Analysis of the plan. Without an analysis such as this, many agents would probably spend most of their time with the $200,000 account. But with a 40 percent chance of getting the business, they would probably lose out. Obviously, more time should be spent with the second account, even though the estimated potential dollar volume is only half of the first. As you can see, this system controls two major variables—the estimated dollar volume and your agent's gut feeling about his chances for getting the business. We all know about the salespeople who chase the potential big spenders and seldom make a nickel, while others work the accounts with more realistic potential and make a bundle. Most successful agencies use a system like this intuitively. However, when it's down on paper, they can have a clear picture of how best to use their time.

This is only the beginning. Obviously, a system such as this will go a long way to getting you your fair share. And when you're fighting for an agency's time, this is good for openers. As stated earlier, this system or a similar one, should not be used slavishly. However, if you can help your agencies put your line into their total perspective, you should have no trouble getting them to give you the extra time that is necessary to make the territory grow for you.

HOW TO MAKE WINNING BUDDY CALLS WITH YOUR AGENTS

There's no middle ground when it comes to making sales calls with your agents. You either do it right and are welcomed by the agents and their customers or your agents will find every excuse in the book to keep you out of the territory.

If you remember that time is money for you and your agents, you're off on the right foot. But this is only the beginning. This question was discussed with a number of manufacturers. George Anderson, president of Ramapo Instrument Company, was especially helpful. Many of the points that follow were supplied by him.

- "Out of sight, out of mind" is more than just a saying when it comes to working with your agents. Agents don't want to be haunted by their principals, but they do want you to visit them regularly and to do it with a specific purpose in mind. That is, don't set up a three-day visit and make it a social occasion only. How often you visit your agents will depend on the number of agents, the time available from them, your schedule, and the real need for visits.

- Set up expense ground rules in advance. When you visit a territory, it's understood that you will pay all your own travel, lodging, telephone, and personal costs. If you're going to make the rounds of the territory with your agent, he should use his car at his expense. It's usually best to split the cost of food. When you and your agent entertain a customer, it's customary for the agent to pick up the tab, but this is not a hard-and-fast rule.

- Let your agents set the scene for each call. Ask your agents what they expect of you on each call. Remember that every person an agent calls on is different and that your agents have already established patterns for handling them. In some cases, they may want you to come on strong and in others to remain passive. Know what your agents expect of you in advance of every call and stick to the script.

- Acknowledge that the agent is the sales professional on the call. Even though you may have spent years in sales, stick to your role as principal and let your agents know that you aren't going to upstage them. If they know that you will stick to products and applications and leave the selling to them, they will be more relaxed and productive. Let your agents know that you will only correct gross errors and that you will do it in a professional manner. Minor problems should not be corrected in front of a customer. You can save yourself and your agents problems by establishing a set of hand signals. A tug of the left ear, for example, might mean that you want to break in to make a point. Signals can be very helpful, but make sure that you practice them so they are not obvious.

> ⟫→ *IDEA IN ACTION*   Every buddy call should be a learning experience. There are three aspects to this learning experience: 1) You should help your agents learn more about your products, applications, and markets. 2) You should learn about your agents' needs and problems. 3) You and your agents should learn how to work closely and effectively together. The last point is perhaps the most important. Working together on calls is only the beginning. When you're in the field you should learn enough about each agent so that all your other interaction will be more productive.

- Don't prevent your agents from selling their other products since they work on commission. You will really get the agents on your side if you let them know that you will not interfere with their sales efforts of other lines before you set foot in the territory. They will, however, no doubt make the decision to concentrate on you and your line as much as possible during your visit.

• Follow up on every field visit. On your way back to the office, while the trip is fresh in your mind, dictate or make notes for a follow-up memo to the agents you visit. It's important to be open and honest about your visit, telling them what you liked and didn't like. When you have specific complaints, deal with them in a positive, non-punitive way by stating the problem and either asking the agent to propose a solution or proposing a few solutions yourself. If you give an agent several possibilities and let him select the approach that he feels is most appropriate, you will have given him a hand in the solution rather than just nailing him with a one-choice command.

• Ask your agent for a report. If your field visits are to be effective, you will need to know what your agents think of what you have done. Ask them to be candid, and don't accept a whitewash if you're given one. Remember, we never stop learning—especially from each other.

NOTIFY YOUR CUSTOMERS IMMEDIATELY WHEN YOU CHANGE AGENTS

Not only is it good manners, but it just makes good business sense to notify your customers as soon as you change agents. This will help to smooth the transition and reassure your customers that you are concerned about their needs. Include in the announcement all the facts: The name, address, and phone number of the new agency, the date when the transition will take place, plus some background information on the people, the other lines they carry, and their business experience. Also, you should plan to make a visit to the major accounts in the territory with your new agent as soon as possible.

ENCOURAGE YOUR AGENTS TO TALK WITH EACH OTHER

Strangely enough, manufacturers seldom encourage their agents to talk with each other. When they see the value of communications, they will form Rep Councils, but rarely do they see the value of regular inter-agent communications.

    ⇨ OBSERVATION We asked several manufacturers if they try to put their agents in active contact with each other. The responses ranged from "Why would I want to do that?" to "Some of the best leads are passed from one agent to another." This is an area where you can do a lot of good for your agents—and for yourself. The following are a few pointers on communication:

1. Insist that the agents communicate with each other regularly. Tell them to pass on leads from one territory to another and to discuss selling techniques that work, new applications, and other tips that keep the orders flowing.

2.   Set up a formal or informal communications network.

3.   Communications can range from informal hand-scribbled notes to formal letters, reports, and even multi-agent teleconferencing.

How to Get the Ball Rolling and Keep It Rolling

1.   One of the fastest ways to show agents the value of talking with each other is the use of a circular letter. When you get information from one of your agents that can benefit the others, put it in a circular letter. A circular letter is simply routed from one agent to another, but with a gimmick. Each agent who reads the letter is asked to respond to it—to make a comment on the letter—before it's passed on to the next agent in the chain. Even if the comment is one word—"good," "lousy," etc.—each agent is to respond. Of course, to make sure that all your agents know what the others said on the circulated letter, you must duplicate the fully circulated letter and send copies to all your agents. It's important to encourage your agents to be up front with their comments. Don't take them to task for shooting down your pet ideas.

2.   A circular letter will get the ball rolling and will help your agents see the value of communicating with each other. You should encourage them to pass on tips, leads, and ideas that relate to your prospects, and the phone is a good way to do this. One way to make this work is to offer to pay that portion of an agent's phone bill that is used to call other agents. But be sure to make it clear that the calls aren't for socializing. Set a time limit if you want.

3.   Teleconferencing is a great way to get all your agents together at one time. It's wise to do it regularly and at a time that is agreeable to all. To make teleconferencing productive, prepare for it just as you would if you were running a face-to-face meeting. Mail out an agenda a few days in advance. Assign specific responsibility to individual agents and tell them what you and they should expect to get from each conference. Be sure to set time limits as phone bills can add up. Remember, time spent on the phone that isn't productive is time that could be spent in a buyer's office. If you have a national organization and the time zones make it difficult to handle, try holding regional teleconferences.

4.   The more agents know about each other, the more willing they will be to participate in such a program. Send descriptions of each agency to all your agents. Include photos of individuals as well. This may sound corny, but it's very practical sales psychology. People like to know what the person on the other end of the line looks like.

SELLING THROUGH OVERSEAS AGENTS

If you sell your products domestically through agents, the chances are that you can market the same way in foreign countries. There are many ways to sell, but your experience with domestic agents can be a big help when you tackle the world.

Regardless of the products you make—high technology or consumer disposables —there is probably a foreign market that can be reached with agents. The question is, however, can the market be penetrated profitably? The same logic applies to overseas marketing as to that done stateside—the cost of sales using agents will be lower than using a direct salesforce. Ironically, American products are found all over the world, but fewer than 10 percent of all American firms actively pursue foreign sales. Dealing with overseas agents is much like working with your American team, but there are a number of conditions you should understand, as follows:

• Make sure you can handle the business before you undertake foreign sales. Setting up an overseas agent network will take time and money. When the orders begin to arrive, you'd better be able to ship the product. If you can't deliver, you will not only lose customers but your agents will desert you in a hurry.

• Determine the market potential carefully before you enter into any agreements. Overseas agents can usually help you with a regional analysis, but you would probably need additional help to get a handle on the total picture. This help can be obtained from our own Department of Commerce as well as from the American-based commercial attachés representing the countries in which you plan to sell. Also, many major foreign governments are represented by international chambers of commerce in major American cities. Their help can be quite valuable.

• Be sure to investigate local regulations that relate to your products in the countries in which you plan to sell. Some special conditions may make it difficult for you to compete. Local health codes, for example, may require product modifications too costly to allow you entry. Agents can often help steer you through the bureaucracy that would seem impenetrable.

• You can set up and manage your own overseas agency network, work through export agents, or use export management firms. Many of these organizations can do a good job, but when you use them you often lose direct contact with those in the country who are actually selling your products. Managing an overseas agent network isn't easy. A lot of time and travel can be involved. However, it's an excellent way to travel and do business at the same time. Make sure that you are fully aware of the IRS regulations relating to these business expenses before you get in too deeply.

• How do you find overseas agents? If you don't have the connections to start with, the International Union of Commercial Agents & Brokers (IUCAB) may be your best bet. Through them, you can have contact with over 100,000 agents and brokers. Headquarters of this organization is in Amsterdam, Holland, but you can obtain information by writing to MANA and asking for a copy of their brochure "Trade Connections All Over the World."

• The Department of Commerce may also be a good source. They offer an inexpensive service called Agent Distribution Service to help locate qualified agents. Their Trade Opportunities Program provides a computerized match with you and appropriate representatives. To give you an idea of the scope of their resources, they maintain a data base of over 138,000 agents, importers, distributors, service organizations, and other businesses worldwide.

• It's not uncommon for European companies to pay bills routinely in 120 days. Be sure to figure in this factor when you make your cash flow projections.

• Have your overseas agents convert your sales literature to their own language. It will probably be more accurate and reflect local idiom often missed by translators who are not familiar with your products. You should supply them with all of the artwork and photographs, but rely on them to have the translated copy set in type and printed locally.

• Watch for local laws. For example, you should make sure that you know the best time for title to pass in each country in which you sell. This simple factor could make the difference between profit and loss from a local tax point of view.

• When you prepare quotations, include all information you would provide a domestic customer, plus gross and net shipping weights as well as the total cubic volume when the products are packed for overseas shipment.

• When you work directly with agents in foreign countries and not through distributors or other import agents, credit is strictly your problem. There are a number of ways to specify payment. If you are not getting direct payment, the use of a letter of credit can save you some headaches. When this instrument is used, a bank commits itself to pay for the merchandise when shipping papers are received.

• If you plan to advertise in foreign countries, get advice from your agents before you attempt to use ads that have been prepared for the American market. Usually American advertising is considered too direct and overbearing. Have an ad agency in the country in which you plan to sell prepare an appropriate version. There is much more to this than just word-for-word translation.

WHEN YOU'RE TEMPTED TO SHAKE UP THE TEAM

Think about what really motivates agents before you fire off some teeth-rattling memos or decide to hold a revival-type sales meeting. Those razzle-dazzle sales films starring big-name football heroes are a lot of fun and will send the gang charging out of the meeting with a lot of enthusiasm that day, but the long-range effect of fiery speeches, implied threats, and most of the other gimmicks labeled "motivation" is not very impressive. MANA has published a special report entitled "How to Motivate Manufacturers' Agents—A Guide to Success with an Independent Salesforce," to help motivate agents. Here are some highlights from the report:

• Motivation and good management are really the same thing. To be successful in managing a team of agents, you must take into account all of the factors that are positive motivators and they must be used regularly as part of your total management program. In other words, there are no one-shot gimmicks that are going to turn low producers into superstars.

• The factors identified as being most important in a practical systems approach to agent motivation are: 1) proper agent selection; 2) communication and feedback; 3) compensation and reward; 4) quality and style of management; and 5) effective training.

• If you want to motivate a team of agents, you must first know and understand each individual. When you learn how to achieve success with each agent, you will be in a position to expect the most from the entire team.

• When you discover just what it is that motivates your agents and what helps them to achieve their goals, you will be able to get just what you want from them. In other words, this method of motivation is designed to help you and your agents achieve your individual and joint goals in a positive, nonthreatening way.

SWITCHING TO AGENTS? MAKE SURE EVERYBODY IS READY

The benefits of using agents are significant, the reasons obvious, and the decision is usually easy to make. However, this is only the beginning.

"The first year we had agents in the territories, sales went up, but so did my expenses," one manufacturer told us. "Of course we were much better off in the long run, but I didn't plan my cash flow properly, and when it came time to pay commissions, I occasionally had to scrounge for cash." He did say that the problem wasn't one of using agents—it was one of not being prepared.

Warning: It's easy to oversimplify. You know that you pay commissions only when sales are made and that you have no fixed overhead as you do with a factory salesforce. But you've got to prepare for the transition. You can't just go from one marketing system to another without careful planning. Make sure that everyone in your company knows what is happening and is ready for the change. The following are some of the areas that are most sensitive:

• Most likely you will have to spend a little more on the production of sales support material—catalogs, spec sheets, direct mail, etc. Agents tend to make more and better use of this material. They know that the more sales literature they get into the right hands, the better the chances are for future sales. Because they make more calls than company people (they carry several lines), they get to see more people who are prospects for your products. Be prepared to reprint the catalog a little more often when you have agents on board.

• Warn your engineering and manufacturing departments that they are going to be pestered—but that it will be productive pestering. When agents sell products, they want to make sure they are delivered as quickly as possible. And when they're on the trail of a hot order and need engineering specifications, they won't let go until they have the information they need. Here's the point: If the people in these departments are aware of this and it doesn't come as an unexpected intrusion, they will be better able to deal with the activity.

• The people who prepare your quotations will be hassled a little more, too. Don't wait until this occurs. Plan ahead, prepare your people, and take it in stride.

• Perhaps the most important place for preparation to take place is in finance. Financial people like to make projections, to plan for smooth cash flow, and to avoid surprises. That's the way they are, and in some respects their attitudes will keep you out of trouble. But when a big order comes through and a large commission check has to be written in a month already accounted for, money-people get very nervous. You may have to hold their hands when they write these checks, or you may have to get tough when they suggest splitting the money to keep their projections on target. But whatever you do, make sure those commission checks are paid on time.

• You may end up losing some contact with customers. Since you are dealing through a third party—your new agent—there can be some loss of contact. However, if you make regular trips to the territory with your agents to meet with your customers, there should be no problems.

• Make sure the inside salesforce understands that they are now dealing with independent—not company—salespeople. Agents tend to be a little more demanding, but only because they are critically aware that time is money.

• Although most agents are mines of information and they usually share it willingly, you will find it difficult at times to get them to participate in formal market research programs unless, of course, they are paid for their time. Factory people do what they are told and are paid for whatever they do. But agents don't make any money when they are making phone calls or are knocking on doors to gather market information for you. However, this doesn't mean that they can't be helpful sources of information.

• You will find that most agents are loaded with ideas for new products or for ways to modify your existing products. This, obviously, is a strong benefit that comes with the territory. But watch out for the "Not Invented Here" (NIH) factor in your new product people. People can be very protective of their turf. And when you pay a new product person to produce but other good ideas come from the outside, there is likely to be friction. However, like any other human relations problem, it can be solved if it's discussed in detail long before it becomes a problem.

• Somewhat related to the last item is the situation of agent aggressiveness. Agents are entrepreneurs, and they are your business partners—not your employees. You will find, on occasion, some of your inside people saying that the new agents are trying to "take over" the company. They may be pushing some of your people to work harder than they did when they dealt with factory salespeople. But we've never known an agent who would trade places with anyone.

WHAT'S WRONG WITH UNANNOUNCED VISITS TO AGENTS?

Have you ever wondered just what is accomplished when you head for the field and don't tell your agents you're going to drop in? Usually you accomplish something, but not necessarily what you intended! We've heard all sorts of reasons for the surprise visit—"Keeps 'em on their toes!" "It's the only way to find out what's really going on!" "What have they got to hide, anyway?" None of these reasons, or any other, holds water.

Warning: It's just plain courteous to drop in on a local agent if you're in the territory. But you'll do nothing but stir up resentment if you make a practice of surprise visits. The best way to handle the unplanned visit is to phone in advance of your arrival and make sure that the agent understands that your visit is purely casual. Perhaps the best way to make sure that this point is made is to ask the person to whom you speak at the agency if it's OK for you to drop in. Of course the answer is going to be "yes," and a brief visit will probably even be welcomed. Keep in mind the following:

• Even if you are trying to build an image as a concerned principal, an unannounced visit is very seldom appreciated. A planned visit does much more for both you and your agents.

• Most unannounced visits are made because the principal feels that something is wrong at a particular agency. The thinking is that by dropping in unannounced, you will catch people off guard. You sure will, and they will be flustered—whether or not there is trouble. If there really are problems at a particular agency, it's going to take a lot more than a swooping, unannounced visit to uncover them.

>>>→ *CASE IN POINT* One manufacturer dropped in on one of his agents unannounced, only to discover that a key inside person had left for home—at three in the afternoon. After he stopped complaining, he found that the person had been in the office until midnight the night before handling paperwork on his account. However, the damage had been done. The resentment and anxiety caused by the surprise visit and the uncalled-for complaints couldn't be reversed. You can imagine how difficult it is to get out of a spot like this.

HOW TO SEND NON-SALESPEOPLE INTO THE FIELD WITH YOUR AGENTS

There are times when you might want to send a non-salesperson into the field with an agent. This situation poses a number of problems that are often quite different from those salespeople encounter when they work the territory with an agent.

>>>→ *EXAMPLE* A major advertising agency used to insist that all of its creative staff spend some time each year in the field, working at a client's company. Artists pumped gas and copywriters sold cigars. They learned firsthand the problems and opportunities in the face-to-face sales situation of their clients.

Obviously, the same approach can be very helpful for people who have no direct customer contact, but who must make decisions based on their impressions of what is happening in the field. However, it's important to instruct them carefully on just how to work with an agent. You can use the following guidelines:

1. Plan the visit well in advance. That is, plan ahead with the agent and give him or her time to plan with the customers.

2. Be sure that you and your agent can give the customers good reasons for the visit. Customers expect to see the sales manager tagging along once in a while, but there should be a good reason for the director of engineering buddy-calling with an

agent. Of course, the best reason, and the one that makes the most sense to the customer, is the one used by the ad agency that sends its people into the field—they should know everything about the people who buy and use the products.

3. Make sure that the roles are carefully defined before the calls are made. The non-salesperson and the agency should decide together whether the visitor's role is to be that of onlooker or participator.

4. Whatever role the visitor plays, nothing should be done to upset the agent's presentation pace. For example, notes shouldn't be taken. This breaks the pace and makes customers somewhat reluctant to talk.

5. Let the agent have full control of the meeting. Even though you, the visitor, may be the top dog in your company, don't expect to speak executive-to-executive to the customer. In fact, do everything you can to make the agent realize that he is in full control of the meeting. Don't contradict the agent during the meeting; save your comments for later.

6. Be sure to follow up with a short note to the people with whom your non-salespeople met. Thank them for their time, summarize any points that were made, and leave the door open for future meetings. Send copies of the notes to the agents you accompanied on your visit.

No matter how well your agent may know the person who is going to accompany him or her on field visits, the presence of others, especially non-sales types, can put a stress on an agent. If you stick to these guidelines, you will do a lot to reduce the tension and to put the meeting on a positive trajectory.

IT'S TIME TO REVIEW YOUR SECOND-IN-COMMAND

"One order lost, one on the edge, and it all happened in less than a week." The sales manager relating this horror story had taken a short trip to visit another agency and didn't realize that the person who was in charge of the team during his absence hadn't held the helm in a long time. "We work together everyday," the sales manager said. "I thought he knew what was going on." But his understudy didn't. He tended to the regular chores, and his boss tended to his. In his boss's absence, problems arose that were beyond the assistant. He tried, but without knowing what his boss had been doing, he made some serious blunders.

Caution: Today most executives have much more responsibility than they had just a few years ago. If running an agency network is one of your jobs and you have an assistant, you should do an audit of that person at least once a year. If the sales manager just quoted had done this, there probably wouldn't have been any trouble. Include in the audit the reactions of your agencies to the work done by your understudy. Apart from sickness, accidents, and other emergencies that may make it impossible for you to run the team, just the press of day-to-day work may be limiting your effectiveness. The following checklist will help put the situation and your understudy into clear perspective:

• How much clout does your second-in-command have? How much clout should he or she have? Whatever your level of need in this situation, be sure that your assistant has the responsibility and knows just how far to go—and take it seriously. It's especially important for you to let all your agencies know the extent to which your assistant can act for you, and under what circumstances. There's no substitute for a short but comprehensive memo to all concerned. Unfortunately, many agencies only discover how far an assistant can go as the result of an emergency. And when one arises, the agencies are really in the dark, unless you have qualified your assistant to them in advance.

• How effective is your second-in-command? You should have a handle on your assistant's ability to handle daily situations just from regular interaction. But unless you have had to turn to the person in a real emergency, you'll never know. "If I'd held a few fire drills, this would never have happened," the sales manager said. And he's absolutely right. We suggest that you hold regular drills. Don't announce them in advance; just create situations in which your number-two must take the helm under a variety of different management situations. When you do this, get feedback from your agencies as well as using your own evaluation. Remember, drills are held to prepare people for the real thing, but they can also help to spot weak areas you and your assistant can work on.

• How does your number-two rate with other members of your management team? If your assistant's image is rooted mainly in your authority within the company, he or she may have difficulty taking over whenever it's necessary. It's very important for your assistant to have a firm, self-standing image, and that he or she be able to interact well with others at the plant as well as with your agencies.

• How self-confident is your number-two? An assistant can appear to be quite confident as long as his or her superior is on the scene and knows that backup is handy. But what you really want to know is how well your assistant will stand up under fire—alone! "My assistant used to make great decisions when I was around," another sales manager told us. "But when he had to make decisions on his own, he fell apart. All it took to bring him around was practice. I let him make more and more decisions on his own while I was in the office. And I threw in a few practice problems for him while I was away. When he had to handle real problems on his own, he was well prepared." This is a very practical way to bring your number-two up to speed.

• How knowledgeable is your assistant? Consider evaluating him or her in terms of product knowledge, the market, product applications, sales policies, and the goals of your department and your company. If you have more than one person serving in a backup capacity, make sure that there is an order of succession. It should be based, in part, on the individuals' knowledge and skills. Be sure that each has the ability to deal effectively with all of the agencies and the key people at your company.

• If your number-two stacks up well on all the points we have outlined, you're in good shape. If, however, you are less than satisfied, you'd better dig into the situation right away. And when you do, do it with an open mind. Find out just why your assistant is falling down on certain aspects on the job. If you're like most executives today, you hold a lot of responsibility close to your vest, and don't give it out easily. If this is the case, an assistant with a few low marks may not be personally responsible. Be open with yourself when you do this evaluation. If you have failed to delegate appropriately, take steps to do it, and be sure to check on your progress.

To have a strong number-two, you have to be a good number-one. Sales managers we know who rate high are self-confident, uncomplicated, and trusting people who keep their word. They also have good product and market knowledge, and they share it freely with their assistants. When your agencies know that you have faith in your assistant, they will too. And when they have faith, they will work more closely with him or her, allowing you to do all of those chores that weren't in your job description a few years ago.

HOW TO HELP YOUR SUCCESSOR TAKE OVER
THE AGENCY TEAM

"The president used to run sales as well as the company," an agency owner said. "But when he got big enough, he hired a sales manager. That was a good move, but he never prepared the guy for the job." Not an uncommon problem.

Whether you're the president and are turning sales over to someone else or are the sales manager and are moving up to marketing VP, you will still be concerned with the productivity of the agency team. And you must make sure that your replacement knows this. Use the following tips to make the transition go as smoothly as possible:

• Take your successor on a trip through the territory. Visit all the agencies, but make sure that they are aware of the visit, have planned for it, and know exactly the purpose of the visit.

• Wear both hats for a while. The new manager is going to need all the help you can give him or her, and the agency people will need you to handle the transition. Even after the transition is officially over, there will be times when the new manager or one of your agency owners will need your help. Don't let either down. But when you do it, make sure that the new manager is privy to everything, and that he is made to realize that you are helping because of unusual circumstances, not because you think he can't handle it. When you hang in for the transition, you will make it apparent to the agencies that you value their efforts, and that you are not leaving them in the clutches of someone else.

• Pass on the little things as well as the major items. For example, when you get to know each agency owner personally, you will learn their interests and habits. And, as you know, it's a lot easier to get moving with a new person when you have this insight. If your new manager can open with a discussion of the standing of the Giants, he's on home ground a lot sooner than he would be if he had to fumble for a connection.

• The person you choose to replace you doesn't have to be your mirror image. He or she must have the skills and abilities to handle the job, though. When you bring in a replacement who likes a good joke but you know that you are on the quiet side, make sure that your agents are aware of the difference. When you point out differences, even though they won't make a difference in performance, you will help smooth the transition.

Do everything you can to smooth the transition but don't prolong the period. If you do, you can inhibit the progress of your successor and can send unintentional signals to the agents that you are not too sure of the replacement. If you're sure, pass the reins smoothly and efficiently.

THINK TWICE ABOUT SPLITTING A TERRITORY

"For the last three or four years, we covered the entire territory for the principal and brought in good business. Now that the economy seems to be on a strong upswing, they're going to split the territory. We didn't even get a chance to add the people they think they need to do the job." The agent speaking wasn't asked for any input—he was just notified of the change. Unfortunately, the switch was made at the end of the contract period and the principal moved unilaterally.

Most agencies are just as interested in building their business as you are. If you think that there's more business that isn't being handled in a territory, talk to your agency about it—talk to them about expansion, what they can do to make it happen, and what you can do to help.

EXPANDING TERRITORY COVERAGE

If the territory has grown and needs greater attention from the agency, you and the agency owner should discuss the specific needs. Additional field salespeople are not necessarily the answer. The addition of inside people or someone to do the phone lead qualification and sales backup may do the job. The point is this: Be sure that you and the agency owner agree on just what it will take to do the job that you now perceive. In other words, work together.

>>>→ *OBSERVATION* Periods of economic expansion and contraction are always logical times to examine the effectiveness of any business system—including an agency network. An expanding economy is important to you and your agencies. Now is the time to plan carefully with each of them. The chances are that you will find the same expansion-minded thinking at each of your agencies. Make it practical for everyone—plan together, grow together.

TWO AGENTS IN THE SAME TERRITORY?

If you have different products being sold to entirely different markets, there's no reason why you shouldn't have two agencies in the same territory. But make sure that the market difference is significant, that both agencies know and agree to the plan, and that the marketing territory description is specifically detailed in your written agreement.

A CHECKLIST FOR MANUFACTURERS WHO MAKE TRIPS
WITH THEIR AGENCIES

There's no substitute for direct contact with customers and prospects. Most of the top sales managers feel that one or two visits a year with each agency in the territory is imperative. The following checklist will help you plan for and benefit from those buddy calls:

1. Plan every trip well in advance with the agency in the territory. It's not uncommon for sales managers who recognize the benefits of these calls to plan up to three and four months in advance.

2. After the date has been set with the agency and the schedule of visits has been agreed upon, don't let everything sit until the date of the first meeting. Keep in touch with the agency—don't hound them, but an occasional reminder, as well as thoughts for the meeting, will be very helpful. And it's smart to encourage the agency people to discuss their approaches to each meeting well in advance.

3. A few weeks before the trip, ask the agency to supply a detailed itinerary of the trip. Don't ask for the itinerary too soon because there will always be changes. When the agency sends you the schedule, do your homework and look into the sales history of each company you will visit. If there are prospects on the list with whom you have had no experience, try to learn as much about them and their business needs as possible. Analyze how their needs relate to your products.

4. Your expenses to and from the territory are yours, as is your lodging. And most sales managers prefer splitting the food expenses by picking up the tab at every other sitting. But why not make sure that you have one good meal at a fine restaurant at the end of the trip, and you pick up the tab. People tend to remember later events better than earlier ones. A good impression at the tail end of the trip is worth a lot. Think about taking the agent's spouse, too.

5. Your agent should provide local transportation in his or her automobile. If, however, the territory travel involves a plane or a bus, each should pick up his or her own fare.

6. Before you leave the territory, make sure that you and the agency agree on just what the follow-up is to be. If you want information on some customers, be specific about what you want and when you want it. Remember, these meetings and trips are for the benefit of you and your agency. Don't leave any lines unsecured. If there is anything that the agency needs from you as a result of the trip, go over it before you leave and handle the follow-up as quickly as possible when you get back.

7. Ask the agency to send you an informal report on the visit itself, and you do the same. Far too many agency people and sales managers stew about little things that could be corrected easily. "He always upstages me," an agency owner told us of his trips with a principal. "When I mentioned it he said that he knew it was wrong, but the salesman in him wouldn't sit still. However, it did after we talked about it."

WATCH PRODUCT MIX WHEN YOUR AGENCIES CALL ON DISTRIBUTORS

Most manufacturers go to great lengths to seek and appoint agencies that carry compatible but not competitive lines. They screen the agency's principals as well as the customers they sell to. However, when agencies call on distributors, most manufacturers pay little attention to the distributors' mix.

A manufacturer we talked with at a MANA seminar told us of problems he encountered when his agencies called on distributors. "Some distributors," he said, "pay very little attention to the way their lines grow. As long as there is some resemblance to the profile they have of the customer for their major lines, they will frequently take on lines with little chance for success. This, in spite of the fact that they must lay out money for stock, can spell trouble for manufacturers. Distributors can get in trouble with this attitude and ultimately cause real headaches for the manufacturers whose products they sell."

This manufacturer had some good advice for agencies who call on distributors for their principals, as listed below:

- Analyze the lines very carefully. Simple compatibility is not enough.
- Review, if possible, the volume done in the lines by the distributor. If a few manufacturers account for the bulk of the distributor's sales, make absolutely sure that the 80/20 rule is in your favor, not working against you.
- Be sure that the special needs of your products can be met by the distributor —service, calibration, installation, and the like.
- Help those agencies who call on distributors for you by preparing profiles of the distributors you want.

A key element of distributor success is training, and if you use agencies to call on them, you should make sure that they are prepared to do a top-flight job of distributor training. Remember, don't try to train anyone how to sell—train them how to sell your products. Distributors need to know everything agencies need to know about your products when the agency sells to users, such as product benefits and features, competitive points, buyer profiles—the works.

PITFALLS TO AVOID IN THE PRODUCT PATH FROM AGENT TO DISTRIBUTOR TO CUSTOMER

Many manufacturers' sales agencies sell their principals' products to distributors and are expected to provide direct and indirect assistance in a number of ways. As products mature and become commodities and as other forms of marketing emerge, the relationship of the agent to the distributor changes.

Caution: Unlike manufacturers' agencies, distributors operate in a number of different ways. Some sell only over the counter; others have many salespeople on the road. No matter what form their operation takes, there are some fundamental changes taking place. And if your agencies are calling on distributors, it would pay to watch the signs.

Training inside and outside salespeople is, for many distributors, limited to some handholding and counseling when problems arise. This is frequently not planned to be this way, but because of traditionally high turnover in distributor sales, training can be expensive. It's hard to tell which causes which, but the fact exists. You can do a lot to improve your sales through distributors by encouraging your agencies to spend as much time training as possible. Of course, the basic problem is that training time is not selling time for agencies. But you can get the time you need with special compensation. "I estimated the daily income one of my agencies got from my line," one manufacturer told us, "and paid that figure every time a training meeting was held with a distributor."

Advertising inquiry follow-up seems to be one of the real hang-ups with some distributors. When you consider that many distributors have a lot of lines, it becomes a little easier to appreciate the problem. But when you are spending thousands of dollars to produce the leads, it's frustrating to see them languish in a distributor's file. Your agencies can do a lot to improve the picture.

"We sort through all of the inquiries very carefully," another manufacturer said. "When we have identified the top-quality leads, we send them by Express Mail to our agencies. The agencies, in turn, hand carry them to the distributor. While they are there, they have been instructed to ask to see the follow-up work that was done on the previous batch. It was embarrassing for some of the distributors at first. But after they came to expect that our agencies were going to check up when they delivered a new batch, we got some action."

It's no longer as easy to move merchandise from the plant to the distributor with regular deals. Earlier distributors ran their operations on the basis of filling shelves as inexpensively as possible and then working like mad for optimum turnover. More products, more competition, and more sophisticated customers have resulted in more sophisticated distributors. But they still need help from the agencies that sell them products. "The agents I listen to," a distributor told us, "have more to talk about than features, benefits and deals. They bring us ideas and practical support from the manufacturers they represent." Since manufacturers must now look at distributors as more than simply local warehouses, it's important for you and your agencies to plan programs that will be of immediate benefit to distributors.

> ⟫→ *OBSERVATION*   Most distributors are privately held businesses that provide the owners with a significant income. Growth often means investment and more work. For some, growth is important; for others a steady-state is primary. It is probably for the latter reason that more than a few manufacturers' representatives have become distributors. They saw the opportunity and took it. For the manufacturer facing a recalcitrant distributor, backing an agency expansion can be a productive move.

In recent years, the lines between agencies and distributors have blurred some. Some agencies now offer warehousing without taking title to the products. Others serve some principals in an agency capacity, and others as a distributor taking title to products.

QUESTIONS DISTRIBUTORS ASK AGENCIES

If you use agencies to call on distributors, you might want to review the following list and try to provide as much ammunition as you can for your agencies.

• What is the history of the company, and what is its competitive position? You may be tempted to brag a little on the question of competitive position—but don't! Distributors will be just as interested in a number-two product if they know all the facts. Frequently there are benefits in these products that haven't been fully exploited. When the product is presented in its true light, the distributor knows exactly what he has and what he can do with it.

• Is the company accustomed to selling through distributors? There have been enough manufacturers who have used distributors to get established before going direct to make that a very important question. Make sure that the distributors know that you are in it for the long haul and that your agencies are going to provide the service they need.

• What is the capacity of the plant? Remember that most products sold through distributors are those that can be stocked in some depth. The value of a distributor to a customer lies mainly in local supply. When the plant can't ship, customers frequently will buy a competitive product from another distributor with stock. It's very tough to get those customers back.

• Is there a demand for the products or will the distributor have to create it? Most likely there will be a demand but it will be up to the agencies and distributors to create the brand demand. If this is the case, the distributors will want your agencies to help in some way. It may be in product training or in making joint calls in the case of some types of specialty distributors. But your agencies will probably have to present a strong picture of aggressive promotion and advertising to make the line attractive.

• What is the potential for growth of the product and related lines? Distributors build strong customer bases by providing good service along with the products they stock. If your firm does its homework and has products on the drawing board that can be sold to the distributors' customers, your agencies will have a much easier time of locking up the best organization.

• What is the possibility for related selling? Cross selling is as important for most distributors as it is for agencies. When you can sell a few product lines to one buyer during a single call, you have a product that distributors will pay attention to.

• What about product quality? Just because this point is near the end of the list doesn't imply that it's not important. The quality of your product reflects directly on the distributor who sells it. By all means give your agencies all the help you can to present the quality picture.

• Do you provide the products in practical containers and, if the products will be displayed, do you provide the displays for use in distributor showrooms? If it's convenient, provide these displays for your agencies to use when they make their calls on distributors. When the distributor sees the product in terms of how it will be stored in his warehouse or how it will be displayed in the showroom, he has a more complete picture than he would with the product alone.

HOW TO DEAL WITH SHIFTING MARKETS

More than a few companies decided not to sell to the federal government when they began tying so much red-tape requirements on the privilege. And companies that got their start in one field have frequently found that they have slowly drifted into other more productive areas.

The drift is product and market driven in most cases. However, it's important for you to keep your agency team aware of the changes. Far too often, a manufacturer will simply shift slowly without planning closely with his or her agencies. More often than not, the agencies will be calling on the people in the new markets because of their specific product orientation. But, when this shifting takes place, you can get a lot of planning input if you seek your agency's counsel. "When they told me they were going to back off on government selling," an agent said, "I was able to bring them immediate business as a result of other lines I carried to the same market. In fact, one of my principals helped by working out a joint venture with the other principal of part of the line." If you see your markets shifting or if you are shifting intentionally, get as much input as you can from everyone, including your agencies.

SETTING SALES GOALS FOR AGENCIES

Goals are an acceptable way of targeting. But now think of this way of stimulating sales: Establish goals that when exceeded will result in a bonus payment. The usual commission is paid for all sales above and below the goal. But sales that exceed the goal result in a small added incentive. It's an idea we have heard from a number of sources and seems to be gathering momentum.

TERRITORY MANAGEMENT THAT HELPS AGENTS GROW

"We have four territories," a sales manager once said. "North, east, south and west." Not very clear, but compared with some other boundaries we've had described to us, it does convey something. Territory is a word that everyone uses, but everyone seems to understand it in his or her own context.

There can never be anything that approaches strict territorial definition and boundaries for everyone. But the approach to territorial development can be shaped to meet contemporary marketing demands, and it's especially important to do this when you sell with agencies.

In textbook terms, a sales territory is an area that must produce sufficient income to be profitable. However, the textbook definition is limited to a manufacturer's perception and is based on selling only the line they produce in the territory. Obviously, a territory must be productive for an agency, too. But the agency can spread costs over several lines to make the territory profitable, where the manufacturer cannot.

Depending on the business, the products, and the distribution of customers, a territory can be defined just about any way you want. However, there are a few guidelines that must be given serious consideration, especially if you are going to cover the territories with manufacturers' agencies. Let's look at the most important considerations:

Sales objectives. We've heard of one agency that covered just one square block in Manhattan. Not very big by conventional measure, but very big when you consider the third dimension of verticality. The objective of creating this territory was to cover every prospect, and there were an awful lot of them crammed into this block. On the other hand, one-person agencies frequently cover several of the rather large states in the west. If the territory potential can be realized, then the territory is adequately defined.

Sales potential. Sales potential and profitability have to be considered together. There may be a lot of business in a territory, but if it costs too much to get it, it isn't profitable. Of course, when you use agencies, this is seldom a problem because of multiple-line representation. However, the trends in a territory are important for principals and agencies to watch carefully. When one or a few customers dominate, there could be problems for you and for the agency covering the territory. Before any changes are made, it would be important to determine with the agency just what kind of effort and investment would be required to change the balance.

Operation costs. Sure, it doesn't cost you a cent to cover a territory—the agency bears all the expense. But remember that you must support that agency and others with advertising, promotion, and sales literature. It makes sense to evaluate each territory in terms of these and other costs in order to help your agencies make the best effort. "We doubled our direct mail budget in one of our big, spread-out territories," a sales manager said. "However the money we spent was peanuts compared with the results it produced in terms of new business and agency enthusiasm in the territory."

Market segmentation. Market segmentation and territory boundaries are seldom the same. You may find that you have several different markets for your products within a territory that might be best served by more than one agency—each specializing in a market. One manufacturer did this, but reassigned territorial boundaries so that all agents had the same potential—no one was penalized.

Competitive activity. No matter where you are in terms of product life cycle, competition should be a major consideration in territorial management. Obviously, you will focus your attention on areas that offer the strongest potential—but so will your competitors. There are no hard-and-fast rules, but your strategy may be to have smaller and more concentrated territories than your competitors in order to concentrate developmental efforts. If you are dominating the market and want to hold onto what you have, you might choose to run a thinner territory. But remember that competitors should be considered as a major influence in planning and managing territories.

Customers. Some of the important questions to ask when you consider customers in a territory are: Just how many are there—really? What about prospects, untapped potential? How many of the present customers have the potential to turn into major accounts? How efficiently can these customers be served by your agencies and what should you do to help the agencies blanket the territory? How about image? What is your reputation with customers and prospects? Is there a potential to increase existing business with present customers? It's important to remember that some products and customers require more frequent person-to-person contact by the agent. An agent whose customers don't require this can generally handle a larger territory than the agent who has to make frequent customer calls.

Agencies. The one question you don't have to ask is: What will it cost to put a salesperson in the territory? However, you must plan carefully with agencies that are in place and with those you plan to appoint if you are still expanding your territories. Be prepared to supply all the information you have on the market within the territory; the agent should already know the companies and the individuals, but he or she should be supplied with all of the market intelligence you can lay your hands on. Territory management is a lot like working with factory salespeople except that they are your working partners, not your employees. However, both should be motivated to build the territory, and this is best done with strong cooperation.

LET YOUR AGENTS KNOW WHERE TO REACH
YOU WHEN YOU'RE AWAY

If you're the key contact within your company for the agencies, let everyone know where you can be reached in an emergency. An agent in the field who needs immediate factory contact doesn't want to chat with your secretary—he wants to talk with you. This may sound like we're telling you that your personal life is open for all, but this isn't so. If you specify the circumstances under which you can be called when you are away from the office, your agencies won't abuse the privilege. Better yet, train someone who can stand in for you and who can reach you when the problem is more than he or she can handle. The point is this, make sure that you can be reached by someone—easily.

HOW TO HELP REGIONAL MANAGERS GET THEIR SALES
AGENCIES' BEST EFFORTS

"We have thirty-six sales agencies across the country and we have six regional managers looking after this team," a marketing VP indicated recently. "As you might expect, some of the territories are more productive than others. However, when we looked closely at productivity, we were shocked to see that agents and territories we thought would be less productive were leading the pack. It turned out to be the way our regional managers were doing their jobs." We have heard similar stories from other manufacturers.

Caution: Regional sales managers are only as effective with the agencies in their territories as they are able to interpret corporate goals and the directions you give them. This means that you must be totally clear in your mission statements to them. It also means that the agencies must respect your regional sales managers. Regional sales managers working with agencies are in a tough spot. Being "one-of-the-boys" may make life easy in the field, but it doesn't get the job done in the long run. You watch them closely: Your corporate manager gets flack from both sides—corporate and the agencies.

Here are a few tips for your regionals to help them lead your agency network:

• Make sure that your agencies know exactly what your regional managers are expected to do and appreciate your corporate goals as well. When you get right down to it, the regional managers are your company in the field. "I make sure that all my regional managers work with people at all levels within our agencies," a sales VP explained. "It's not enough for our regional managers to work only with the owners or top people in each agency. I expect them to be on a first-name basis with everyone in each agency in their territory. That includes the clerical staff as well as salespeople and agency management people."

• Take a firm but friendly hand in the field. "Agents are entrepreneurs," the president of a small firm explained. "They often get annoyed when a regional manager is placed between them and a principal's management. I know this from very personal experience. However, when they understand that I, or my marketing VP, can't do everything, they take our regional managers seriously. When your agencies know that your regional managers thoroughly understand your sales as well as corporate policies and are able to interpret and implement them in the field, the regional manager concept works beautifully. However, and this is very important, I let every agency owner know that I am always available to them directly. But I make sure that they know that they are not welcome with routine questions and problems. They have to know that our regional managers are our day-to-day contact for them in the field. And they know that they can get to me if they need to."

• Regional managers must be able to respond quickly. You put regional managers in the field for a number of reasons. But one of the most important reasons for their existence is that they are there when you are not. If they are not empowered to act and if they have to get back to you with everything, you aren't making the best use of some pretty high-priced people. Make sure that your regional managers know what authority they have and the circumstances under which they can and are expected to use it. And make sure that all your agencies are aware of this, too. As important as it is for your regional people to act quickly, often without consulting you, it's just as important for them to keep you posted on everything they do. You may not expect them to call you for every decision they have to make, but you should expect them to keep you current on everything they do in your name and in your company's name.

HOW TO HANDLE THE SWITCH FROM DIRECT
SALES TO AGENCY SALES

"The first thing many of our customers asked when we told them we were going to switch from direct to agency sales was—'How will our relationship change?'"

⋙→ *WATCH THIS*   Once you make the decision to switch from direct sales to agency sales, you must plan and execute the strategy very carefully. Everyone has to know why the change is being made and exactly how it will affect them. This means getting the story out to your customers or to the distributors, if you will be selling to them through agencies. It's not usually a question of going to a less desirable system, it's a question of going to something new. People just don't like change, especially if they have become comfortable with something that is familiar. Here are some tips to help you make the transition:

- Define your strategy clearly and make sure that everyone in your company and every customer knows why the switch is being made and how it is going to be done.

- Allow plenty of lead time for the process to take place. An overnight switch suggests panic to everyone.

- Make sure that your announcement is clear and circulated to everyone— those in your company, suppliers, customers, and the agencies that you have switched to.

- Make sure that your customers know that they still have access to individuals within your company. You don't want customers and prospects to perceive the shift as isolating them from you and your organization.

- Assure your customers that the switch is being made for their benefit as well as yours. The continuity factor is especially important for customers.

- Take an active role during the early stages of the transition. Your visibility to all parties will be a critical element in making the switch work without flaws.

- Follow up on all glitches, no matter how insignificant they may seem. Small problems have a way of becoming big problems, especially in an agency transition if they are not monitored regularly.

- Do everything you can to help the direct field people, who have been replaced, either to find new employment in your company or with other organizations. The switch from direct salespeople to agencies often takes place when management sees the need for much more extensive coverage than can be handled with a salaried force. More often than not, the experienced direct salespeople are given the assignments of regional managers, working closely with the new team of agencies.

- Try to publicize the shift in the magazines that cover your field. If you can arrange to have a story published that explains why and how the switch was made, you will stop short the rumor mill before it has a chance to grind out some damaging misinformation.

HOW TO HANDLE UNPROFITABLE ACCOUNTS

The chances are that your agency will consider an account unprofitable before you do. But there often comes a time when it just doesn't pay to continue to handle certain accounts. It isn't easy for you or for your agencies. But the following are some thoughts that can be of help:

• Try to determine exactly why the account isn't profitable. It could be a small volume. It might be that it's always necessary to underprice in order to meet competition or be the result of excessive service requirements. Or it could be a number of things. But before you take any steps, make absolutely sure you know why the account is unprofitable.

• Your next move should be to determine what steps could be taken to remedy the situation. They may not be practical, but make a list of everything that could be done.

• You might want to consider reducing the frequency of service and sales calls. This, of course, is critical from your sales agency's point of view. Since your agencies are solely responsible for their selling costs, it's important to discuss this in detail with your agencies before making any changes.

• If service is the problem, consider the possibility of charging for the service. If your agencies are performing the service work, they should be consulted. Most manufacturer/agency agreements that include a provision for service work specify either a fixed fee for service or some modification of the commission to cover the work.

• The other possibility is to raise the price of the product. If this is impossible in the face of stiff competition, you might have to find some other ways to make your product and service of value in order to get a margin that leaves enough for everyone.

SALES AGENCIES HELP YOU GAIN MARKET PENETRATION FOR A NEW BUSINESS VENTURE

Diversity has always been an important fact in the expansion of mature businesses. However, more than a few expansion-minded businesses either failed to take advantage of their existing technology or failed in the marketplace simply because they relied only on the marketing strategies that have been successful in the past.

The selective use of alternative strategies for entering new businesses should include much more than the evaluation of current capability. More than a few companies have broadened their base considerably by entering fields that were almost totally alien to them. Part of their success can be attributed to a flexible view of marketing that included the use of agencies-in-place rather than working with an existing salesforce or recruiting a salaried sales team for the product.

LIMIT COMPETITION AMONG YOUR AGENCIES

Healthy competition among agencies not only improves productivity, it improves the morale of the entire agency team. However, a system of rewards that pits agencies against each other in intense competition can usually be counterproductive.

When agencies strive to outperform each other, conflicts can develop. This is unhealthy and should be avoided.

HOW TO BALANCE YOUR CONTROL OVER YOUR AGENCIES

Too much control can stifle agency creativity, motivation, and autonomy. Too little promotes chaos. An agent recently complained about a principal who had seriously cut into the agency's productivity by demanding approval on every step of a specific sale. Demanding excessive feedback not only slows down the selling process, it also gives the competitors a lot more room to maneuver. However, any feedback that moves the sale ahead is very important.

HOW TO BE AN EFFECTIVE AREA SALES MANAGER

Manufacturers with many territories and many agencies in them frequently place their own people in areas to serve as regional managers for a group of agencies. Based on conversations with some of these regional managers and a few of the executives to whom they report, here are some tips to help you do a first class job in the field:

- Identify your company's mission in the territory immediately. Make certain that your supervisor at the home office and the agents you work with in the field agree exactly on your mission and how you are to accomplish it. It's best to put this in writing and see that the agencies get copies.

- Define the limits of authority. It's important for you to know exactly what kind of action you can and cannot take without a supervisor's approval.

- Make sure that you clearly understand the person to whom you report. This means that you should have a clear picture of this individual as a person and as a professional.

- Understand how your performance will be evaluated by the person to whom you report in the company and by the agencies with whom you will be working.

- Don't try to steal all the glory. Realize that your role is to promote the effectiveness of the agencies in your area. When the agencies in your territory do well, the credit will be shared.

SETTING AGENCY GOALS—AND WORKING TOWARD ACHIEVING THEM

Effective goal setting is a prerequisite for sales agency productivity. Even the most effective and efficient agencies can't contribute to your sales success unless they have goals that are realistic, challenging, and clearly defined. As one sales manager said recently: "I'm judged by my agencies' record of achievement. My personal goals and the company's goals are locked together, and I know that without goals set and achieved we're all in trouble."

Caution: We're talking about goal setting, not quota setting. Sales quotas are counterproductive for agencies. The goals that are important include such targets as opening new accounts, reviving old accounts, and gaining more market share. All of these ultimately translate into increased sales. But specific sales increases are not appropriate goals when you're dealing with business partners—your agency team.

Keep the following points in mind:

- *A plan for setting agency goals.* Goal setting can proceed from the top down, or from the bottom up. There are advantages to both in some types of situations, but in the agency/manufacturer relationship the best approach is a combination that taps the experience and leadership skills of both parties. Some manufacturers set goals individually with each of their agencies; others work out a general goal program with the members of their rep council. The latter approach is often easier to manage logistically, but it does not give room for individual consideration of the strengths and weaknesses of all agencies.

- *How to identify agency/manufacturer goals.* Agencies and manufacturers have goals that must be achieved if they are to prosper. Often these goals are stated in short- and long-term expectations. Far too often though, goals are merely unspoken ideas in the minds of executives. Both manufacturers and agencies must review their own organizations' goals before they can identify the goals that they should have in common. From this effort, preliminary drafts of their common goals can be created. These goals should be distributed to all those in both organizations who will have responsibility for approving the goals and for seeing that they are achieved. Once this has been done, the objectives can be translated into goals that are appropriate for the agency and for the principal.

- *Setting agency goals.* Once agency and manufacturer goals have been identified, clear and measurable goal statements should be written. It helps to use active verbs when you write goal statements. For example, to open new accounts, to revive lapsed accounts, etc. Then set specific and measurable targets. Goal statements must not only be challenging but they must be achievable.

DON'T MAKE PRICE CONCESSIONS TOO QUICKLY

There's no question about it—high prices can put you out of the running. However, when you make price concessions too quickly and too drastically, customers wonder just what's going on.

An agent who sells products for his principals that have room for price maneuvering told us that his principal blew a big order out of the water by dropping the price too fast and too low. "The manufacturer had slack time and wanted to keep his machines operating," the agent explained. "Before we realized what he was doing, he came in with a price that was well below all of the competitors. It was so low in fact that the customer figured something was wrong and bought from the next highest bidder." There was nothing wrong—except for the fact that the manufacturer didn't consult with his agency in the matter. He just plunged ahead thinking that the customer would buy on price alone. Before he and the agent knew what happened, the order went to a competitor for a slightly higher price.

We've said it before: Include your agents in these decisions. Some people don't buy on price alone. Some are convinced that a low-ball price has a lot of strings attached to it. Let your agents in on these decisions in time to permit fast reactions.

HOW TO PROTECT YOURSELF AGAINST FOREIGN BAD-DEBT RISK

An agent who sells domestically as well as in the international market told of a problem he and his manufacturer-principal had with bad debts. It was a classic no-pay situation, except that the customer was a few thousand miles away in a foreign country. It used to be that you could demand an irrevocable letter of credit from foreign customers. Now, however, foreign competitors are heavily in our export markets and many are offering very liberal credit terms—up to 180 days in some cases. Many American manufacturers have been forced by this to ease their credit policies. And many of these companies are turning to foreign credit insurance for protection against the possibility of bad debts. The main source of this insurance used to be the Foreign Credit Insurance Association on behalf of the Export-Import Bank. Recently, however, commercial insurers have gotten into the business and in some cases the cost of this insurance is no more than the cost of a letter of credit for the same amount. Protect yourself; protect your agencies!

HAVING TROUBLE COLLECTING BILLS?

Recently an agent told us that one of his principals had put a lot of heat on him to help collect some past-due bills. As a matter of course, most agents will cooperate, but this was a situation that required more than a call from the agent. Here are some thoughts to help you collect those past-due bills.

- Your initial collection letter should refer to the business that has been completed, and it should ask for a reasonable explanation of why the bill hasn't been paid. Request payment at this time, but don't offer terms. The letter should be firm, but courteous.

- If you don't receive payment or an acknowledgment, make your next letter quite firm and formal. Restate the amount owed and the date of the billing. Be sure to state a final payment date. When you include interest charges and send the letter by certified mail, you will probably get the attention you seek.

- Keep your letter to four or five sentences. Invite cooperation. Don't let your anger get the better of you in the letter. Don't use any threats unless you are prepared to back them up.

- It is imperative that you keep your agents informed of these circumstances. It could become awkward if he keeps calling the customer to ask for orders and your collection department has been having active communication. Sometimes, too, an agent can go to the customer and say "The company says you've got some unpaid invoices. Is there a problem?"

HOW TO MEET DOMESTIC AND FOREIGN COMPETITION

Most businesses tend to be more than a little myopic. That is, when sales drop off they look for the *one* answer to the problem. There may be times when there is a single answer, but more often than not the solution lies in shifting the emphasis on several elements of the marketing mix. In the past, competitive onslaughts were met by drastic product improvements or by making major advances in the service provided by the customer. Today, the picture is very different.

Caution: We talked with agency owners who represent manufacturers whose sales have been lagging, mainly from the effect of strong competitive forces. More than a few of these agents claim that the products they sell that seem to be most resistant to competition are those that have features that make them a definite standout from look-alike competitive products. And in most cases the factors that were responsible for success were a combination of product features and service factors that were especially important to customers. None of the products were so different that they stood out on the basis of one major factor; they had a strong combination of benefits that made them popular with customers.

Here are just a few of the factors that the agents mentioned:

• One agent we talked with who sold electronic components to the O.E.M. claimed that he suggested a change of packing to one of his principals that not only took less space on a customer's shelf but the packages could be used right on an assembly line to save assembly time as well as to make it unnecessary for the customer to have to invest in line equipment to speed production. Nothing whatsoever was done to the product—it was already accepted as a quality part—but the advantage was turned by a package redesign.

• Shipping and storage are growing cost factors in most businesses. Another agent suggested that his principal investigate the new foil-lined cardboard packages for the liquid product they were making to replace the conventional round bottles in which the product is shipped. This simple change in package geometry made it possible to ship the material in smaller containers and for the customer to be able to store the product in less space. The agent called this a quality fringe benefit and claimed that it was an important step in beating competitors.

• Another agent who was selling his principal's product direct to users determined that local stock would make the product more valuable to the customers. The agent added a warehouse and stocked for fast delivery in small lots. The idea worked so well that the manufacturer helped other agents set up warehousing for the product. This, of course, provided added revenue for the agencies and it also provided that added measure of quality service that can make the difference in a tight competitive situation.

The old idea of the suggestion box still works, and when you ask your agents for ideas that will help make your product more competitive, you will probably have more than enough to choose from. Most agents will give you their ideas without charge. But many manufacturers have found it very helpful to offer prizes for successful ideas. One manufacturer even pays royalties on the sale of a modified product submitted by an agent.

AGENTS ARE THE BEST WAY TO CARVE OUT A NICHE IN THE MARKET

Today, business focus gets tighter and tighter. It's the age of specialization. And, as marketing consultants have always advised: Look for niches in big and fast growing markets—not in shrinking ones. Since manufacturers' agencies are, by nature, niche specialists, they are in most cases the ideal way to carve that position for yourself. However, in the haste to lock onto a niche, some manufacturers often overlook some trouble spots.

We recently heard of one such manufacturer who had designed and built some lower cost home health-care equipment. It turned out that even though the products were in some ways better than those made by competitors, the distributors to whom the agents sold them weren't too excited about the lower margins based on the lower selling cost. In addition, there was public distrust of a product of "such importance" that sold for so low a price. There was a market, but the niche this manufacturer had tried to carve out was based on some erroneous perceptions. The agent in this case had warned the manufacturer, but they went ahead anyway. The moral of the story is to first make sure that the niche exists.

IT TAKES AN EXPERIENCED HAND TO MANAGE A TEAM OF AGENCIES

An agent with a lot of experience under his belt told us that a newly appointed sales manager was making a mess of things. "This guy had some field sales experience," we were told, "but he had never worked with or for an agency in his life. Apart from treating us as though we were company employees, this guy is now making noises about reducing the commission rate. He's going to wreck the system."

Although we refrain from offering direct advice, we did suggest that the agent talk directly with the president of the company. This wasn't really an end run since the agency people and the president knew each other well. The point, however, is that it can be very difficult for people who have no experience with agencies to manage a team of agencies. Even a very experienced direct sales manager would probably find it difficult to make the transition. If you can't find the right person, you might want to turn to your rep council for advice. It's a short-term suggestion, but it's better than having someone ruin a well-running machine.

6

Planning and Running Effective Agency Training Programs

Most manufacturers' agents start their business after a number of years of successful selling as an employee. Therefore, their training should not be in the form of sales training but in product application training.

This chapter highlights product application techniques. From helping agents understand your products to successful field coaching, the guidance given is based on many major manufacturers' hands-on experience.

A survey conducted by MANA revealed that manufacturer training, which was considered ineffective by agents, was essentially of the one-shot variety. That is, trainers did their job and then forgot about the agency. In the sections that follow, you will be given tested techniques to help you establish and run an effective training program and a solid follow-up program.

To be most effective, training has to be evaluated. While sales are the ultimate test, there are other ways of determining the effectiveness of the training. This chapter will show you how to do an effective training evaluation.

HOW A ONE-TRACK MIND CAN KEEP AGENTS FROM SELLING EFFECTIVELY

Many agents have been weaned on one product and know how to sell it effectively. But those same tactics may not work when they try to sell your line. Correcting this problem is another good reason for holding regular sales meetings. Without some exposure to your direct people and other agents, some agents may never learn how to present your product properly to potential buyers.

>>>→ *IDEA IN ACTION* At your next training session use the best agents you have to present their style of selling for your company. You may find that your poor performers will become more effective after such simple instruction.

PROCEDURE MANUALS FOR AGENTS ARE
PRACTICAL AND HELPFUL

It's not unusual for modern, up-to-date companies to develop a procedure manual for operating departments within the organization (sales, accounting, production control, and inspection) but to ignore the outside salesforce completely. Often, new agents are appointed, given a cursory trip through the plant and some descriptive literature, and turned loose without having the faintest idea of the operating policies of the company they represent out in the field.

Caution: New agents often enter a purchasing agent's office knowing only that you make, for example, the finest widgets in the Midwest. But what they don't know is how an order is entered, how long it takes for quotations to reach the customer, the general policies governing distributorships, how rejects are handled, who to contact at the home office when things go wrong, and a myriad of details about the inner workings of your company.

Procedure manuals can be of tremendous help to your agents. Picture the new agent, just signed up by you and told what your virtues are and how you can make widgets on three shifts. He's impressed, but what happens when a buyer asks if stock items can be returned without a handling charge or if prices include freight on large orders. The agent's immediate and typical reply is, "I'll check with the home office, Sam, and let you know later today." If the agent knew what your policies were in each instance, he'd know the answer immediately instead of learning the ropes through a series of mistakes.

>>>→ *HOW TO DO IT*   The important things to include in a procedure manual are the basic policies of your firm. For example, who's in charge when the chips are down and you're out of the office; when a buyer yells about poor quality, what should a rep do; whether commission checks are payable by the fifteenth of the month.

Too many firms simply do not attach enough importance to starting an agent out on the right foot. By providing indoctrination advice and information that will put the agent on a familiar basis with your operating procedures, you will make him or her look like an informed member of the company when sitting in front of Mr. Purchasing Agent. The procedure manual can be in loose-leaf binder format so that it can easily be updated whenever necessary. A little time spent on a manual will go a long way toward giving your agents the confidence they need when selling for you.

WHY AGENTS NEED A THOROUGH BRIEFING

Each company has its specialties and nonspecialties—things they do well and things they do poorly—and these aren't readily apparent to someone from the outside, including the newly contracted agent. The agent will take the company at its face value in the absence of "inside" knowledge and as a result often makes a number of avoidable mistakes in the first few months.

Caution: Company literature is usually painted with a very broad brush and the range of products and sizes may be quite wide, as illustrated in the company's 4-color brochure. For instance, a foundry may be very good at making small and complicated castings and, while it may be able to make the larger and simpler castings, it cannot do so competitively. In the meantime, the agent is out promoting the sale of all of the company's castings to his best customers and often looks foolish when the principal "no quotes" or comes in with unbelievably high prices.

Level with your new agents. Tell them exactly what you can do well and what you can't do well. This will give them a lot more confidence in selling your products. It will also save them a lot of time and energy since they'll be emphasizing your strong points and won't waste time trying to sell the weaker units in your line.

HOW AGENT TRAINING CAN PREVENT A LAWSUIT

In his enthusiasm to sell your product, it's entirely possible for an agent to overextend his knowledge and intimate to the buyer that the product can do a few things it really isn't designed for, or that will make it dangerous. This can lead to problems with the customer and even to court.

In its *Marketing for Sales Executives,* the Research Institute of America points out two precautions salespeople can take to minimize the chance of saying the wrong thing:

1. Probe for every application the buyer has in mind. A buyer may assume qualities for your product that it doesn't possess. He may buy it for one use and, because it works well, try it for another application. Ask the buyer just exactly how the product is going to be utilized.

2. Take the probing one step further—look around. Even though the buyer has no intention of using your product in another fashion, by looking around the customer's plant it may be possible to spot other potential uses for which your product was not designed. If so, caution the buyer at once.

These simple precautions can help the customer and help you, since legal arguments are expensive to both of you.

FIELD COACHING

"Once a year, the sales manager hires a training consultant. They both make the territory rounds, but the trainer has never sold the products we handle. He doesn't know anything about the market and the people who buy the products. Can you imagine this ivory-tower type telling my guys how to handle a sales call?" That's what one agent told us recently when we were discussing sales training.

Another agent said that he has never had any training in the six years he has handled his major line, and that he wished that someone from the plant would hold a meeting to bring his salespeople up to date on new product developments and applications. The point is this: You're damned if you do and damned if you don't. But you'd better do something!

Warning: Every agent's needs are different, and your training should be planned to meet those needs. Don't be mislead by stereotypes. Agents look more for product and application training, but they can benefit from some of the new selling techniques that have been developed as well. However, don't make the mistake of putting on a basic dog-and-pony training show when your agents have been selling successfully for years.

>>→ *HOW TO DO IT*   The best way to help your agents with product and application training as well as the new selling techniques is by way of field coaching. Field coaching isn't easy, but it's one of the most effective ways you have to help your agents grow.

Field coaching requires more effort than most other techniques. Field coaching is a one-on-one system, and it's best done by the person to whom the agent reports at the factory. The system is less effective when it's handled by someone at the plant who is several steps removed from day-to-day agent contact.

Field coaching is a two-person call, but with a difference. There should be little or no sharing of the selling task during a customer visit. And the factory person should not use the call to demonstrate how he feels that sales calls should be handled. This isn't basic training; most of your agents should have gone through boot camp many years ago.

How to Handle Field Coaching

Let's assume that you are the one doing the coaching. To do the job, you observe the agent in action and try not to take an active part in the selling. This isn't going to be easy. Most of you got where you are by selling successfully. Sitting back and watching someone else do it differently than you might take a lot of willpower. However, if you do see problems that should be put right, take some action. But don't jump in and try to "save" the situation. Rather, it's better to make a suggestion at an appropriate time and let your agent pick up the ball.

What Can Be Accomplished During a Field Coaching Session

If you are trying to help an agent expand his product knowledge, pick a prospect you know is not well-acquainted with the product for the call. The questions asked by the prospect and the answers given by the agent will provide the framework for the coaching session that will follow. But first let's look at the steps in successful field coaching, as follows:

1. Set specific objectives for each coaching call you and your agent make.
2. Remain a passive observer during the call. Of course, it's impossible to sit there and say nothing at all. The best thing to do is to agree with the points made by the agent whenever possible and speak only when you're spoken

to. Be sure to tell the agent to talk to you as little as possible during the call.

3. You won't be able to make notes during the meeting, so you will have to sharpen your listening, observing, and memory skills.

4. Hold the coaching session immediately after the meeting. Do it in the car, at a near-by coffee shop, or over lunch or dinner—but do it right away. Because you will not have been able to make notes, you want to make the right points before memory fades and perception changes your evaluation of the call.

How to Plan for a Field Coaching Session

Plan the call with your agent first. Ask what he feels will be most helpful. Just to prepare yourself, you might review the territory records and look for the high spots that suggest where you can be most helpful. If, for example, it turns out that your agent has a good record in one market in the territory but isn't making a dent in another that you know exists, this might be a good place to start. The agent just might lack the appropriate application knowledge to move products in the untapped market. One or two field coaching sessions might do the trick.

How to Handle the Field Coaching Conference

Once the meeting is over, the conference should begin. But remember that this is a face-to-face situation and that you are there to help the agent and not to show him just how smart you are.

Follow these steps and your coaching will be most productive:

1. Be upbeat. Compliment the agent for everything he or she did to move the sale forward. This reinforcement of the positive aspects of the call is just as important as correcting the glitches you noticed.

2. Limit your comments to the few most important points. Pick out the actions that you felt were most positive and praise the agent for them. Then get to the points that need strengthening. However, don't haul out a laundry list of goods and bads. Stick to the main events.

3. Involve the agent in the conference directly. By this we mean don't simply lecture, but ask for his or her own evaluation of the situation. Begin with general questions and then move on to the specifics. This approach will help the agent to reach his or her own conclusions. More often than not, you will find that carefully guided sessions will result in your agent coming to the same decision as you did. This consensus makes the points even more important and helpful to the agent.

4. When you spot need for improvement, make it a suggestion rather than a command. Saying something like, "Most people find that if they mention the high-capacity feature, they get the order," is much more effective than simply telling the agent to use the point.

5.   Keep the sessions short, friendly, and productive. To make the most of them, ask your agent to summarize his or her impressions of the meeting and the points you have made to help. Not only will you have a measure of the learning that has taken place, but the act of restating what has been discussed further reinforces the points that have been made.

ENCOURAGE YOUR AGENTS TO USE SELECTIVE SELLING

"Some of my agents are skimmers—they just hit the high spots and neglect everybody else." This is what one sales manager told us the other day. It's nothing new, but the times have changed and so have the rules we have been playing by. Not that the small prospect should be ignored, but now is the time for a fresh, and possibly refreshing, look at a proven selling system for tight times.

When products are sold through manufacturers' agents, coverage of the important territories—and important customers—is often the main determiner of success. It's not uncommon for 20 percent of the customers to represent 80 percent of the business. However, most manufacturers constantly lament the business they are not getting from the remaining 80 percent of the customers they claim their agents are not covering.

When gas was cheap and other business costs relatively inexpensive, a sales manager had a point when he pushed his agents to call on the nickel-and-dimers. But now that survival, let alone growth, is uppermost in the minds of many managers, it's time to look at measures that will insure volume and place the company in a position to grow in the years ahead. Selective selling may be the answer. Let's look at how your agents can use it effectively.

Caution: All customers are just not equal. This is another way of looking at the 80–20 situation. Whether you agree with it or not, agents who are often derisively called skimmers have intuitively recognized the situation. True, there are some who have milked territories by picking off only the easy prospects. But most good agents have long known where their bread, as well as yours, was buttered. During these times, perception of this fact is important for you to understand.

The best source of increased sales is often your present customers. These are people who have bought from you and appreciate your product, your service, and the benefits of dealing with you and your agents. If you know this, so do your competitors. Therefore, their agents are going to be chipping away at your business. Spending time chasing low-potential smokestacks just isn't going to be profitable in the months ahead. Paying close attention to your high-volume accounts and cultivating high-volume prospects is important.

Whether you are talking about prospects or present customers, selective selling will be most effective when you carefully consider these following points:

1.   *Market position.* You want to sell to the movers and shakers. This doesn't necessarily mean that you should have your agents limit their calls to large companies, but it does mean that they should carefully evaluate the past, present, and future status of each. Obviously, a company buying a large volume of your products

is to be nurtured and protected. And, of course, those who buy in volume from your competitors should get first-class attention. Watch the small companies on the move. Even in these high-interest, inflationary times there are many small companies that are going to be big in a hurry.

2. *Credit position.* No one can afford to be strung out for very long. Believe it or not, there are still many companies in every field that discount their bills. Sure, they could make money on this money (your money if they chose to hold it and invest it), but executives of many well-managed companies recognize that short-term interest is often of less value than long-term good relationships with suppliers. Even if you have to extend your terms, you should seek out companies that have good credit histories.

3. *Competitive position.* Everyone has competitors, and you would be wise to see who's nudging who in this front. Even though you may sell to two or more companies that compete, you should tailor your sales effort to go after those who are leading the pack. Selective selling is a matter of setting priorities, and you might as well pick and sell to those who are in the driver's seat.

4. *Kinds of goods being manufactured.* You're going to have to play futurist here. Some industries are losing ground and others are expanding. Some are obvious and others subtle. If you sold to people making vacuum tubes and refused to acknowledge the importance of semiconductors a few short years ago, you'd probably be out of business now. Make sure that your agents are informed of where you think the growth and declines will take place.

5. *Location may be important.* The cost of shipping goods is getting more and more expensive. Not that you would consider dropping customers at great distances, but you should review alternative ways of getting the merchandise to them. Regional warehouses can cut costs. You might even think of regional manufacturing or assembly if your product lends itself to that. Selective selling can help you pinpoint the areas where this might be profitable.

This doesn't mean that you should forget about smaller accounts. What we are saying is that selective selling is one of the best answers to the short-range problem of making money in a very tight economy. If you feel that there might be some good potential among the smaller, more-expensive-to-call-on prospects, try to qualify them first by mail and phone. If you can determine a good potential, relay the information to your agents and have them make personal calls. In the meantime, help your agents to use selective selling to protect the volume you have and to build a base for the future.

HOW TO INCREASE THE EFFECTIVENESS OF YOUR AGENCY TRAINING PROGRAM

Remember, training for your agencies doesn't include sales training. It's product and application training that counts. But how well does it count a week after the session? A month? Six months? There's probably a big dropoff. This factor is not mainly the result of poor training, although that can be a major problem. It's a problem of time and lack of reinforcement.

Most of what everyone learns is forgotten rather quickly. However, there are ways to make training more effective and to reduce the fading of training material. When you spend time and money to help your agencies learn about the product and its applications, you should also go a few small steps further and reinforce the material you have presented.

The following are a few ways to make the most of your agency training program:

• Follow up after you have observed your agents use the material in a real sales situation. Buddy calls or field coaching sessions are ideal diagnostic situations. However, to make the most impact you should respond in writing as well as verbally to the person with whom you have made a call. And your verbal and written responses should be upbeat, not negative. Rather than say, "You shouldn't have mentioned the specifications until you had covered the features," you should say, "Why not cover the features first. It helps the prospect get a firm grasp on the specifications when you discuss them later." We don't mean that you should sugar-coat everything; you are dealing with grown people. But you can be much more effective with positive statements than you can with a negative brickbat.

• Provide brief summaries of the main points of your training. It may be impossible for your agents to remember a page of specifications, but when you provide easy-to-use cues, a lot of material presented at training sessions can fall right into place. This association of ideas is a psychological fact that you can use to considerable advantage. You may think of the little pocket cards given at sales training sessions as being a bit childish, but they do work. And they work with everyone, regardless of the level of sophistication. These briefly stated facts help people to associate the other ideas they learned at the sessions. And the more often these ideas are associated, the more readily they are available from memory. Think about using the pocket cards with the main points of your product and application training course, or just a single typed page of material that each individual can review at odd moments and just before an important meeting when the points will be discussed.

• Help your agents to rate themselves. It's fine for you to do your own rating, but when your agents are given material they can use to rate themselves, they feel less threatened and are more likely to do something about correcting the deficiencies that they turn up—themselves. The rating can be done with simple check-box forms or multiple-choice questions. However, it's best to avoid any kind of self-checking system that requires long written answers. There are two reasons for this. First, most people resent having to take any such "test." Second, when you provide a simple check-box or multiple-choice quiz, you should also provide the answers. When the agents correct their own quizzes, the sheets can serve as a reinforcer.

• Encourage your agents to report on their use of the material. This technique not only encourages its use but it provides feedback to help you help them and to correct any problems that may turn up in the training package as a result of such field input.

• Demonstrate that the training does work. After you have had some experience with your program and have gotten enough positive feedback, it's usually a good idea to develop some case histories that will help those who are now taking the training. The case histories should be related directly to the material and the techniques that were presented in the training sessions.

Warning: Some very fancy training programs have turned out to be complete flops simply because the material wasn't useful. You can plant a lot of information in the heads of your agents, but unless it's practical and useful in their daily work of calling on your customers and prospects, you will waste time and money.

ENCOURAGE YOUR AGENTS TO PARTICIPATE IN BUSINESS SEMINARS

Most manufacturers provide some training for their agencies. The most appreciated training seems to be product and application training—not sales training. Now that manufacturers and agencies are working more closely business-to-business, some more progressive manufacturers are providing other types of training to their agencies. Frequently this training is not directly relevant to the sale of the products the manufacturers make. But the effort and expense pays off in terms of the strength of the business relationship. "We have encouraged our agencies to take part in seminars that will help them build a better and stronger business," a manufacturer told us. "We feel that the better equipped they are to run their business, the better they will be able to serve our customers."

Some of the seminars and programs that fall into this category are the basic and advanced business courses such as accounting, data processing, management, and sales promotion. However, all courses and seminars are not created equal. If you feel that you want to build stronger ties by making seminar learning programs available to your agencies, the following is a checklist to help you make sound decisions:

1. How many times has the seminar been run in the past year? In general, the more often a seminar is run, the better it gets. Speakers gain experience with specific topics; they learn from the questions asked and are better prepared at future sessions to answer when others ask the same or similar questions.

2. What are the qualifications, experience, and background of the seminar leader and the panelists? If the program you have selected deals with real-world problems, make sure that enough of the panelists have real-world experience. Academic professionals frequently go on the seminar circuit, and many of them have important things to say to agents. But, for the most part, the most helpful information will come from individuals whose professional experience includes facing and solving the problems that most concern the audience.

3. What, specifically, will the agent be able to do better after attending the seminar? Again, don't waste your money and an agent's time by offering to pay for any sales skills seminars. Most agents are interested in learning more about data processing. Our research indicates that many MANA agency members are using

computers regularly in their business. Even those who have gone deeply into electronic data processing feel that they can use fresh insights just because the field is changing so rapidly.

4. How much time is devoted to each topic in the seminar? In general, the fewer the speakers and the more there is of group interaction, the better the seminar. Beware of the one-day seminar with ten panelists. These seminars are frequently the product of promoters and consultants looking to turn up contracts. The one-day seminar with three or four panelists and two workshops—one in the morning and one in the afternoon—generally provides for the most efficient information transfer.

5. What are the characteristics of those who have attended previous seminars? Most individuals and organizations who produce seminars should be able to provide you with a profile of the type of individual who has attended previous seminars. This may not seem to be too important, but knowing the characteristics of the audience is very important. The workshop part of any seminar will set the tone for the material that is presented. If the people who attended previous sessions did not ask the panel the types of questions that your agents might ask, then the seminar may not be of much use to you or your agency people.

USE THE TELEPHONE TO TRAIN YOUR AGENCIES

It's no secret that it costs a bundle to bring an agent into the plant for product training. However, product training is critical for success. And continued training is just as critical as is the initial training. A marketing VP told us that he always brings his new agency people to the plant for their initial training. "It's absolutely necessary for them to see the plant, see how the products are manufactured, and to meet the people," he told us. "However," he added, "follow-up training can be done over the phone. It's a lot less expensive—we pay for everything and it takes less time out of the field for the agent."

This marketing man puts on a thorough training program at the plant, as he stated, but we think he has a unique idea for keeping that training in motion. Here's how he explained it:

;;;➤ *EXAMPLE* "Once the agencies understand the product, know how we make it, what the benefits are, and who they should talk to at this plant, we feel that the best continuing training is product application training. We make paints and coatings and are forever turning up new and interesting applications. It's these applications that make up the bulk of our follow-up training, and we do it by telephone. We tried making tapes and playing them over the phone to the agencies, but this was a bad step. Now, we prepare an outline of new and interesting applications and mail them out to each of our agencies. We tell them in the mailing exactly when we are going to call—the day and the hour. This gives them an opportunity to read the material and to discuss it with us when we call. You may think that it's redundant to mail information and then call about the same material. Well, it isn't. Somewhere I heard that people forget about 75 percent of what they hear and read within an hour. When we call, we first go over the basic material and then turn the call into a brainstorming session. We ask the agents to imagine how the applications we sent them might be applicable in their own territory and with the customers they serve. This isn't a one-sided classroom situation—it's a dynamic learning laboratory. The agents are encouraged to take part rather than just read the material and listen. And it works."

The marketing man who described this unusual system went on to explain that he follows up these calls with answers to agent questions and with more information that relates to specific customers. "This is more than training," he claimed. "It's good sales management."

We agree!

TRAIN YOUR NEW AGENCIES IMMEDIATELY

"Four months after we signed the contract, they decided to come around and tell us about their product and market. By that time, we had just about lost interest," an agent told us recently. It's what happened to the manufacturer in terms of diminished enthusiasm that's important here.

Experts claim that training should be done almost immediately after the agreement has been signed. Interest and expectations are highest at this point. One manufacturer related that he signs contracts and does the training at the same time. "Signing the contract with all of the agency salespeople watching has a dramatic effect," he said. "And then we get right into the training. It works for us!"

FOLLOWING UP ON AGENCY SALES TRAINING

Agency training doesn't end when the formal training program has been completed. Strong follow-up is necessary to reinforce the program and to insure that the information that was presented is being used effectively in the field. The following are a few follow-up tips:

• Provide additional material for the agents to use after the program. If, for example, your program concentrated on product applications, you can make the most of the program by sending your agents, on a regular basis, additional application case histories. Relate these cases to the points made in the original training program.

• If it's possible, have the person who did the training make a visit to the agency about a month after the completion of the program. The purpose of the visit should not be to test the agency on how much they have retained, but to answer any questions that may have cropped up in the meantime.

• Ask your agencies to document their efforts to make use of the material that was given to them during the training. You shouldn't ask for nit-picking details, but you should have them give you the broad strokes of their efforts to use the material.

Again, the intent is not to judge but to provide an opportunity for the agencies to step back and look at what they are doing. The step-back process is important; it's usually impossible to evaluate any new techniques you're using at the moment of use. However, looking back and evaluating their use and perceived effectiveness not only identifies weak spots but it reinforces the strong points.

• One of the best ways to make effective use of training is to have those who have been trained pass on their knowledge to others. When your agents have regional meetings, this is not only a good way to make effective use of training, but it's a good way to get agents to mingle.

GAME PLAYING IMPROVES TRAINING RESULTS

According to training experts, programs that include interactive games help agencies absorb complex material more quickly. The games seem to reinforce the agent's understanding of the product and its applications, and they make it easier for agents to learn difficult subject matter.

One sales manager we talked with who uses the game approach in his agency training programs said: "Game playing allows us to interact with our agencies in a nonthreatening way. The traditional classroom training situation is threatening, no matter how well we know each other. Once someone takes the role of teacher and others are students in a classroom, lines are drawn. But when games are used to facilitate the training, the threat disappears."

REVERSE TRAINING PAYS OFF

An agency that sells OEM parts to electronic manufacturers recently related that it was able to put an end to late deliveries by having its principal's shipping manager spend a day talking with customers. "We showed him what happens to a production line when parts are late. And we showed him shipping schedules proposed by competitors. We had been telling him this story for a long time. But it took a firsthand experience to make it real."

HOW TO EVALUATE YOUR AGENCY SALES TRAINING

As we've already said, agencies really don't want and don't need the kind of sales training that deals with the subject from a skills perspective. However, most agencies welcome sales training programs that are product and application oriented. According to the professional trainers, the following checkpoints will help you get a handle on the effectiveness of your training:

• Determine if your current training program is relevant to the experience your agents have with customers in the field. If, for example, your agents are meeting resistance in terms of certain application factors, it doesn't make sense to stress product quality, price, and delivery.

• Ask whether or not the training program has produced measureable results. This doesn't mean that a passing grade after a training program is the be-all and end-all. It does mean, however, that you should see some positive effect in terms of sales activity after the training has been completed. You should expect positive benefits, but it's important to know when these benefits should appear. Too many managers feel that sales should jump immediately after training. This may be true for door-to-door salespeople who bring in cash at the end of each day, but it certainly isn't true for most products sold by sales agencies.

• Make sure that your training is consistent with your overall marketing program and objectives. Far too often training programs are used over and over again, while the marketing plans are changed to suit market conditions. If there is no synchronous activity, you could be spending a lot of money on very unproductive training.

• Is there full management backing for your training? You, as the sales manager, may be fully committed to your training program. However, if top brass pays only lip service to the program, the chances are that it will not be very effective. And all the other people and departments within your company that deal with the agencies should support training. There's nothing that can sabotage a training program more than a disinterested chief engineer making an offhanded comment to an agent that he thinks the training program is for the birds.

• Do you have the appropriate tools to evaluate the training? The most important tool you have is your voice. Talk to your agents and ask them if they feel the program is effective. What they think could be added or subtracted. Ask them for their input before and after the training. You might want to do this anonymously or face-to-face. It all depends on your relationship with your agent.

• Increased sales are not always the best way to evaluate sales training. Sales increases are critical for growth, but to evaluate your training, go back to its specific objectives. If the goal is to build contacts, that's the measure to use. If the goal of the program is to do more product demonstrations, then use this as a measure. The bottom line, of course, will be sales increases. But to judge the program, use its goals and the bottom line.

GETTING THE WORD OUT WITH A VIDEOTAPE

About fifteen years ago, manufacturers who wanted to be on the leading edge of training could spend ten to fifteen thousand dollars on video equipment. Today, for about two thousand dollars, you can buy a camera and a VCR that does a lot more than the early equipment could ever do. We have heard from more than a few manufacturer readers who are using cameras at customer sites to tape product installation and operation information for their agents.

>>>➤ *OBSERVATION* According to industry studies, more than one-third of American homes have VCR equipment. Even if your agents don't have equipment in their office specifically for training, they will probably have one at home.

The following are some of the uses manufacturers have made of their recording equipment for their agencies:

• Training manuals are necessary for the operation of complex equipment. However, it's not always easy to set up and operate equipment by simply reading the book. And when your agents are involved in product use training, their time is always limited. Using a videotape to take a customer through step-by-step procedures backs up the agent and also provides a "live" record of operating procedures for the user when the agent isn't available to help or to answer questions.

• Several manufacturers we talked with told us that they have taped technical sales sequences in which product application and demonstration sequences were crucial to the sale. "There isn't an agent around who doesn't understand the sales closing process," a corporate marketing VP told us recently. "However, closing with our equipment, which is expensive and complex, is not an easy job. To help our agents, we created tape scenarios that were based on actual sales and sent them to the agents. The feedback was very positive."

• You can also use videotapes to get the word back as well as out. We've heard of a few manufacturers who have supplied their agents with small, portable video cameras. These manufacturers asked their agents to tape the operation training that they gave to their customers. The goal of this project was to analyze the training process to see where it could be streamlined. It also turned out that the product design people were able to see ways to improve the product when they saw the same problem crop up a number of times in each training sequence.

• Videotapes can be used effectively in selling situations. However, those who use them stress that the tapes should only be used in short sequences to support the personal presentation. We all know how dull and boring it can be for the salesperson and customer to sit in a room looking at a tape that is supposed to do all the selling.

7

Motivating Sales Agencies

The perennial question asked by manufacturers who sell through agencies is: How can I get more of my agents' time? Those who have sold successfully through agencies know that it's not a matter of getting more of an agent's time, but motivating him or her to make the most productive use of the time allocated to a specific product line.

Surprisingly, motivating a manufacturers' agent is not at all like motivating an employed salesperson. Most agents simply don't respond to sales contests, even when the prizes are significant. And the usual rah-rah type of motivation often has a negative effect on them. However, when agents are treated as working business partners, their motivation is high.

In the sections that follow, practical and easily used techniques for manufacturers to maximize their work with sales agencies are revealed. For example, an eight-point checklist is given to get a new agent off to a good start. As your company grows, you will want your agencies to grow too. In one of the reports outlined, you'll find ways to insure parallel growth.

HOW TO ASSURE AGENTS' FOLLOW-UP SERVICE

A major concern among capital equipment manufacturers who provide a guarantee or warranty on their products is the difficulty they have in stimulating agents to investigate customer complaints. It appears many agents, after receiving their commissions, show little desire to service the customer in the style promised by the manufacturer.

>>>→ *SOLUTION* Immediately after shipment or after payment has been received from the customer, pay the agent only 75% of his commission . . . mail the 25% balance after the warranty period expires with the condition that the rep provide satisfactory customer follow-up during this period. A change such as this naturally requires a contract change— not just a verbal agreement.

Sales managers whose firms make expendable products are usually selling continuously to the same customers and seldom experience this problem, as their agencies must provide follow-up service to justify additional orders.

WHY SO MANY TERMINATIONS?

The pressure on sales managers to increase their sales has been one of the reasons for the turnover of agents. And lately there have been more reverse terminations—agents shedding principals—because of that same pressure.

Caution: The business cycle has a lot to do with these pressures. In good times companies can't meet production schedules so they expand their facilities to meet customers' needs. When business drops off or more competitors enter the field, they find themselves with excess capacity. When this occurs, the sales manager is hauled up front and told to boost sales as quickly as possible.

This type of pressure is bound to cause some irresponsible actions guaranteed to increase terminations such as badgering agents at home for a report on the day's activities, coming into the area too frequently, and setting unrealistic goals. All these create friction between the two parties and as relations worsen, so do results.

When pressures mount, try some of the tried-and-true rep motivating methods: higher commissions for new customers or blanket orders, special pricing for short periods, regular or increased mail communications, and good down-to-earth advertising and promotional aid. It may not bring the immediate results management wants, but it will hold terminations to a minimum and help you get through that shaky period.

SOMETIMES EVEN A GOOD AGENT CAN'T SELL YOUR PRODUCT

Have you ever appointed what you thought was a truly professional agency and sat back and waited for orders . . . and waited, and waited, and waited? This happens to every company now and then, and the reasons are not always too clear.

⟫⟶ ***OBSERVATION*** A major cause of this type of performance often lies in the salespeople's inability to sell your product. They may be great salespeople and even have a pretty thorough knowledge of your product, but they may not know the selling techniques that can really put your product across.

When this happens, don't wait too long. Get out of the office and into the territory. A one-week trip can usually spot the problem. Chances are the salespeople are as puzzled as you. Occasionally it may be because the agent doesn't understand the real benefits of your line, or he may be working through the purchasing department instead of the maintenance foreman or the project engineer.

Don't approach the trip as a do or die effort but as a cooperative venture designed to help the company sell its product and help the representative make commissions. Finding a good agency is hard enough, don't just let them sit there making mistakes.

At the end of the week sit down with the agent and go over your visits. Point out where things went well and where they didn't, and why. A professional agent will welcome your help and you'll both benefit.

HELP YOUR AGENTS WEATHER A RECESSION

Let's examine some of the things you can do to help keep your agents solvent so they can survive an economic pause and go out to sell for you again.

1. If you have some inside information about declining demand, let your agents know about it just as soon as possible—they're not economic experts.

2. As soon as you detect a lessening of demand, start concentrating on innovative sales strategies that will help your agents have "that little extra" to sell. Generous discounts, extended terms to good customers, and offers of more technical assistance can keep buyers tuned in to your company.

3. Alert inside personnel to be quick to react to any requests from your agents. Give them that little edge they'll need to beat out competition.

4. How much does your business decline in a recession if it's 20%, for example? There's 80% left which requires more than normal servicing.

You'll be having troubles of your own if a recession arrives, but a good outside sales staff is difficult and expensive to recruit. Anything you can do to help them over the hump will give them a head start when the economy picks up again.

DON'T OVERSELL YOUR AGENTS

When a new product is introduced, it becomes one of the most important focal points of your entire organization. Usually it's the result of a lot of energy and a substantial investment, and you attempt to promote a lot of enthusiasm for it. One of the dangers of this natural enthusiasm is an "oversell" to agents on the part of sales management.

Even though your management wouldn't make exaggerated claims to customers, they often can't resist overemphasizing the qualities of the new product to the sales teams in order to "rev them up" and send them out with an enthusiastic charge.

>>> *IDEA IN ACTION* Instead of overdoing the promotion to your own team, the following are several realistic approaches that can be taken that will make the salesforce attentive to the need for selling the new product:

"Why are we coming out with this product at this time?" Let your agents in on management's rationale for the decision. If it's to fill a gap in a product line to meet a customer or market need, say so rather than simply "to give us the most comprehensive product line in the business."

"Why is the product priced as it is?" To tell the agents that "no one can touch our price," isn't good enough even if true. Actually, anyone can beat any price the day they decide to. Instead, tell the agents why the price is positioned where it is—for example, to make it easier for them to trade up to (or down to) another product in the line.

"These products (name them) are likely to be your primary competition." Sales agents are always aware that they're selling against a specific company or product. Words won't change that and it's a mistake to try to persuade people that "we're in a class by ourselves." Agents who relay that line to customers are met with skepticism.

"These types of customers (name them) are likely to be your best source for sales." You've researched the market; you know who the prime prospects are, maybe even where they live. Don't keep this information secret—though you might be tempted to because you realize your research might not be perfect and you want agents to expand the market if possible. Instead, always level with them.

If you're perfectly honest with your agents, you're likely to generate more enthusiasm than if you exaggerate. Most of them are veterans and have been through the new product syndrome before. Treat them like the experienced pros they are, and they'll go out and sell for you.

DEALING WITH THE UNDERACHIEVING AGENT

Every company has an underachiever or two in its sales department, if for no more reason than the fact that someone has to bring up the rear when it comes to sales results. Whether these persons are really underachievers is open to question, since they may be doing as well as possible under the circumstances—a poor territory, aggressive competition, or product quality lapses.

However, by a thorough analysis of the person's personality and his or her territory and management of time, you can pretty well identify whether or not the salesperson is living up to his or her potential.

It's not easy with agents. How do you spot the underachiever from a distance, which is the only way most of your appraisals occur. Is that guy in the field really doing the best he can and coming up short, or are there other reasons why he appears to not have the potential you attributed to him when you contracted for his services?

First, let's review several reasons why he may not be bringing in the sales you expected:

1. Some other sales manager has his finger on the agent's "hot button" and is doing a better job of motivating him.
2. You may have overestimated the potential for your goods in the agent's territory.
3. An exceptional local supplier may be marketing aggressively in the territory making it difficult for out-of-state firms to compete.
4. For one reason or another the agent finds your product more difficult to sell than his other lines.

These are just four of perhaps ten or twelve reasons why an agent may look like an underachiever to you, but in reality may be a very good salesperson. He may be doing well, in his opinion, since he's making a good living, but that won't keep your boss from asking why Harry Johnson never seems to increase his yearly sales as much as your other agents.

Frankly, there are few underachievers in the agency business—they simply can't survive by not living up to their potential. But one or two may appear to be underachievers, and there's only one way you can change this impression. Travel with those agents, and do it quite often until you've either improved results or decided the person is doing a pretty good job with the tools at hand.

On the other hand, you may find that your "underachiever" simply took on your line to pay the phone bill or that he's happy with the amount of commissions he's making from your line and doesn't want to put out the extra effort that's necessary to increase sales. If either of these two situations are obvious, then it's time to have a heart-to-heart talk.

GETTING MORE OF YOUR AGENT'S TIME

The Comfort Level Factor

Ego—the pride of accomplishment and winning are the strongest internally generated factors that drive an agent. Far too often, sales managers neglect and overlook this point as they attempt to find methods to control and motivate their agents.

For over 30 years on one side or the other of the agent/manager relationship, we have seen sales motivation techniques that run from 2 percent commission incentives to the threat of cancellation, from trips to the Islands to territory reductions, from new account bonuses to a 2 x 4 with a nail in the end. And invariably, the same sales manager will try one, then the other, then another—with little long-range success.

The best method that we have witnessed to control and motivate sales agents and to have it work for the long term is what we call the "Comfort Level Factor."

Your Competition Is Not Who You Think It Is

If an agent has 6, 8, or 10 lines, all of them do not realistically get an equal 16 percent or 12 1/2 percent or 10 percent of the agent's time. Those other 5, 7, or 9 lines are your competition. You are first and foremost competing for more of your agent's selling time. Those 2, 3, or 5 lines that get the top attention of the agent have motivated him, not by meaningless incentives or threats but by the "Comfort Level Factor."

When it is time to pull a line or a product out of his briefcase, the products he most eagerly, most earnestly, and most often promotes are those that he is most comfortable with. When push-comes-to-shove, the agent will promote those lines he feels competent to discuss, familiar with in jargon and technology, confident of its quality and support, and sure of the manufacturer's character behind those products.

How then do your products stack up against the "Comfort Level Factor"? There are only two grades in this examination—pass or fail. If you are one of your agent's top two lines, you probably pass. Otherwise, you are missing the best opportunity to control and motivate your agents to higher and higher volume sales and better sales and marketing feedback.

The Comfort Level Factor Test (Rate Your Company)

Grade yourself 0 through 5 for each question. *0* is not at all–never. *5* is often–regularly–every possible time. Grades *1* through *4* are between never and always.

1. We publish or print current and new product literature, made available to our agents, and reflecting something new for them to discuss with their customers and prospects?

2. We regularly keep our agents informed about new facilities, capabilities, products, applications, customers, and ideas we are considering?

3. On a regular basis (annual or biannual) we hold a sales conference where we bring our agents up to date on technology, product changes, company objectives, personnel changes, advertising programs, and other factors that will help them sell our products and our company to the marketplace?

4. We encourage our sales, technical, and management people to be available to our agents to help in sales activity, specific account penetrations, and key program closings?

5. We make it easy for our agents to be a part of our company?

6. We make it easy for our customers to do business with us?

7. We are easy to communicate with and respond well to questions, inquiries, and suggestions?

8. We spend time in the territory with our sales agents working not only on specific customer calls but also on planning, ideas, objectives, and their selling problems?

9. We seek our agents' advice on products, advertising, literature, and on communications strategies?

10. All of our owners, managers, and other key personnel know our agents and regularly get an opportunity to meet, know, and understand the other?

How did you rate in the Comfort Level Factor Test? 40 or above and you are probably getting top billing from your agents. 30–40 and a little extra effort will make your agents feel more comfortable with your products and will push you ahead of three or four of your competitors. Below 30 and you probably need to do some replanning of just what you can do to gain your agent's interest and get your product first out of the briefcase with all your salespeople. Remember that the first thing you must do is sell your agents. Then hold them responsible for taking that sales message to your prospects and customers.

Are your agents confident to discuss your products and your company? Are they sure of the capability and the technology? Are they familiar with the jargon, the quality you represent, and the support you offer to them? Are they completely comfortable to discuss your product with the customer?

If you work to improve the Comfort Level Factor of your agents, you'll see a rebirth of spark, new energy, and motivating force that far surpasses most others. The field salesperson wants to promote comfortable products, not unsure ones. Make your products and company more comfortable than that of your competition.

HOW THE ONE-MINUTE AGENCY MEMO GETS INSTANT ATTENTION

It seems that the one-minute manager has spawned its share of clones and looka-likes. However, we recently heard a sales manager explain that he sends general memos to all his agencies every week, and that each memo is carefully worded so that it can be read in only one minute. In fact, he even had a masthead printed for his memos in which the words One-Minute Memo appear in bold type across the top of the sheet. "This tells the readers that I'm not going to bore them with a lot of reading," the sales manager was quoted as saying. "It also says that I have respect for their time." Not a bad idea, is it? Why not give it a try . . . if you're not already communicating effectively with your agencies.

Make It Easy for Your Agents

Too often manufacturers make it difficult for their agents and customers to do business with them. They destroy the "comfort level" of agent and customer, thus inhibiting increased sales, sales penetrations, and lessening opportunities.

Sales managers are constantly saying that they can't control their agents, can't motivate them, don't get any feedback from the field, and don't have enough communication from the field. Yet many of those sales managers don't make it easy for the agents to accomplish these motivating and controlling functions.

On the other hand, companies that attempt to make it easy for agents and customers to do business with them usually enjoy steady feedback, a strong sense of control and understanding, and a salesforce that is comfortable with the line, motivated toward new customers and higher volume sales.

Making it easy costs less, motivates better, controls stronger, and produces more than making it difficult.

Sixteen Steps to Greater Control, Motivation, and Sales Volume

Make it easy for your agents to

1. Understand your company
2. Learn about your products
3. Plan to sell your products
4. Understand the direction you're heading

5. Know what not to sell
6. Secure sales aids, literature, and tools
7. Get answers
8. Communicate with you
9. Solve problems with you
10. Service your customers
11. Secure new customers for your products
12. Learn new applications or product uses
13. Know about upcoming new products
14. Know who is talking to whom
15. Be totally comfortable with your products
16. Sell your products.

Working hard to continuously accomplish these sixteen easy steps, the sales manager and factory management will place their products and company atop the agents' "comfort level" lines. As a result, the factory can reasonably expect more sales penetrations, more new accounts, greater field communications, better control, and more idea generation from the field sales team. Motivating the sales agents to promote your lines better is reflected at the bottom line, i.e., more sales and higher profits for both the factory and agent.

MOTIVATIONAL POTPOURRI

There are traditional motivational techniques used by many sales managers in pepping up their agent salesforce; prompt commission payments, good competitive pricing, on-time deliveries and no house accounts. Here are a few not-so-traditional goodies that can have a positive effect on an agency group whose recent results are not up to par.

• Bring the CEO along on the next field trip. He may not take to the idea, but having him present on quick one- or two-day trips will impress your agents and customers.

• Mail all correspondence promptly. Believe it or not, there are companies that hold all agent correspondence (copies of quotations, letters, orders) until Friday and mail it all in one big envelope to save 50 cents in postage—meanwhile possibly losing thousands because of delayed follow-up by their agents. Also, large mailing envelopes, even though carrying first-class postage, often are delayed in transit because of their bulkiness.

• Make product samples, catalogs, and literature first class. Some firms send rejected parts to their agents to use as samples. If you expect your prospective customers to think highly of your company, make sure your agents are armed with top-grade literature, sparkling catalogs, and the very best product samples . . . it helps convince your agents too, and that's important.

• Feature your agents in your advertising. Good agents will stay with you a long time, eliminating the danger of an ad going stale because of changing personnel. This not only makes the customer know you think highly of the people you've charged with the responsibility of selling for you, it also gets the same message across to the agent.

• Use bulletins and newsletters monthly. A monthly bulletin or message to the entire agent salesforce makes them all part of the family. Everyone likes to see his or her name in print, particularly if you have something good to say about them. Mention their plant visits, new customers, innovative selling techniques, and any other accomplishments worthy of publication.

• Bring agents to the home office at your expense. Whether it be a sales meeting or just a yearly visit, pick up the tab for a plant visit and don't skimp on accommodations. A luxury hotel or motel may cost only $20–$30 more than a run-of-the-mill hostelry, but it indicates a first-class operation and instills the agent with pride in your organization.

If you stand head and shoulders above your agents' other principals when it comes to thoughtful actions which unspokenly transmit respect for your agents, you'll have a group that will be happy, loyal, and productive.

HOW TO GET A NEW AGENT OFF TO A GOOD START

"Okay, Martin, how do you plan to get this territory moving and turn it into a moneymaker?" These were the gruff words that greeted Tom Martin, head of an agency, as Larry Monaghan, the marketing VP from the factory stepped off the plane for his first visit.

    ➤➤➤ *EXAMPLE*   Tom Martin is a good agent, respected by his colleagues and customers, and by all standards, very successful. But now he wasn't sure just where he stood with his new principal. Monaghan had chased him for months to take his line. Martin was already representing several companies managed by tough, take-charge guys. But Monaghan's greeting had more than a challenge in it.

Agents are like new employees, but they are strongly motivated people who have the entrepreneurial traits that set them apart from those who choose to work for a paycheck. But they do like to get to know you before you turn up the heat. The following are some suggestions for making the honeymoon pleasant as well as productive:

• Don't cut and run once you tell the world that Cleveland is now covered by Smith & Co. Agents are very individualistic, but they want and need support in the first few months. Larry Monaghan, for example, said to Tom Martin after he realized that he was pushing too hard: "I know you know the territory and the market. It's just a matter of getting to know us and our products. Let's spend the first few days getting to know each other." A good marketing person will pull the strings for a while, but never enough to tangle up a new agent before he ever gets going. And he knows when to let go.

• Let your agents do it their way. Sure, you know what you'd do if you were an agent—but you're not! Remember that your responsibility is for the bottom line. As long as your agents adhere to company policy, let them use their skills and imagination unhampered. However, you should encourage new agents to discuss their ideas with you. Don't be judgmental unless you know for sure that they won't work. A simple, "Let's see if it works," is usually enough encouragement to let a new agent know that the arrangement is a two-way street.

• Don't force the pace of your new agent's development. Every individual and company is different, and each will get the job done their own way. Of course, if things drag badly, you'll have to speak up.

• Make it very clear that you expect high performance. Nursing a new agent into productivity often requires reduced expectations early in the game, regardless of the territory potential. But make it absolutely clear what is expected and when you expect it. Don't leave room for misunderstandings.

• Be tolerant, though not protective of mistakes. Everyone goofs once in a while, especially in the early stages of the manufacturer–agent relationship. Let your agents know that you consider mistakes to be learning experiences.

    ⟫→ *HOW TO DO IT* Far too many manufacturers appoint new agents, hand them catalogs and samples, and then just point them to the territory. The following are eight points to keep in mind when you're launching a new agent:

1. Provide complete and comprehensive material on all products and sales policies.
2. Answer all agent inquiries promptly, no matter how trivial they may seem to you.
3. Tell your new agents where and how others have succeeded. Similar opportunities may exist for new agents.
4. Tell your agents about new products in the planning stages—not when you tell the rest of the world.
5. Provide a sales and operations manual that not only shows the agent how he fits into the organization but specifies his contacts within the company.
6. Give your agents all the facts on your competitors. Don't gloss over the details no matter how much it hurts.
7. Spend time in the territory early on. Make sure that you have specific goals to accomplish. Discuss the plans with your agent in advance of your visit.
8. Screen your advertising inquiries before you send them to the field. This is especially important for new agents to prevent them from wasting a lot of time and becoming discouraged.

HOW TO GET YOUR AGENTS TO SPEND MORE TIME
WITH YOUR LINE

We asked this question and got a number of provocative answers. Fred Harding, national sales manager of Wilder Mfg. Co., Port Jervis, NY, sent in his thoughts. They summarize most of the ideas of others. He calls his approach the T.I.M.E. formula. Here it is in an editorial nutshell.

Thoughtfulness Establish rapport—listen to problems—be sincerely interested—be a teammate.

Invasion Carefully prepare personal visits with agents—avoid interrupting normal routine.

Money   Make it financially worthwhile for your agents to handle your line.

Education   Give a steady flow of helpful information on all aspects of the agency/manufacturer relationship.

HOW TO USE THE SUCCESSES OF SOME OF YOUR
AGENTS TO HELP OTHERS

Even though agents talk with many people all day long, they lead a lonely life. It's lonely in the sense that they seldom have the opportunity to discuss their successes, failures, and problems with others in a similar situation. After all, agents are usually given exclusive territories and rarely see and talk with your other agents. Many of them are faced with reinventing the wheel when they should not have to go through the exercise.

Getting the word out to your agents on how others have solved problems has never been easy. Agents are seldom willing to take the time to write about how they got or lost a big order, and the means of communicating has always been a time-consuming memo or newsletter. Both can be effective, but there is a better way—tapes.

Relatively inexpensive equipment is now on the market. There's no need to buy commercial recording equipment or have the work done by a professional studio. A good stereo system with a built-in tape facility and an outboard deck can be combined to make all the tapes you need. And, of course, when the equipment isn't being used to produce tapes, it can provide music for your office.

   »»→ *HOW TO DO IT* Tapes are very personal and effective. When you ask your agents to give you a short tape on how they handled a sale that you know will benefit your other agents, be sure to give them an outline to follow. Perhaps the best outline is found in the journalist's Who, What, When, Where, Why, and How.

Here's how to make the system work.

1.   Make sure that all of your agents have tape recorders. If they don't, consider buying inexpensive units for each. There are some very good recorders on the market for about $50 that record as well as play back.

2.   Tell each agent about the program. Don't write it; send a tape along with the tape recorder.

3.   Contact each agent regularly by phone to discuss sales situations that would be of value to the other agents.

4.   Have each agent who has a story to tell, record it in his or her own words on the recorder. Be sure you emphasize that they follow the outline to keep them from rambling.

5.   When you receive the tape, duplicate it on your stereo equipment and send copies to all of your other agents.

6.   Encourage your agents to keep these tapes after they have first listened to them. The tapes can serve as resource material when agents face similar situations and need information on how another might have solved a similar problem.

7.   Encourage your agents to communicate directly with each other to share their experiences. You will find that many will use tapes for this or will begin talking regularly with each other by phone.

8.   After every four or five tapes, it's a good idea for you to prepare a summary tape in which you review and comment on the material that has been sent in the past. This wrap-up serves several purposes. First, it reminds the agents of material that they may have forgotten. Second, it provides an opportunity for you to reinforce the points that contribute to success. And, of course, it gives you an opportunity to give your agents a verbal pat on the back that all will hear. This is not only good for sales, it's great for morale.

HOW TO MAKE THE MOST OF A MAJOR AGENT ASSET—INITIATIVE

A sales manager told us recently ". . . the best reason to use agents is to benefit from their initiative." He went on to talk about all the obvious benefits that everybody knows, but he finished his story by saying, "Anybody who uses agents and rides hard herd on them will kill their initiative. And without that, all you have is a bunch of salespeople who are selling your products along with someone elses." An interesting comment, isn't it? A quick look at some manufacturer/agent relationships shows that our friend seems to be right—very right!

The word initiative implies the beginning of something. In the case of agents, this can mean getting something done without having to ask for it. When we talk about initiative, we are talking about ingenuity and resourcefulness—two characteristics that make the agent stand out from other salespeople. But how do you encourage your agents to use their initiative on your products when they carry many others in the bag? How do you help them to think of you first, and to think creatively when the situation calls for it? How do you encourage them to think the way you do without stifling their creativity?

These questions will be answered shortly. But keep in mind that most agents are far more resourceful than they are given credit for. Unfortunately, corporate marketing executives often put so many restraints on their agents that they never get the benefit of the resourcefulness that is the hallmark of those who stick out their necks to work for commissions. Let's begin with a little soul searching.

1. *Assuming that conditions are the same in every territory.* The situation in each territory is different from that in another. Unless you view each territory separately and encourage your agents to solve their problems independently, they will not use their initiative. Pat answers for all territories just don't exist.

2. *Unwillingness to accept that each agent has a unique way of doing business.* You must allow for human differences and let each agent exercise his or her own brand of selling and management on your account. You can define the limits, but be sure to emphasize that all the space in between is for individual action.

3. *Demanding conformity.* The bottom line is sales and profits, yet many a sales manager gets poor agent performance simply because he demands that company policy be followed slavishly.

4. *Negativism and lack of recognition.* Some sales managers tend to judge their agents' performance by their mistakes rather than by their successes. Sure, we all goof once in a while. And the goofs shouldn't go unnoticed. But when more attention is paid to errors than to accomplishments, the relationship is in for trouble.

5. *Lack of long-range planning.* The company that confines the guidance of its agents to day-to-day directions does itself a great disservice. Agents won't know how to plan their work and will tend to wait for specific instructions. Plan ahead and keep your agents aware of what's happening and what's going to happen.

That's the long and short of stifling initiative. If you see any of these trouble spots, do your best to correct them. Now let's look at what you can do to encourage those entrepreneurs who are just as interested in making you rich as they are in making a fortune for themselves. Take the initiative yourself—let your agents know that you respect their individualism, and that you want them to do more than follow the company rule book to a fault.

HOW TO ENCOURAGE YOUR AGENTS TO USE THEIR INITIATIVE WITHOUT LOSING SIGHT OF YOUR GOALS

1. Make an effort to know and understand the individual problems each agent faces. When you can discuss their plans and problems personally, each agent will know that he or she is being treated as an individual, not as just another agent.

2. Develop open and regular personal communications with each agent. The monthly memo and the company newsletter may be okay for some things, but for the job of communication with your agents, nothing beats regular, direct, and personal contact. Use the phone on a friend-to-friend basis. Write short notes occasionally that encourage and let each agent know that you appreciate specific things they have done.

3. Accept responsibility yourself and be sure that all your agents know it. If you've done something that deserves a pat on the back, pat yourself. If you've

fouled up, let your agents know about that too. Agents are seldom willing to take the initiative when they know that a sales manager won't acknowledge his own problems. It's a two-way street.

4. Acknowledge each agent's suggestions and put them in action whenever possible. Be sure to let all your agents know when the initiative of another is appreciated.

5. Don't use the Not Invented Here (NIH) factor. The person who uses it as part of his or her personality defense system is really saying that nothing anyone else can think of could possibly be worthwhile. This is very stifling—learn to recognize it and avoid it.

6. Encourage your agents to try new ideas on their own. If you know what's happening in each agent's territory, you should encourage them to develop initiative solutions to their problems and better ways to build sales. If the solutions can be used by your other agents, pass them along and be sure to give appropriate credit.

7. Use a challenge to stimulate initiative. Simply using a challenge has a very negative effect. But if the challenge has within it an element of personal involvement that can be ego satisfying, you will get all sorts of positive input. And, of course, most ego satisfaction is expressed in terms of personal recognition.

TWELVE WAYS TO MOTIVATE YOUR AGENTS

Don Christman is a partner in the Specialized Training Group (SpecTra) and has developed training programs for such diverse organizations as The Harvard Graduate School of Business, the New York City Police Department, and many international marketing firms. We asked Don to give us the elements he has observed as being the most effective when training an agent salesforce. Here is a brief summary of a two-hour interview.

"Asking how to motivate an independent agent is like asking how to cook a chicken. There are as many ways as there are people you can ask. All usually work, but the methods are quite personal and they depend on specific situations. But here in a nutshell are the major factors I have observed and used in my training programs . . .

Provide a reward for performance. Not just a commission check but a pat on the back, a phone call, or even a bonus for a job well done. Do it whenever it's deserved . . . Don't threaten. If there are problems, lay them out and spell out the alternatives, but don't use force or threaten an agent . . . Provide the support that each feels is necessary for him to do an optimum job. If you can't, be sure that the agent knows why you can't and that he or she understands the problem . . . Make sure that your agents know how their effort relates to the total effort of your company. Make sure that the agents know that they are part of a winning team . . . Individualize your supervision of the agent network. Even though you may have many agents, be sure that each gets personal attention, either from you or from someone on your staff . . . Provide immediate feedback for jobs well done as well as for jobs that are not so well done . . . Show that you have confidence in each agent. If you publish an internal newsletter, play up your agents in each issue . . . Make sure that there is a climate of trust and open communications between your company and every agent in the field. Make sure that each agent can get your ear personally when he or she has problems. Don't delegate this personal counseling to any of your subordinates . . . Don't criticize people—criticize behavior. By this, I mean you should avoid making a personal attack when you have problems with an agent . . . Encourage your agents to try new and novel ways of doing business. And be sure to reward them when they are successful . . . There's a lot being said about stress these days. Stress at moderate levels is what makes for business and personal success. Don't try to make a bed of roses for your agents, but at the same time don't try to motivate them by creating high levels of anxiety."

HOW TO HELP WHEN AN AGENT NEEDS ASSISTANCE WITH A SALE

Agents, like the rest of us, can get in over their heads at times. And when they do, you have two problems: You must find some way to save the sale, and you must also find a way to help the agent without bruising his or her ego. Most agents know when they need help and aren't afraid to ask for it. But occasionally an overeager or less experienced agent gets into trouble, and you may have to throw him or her a line.

Growth is as important to agents as it is to the manufacturers who use them. And with growth comes unfamiliar territory—larger and more sophisticated customers, more complex selling situations, and highly involved applications for some products. However, it's the challenge of growth and the unknown that not only makes business fascinating—it makes business profitable. When one of your agents has reached a point where he or she needs help, you will probably notice it, and you may be reluctant to interfere. However, if you do, the chances are that you will find the agent relieved and receptive to your help—if you handle it right.

The following offers ideas for handling this touchy situation with tact and skill:

• Most likely your agent is just as aware of the problem as you are and he or she has already spent a few sleepless nights trying to solve it. Whether the agent comes to you or you suggest a helping hand, the agent will probably be relieved to get help with the problem.

• The chances are that by the time you're on the case, speed is important. However, in haste to get the sale that is in jeopardy, don't trample the agent's ego with lectures.

• To make the most of the situation, be sure to point out exactly what the agent did right up to the point where you had to step in. For example, mention the skill the agent used in locating the prospect and getting him or her this far and discuss the preparation that went into the presentation. Explain very carefully that your reasons for becoming involved don't reflect poorly on the agent's sense of self. This will not only protect the agent's self-esteem, it will also provide a positive learning experience that can be applied in future situations.

- Whatever you do, don't cut out the agent when you step in. The agent is still the territory contact with the customer, and whenever it's practical, work through the agent to the customer. If time is critical and this is impossible, you should explain the situation to the agent and make sure that he or she is told of everything you are doing directly with the customer.

GETTING THE MOST FROM YOUNG TIGERS
AND THE OLD GUARD

At a recent MANA seminar, a lively discussion erupted at one point when a manufacturer asked whether it was better to sign up "lean and hungry" agents or to seek out seasoned and successful pros. It should be a matter of strong concern to all sales managers who work with agents to keep a healthy balance between growth and stability—to maintain a dynamic interaction between the young tigers and the old guard.

> ➡➡➡ *OBSERVATION* Early in the seminar discussion, it became quite clear that those who were taking firm stands for one group or the other were not necessarily differentiating by age or time in service; they were talking about attitudes. They were talking about their perceptions of sales success and relating them to levels of agent activity. This is the kind of discussion that is difficult to resolve, simply because no two manufacturers have the same needs. However, if you recognize that both groups have a lot to contribute to your growth and to the success of other agents, you will be on the right track. Let's examine how you can benefit from both.

- Unfortunately, young tigers and the old guard, both as groups and as individuals, often are at personal sword's points. This is usually most obvious at sales meetings and at rep council meetings. However, since it's your show, you can pull the strings and get the most from the interaction. But you must remain in control and not let one group dominate the other. If the old guard dominates the tigers, there will be no one left to challenge ways that may have become ineffective. And if the old guard is put down, there will be no one to provide the hard-won know-how and experience the young tigers so often need.

- Since you benefit most when you make the best of both groups, let's see just how you can handle the situation. New ideas are the lifeblood of any industry. Whether these new ideas take the form of new products or new ways to sell old products, they are extremely important. More often than not, you will get these ideas from the young tigers. Sure, some of them will be off the wall or just plain impractical. But, for all the ideas that won't fly, there will be some that will make important contributions to your operation and to the effectiveness of all of your agents. The best thing you can do is to encourage this independent thinking—nurture the creative process.

You're going to find, however, that the old guard can be more than a little resentful at times. Remember that they already figured out how to do it. They have gone through the process and sorted out the systems that won't boost sales. They have sharpened the ideas that do work. But there can often be resentment on the part of the old guard when the tigers come up with ideas that you like. There's no easy way out—you need the support and the input of both groups. You're going to have to encourage both and let both know that their ideas are welcome.

In such situations, nonconformists—those who want to do it their way—can be turned off quickly by those who have grooved on a successful track. If these innovative people get the message that the price of being different is too high, they will forget the whole thing. While you may be bothered at times when your young tigers reinvent the wheel, the best thing you can do is praise and encourage initiative while gently pointing out why the particular idea is impractical. Don't turn off the enthusiasm, though.

How to Encourage Creative Input

• Be sure to praise and reward originality. Do this with words as well as actions. If you publish an internal newsletter, let the other agents know what the young tigers are doing and how their efforts have enhanced the operation.

• Let all of your agents know that you are looking for innovation. Don't make the mistake of talking only with those who you think are the young tigers. More often than not, the old guard is just as ready and capable of providing creative solutions to marketing problems. They just aren't as visible as the young tigers simply because they have already worked out the solutions to their problems and are now using them to make sales. When all your agents know that you respect them for their ideas as well as their ability to sell your products, you will be surprised at the quality of the creative input.

In your haste to encourage creative thinking from the young tigers, don't dim the enthusiasm of your stable producers—the old guard. As mentioned, you can expect as much creativity from them as you can from the tigers. In addition to this, the old guard provides perspective and can help evaluate the ideas produced by the tigers. They may discover that the ideas have already been tried in the past and have been abandoned for very sound reasons. When this information is available, much wheel-spinning can be avoided for both groups. The most productive role you can play as a manufacturer is to mediate the interaction and to get both groups to work together for the common good—theirs and yours.

• Mixing the old guard and the young tigers can often be a stimulating but explosive experience. However, if the rules for the meeting are well established in advance, you should have no trouble. These meetings can take place as part of rep council sessions, in conjunction with a sales meeting, through teleconferencing, or the use of a direct mail roundtable.

• It's especially important for you to remain in complete control of the situation. The best way to do this, in addition to establishing firm rules in advance, is to make absolutely sure that you favor no group over the other. Such behavior instantly cuts down the enthusiasm of the group not favored and eliminates your credibility as a mediator. But if you remember that agents are creative and imaginative people, regardless of whether you classify them as young tigers or the old guard, you will have a collective resource that can unleash incredible power.

WHAT TO DO WHEN YOUR AGENTS ARE
RELUCTANT TO GROW

"The territory has twice the potential, but the agency in it just can't get to see everyone. Sure the owner and his one salesman are doing a terrific job—with the people they get to—but we're missing too much business." The sales manager who said this wasn't exaggerating. He knew that the additional volume was there, and he was frustrated because he did not have a crackerjack agency, but he couldn't convince the owner to grow.

Caution: On the surface, every businessperson, whether he or she is running an agency or a manufacturing firm, wants to grow, expand, and make more money. But when it gets down to the nitty-gritty, there are a lot of problems that can come with the benefits. The following analysis of the situation may give you and your agencies some practical ideas you can use.

Let's first look at it from the agency point of view. Before we get into the specifics, keep in mind the profile of the average agent. He or she is highly motivated, risk-oriented, and entrepreneurial. He or she is not impulsive though, and takes risks only after a careful assessment of the odds. Yes, he or she will take greater risks than most other businesspeople, but he or she wants to know his or her chances first.

Let's look at expansion as an *agency owner* would see the problems.

1.   "One of my major principals encouraged me to grow. I added people and built up the territory. Then they took it away and put in factory people." Not an uncommon lament; and it's one of the reasons many agencies control their growth very carefully. What would you do? We have some answers. But let's look at the other problems first.

2.   More than a few agency owners have said to us: "I added people, took on the responsibility of managing them, built sales for my principals, and found on April 15 that my personal income was no better than it was when I carried the bag into the territory myself." This is usually a temporary situation. The benefits of agency expansion extend to much more than taxable income.

3.   Related to item two is the problem of complicating a lifestyle. Most agents left industry because they were frustrated by bureaucracy and wanted to win or lose on the strength of their own efforts—not on the whim of others. Adding people can remind an agency owner of the reasons why he started his own business.

4.   Because of the relationships that develop between agency salespeople, principals, and customers, those salespeople hired to expand a business occasionally tear it apart by walking away with key principals and accounts. It's easy to say that good managers wouldn't let this happen. But it does happen to good and bad managers. People who own agencies, and those who work for them, are highly motivated. And

so are the many manufacturers who left their employers to start competitive manufacturing businesses. Apart from the ethics of the issue, this is a problem that is a fact of life for every agency that considers expansion.

These are the problems that cross every agency owner's mind when a valued principal turns up the heat for expansion. There is the drive for self-preservation. Expansion can bring not only the obvious benefits but also some serious problems. Remember, most agency owners want to grow, make more money, and build a company that will go on when they decide to call it quits. But you should look at these problems through the eyes of the agency owner when you push for expansion.

Now, let's look at some of the solutions. You know that it serves your purposes to have your agencies expand in the territories that are not fully covered. And, in general, you know that it can be beneficial for your agencies to grow. Inasmuch as you and your agencies want the same thing, it becomes a matter of solving the problems that you have just seen from your agency's point of view.

1. Since a single agent in a territory doesn't cost you a cent until a sale is made, additional people on the agency staff won't cost you anything either. It's easy, then, for you to encourage an agency to grow. But every time a salesperson is added, it costs the agency. Sure, many agencies pay base salaries and commissions on sales made, but the fixed expenses can eat an agency alive until the new salesperson becomes productive. Most agency owners know the numbers by heart. They know the slim margin of success and failure. This is especially true in the early stages of growth—adding the first few salespeople. It is less of a risk with larger agencies, of course.

The solution: Be up front with your agencies. If you want the territory covered in greater depth and it will take investment on the part of the agency owner, assure him that you're not planning an end run for salaried staff when the volume is there.

2. The push to get more from a territory is always based on the assumption that there's more to get. Before you push an agency owner into an expansion mode, make sure that the territory has the capacity. This means doing some serious market research—not the off-the-cuff analysis many manufacturers do when they travel the territory for a day with their agencies. You can often get good estimates from the editors of the trade magazines serving your field and from associations that serve your industry. Wherever you get the numbers, be sure that they are valid before you lean on any agency.

3. Suppose that the agency owner you want to expand turns pale at the thought of the paperwork and administrative details he would have with added people and responsibility. Obviously, you and your agent have to maintain an independent relationship in the eyes of the tax people, but there's nothing wrong with providing him with some advice on how to make the most of an expanded agency without being buried alive in paper and details. One of the best ways to approach this problem with a reluctant agency owner is to explain the benefits of the expanded business once the details are ironed out. Talk about the additional free time

that will be available when the systems are in place and running. And discuss the continuity that is only possible where there is more than one person in the company.

4.   You should also point out that added salespeople will not only be selling your products, they will be selling the products of the agent's other principals. This, of course, easily translates into increased sales across the board.

Many big agencies got big because their principals wanted them to grow. But the principals looked at expansion through their agent's eyes and made sure that it was a joint venture—with no surprises for either party. If you assess territory potential carefully and work closely to help your agencies expand, you've won most of the battle.

A Way to Grow—and to Help Your Agencies Grow

"I became an agent because I like selling, and I'm good at it. If I wanted to be a distributor, I would have done so in the first place." You can see the direction we're going when we talk about one avenue of growth for you and your agencies. But we're not out to turn every agent into a distributor.

>>>→ *OBSERVATION*   Standard products that are not high priced and often needed in quantity can usually be stocked locally to give you and your agencies a significant competitive edge. Even spare parts for capital equipment can fit this model.

Let's look at the important considerations that should be of interest to you and your agencies.

1.   One of the major differences between a distributor and an agency is the way orders are developed. Distributors tend to provide local sources of parts but do little aggressive field selling. Those running agencies, on the other hand, spend most of their productive hours beating the bushes, but they seldom carry stock. The curious combination of agency and distributor, often referred to as the specialty distributor, can in some cases offer the best of both worlds to you and some of your agencies.

2.   Most specialty distributors are really hybrids. That is, they do provide a local stock of some of the products and parts that they sell, but they also have a strong field sales team for the lines they stock and the lines they represent.

3.   Local stock can sure help get the jump on competitors in some fields. Think, for example, about electrical and electronic components, fluid control systems, hardware, fasteners, and similar products.

4.   Most of the people who run agencies do it because they like that way of doing business. They are not really interested in the details that can bog down an aggressive salesperson when warehousing and stocking are undertaken. There are two creative alternatives . . .

- Consigning stock is often a good way to handle the problem. When this is done, you maintain title to the stock and continue to bill the customer. But the stock is shipped to the customer immediately—a very strong competitive advantage. Essentially, you can help put an agency in the warehousing business. Agency owners often see this as a way of investing and building equity in a business that seldom has much visible value when the time comes to sell. If an agent agrees to stock products and handle local shipping, additional financial arrangements must be made, of course. The agreement alone is often enough for an enterprising agency owner to get the financing needed to build a building—and equity.

- The pure agency and the pure distributor still dominate both marketing systems, but the lines are blurring. Many agencies actually perform full distribution services for some of their principals, and many distributors just represent and don't distribute some of the lines they have. A step in either direction could be beneficial for both parties, but both should know what they are getting into.

  Remember, it's not the magic answer, but local stock no matter how it's handled can often do a lot to cement customer relationships and to lock out competitors. Most agency owners who have gone this route soon see the system as an excellent way to add a measure of security to a business that is, under the best circumstances, precarious.

HOW TO ENCOURAGE YOUR AGENTS TO BRING THEIR IDEAS TO YOU

"We found that we could make solid initial contact with electronic parts buyers through the members of local radio amateur and video user clubs. Most of the hams work as engineers, and if they don't have buying responsibility, they sure can put us in touch with the right people. However, when we told our principal about our system, he thought it was a joke." The principal who thought the system was a joke made a big mistake. First, he probably missed a lot of business by not listening and passing the ideas to his other agents. Second, he turned off the agent who told him about the system so that he'll never get an idea from him again.

Running a team of agents is often a lonely job. You seldom get to see your agents and exchange ideas. Those who direct employed salesforces see their people regularly and can have that give-and-take that is important for the salesperson as well as the manager. Since ideas are the lifeblood of sales and since your competitors are all trying to outsmart you one way or another, here are a few tips to help you encourage your agents to share their ideas with you.

- *Be enthusiastic.* Sure, a lot of the ideas you get you will probably have heard before. And many of them will not work, at least with the rest of your agents. But when you react with enthusiasm, you show your agents that you are interested in them and take them seriously. When you have to reject an idea, you will at least have given it careful consideration, and the agent who submitted it will know that.

• *Listen carefully before you respond.* We all have the tendency to anticipate —to form an image of the direction the person who is speaking is headed. Even if it's absolutely obvious and you know from experience that the idea is not practical, listen to it completely. First of all, your impressions may have lead you to the wrong conclusion. And second, by listening to all the details, you may be able to come up with a way to make the idea work, where it hasn't in the past.

• *Give credit when credit is due.* When an agent comes up with an idea you like and it works, spread the word. Make sure that the agent gets the credit immediately and that all of your other agents know of the accomplishment. The agent whose idea you have used should be rewarded with praise at the very least and other rewards if possible. And when you make sure that your other agents are aware of the successful idea, you will encourage them to speak to you with their thoughts and ideas. It's a pump-priming process that pays lots of dividends.

• *Explain why you reject some ideas.* You owe it to the person who took the time to give you the idea. And, apart from the courtesy that is due, an explanation may put the idea into sharper focus for you and for the agent, with the result that a modification could make it work.

If you have a rep council, circulate a newsletter, or have any other form of regular communications, you can get the idea mill in gear easily. It's more difficult to cultivate ideas from agencies simply because each of your schedules make it difficult to meet regularly. But with encouragement, you will turn on one of the best idea sources you have. *Note:* Keep all ideas in a file, even those you must reject. Often ideas that won't work today will work in the future under different circumstances. If you do use a previously rejected idea, make sure that the agent who originally submitted it gets the credit.

HOW TO DEVELOP A SPIRIT OF CREATIVE COMPETITION WITH YOUR AGENTS

Strictly speaking, agencies don't compete with each other. They work their own territories, and only meet each other during sales meetings. However, as every sales manager knows, competition is a strong motivator. "When I worked for another company, I managed a team of salaried salespeople," a man who now manages a network of agencies told us. "When I moved and took over an agency team, I applied a similar philosophy and not only built sales, I created a closer sense of belonging for the agents." There are ways to use the benefits of competition to enhance your agency operation.

Warning: The usual sales contests are, for the most part, wasted on agencies. Those who own agencies and those who sell for them are highly motivated, but they seldom respond to the trip to Cleveland contests that can motivate salaried salespeople. Competition, used properly, can spur agencies to greater performance. However, unless it's used carefully, it can be counterproductive. Don't, for example, push people and agencies beyond their limits.

The following are some situations in which competition is a positive factor:

• When essentially all of your agencies are evenly matched, you can create competitive situations that will have a positive effect. Each agency owner knows that he or she has a chance. But when the team is dominated by an agency that, for one reason or another, dominates all the others, there is little likelihood that the others will have any interest in competition. You can, of course, set up a system of handicaps to even the odds. But even with this approach, a dominant competitor makes it difficult to use competition as a motivating force with a team of agencies.

• You can use a competitive system when all of your agencies are not overloaded. If any members of the team are burdened more heavily than others, the chances of success are slim. One agency, for example, may be going through difficult reorganization. The stress of such a situation makes it difficult for that agency to put forth its best effort. There is a big difference between using competition to create the positive tension that builds sales and using it to put the heat on someone who is, at the time, unable to put forth his or her best effort.

• When there is a spirit of unity with your agencies, competition can be a very positive force. It can stimulate agencies that are falling short of the mark to put on the pressure, and it can motivate the top performers to do even better. However, when there are intense rivalries and the agencies avoid cooperation, any competitive elements you introduce will do nothing more than add fuel to the fire. Usually those manufacturers who run effective rep councils have developed cooperation to a high degree with their agencies.

Caution: To be most effective, a created competitive situation should be short-term. Competitive situations of short duration make the most of people's normal behavior cycle. They push hard for a while, then relax. Nobody pushes hard forever.

• You can create situations where agencies compete with each other or where individuals compete with themselves. Most motivated people prefer to compete with themselves rather than with others. They see such competition more as a personal challenge and usually respond much more favorably to it.

These are the conditions under which manufacturers' agencies are likely to respond most favorably to any kind of competitive situation. What kinds of competition are practical for agencies? As mentioned, most sales contests are marginally effective. However, don't rule them out altogether. They can be effective when more than a trip or obligatory dinner is involved.

Use contests when the contestants have a chance to demonstrate their sense of personal accomplishment. Use them when the chances for success apply to all agencies on the team. Use competition in the team sense, and you will have a powerful tool at your disposal. To do this, for example, you might create a competitive situation in which your agencies are challenged to exceed the growth of the agencies selling competitive products. Every agency benefits when sales go up, but some agencies will be given awards for outstanding performance.

Competition, carefully used, is a powerful motivator. But when it's used to pit one agency against the other in a win/lose situation, you're off on the wrong track.

HOW TO MOTIVATE YOUR AGENCIES BY TAKING THINGS AWAY FROM THEM

There are probably as many schemes to motivate salespeople, including agencies, as there are people selling. And most of them center on giving something for a positive performance. How about taking something away from your agencies to motivate them?

Money, trips, awards, gifts—these are things that most sales managers think of when trying to motivate their agencies. But you can do just as strong a job by making life less complicated for them. You can remove some of the tasks they are to perform or you can make them less onerous. This, psychologically, has the same positive motivating effort as giving them something.

The following are some ways how to do it:

• Back off on some of the pressure. If you have been pushing an agency pretty hard, you can do a strong job of motivating by relaxing the push.

• Reduce some of the routine work you expect your agencies to perform. For example, if you expect them to do some of the inquiry qualification, you might take on all of the qualification yourself. A lot of manufacturers are doing this now with telemarketing systems.

• Reduce roadblocks that may exist between the agency people and those at the plant with whom they must communicate. There shouldn't be any obstacles in an ideal situation, but the world isn't exactly an ideal place. Just by acknowledging and removing them, you will show your agencies that you are interested in them and in turn will motivate them. Remember the G.E. Hawthorne studies. Just by changing lightbulbs in the plant, work improved. The workers perceived it as positive attention and responded with greater output.

You may have noticed that all the things we suggested are those that most experts consider to be the essence of good agency network management. However, it's frequently easy to slip into bad habits. And when these habits have a negative effect on an agency, the act of changing them usually has a very dramatic effect— an effect that lasts.

WHEN TO USE MONEY TO MOTIVATE AGENCIES

You may want to introduce a new line or bring an old line up to snuff. Or you might be faced with a competitive problem that an increased agency incentive might help. Should you consider giving more money? Surprisingly, the answer is that money incentives work best only under certain circumstances.

Research has indicated that the following are the circumstances under which additional money will motivate:

• When the level of trust between the manufacturer and the agency is high. It's not easy to come up with a sound reason for this condition, but it seems that money motivates when the relationship is good.

• When the expected performance can easily be measured and related to the additional incentive. Agency owners are practical people, true entrepreneurs. As such, they see and appreciate cause and effect situations. And added commission to move a slow product will give the agent more than money. He or she will see the additional money as compensation for an added effort and will also see it in terms of a long-term payoff.

• When it's significant, but this is not a plug for big plugs. Most agencies are quite profitable and added incentives may not loom large in their financial scheme of things. Remember, when a shiny dime in a direct-mail market research letter would get you to respond? Now it takes a crisp buck. However, the added incentive can be a combination of more money and other benefits such as recognition and nonmonetary awards.

• When they are directly tied to superior performance on the part of the agency. In other words, most agencies don't go the Little League trophy route.

HOW TO GET TOP CREATIVE EFFORT FROM YOUR AGENCIES

No matter how creative your agency people may be, there is no way that they can succeed without making calls persistently. However, the difference between good and great sales is often the distinction between an ordinary effort and a creative effort.

Although the word creativity can conjure up many images, those who study the process seem to agree that a creative idea is one which is based on a novel solution to a problem and which is appropriate to the situation. Sales managers and the agencies they work with are frequently faced with situations that can be solved with the tried-and-true, but usually there is a low probability of success. Or, hopefully, you'll be more interested in trying a new technique.

To help you, here are the characteristics of creative organizations as seen by industry psychologists who have worked with salespeople:

• A creative company maintains open communications among the members.

• A creative organization maintains open communications with individuals and organizations outside.

• Creative organizations contain a variety of personality types.

• Problems are solved by creative organizations by looking carefully at all of the issues: stereotyped approaches are avoided.

• Those in creative organizations are not afraid of change and they enjoy experimenting with new ideas.

• People in creative companies are always seeking to acquire new knowledge.

• Creative organizations generally credit part of their success to flexible scheduling.

• Leaders of creative organizations define their goals carefully and commit themselves to achieving them.

• The individuals in creative organizations make decisions without undue fear.

Much of the work done in a manufacturer's sales department is routing—order processing, inquiry handling, and all sorts of follow-up. However, the manufacturers that have the most success with sales agencies do more than the routine work; they provide creative input.

Minds well-stocked with information are more likely to come up with creative ideas than those that are not. But for this to happen, it's important for a free interchange of information to take place within the department. It's unfortunate, but the information that is frequently most responsible for creative responses seldom gets transmitted in the formal channels of communications.

>>>→ *EXAMPLE*   To overcome this problem, many companies provide opportunities for individuals to seek and exchange information from others on an informal basis. At one company, managers are chosen randomly from the different functional areas to go to lunch with each other once or twice a week for several months. The only goal is for these individuals to identify company problems that they share and to generate alternative solutions.

The same process that works internally can work as well with your agencies. Rep councils, if they are structured to stimulate an open exchange of ideas, can be a major source of ideas and solutions to problems.

WHEN NOT TO FOSTER COMPETITION WITHIN YOUR AGENCY TEAM

"None of my agencies compete with any of the others," a sales manager said recently. "They all have individual and protected territories. I feel that inter-agency competition weakens rather than strengthens it," he said. This does make sense. After all, agencies frequently have to help each other when products, for example, are sold in one territory and installed in another. This sales manager was speaking specifically in terms of sales contests for his agencies. His view is to reward each agency for individual performance, based on its own standards, and not to pit one agency against another for a grand prize.

UNDERSTANDING AND MOTIVATING THE THREE TYPES OF PEOPLE WHO BECOME AGENTS

Too often, those who write about motivating salespeople tend to think that all salespeople respond to the same kind of motivating force. Recently, however, researchers have determined that there are really three distinct types of people in business and that you have to approach each differently to make the most of the relationship. This is especially true for manufacturers' agents. Let's see how you can identify the three types and how you can motivate each.

1.   Practical, systematic, and very orderly people are frequently doers rather than leaders. These are the agents who generally build large and successful agencies, but who weren't too spectacular as managers when they worked for other people. *How to motivate:* These people respond to attention, are very concerned

with fairness, and strive to build long-term stability into their agencies. Treat them fairly and see that they know the relationship is going to last, and you will have solid team members.

2.   The risk-takers are confident and often innovative as agents. Unlike the first group, they are change-oriented and seek leadership positions. They may seem pushy and somewhat insensitive, but this is more a picture of impatience than anything else. *How to motivate:* Give them a lot of recognition and challenge and they will thrive.

3.   The optimistic, people-oriented agents are those you think of most frequently when you think of successful agents. They are helpful and talkative. They provide a lot of support and motivation for others. *How to motivate:* This group responds to appreciation, personal warmth, and being allowed to express themselves. Listen and you will automatically motivate.

You'll find all three types on your agency team. Just because each is quite different than the others doesn't imply that one type is going to be more successful. It does mean, though, that you should identify each type and treat each individually.

    ⋙→ *IDEA IN ACTION* When presenting problems to agencies, ask them to provide two solutions. This develops creativity and encourages innovative answers.

HOW TO BUILD LOYALTY BY ENCOURAGING AGENTS TO COMPLAIN

The lessons learned in marketing consumer products have a direct corollary in agency/manufacturer relations. Research has shown that customers who complain are more likely to be repeat customers than those who are dissatisfied but who don't complain. If the informal poll we took is any indication, the same effect operates with manufacturers and sales agencies. When agencies are encouraged to air their complaints to their principals, they seem to have a stronger and longer relationship. It stands to reason. When there are problems and they go unresolved for a long period of time, the result is usually a big blowup. However, when agencies are encouraged to let their principals know when they are unhappy about the relationship, the problems are nipped before they become big explosions. The moral: Ask your agents to complain.

HUSTLE IS THE NAME OF THE GAME

In a past issue of the *Harvard Business Review,* it was stated: "Intense preoccupation with competitive strategy is declining. Sophisticated managers return to basics. They know that growth and handsome returns come directly from superior execution, not strategic planning by itself. Their method: Hustle and getting it right." This is pretty strong medicine, and it's the kind of thinking that points directly to one of the most important characteristics of the agency method of selling.

Further on into the article, the author, Amar Bhide, states: "Emphasis must be on the quality of recruiting and training for marketing and operations. No overriding competitive strategy beats hustle linked to the discipline of detail and a generalized vision of where the company needs to go." All we can say is that it's reassuring to read these words in this prestigious publication.

TO HELP YOUR AGENCIES SUCCEED, ENCOURAGE THEM TO FAIL

No, this isn't a typographical error. Of course, you want your agencies to succeed, but if your control is too tight and your expectations are unrealistic, you will find that your agencies will avoid taking the kinds of risks that lead to growth. But when risks are taken, there are bound to be some failures. And when you take your agencies to task for their failures, you are sending them the wrong messages. By their very nature, those who start and run sales agencies are risk-takers. Who else would go into a business that depends entirely on commissions? When you encourage your agencies to take only the safe path and to avoid some of the riskier avenues, you are inhibiting them and reducing your potential for growth. There is, of course, a fine line between wild ideas and measured risk-taking.

8

Evaluating Sales Agencies

You may think that the only worthwhile test of an agency is sales. In the long run, this is true. But there is much more to a manufacturer/agency relationship than just this. In some cases, a territory must be worked for a long time before any sales results. This chapter reveals how you can tell if the agency is effective during this interim period.

Your agencies are, in effect, an extension of your business. They are your representation in the field. To help you determine how effective any agency is, you should be able to measure the impact the agency is having on your customers. You'll find guidelines for this task in the pages that follow.

Most manufacturers are in a quandary when it comes to determining whether a large or small agency would be best for a specific territory. The questions of large versus small and single-person versus multi-person are also answered.

As important as it is for you to evaluate your agencies, it's just as important to recognize that your agencies are constantly evaluating you. This chapter gives guidelines to get high marks when your agencies are evaluating their principals.

BEWARE OF AGENTS WHO PROMISE FORMAL REPORTS

A southwest foundry owner was romanced by partners in an eastern agency who promised a paper work blizzard—follow-up reports, engineering critiques, formal forecasts, and monthly account analyses. The owner couldn't wait to get his name on the dotted line so that he could start receiving all these goodies.

It turned out that this was a puffed-up front for a lack of field effort. The partners delighted in working up new forms, writing all kinds of direct mail bulletins, and spending their time dreaming up ways to stay dry during the rainy season. The result was that the owner received no orders . . . and no reports.

Agents should have good professionally prepared letterheads and literature, but check carefully when they start looking more like a public relations firm than a sales agency.

WHY LONGEVITY COUNTS

Sales managers who jump from agent to agent seeking to find the ultimate salesperson lose that one indefinable asset that can eventually mean improved sales results—familiarity. Familiarity is essential to the seller of goods: He must be familiar not only with the product he sells but with the company whose products he sells. Only after years of working with a principal can an agent confidently answer most questions a buyer will ask about the company's products and policies.

When you are tempted to change, try staying with your present agencies. Work on improving their weaknesses while benefiting from their strengths, and watch sales results improve as the familiarity factor goes to work for you.

COMPATIBILITY OF PRODUCTS

There's a Texas agent who sells everything from bath towels to diesel engines successfully. But he's an outstanding exception to the rule. Usually this would be an extremely risky operation for his principals. But in this case, the agent has balanced these various lines with imagination and a tremendous personal drive.

The closer your product line is to other lines your agents are carrying—providing there's no glaring conflict—the better luck you'll have. Compatibility means crossbreeding: the ability to fill a customer's needs from one of the several lines your agent carries. And crossbreeding is the basic strength of the agency method of selling.

Caution: A little conflict can't hurt. Don't get upset if your agent asks about handling another firm with some slight product overlap. Many sales managers have sacrificed an agent's effectiveness by adhering strictly to a policy of noncompetitiveness in their agent's other lines.

The most important factor is the compatibility of the agent's lines. An agent who calls on too many companies for too many types of products dilutes his effectiveness at any one customer. When he can offer a close range of different products, he is more valued by the buying influences at his customers' plants—and will be a more valuable agent for you.

"BOY, IS HE A LOUSY AGENT . . ." TRUE OR FALSE?

Probably false. If an agent is in business and is financially solvent, he's probably a good agent for someone, but maybe not for you.

It takes a lot to survive in the agency business. If you've appointed someone from lower Transylvania and can't figure out when the orders will start coming in, you're not alone. Many sales managers have the same problem.

Most agents, in order to survive, will concentrate on any line that pays their rent, electricity, and travel expenses. If you have no existing business in the agent's area, he may relegate your product line to the back burner until he can afford to do some pioneering for you. This is tough to take but true. If you want to improve results, try a small retainer, attractive pricing, or perhaps concentrated field trips to his area. If you help him, he can afford to help you.

HOW TO GAUGE YOUR PERFORMANCE

Are you performing up to your potential? Are you getting the most out of your agents? Could you do better?

These are haunting questions for the average sales manager because there are no definitive answers. How can you tell if you're accomplishing the maximum when you have no basis for comparison?

Sales managers in competing companies have the same problem, but they're not going to confide in you because too much is at stake. In the meantime, you continue with your agency sales program doing your best to increase sales—the ultimate goal of every sales manager.

>>>→ *IDEA IN ACTION*   The real judges of your performance—your agents—are as close as your telephone, but don't bother to call them because it will be hard for them to be perfectly candid with you. To a degree you control their income, and if pressed for an answer, they may give you one. But it will probably consist of platitudes and compliments rather than an honest and frank appraisal. Yet, through their day-to-day experiences with eight or nine different sales managers, they're the best judges of effective sales leadership and, chances are, they've already ranked you.

Although it's hard to determine your ranking by your own agents, there is a way to get some helpful advice from other agents independent of you. These agents will be able to analyze your techniques and procedures and aid you in an honest self-appraisal.

>>>→ *HOW TO DO IT*   Find an agent who is servicing another industry—one not too far removed from yours. If you don't know of someone who fits this description, ask your purchasing agent to introduce you to one or two agents who call on him. Make sure he understands that you'd like to visit with those he considers professionals.

Buy the agent lunch or dinner and lay out your program. Show how you appoint agents, how you pay them, what incentives you use, and how you terminate them. Ask for an honest critique, and answer the agent's questions honestly.

Agents love to give advice, and if your choice should be a former sales manager, so much the better. His comments will be doubly helpful. Having worked at your job he'll identify with you, and his comments will be relevant and to the point.

Selling through manufacturers' representatives is a constant challenge, and trying to figure out your effectiveness is extremely difficult. Don't be afraid to ask for help.

SHOULD YOU APPOINT A BIG OR SMALL AGENCY

If you're a large company with good existing business in the agent's area, consider how much attention you'll get from each type of agency.

A small agency is almost guaranteed to give your line a lot of attention, particularly if you're one of its biggest commission producers. You'll be a big factor in the success of the smaller agency, so its personnel must keep active for you. On the other hand, you may be one of several good lines a larger agency handles, and you'll get average attention from its salespeople—but you may get average attention in a lot more places.

Caution: This is a difficult decision for most sales managers, but by and large they tend to go with the larger agency. By doing so, they're taking less of a chance and can't be faulted by company management if it doesn't work out well—they've gone with the biggest and the best. Many sales managers, however, have been pleasantly surprised with the steady results received from smaller agencies.

WHEN TO REPLACE A REPRESENTATIVE WITH A DIRECT SALESPERSON

At what income level should you terminate your agent and hire a direct salesperson—one who would be an employee of the company?

Apparently something is right with the relationship when this question comes up. You obviously have worked well with your agent and he has worked well with you since his commissions are approaching the point where you're wondering if, for economic reasons, it would be better to have a direct salesman.

The question is, why break up a winning team? It's so difficult in these competitive times to find the right combination, a combination that can develop sales in an area to the degree that makes it necessary to consider alternative methods of selling because commissions are too high.

>>>→ *IDEA IN ACTION*   The one big advantage that you have going for you—and that you may not have with a direct salesperson—is the agent's permanence in the territory. He's not going to leave that area (he has too much to lose) so he'll be around selling for you for a long time—if you'll let him. On the other hand, almost any direct person you hire is subject to overtures from competitors, particularly if he's good. You may find that you've saved $30,000 in commissions but spent $20,000 to train a new salesperson—for somebody else. And he may not be as good as the agent you had in the first place.

Sure, if commissions are too high and he's not putting on an extra person, talk to him about it or negotiate a slight change in the commission structure. But don't jump off the deep end without giving it a lot of thought.

Another real danger of terminating a representative who's doing an exceptional job is that if an agent is successful in building up a good business for you in the area, he's perfectly capable of doing the same thing for a competitor. Perhaps he'd rather stay with you. But if you take away his livelihood, it's only natural that he will seek out a competitor or take one on that's been after him all along.

There are times when termination is called for. If the greater sales are due mainly to the company's efforts in selling, promotion, and advertising and the agent makes only token efforts but reaps the benefits, then it's time to say goodbye. But make sure this is really the case before sending the cancellation notice.

QUARTERLY QUESTIONNAIRES LET YOU KNOW HOW YOUR PERFORMANCE STACKS UP

Getting feedback from the field may be one of the toughest jobs you have, and it won't improve much unless you do something about it.

Caution: Although agents realize the importance of feedback, your problem is coaxing them to sit down and compose a letter providing you with necessary information. Most agents resent the time this takes from their selling and abhor this type of detail. Therefore, they tend to set it aside for later and never get it done.

To make it easy for them and assure yourself the needed feedback, do most of the work yourself. If you're following up a quote, put all the information on the form—customer name, date of quote, parts covered—then ask important questions such as: Were we competitive? Was our delivery promise OK? Leave blanks so that the agents can check off the appropriate answer.

Also, specify a return date; it creates urgency. This technique works in direct mail and it can work for you. Give them a two- or three-week deadline and you'll find more feedback coming through.

"HOW ARE WE DOING?"

Have you ever taken the time to ask your representatives what they think of your company's performance? Probably not. Part of this stems from management's natural antipathy toward upward communication.

This is a common fault within companies. Management people are often reluctant to open the communication door for fear that the comments they hear won't be favorable . . . and some of them won't be. On the other hand, you can't improve poor performance if you don't know what the problems are and how they're affecting your company's reputation in the field.

An easy way to get started is to send your agents a questionnaire asking for their frank appraisal of all aspects of the company's performance as it affects them and their customers. You may pick up a few good ideas.

WHAT'S YOUR BATTING AVERAGE?

If a professional baseball player consistently hits over .350, he'll probably be paid several hundred thousand dollars a year and ultimately be inducted into the Baseball Hall of Fame. If a sales manager bats at this average, he may lose the key to the executive washroom.

We're talking, of course, about the success rate you have with your sales agents. If out of ten agents you have only three or four who are truly producing up to your expectations, then you're batting between .300 and .400. This doesn't appear to be a satisfactory level for a firm using manufacturers' representatives to sell its products. Yet it really isn't too bad.

A top-notch agents' sales program may produce a .500 average and a truly exceptional one may reach .600, but frankly the average is lower. Most sales managers have about 40 percent of their agents performing at the rate the company deems satisfactory. So don't feel too bad if you're in this category.

Why such a low average? There are several reasons, as follows:

• Agents are generally excellent salespeople. But like direct salespeople, they're not all superstars, so you'll have to have a few top producers and some that are merely average.

• Unless a company manufactures a specialty product, it may truly be competitive only in its regional area rather than on a national scale. A distant representative may be one of the best salespeople in his area, but can't sell a product that isn't competitive.

• An agent will always perform best for the company that motivates him most effectively, whether it be through generous commissions, competitive prices, or on-time deliveries. If your company doesn't provide the proper incentives to gain his attention, he may concentrate on other principals' products with resultant below-average returns for you.

• Perhaps you really don't have the best agent available in each territory, but then the best agent may already be working for your competitor and there's not too much you can do about that if the competitor keeps him happy.

These are just a few of the reasons why it may appear that you have just an ordinary agent sales group, and it's difficult to improve the average. Yet it's worth trying because just one agent producing at a higher rate than normal can increase your company's sales by several hundred thousand dollars.

A few hints for improved performance include better interviewing techniques when contracting for agents' services, more communication, closer field assistance, productive sales meetings, and good service backup. You'll find that improving one or two of your company's weaker points may just be enough to raise the batting average of your entire representative salesforce.

HOW DO YOUR TOP AGENTS SELL?

If your fortunes are similar to those of other sales managers using agents, you have several doing an outstanding job and the balance performing about average. Have you ever tried to find out why this difference exists?

Allowing for territorial inconsistencies, such as trying to sell snowmobiles to Texans, there are often widely varying practices used by agents, and some are much more successful than others.

⟫→ *HOW TO DO IT*   On your next few trips into the field, pay close attention to how each agent sells your goods. Does one make appointments only with purchasing people or does he try to get technical personnel involved? Does another push other principals' wares in addition to yours, thereby diluting the effectiveness of each sales call?

The purpose of this analysis is twofold. First, if you can discover why some agents are so successful with your line, perhaps you can pass along their secrets to the rest of your group. Second, if there are certain personality types that seem to be able to sell your products easily, try to spot the same traits in candidates for new territories.

WHAT DO YOUR AGENTS THINK ABOUT YOU?

Ed Koch, the mayor of New York, has a habit of asking people he meets, "How'm I doin?" Some people tell him great and some tell him off. Either way, the mayor is sharp enough to realize that running a city requires him to stick out his neck once in a while. Running a network of agents calls for the same courage.

Most manufacturers ask their agents to submit reports on customer and prospect sales activity. However, they seldom ask them how they shape up as principals. Those who do claim that they have gotten good information, even when it hurts, have built an agent force on trust and understanding.

A quarterly reporting system in which you ask your agents to rate your performance as a principal not only establishes you as an open and progressive company, it provides you with the kind of information you need to keep your agent salesforce in strong shape.

The following are some points you should cover:

1. *Promotion.* Ask your agents to tell you how they rate your advertising, publicity, and trade show program in general. This is not the time to ask them to nit-pick each inquiry. All you want to know is if the program is on target from the agents' point of view.

2. *Follow-up letters, phone calls, visits, requests for quotations, and expediting.* Ask them if they are getting what they need when they need it.

3. *Quality of follow-up.* Your agents may get their answers in a hurry, but can they depend on them?

4. *Product delivery.* If your delivery is off schedule, it's the agent who usually catches the flack. Ask them to rate you on this score. Have you lost business because of late deliveries?

5. *Financial facts.* Most principals pay before the customer pays. If there is an opening in this chain of communications, the agent may be able to close it. But you'll never know unless you ask.

6. Think of specific activities that relate to your business and include them in your questionnaire.

When you have this information, do something with it besides gloat or lick your wounds. Thank the agents who gave you high marks and contact those who feel that problems exist. This is the kind of cooperation that builds trust and profits for everyone.

IDENTIFYING OUTSTANDING AGENCIES

Outstanding agencies, whether one-person, or multi-person, are a reflection of the individual at the top. Some sales managers may think of these high achievers as oddballs, but most wouldn't trade them for ten ordinary agents. According to sales psychologists, here are some of the characteristics that top performers have:

- Very high drive and energy levels. They frequently work twelve-hour days and are thought of as workaholics. But they enjoy every minute of it.

- They are selling all of the time. When they aren't selling customers your products, they will be "selling" you. We use the word in quotes in a positive way. They are super enthusiastic and generally have many ideas they will pass along to you.

- Even though most of them give the impression of being extremely self-confident, they are like all the rest of us—they need to be praised! Don't lay it on if it isn't deserved, but when a job has been done well, be sure to let them know and, if possible, do it publicly.

- They tend to dominate a sales situation. If you make buddy calls with your agents, you can make the most of the team effort by playing the subordinate role. Let the agent have the floor and provide support when it's called for.

- They pile up records and like to have them acknowledged. This doesn't mean that the usual sales contests will double your sales through agencies. But it does mean that you should provide goals (not quotas) and help all of your agencies achieve the records that help to build pride in achievement.

- They build long-lasting relationships but not at the sacrifice of bowing to unreasonable demands. Treat your agencies as a joint venture and you will get their best effort.

HAVE YOUR AGENTS JUDGE YOUR PERFORMANCE

One sales manager we know sticks out his neck once a quarter. "I get some bruises, some pats on the back, and some answers. I just don't know how to evaluate," he said. "But I will tell you this: Since I started asking my agents to tell me how we rate, I've had fewer problems and a hell of a lot more cooperation." This man is convinced that knowing the good and the bad is the best way for agents and principals to make progress.

You will need to know how your agents evaluate your performance on matters that mean a lot to them. When you know both sides of the story, you will be in a position to help your agents and yourself grow and prosper.

⋙→ *HOW TO DO IT* We have reproduced the questions manufacturers like answered most about themselves. Not all of the questions will be applicable to every reader. And you will probably have a few questions that will be meaningful only to you and your agent sales network. In other words, you do not have to use every question listed. Choose those that relate to your needs, add those that are specific to your operation, and judge the responses accordingly.

Let's take a look at the questions before we discuss the evaluation process.

Principal Evaluation Questionnaire

1. Have we supplied you with complete, comprehensive, and practical product literature?
2. Do we reply promptly to your questions and requests?
3. Are the case histories and application information we send you helpful?
4. Have we kept you well-enough informed on our product development programs?
5. Are we keeping you up to date on the competitive situation as we see it at the factory?
6. Are all our policies spelled out, clear, and enforced equitably?
7. Are our advertising and product publicity inquiries worthwhile, well-screened, and sent to you in time for you to make the most of them?
8. Are our visits to your territory helpful?
9. Are the people at the factory who are assigned to work with you as helpful as they could be?
10. Do you feel that our field reporting system is practical and helpful?
11. Do you feel that your comments are given fair consideration by those at the factory to whom you submit them?
12. Is our commission system in keeping with those used by other manufacturers you represent?
13. Is the agreement we have made with you comparable with agreements you have made with other manufacturers?
14. Are our customer service policies effective?
15. Is our credit policy practical?
16. Do the people at the plant level with you when there are problems?
17. How effective is our Rep Council?

How to Use and Evaluate the Questions

1. When you prepare your questionnaire, use a 1 to 9 rating scale. One will be the lowest rating you can get, 5 is average, and 9 is a winner.

2.   Any score is difficult to interpret and use in its absolute form. You will be interested in the scores you get on the first questionnaire you send to your agents, but the real worth of this system is the differential view you will get from one rating period to the next. The sales manager we quoted sends out his questionnaire four times a year. This is a good frequency. Enough time elapses between forms for change to take place, and it's not too frequent to bother your agents with more paper work.

3.   Some manufacturers prefer to have their questionnaires answered anonymously. They feel that they will get more honest answers. This may be true; however, you will rarely have the same problems and positive events occurring with each of your agents. If all are to benefit, you should know who is speaking through the checkmarks on the questionnaires. However, you should assure your agents that their responses—good and bad—will be welcomed and not used against them.

4.   Be sure to communicate with your agents after each evaluation period. Remember that this is a two-way street. Your agents want to know if you are serious about solving the problems they will identify for you in their responses. If it appears that your questionnaire is merely a red herring, you will not only get very little out of future requests, you will lose the respect of your agents.

5.   Act to solve the problems that have been identified and move quickly to spread the word about the successes you spot in the responses. Information is only of value if you and your agents use it.

DO YOU HAVE STRONG AGENT APPEAL?

Not all agents are created equal; the same equation holds for manufacturers. It's like any human relations problem—you relate more effectively to some people than you do to others.

There are certain manufacturer characteristics that agents respond to which make them more productive. Call it personality chemistry or define it in terms of specific, observable actions, but when you know and understand these elements, you will greatly enhance your agent relationships. We're willing to bet that you will find that agents you perceive as being the most productive for you are those for whom you have been doing all or many of the items in the following list. In a sense, this is an inventory of your agent appeal. But it's not a popularity contest, it's an inventory of activities that help make your agents productive.

1.   You screen your advertising, publicity, and trade show inquiries and don't send the other slush with the request that your agents do the dog-work research. And you don't insist on detailed reports on all inquiries sent to their offices. You just request information on promising leads.

2.   You provide strong marketing communications backup: catalogs, data sheets, product application stories, press releases for use specifically in an agent's territory, current price sheets.

3.   Your pricing is realistic. It may be higher than the competitors, but if it is, you can justify the difference with quality, service, and delivery. Or at least you can justify the price relative to a specific competitive situation.

4.   You provide quotes on time, you immediately follow up phone quotes with written confirmations, and you respond to all requests promptly, thoroughly, and courteously.

5.   You provide product and application training—not the usual sales training baloney that insults successful professionals.

6.   You consult with your agents on product development, asking for suggestions concerning the potential for ideas that are on your drawing board.

7.   All of your policies are enforced equally with all of your agents.

8.   You deliver on time. If you can't make it when the customer wants it, you level with the agent and try to work out the problem realistically.

9.   You accept the loss of income when you appoint an agent in a territory that was previously factory covered until the agent can get going. In other words, you don't withhold house accounts.

10.   You accept the fact that your sales support budget will go up as you appoint more agents, and you don't try to shortchange other agents to maintain a fixed budget.

11.   You pay your commissions on time. And when distributors are involved, you pay discounts promptly.

12.   As your agent network grows, you don't lose personal contact with any of them.

Companies that can answer yes to all or many of these characteristics seldom have any trouble getting cooperation and sales from their agents. Those manufacturers who seem to complain about their agents are usually those who set down and enforce rigid rules with no thought as to the flexibility of the marketplace or of the individual differences between agents.

JUDGE YOUR AGENTS BY EVERYTHING THEY DO

Today, the bean counters have the reins in many businesses. When it comes time to review the agent salesforce, they often rank the top ten and replace the others simply because they see nothing but the bottom line.

It takes more than sales to measure the full value of an agent. Obviously, your goal is to make as much money as you can, but that goal is best reached when you consider everything your agents are doing when evaluation time rolls around. Here are some points to consider:

•   *Agency development.* Has the agency grown in terms of staff, facilities, selling skills, or whatever?

• *Market development.* Has the agent expanded his or her basic markets, as well as expanded into new areas? New markets involve a certain amount of risk, but without trying, you and your agents run the risk of kicking dead horses.

• *Territory development.* Even if your agent is bringing in a lot of business and you are pleased, you should know what he or she has done to expand the territory's potential. You can help by pinpointing prospects which turn up in your advertising responses that seem to have potential.

REVIEWING YOUR AGENT SUPPORT TEAM

One agent passed along a horror story about a principal's support system. "I had been working on the project for over two months," the agent said. "The guys in sales had done their job getting me price and delivery, but I was waiting for word from engineering on a minor modification to meet the customer's spec. I was told to call on a certain day to get the information from a specific person in the engineering department. When I called, the guy was out of the office on a field trip and hadn't given the information I needed to anyone else." To make a long story interesting— and sad: The agent who had the sale in the palm of his hand lost the order to a competitor because a member of the manufacturer's support team let him down.

In every business there are jobs that have to be done on time and correctly. Handling the field support of an agency salesforce is often left to people lower on the table of organization than those who originally set the policy. Much of this work is routine—sending sales leads, responding to requests for literature, and so on. Despite the repetitive nature of the work, it has to be done on time if your sales agencies are to succeed.

The following are some guidelines you can use to perform a good review of your agency support team:

1. Which of the agency support functions within your organization are most important to you and to your agents? The answers to this question will vary widely from company to company. For example, some companies and their agents live or die on the rapid fielding and follow-up of advertising inquiries.

2. On-time responses to requests for quotations are especially necessary, and a one-week foul-up in either of these areas could result in one week of lost sales for such a company. These functions may be of minor importance in other companies. It's important for you to know which support functions are vital and to place all the orders in rank order.

3. You should know whether these functions are being adequately covered now and if they are being covered by the best-qualified people. Often routine support functions are assigned to juniors or less-qualified people. When this is the case, these people should be well supervised. Remember that the job of packing and shipping literature to an agent may be dull and boring, but it has to be done— and done on time. In this case, the person doing the packing and shipping should be carefully supervised.

4. Do you have backup personnel trained and available? No business can afford full redundancy, but everyone on your agency support team should have another person in the company who can pitch in on overloads or take over during an absence. And it pays to hold "fire drills" once in a while. If any of your backup people are a little sloppy, have the person with the full-time responsibility for the job do some refresher training right away!

5. Know which jobs must be done regularly and which are done only when the need arises. Understanding this will help with your manpower planning and will ensure that your agents get the support they need when they need it.

Poking into routine operations may not appeal to you, but you really should know the status of your agency support system. If you don't have the time or feel that it might be difficult to pick up the clues you need inside, get the facts from those who live at the other end of the lifeline—the agents themselves. Don't make a big deal out of it, and don't give the impression that you are on a big mission. But you can get a lot of very good insight on the effectiveness of your inside agency support system right from the people who are being supported.

To give you a running start on solving internal support problems, you might want to make a checklist of the services performed by your support team and get the following information for each item:

1. Is the job vital for day-to-day operations?
2. Is the job done regularly or occasionally?
3. Who has primary responsibility for the job?
4. Who is the backup person?
5. When was the last time the backup person did the job or had refresher training?

When you have your own list, use it! First, make sure that all management people who interact with the sales department and the agency salesforce have a copy of the list. Second, provide a copy of the list to each of your agents. If the agent we just mentioned had a copy of such a list, he might have been able to find someone with the information he needed.

THE BOTTOM LINE IS ONLY ONE MEASURE OF SUCCESS

"Top management thinks more of the bottom line than they should. Sure, you have to make a profit, but there's a lot more to success with an agency team than just black ink on the balance sheet." These are the feelings of a lot of marketing people. Success is not something that is determined once a year on the final statement. It's a succession of accomplished goals in a variety of marketing areas.

Too often, sales managers running agency networks judge their own personal performance and are judged by management only by the profits they turn in. It's part of the short-range-goal myopia that has gripped so many companies in the past few years. With the economy looking up now, we hope that the long view will be taken and that sales managers will turn to activities that do more than turn in just good quarters. Look at some of the long-range activities that build strong agency teams.

1. *Territory expansion.* The 80–20 rule may keep some accountants happy for a time, but when 80 percent of your business comes from 20 percent of your customers, there's bound to be trouble sooner or later. Smart sales managers not only urge their agencies to do more business with their present customers, but they also do everything they can to help them develop the territory. The sales managers who pushed their agencies to sell existing customers harder during the past few bad years learned very quickly that inventory had a way of piling up on customers' shelves. When this happened, buying seldom slowed down—it came to a jarring halt. However, those sales managers who took the opportunity to work with their agencies in territorial development not only weathered bad times but they will reap increased benefits in the now-strengthening economy.

How can you help your agencies develop territories? First, you can promote more aggressively. Expand your advertising program, take part in the better trade shows, and spend time in the field with your agencies finding out just what they need. There are many things that will collectively benefit all of your agencies. But remember that each agent has his or her own timetable and priorities. Tune in to each one of these elements and help make them happen.

2. *Agency staff development.* It's not too difficult for a sales manager to make a swing through the territories, hit the high spots, and bump up sales. But agents who feel that principal sales managers are helpful all report that those who take the time to work with agency salespeople in the field are the most productive. Skip the sales training and emphasize product and competitive knowledge. Hit the road with the field people and handle the customers' problems as an agency/manufacturer team. Discover the needs of customers and the needs of the agency salespeople who are on the firing line.

3. *Sales lead qualification.* It's no trick to run an ad offering a free catalog and pull a few thousand leads. But the real trick is to qualify these leads in a way that makes it practical for your agencies to follow up. Don't judge your success by the number of qualification forms you get back; use the amount of new business that results from the leads that have been qualified before they were sent to the field.

4. *Non-sales goals.* So far, we have talked about things that can be measured directly. However, there are a lot of personal things you can do that will help the bottom line but can never be measured. For example, have you really made your agents your friends? You don't have to be buddy-buddy if that isn't your style. But just doing the things one friend does for another can be very important. For example, if you read business publications regularly, the chances are that you will spot items of interest. Why not send the clips? If you spot an item that might help one of your agencies sell products manufactured by another principal, send it along. Most sales managers spend an inordinate amount of time trying to get the lion's share of

their agencies' time. Throwing business their way for one of their own lines shows that you are really interested in them and not just what they can do and are doing for you. This will do more to cement relations than just about any of the motivational management you read about in the erudite business journals.

There's more to achieving success with agencies than just hard-nosed management. Manufacturers who build strong relationships with their agencies get much more than sales in return. They get marketing input, product ideas, and personal advice that is seldom offered by agencies who are driven by principals with nothing more than bottom-line thinking.

HOW TO USE PERFORMANCE REVIEWS

If you're like most manufacturers, you're uncomfortable about doing performance appraisals. Just remember that the agencies you're reviewing are probably more uncomfortable—no matter how well they have done. The following guidelines will make it a lot easier for you to do the job and will have an added benefit: You will not only get an idea of the level of performance, you will also have some ideas that will help enhance performance.

1. Concentrate on specifics. Any kind of agency performance evaluation that doesn't zero in on the details of the job that was *expected* to be done and the job that *was* done will be an exercise in futility. We all have our biases, and when these personal points creep into an agency appraisal, you're in for trouble. If the agency was expected to open a new market and you had specified the results you wanted, stick to the assigned task and the results. If the agency was to do telephone qualifications of the advertising leads that you had selected, stick to those facts.

2. If you find trouble spots, identify them, but then go on to stress solutions. Harping on the problem doesn't do anything for either of you.

3. Provide the agencies being appraised with immediate and accurate feedback. If you remember your school days, it was agony waiting for test results. It's the same for an agency waiting for its performance evaluation.

4. If possible, do mini-evaluations regularly, rather than doing it just once a year. Little problems tend to be magnified when they are left to run their course for a year. Sure, if there are big problems that you can spot without doing an evaluation, you should do something about them immediately. But most people tend to let small problems go without saying anything about them. By the time an annual review comes around, these small problems really loom large. It's the burr-under-the-saddle problem in spades.

5. When you discuss your appraisal with your agencies, keep your suggestions and evaluations positive. Rather than saying, "Here's where you had real problems," it's much better to say, "Here's where you could have done better." Remember, an appraisal isn't an occasion for humiliation; it's a situation where you and your agencies discuss ways that both of you can benefit from some changes, if they are necessary.

HOW DID FORMER AGENTS LIKE BEING ON YOUR TEAM?

Agents are not employees, but when agents terminate their contracts, you might draw upon a technique used by human resource professionals when they must deal with employees who quit. The technique is the post-termination interview, and it can be done face to face or with a brief questionnaire. The goal of the interview is to gain insight that might prevent future agency defections. If you take this step, don't do it upon termination; wait a month or two. Even if the parting was amicable, there is a lot of emotion in the situation. After a few months, the former agents can give you a better picture of the problem and help you avoid the same problem with other agencies.

Here are the most important questions you can ask:

1. When we began working together, were your responsibilities explained clearly to you?

2. Did we make clear our responsibilities to you?

3. Was the compensation program clearly explained?

4. Do you feel that the product training and market indoctrination we gave you was sufficient to do the job we expected of you?

5. Were our people helpful to you? Did they respond to your requests on time? Did they get the answers you needed?

6. When you had problems at the factory, were you able to resolve them through the people to whom you reported? Did you have to seek the help of other individuals at the plant?

7. Would you elaborate on your reasons for terminating your agreement?

8. If you are taking on a line competitive to ours, would you tell us what we could have done to maintain our relationship?

9. We would appreciate it if you would comment on what you feel we could do to help the other agents on our team succeed.

All of these questions but the last are closed-ended. That is, they require direct answers. The last question is open-ended and allows the agent to open up. Use the answers in this section to check what was said in response to the closed-ended questions. You should get a good picture of any problems that might not have been made apparent at the time of leaving.

HOW TO CREATE A SET OF STANDARDS TO EVALUATE TOTAL AGENCY PERFORMANCE

"I've got guys making a bundle on my line who are coasting in fat territories, and others who barely get by breaking their chops in thin areas. The first group needs a kick in the pants and the second needs all the help I can give them. But how do I judge the performance of each?" This is a seasoned sales manager talking about his network of agents. He's not a beginner; he's been an agent himself. And he's saying something that is a common problem.

Caution: Most territorial sales data show just the tip of the iceberg. And using the data without careful analysis will tell you nothing about the reasons for the problems—or the successes. The high producer may be contributing less to your profits than those with lower sales. It's not enough to look at sales figures relative to territorial potential, you've got to establish a yardstick that gets rid of the apples and oranges.

⟫→ *HOW TO DO IT*   Begin by establishing your own objective standards. The goal of this system is to create a picture of successful agency performance that can be used as a guide to help evaluate your current agents, as well as define the characteristics of those you are considering using.

In order to create objective standards, you should take the following steps:

1. Identify the component elements of the task of selling your products.
2. Separate those elements that can be measured objectively.
3. Set up a system to measure and record each agent's performance on each criterion.
4. Create a weighting system for each element that relates to your business, your goals, and the unique conditions of your business and market.

Remember that you are evaluating independent agents, not employees. You can dig into a staff salesperson's work habits just about all you want. However, you're on shaky ground when you stick your nose into the business of an agent. But when you seek your agents' cooperation by assuring them that the effort is for everyone's benefit, your work will be a lot easier.

Every company will have different requirements, but these characteristics seem to be most important with those selling through agents:

1. Product knowledge
2. Preparation for sales calls
3. Ability to do basic prospecting
4. Sales presentation ability
5. Service and follow-up
6. Competitive tracking

Establish a rating scale for each requirement. This can be done any number of ways, but a simple one-to-ten system for each point will work best.

Caution: You must have a base line. Any scaling system must refer to a standard, otherwise the numbers you come up with will have little value. The best way to do this is to give the test to your successful agents, those who have been on board for a relatively long period of time and have been successful by your standards. Even though you are starting out with the winners, you will probably turn up some deficiencies you never knew existed. Don't let this discovery throw you. No one is perfect. It's a combination of characteristics that make for success, not necessarily top scores on every item. You will find that the system will not only help you evaluate your new agents, it will aid you in your work with those who have been with you for a long time. Above all, keep the scores to yourself and don't use them to play one agent off against another.

Establish economic performance curves for each agent. Because each territory will represent different dollar potential, your curves must be made on a relative, rather than an absolute, basis. In other words, convert dollars to some units as they relate to territorial potential. A scale of one to ten, again, is most helpful.

Example: Let's look at a typical situation. The first curve shows a typical growth situation for an agent over a five-year period. During the first year, a lot of learning took place and sales were relatively flat. Then, with advanced product knowledge and the payoff of early effort, sales shot up. After this, there is the usual steady climb you'd expect to see in a territory in which an agent has control and is exploiting the market.

Compare the sales growth curve with the rating data. Note the shape of the curve based on the ratings given by the sales manager on the six major characteristics over the same period. The trends correlate and the data can be used to evaluate the relative success of other agents when the same steps are taken with each.

The information shown in these curves represents only the first five years of a typical agent's service with a company. The same approach can be taken year after

		Years				
		1	2	3	4	5
(1)	**Dollars, adjusted for individual territories**					
(2)	**Measured standards** Product knowledge	3	4	8	9	9
	Preparation	5	5	7	7	8
	Prospecting	5	5	6	6	6
	Presentations	7	7	8	8	8
	Follow-up	4	6	8	9	9
	Competitive tracking	8	8	8	8	9
	TOTAL SCORES	32	35	45	47	49
(3)	**Total Scores (above) plotted**					

year, as long as exactly the same standards are applied each time. If, for example, the dollar curve showed a decline and it could not be attributed to an outside event such as the shutdown of a major customer, the problem might be spotted in the standard measurement.

There is always a danger in using tabulated data only. There is usually much more to consider than just observable information. However, with this data and the use of good subjective observation, the manager using a network of agents should be able to make sound decisions.

Here are some of the subjective factors you should consider:

1. Is the agency well motivated? Is the owner anxious to get and keep your account?

2. Is there a good personal match with those in the agency and the individuals at corporate headquarters?

3. Does the agency do more than sell? That is, do they provide helpful feedback whether or not it's required?

4. Does the owner as well as the staff accept direction when it's needed?

5. Does every person in a selling capacity at the agency have top selling skills, and do they continue to develop by reading, attending seminars, and taking courses?

6. Is the agency and all its employees efficient? How fast do they react when you need help? Are they able to discern between activities that make money and those that just waste time?

Now *you've* got to be put to the test. Any agency/principal relationship is a two-way street. You simply cannot judge an agent's performance without evaluating your own.

ASSESS AGENCY POTENTIAL AS WELL AS PERFORMANCE

Manufacturers' agencies, like the manufacturers that sell through them, are constantly evolving. Nothing stays the same in any business. Potential is as important a part of agency evaluation as is current performance. An East Coast sales manager helps his agency team develop by assessing their potential and then placing each agency into a specific category. Here's his system:

• *The Hard Workers*—According to the sales managers who conceived these categories, most agencies fall into this category. This is a profile. The "hard worker" agency, as the name implies, does a lot of work. The agency is productive. However, most of the agencies in this classification seldom grow into big agencies. In some cases, there is no need for the agency to grow or for the principal to have a bigger and bigger agency in the territory. But if expansion is necessary, the hard worker agencies generally respond to their principals' growing needs when they are given specific assignments and are asked to report regularly on their progress. This kind of direct involvement reveals the potential for both parties and thus growth takes place.

• *The Super Stars*—These are the agencies that were usually in the hard worker classification during the first few years of their business existence. Once on their feet, they get a second wind and frequently have a big impact on the growth of their principals. Any assessment of agency potential should include watching for the signs of a "super star" in the making. These agencies are staffed by motivated people. They stir up a lot of activity—and they look for considerable feedback from their principals. It's often easy to misinterpret this need for feedback as insecurity. But when you look below the surface, you'll see that the information that they are looking for is specific and is needed to make important decisions within the agency.

• *The Problem Agencies*—In almost all cases, there are agencies with real potential but that are not living up to the potential. Between periodic flashes of spectacular sales behavior, the "problem" agencies seem to slow down. Their performance is inconsistent. Most of the agencies in this category are relatively new and are still feeling their way. Their potential demands that the manufacturer's sales manager take the time to provide them with regular counseling and encouragement. Even when a person has been selling for many years, shifting to running an agency brings on different demands and expectations. The encouraging manufacturer's sales manager who spots the potential and takes the time to help is usually well rewarded for that effort.

• *The Other Agencies*—The "other" agencies make up less than one percent, according to the sales manager who described this system of assessing potential. They may be run by people who shouldn't have gotten into the business or those who are planning to retire but aren't doing anything about agency continuity. This may be the toughest group to deal with. But, there is still considerable potential in their ranks. Frequently, consistent direct counseling will do the trick.

MEASURING AGENCY PERFORMANCE

Manufacturers that have been selling with agencies for a number of years seldom have any problems measuring the performance of their team as a group or as individuals. They have history on their side. However, those just starting out with sales agencies often don't know what to measure when they decide that they must, indeed, measure performance.

It may be a mistake to make money the sole measure when you evaluate agency performance. "We didn't know what we should have measured," a small company president related recently. "Since we base much of our own growth measurement on financially based information, we simply took the same approach when we evaluated our agencies. In our particular case, we should have looked at the number of new accounts the agencies opened, rather than sales volume. In our case, sales volume follows new accounts. Now we know how to factor in the lag and can do the evaluations as they should be done."

• Make sure you know which variables, when measured, will give you information you can use to plan with. It may be, as in the case cited, that the number of new accounts is the most important variable. It may be that just the number of sales calls made can be translated into a performance measure if you have some historical data to work with. But the point is this: Don't assume that increase in sales volume is the only measure by which to judge your agencies.

• Once you have decided how you will measure performance, make certain that the information you use relates to the performance you want to evaluate.

• Measuring performance implies that the information you gather will be used for something. Make sure that you know just how this information will be applied before you begin any measurement work at all. It's a big risk to gather data and then, after reviewing them, decide what you will do with them.

• Be sure that your agencies are aware of your plans and that they not only share in the development of the information but that you share the results with them. Evaluation should be done with an eye to improving things, not with the goal of using the information as a club.

HOW TO CONDUCT PERFORMANCE APPRAISALS OF YOUR MARKETING DEPARTMENT EMPLOYEES

Be sure that performance reviews are thorough and that company management includes reports from the agents the company employee marketing people work with. Agency performance is directly correlated with the performance of manufacturers' salespeople who work with the agencies. Discontent in the marketing ranks finds its way into the field quickly. These suggestions will be especially helpful if your agencies are involved in the performance appraisal process:

• Conduct annual and comprehensive performance appraisals in which you stress personal achievement, productivity, and company loyalty. Input on your salespeople from the agents can often provide interesting highlights on which to make your judgments.

• As a result of your appraisals, set objectives to improve performance, open lines of communication, and improve relations with agencies and the customers of the agencies.

• In addition to gathering your own objective data about your sales employees, ask each to give you their own self-appraisal. Specifically, ask them to tell you how they feel they have performed in terms of managing an agency salesforce. Correlate this information with your own views and the views supplied by your agencies.

• In addition to using the typical review techniques, some personnel professionals suggest that you make visits with the personnel being reviewed. These visits should be made to the agencies in the territory involved and to some of the customers in the territory.

• Input from your agencies should be an important part of performance appraisals of your sales staff. In addition to providing personal information, agencies can often provide feedback you can use to help other marketing people on your staff.

9

Improving Agency Relations with Rep Councils

The rep council is the forum by which you can exchange ideas with your agencies. It's important to recognize that a rep council not be considered as any sort of bargaining agent.

The tips and tactics in the sections that follow will help you make the most of this very practical way of working with agencies. They answer the questions most often asked by those starting rep councils and by those with extensive council experience. You will discover how to set up a revolving board so that it won't be necessary to indoctrinate an entirely new board every year or so. You will have guidelines for planning council meetings to ensure that a maximum amount of work is accomplished in a short period of time. And you will have guidelines to use in setting up an information flow system to keep your other agencies informed of the work done by council members.

Not all agents make good rep council members. In one of the reports in this section, you'll discover how to spot the agents who will be the most productive members of your council. Surprisingly, the most effective members are not always those who are most interested in serving.

THE REP COUNCIL—A BONUS FOR THE MANUFACTURER

Independent advice is often the most valuable type of advice that can be given, as in the case of outside consultants, for instance. Every manufacturer working with agents has the same opportunity to obtain this type of advice, but without the expense that goes along with consultants.

A rep council, consisting of a representative group of your agents, can contribute many relevant suggestions regarding your current and future policies and offer the added advantage of not having to learn your product line.

Example: Chuck Tate, Southeastern Regional Manager of the Smith and Loveless Division of Ecodyne in Lilburn, Georgia, says their rep council is very helpful in providing guidance to sales management on several important topics.

Smith and Loveless has 38 agents throughout the United States and limits its council to 6 to 10 members. They meet on a periodic basis to obtain the views of this experienced field personnel group. Prior to the meeting, members of the council are mailed a proposed agenda, which gives them a chance to formulate suggestions and ideas well in advance of the meeting.

Contrary to some industry practices, council meetings are not held in conjunction with sales meetings. Smith and Loveless feel its council meetings are so important they prefer not to run the risk of having the input diluted by trying to run a sales meeting at the same time.

Another interesting facet of the Smith and Loveless arrangement is that the membership of the council changes, depending upon the subject under discussion. If future marketing plans and new products are up for review, a group of agents well versed on these topics will be invited to company headquarters. A different group may be invited if the subject touches on current practices and policies.

Tate says his company is pleased with its results and intends to continue seeking the independent advice of its agents on a regular basis.

MAKING REP COUNCILS WORK:
THE MECHANICS OF A PROGRAM

The basic key to success in forming an agent group is the careful selection of those representatives who will serve on the council.

>>>→ *WATCH THIS*   When the group is first formed, it's essential to choose agents who have had some longevity with the company. Because this will necessarily be a trial effort, with management casting a wary eye at the suggestions coming from the council, it's important that the initial representatives chosen to serve are familiar with the company's practices and policies.

Avoid appointing newer agents and those who have exhibited an inability to work in harmony with company personnel. The new agents are as yet untried. If they prove to be good company agents over the coming years, then at a later date, they'll be able to contribute to the work of the council.

Most councils meet once a year, usually at a time apart from the annual sales meeting. This imparts a sense of importance to the function of the council, as opposed to holding the meeting in conjunction with the sales meeting. The latter timing downgrades its importance to an afterthought.

Also, adding to the prestige of the council is the absorption of all expenses by the company. If the agents are willing to give up selling time to serve on the council, then the company should contribute toward the entire cost of the meeting.

The beginning or the end of a week is the most opportune time for agents to leave their territory for the council meeting. Midweek sessions kill the entire week for the agents, and they'll be less responsive.

Here are some tips to make your rep councils successful:

- *Optimum:* Three or four members will function effectively. More means members won't feel personally responsible for results. Fewer limits the input.
- Assign definite responsibility to each member.
- Rotate membership on the committee periodically. That provides a steady flow of ideas and breaks up stagnant thinking patterns.
- Set goals. To solve a problem (rather than merely move it elsewhere) aim for specific results. A committee that isn't expected to produce a substantial result, won't.
- Monitor progress. Review the level of cooperation. A committee dominated by one member often produces insignificant results and frustrates other members.
- Set a time limit for work to be completed. Get periodic progress reports if the assignment is a multi-stage one.
- *Recommendation:* If committee proposals are rejected, the reasons for rejection should be explained carefully. If the proposals are accepted, they should be implemented promptly so the committee can see the effect of its efforts.

Setting goals is the one most important assignment to give the committee. To merely meet once a year and have a general discussion is not productive and is a waste of time for both company personnel and council members.

The sales manager can easily develop meaningful assignments for the council by reviewing, at the end of each month, the problems that were the most nagging and difficult to solve, as well as problems that continue to plague him despite the implementation of remedial action. Often council members, with no personal involvement in the day-to-day running of the company, can provide a fresh new outlook to a problem that appears to be unsolvable.

If you choose your council members carefully, you may find that you have a group that possesses a diversified knowledge difficult to hire under any circumstances.

Agents are privy to the policies and philosophies of several companies—their other principals. They may have witnessed successful solutions to some of the very problems you present to the council. Because their success is tied to the success of your company, they have a very real interest in helping you solve your problems. And there is no charge for their council services (aside from expense), a feature that does not apply to paid consultants.

A rep council also gives you flexibility. If one member is not contributing substantially to the work of the council, he can easily be replaced.

Often a member who is not doing a good job never really wanted to serve in the first place and agreed only because of the desire to maintain good relations with your company. Keep in mind that some agents went into their own businesses to escape committee work. Their wishes to not serve on a council should be respected without prejudice.

To get your council started on the right foot, make the first assignments noncontroversial. Later, as you observe the competence and capabilities of council members, you can expand the scope of your assignments. For starters, you may want to consider such topics as:

How does our company stack up against your other principals with respect to sales/service performance; and what suggestions do you have to improve any shortcomings?

Are we missing the boat on any new product ideas?

How often and for how long should the sales manager visit the agents' territories?

What form of company assistance will increase our market penetration in the territories; more technical visits, better pricing, on-time deliveries?

It's mandatory that topics to be discussed be presented to council members a month or more prior to council meetings. This allows each member to give consideration to the assignments and will result in more productive output at the meetings.

Is a rep council for you? That's a decision for you to make. However, judging from the benefits many companies are receiving from their councils, it certainly is worth a try.

HOW TO MAKE REP COUNCILS WORK

Anyone who thinks that rep councils are nothing more than gripe sessions for agents and soapboxes for manufacturers should talk with some of the agents and manufacturers. "Sit on a good council, and you'll wonder why you didn't start one sooner," is the way one manufacturer put it. A long-time successful agent said, "Our job on the council is less to solve the short-term problems than it is to create ideas that will make business easier and more profitable for everyone—the other agents on and off the council as well as the manufacturer." And, as another agent put it, "Even if you don't accomplish as much as you set out to, the rep council is a great place to meet the other members of the team."

Manufacturers who go to the bother and expense of setting up and running rep councils wouldn't do it if they weren't beneficial. They take time and money that others in the organization might like to spend on different projects. However, when a rep council works well, it helps solve problems as well as plan for the future. Remember that a rep council shouldn't be thought of as either a bargaining body or a legislative group. The job of the members is not to solve any one agent's problems but to work on issues that impact on everyone. Individual problems should be handled by the people involved—but not at council sessions.

Getting the Most Out of Your Rep Council

• If you are starting a rep council from scratch, make absolutely sure that your agents know in detail what the goals of the council will be, what is expected of those who serve, and that the purpose of the council is to cement the team into a strong working unit. If you have any hidden agendas in mind, your rep council is doomed. Don't make it an "in" club for your favorites.

- The first agents chosen to be on the council should be those who have been on board for some time and are thoroughly familiar with you, your company, your products, and your markets. Because a new rep council will be feeling its way initially, it's best to have participants who can get down to cases quickly and who have the knowledge and experience needed to make the council effective. Newer and less experienced agents can be appointed later on, after the council has had its sea trials and is a functioning unit.

- Membership in the council should rotate every year or two. However, plan your appointments to make sure that the entire council doesn't retire at once. You will need strong continuity to make it work.

- Even though you won't have every agent on the council at one time, make absolutely sure that every agent knows of the council and its work. Those who claim to get the most out of their councils say that they circulate memos of the meetings to the other agents. Some even seek write-in comments on issues that the council feels are too important to act on alone.

- When you meet, be sure that your company is represented by a senior executive. If your agents take the time to plan for and attend council meetings, those representing your company should be capable of doing more than carrying messages to higher executives.

- How large? It really depends on the size of your agent salesforce. If you have fewer than twenty agents, the council will probably be most effective with no more than four or five members. A larger network should be represented in essentially the same proportion. It's important to note that large councils get cumbersome and less decisive.

- Rep councils should be active all the time, although they may meet only several times a year. The meeting is the place for active interchange, but the time between meetings is when most of the work is done by individual members.

- As we mentioned earlier, specific goals for the work of the council should be established. Carrying this idea to its most effective conclusion, you should also set individual goals for each meeting. If the council is to be effective, this agenda must be sent to the members at least a month before the meeting so that they will be fully prepared to contribute their ideas. Members should also have a voice in establishing the topics to be covered at the meetings. Rep councils are most effective when all the members have done their homework and come thoroughly prepared.

- The expenses are yours. If you bring members to the plant, you should not only pay for their transportation, but you should pick up the food and lodging expenses. Some rep council meetings are held at resorts, but this can smack of rewarding a favored few. Oddly enough, those agents who are most interested in the work of the rep council usually prefer to avoid the resorts and instead attend a one-day solid, productive meeting at the principal's plant.

• Make sure that the topics that are discussed relate to all of the other agents on your team. Council meetings, if they are not managed tightly, can often drift into personal problems faced by individual members, which have no bearing on the agent force as a whole.

• Monitor progress and make sure that everyone knows what the council discussed and what was decided, even if it has little direct effect on the other individuals. First, this is just good communications policy. Second, when nonmembers are aware of what is going on, they will become effective members more quickly when their time comes to serve on the council.

• What are some of the topics most often covered? The competitive picture, new product ideas, sales policies, compensation, training, advertising, sales lead usage, finding good agents, contracts and other legal issues, product liability, plus much more. However, be careful not to let the council turn into a gripe session for the agent members or a podium for your pet problems.

USING THE REP COUNCIL AS AN INNOVATION CENTER

If the corporate culture fosters collaboration and its structure encourages agencies to innovate, manufacturers are likely to get the best of the entrepreneurial output the agency team has to offer.

The rep council can be an extraordinarily powerful system in the hands of insightful management. A few guidelines should be observed in order to make sure that the council operates for the benefit of the agencies, as well as for the manufacturers that establish them. First, you should understand the nature of agency people who are effective rep council members. According to business psychologists, these are among the most important characteristics:

• Good rep council members are comfortable with change. Uncertainties don't make them restless. In fact, when questioned, they usually say they are uncomfortable when everything seems to be running too smoothly. They see unmet needs as opportunities.

• They have a clear vision of their directions. They tend to select projects with long-term potential and usually view setbacks as only temporary.

• They are thorough; they prepare well for meetings and usually have insight into organizational politics that prevents them from being drawn into conflicts that don't involve them—but that could prove fatal to their relationship if they butt in.

• They run their agencies as participative managers. They encourage their employees to work hard and they share the rewards with them.

• They are persistent. They know that most goals can't be achieved overnight.

Researchers—and the practical experience of people who have worked with agencies for many years—have shown that the solution of tricky rep council problems requires not just the opportunity to serve but the incentive to reach beyond the formal constraints of their agencies and the structure of the rep council. Here are some suggestions you can use to create the opportunities for rep council members to be most effective:

- *Create multiple reporting relationships.* When you give your rep council members access to people within your organization whom they wouldn't ordinarily contact, you open the door for the cross pollination that leads to innovation.

- *Ensure a relatively active flow of information.* Most rep councils meet only once or twice a year. But when each member and the corporate contacts stay in touch regularly on topics other than the day-to-day operations, there is a much greater chance of innovative output.

- *Install a reward system that stresses personal efforts.* Far too many manufacturers contact their rep council members only when there are problems. This nit-picking has a very bad conditioning effect, especially when you remember that the agency people don't see and talk with the factory people too often. When every phone, telex, or fax message is negative, you simply won't get the best effort. Let the members know that their efforts are appreciated, and do it regularly.

HOW TO SPOT THE AGENTS YOU WANT ON YOUR REP COUNCIL

A place on your rep council should be more than a reward, although an achieving agency is usually an agency that has a lot to offer a council. These factors are prime in influencing your choice of rep council members: organizational skills; the ability to conceptualize; problem-solving skills; the ability to not only deal with change but to make it work positively; and initiative. Many manufacturers rate conceptualization very high. "I like to work with agents who can identify patterns in things that seem random to others," is the way one manufacturer explained it.

HOW TO BUILD A BETTER REP COUNCIL

"I didn't have the vaguest idea of what a rep council was supposed to do," a relatively new sales manager told us. "Although we did have good agents who wanted the council to succeed," he continued, "my lack of experience made it difficult for them to be most effective." Most people have heard of rep councils and many have taken part in them at one level or another. But since so many people have questions about them, we'd like to outline the elements that lead to success.

The key to building a strong and effective rep council is to create a group personality that is more productive, brighter, and more innovative than the sum of the individual members. This is a common management concept that can be applied to any working group. The difference, though, lies mainly in the coaching ability of the person who will direct the council. He has to be able to elicit dedication and commitment from every member of the council. Here are the steps to building a strong and productive rep council, according to many manufacturers who have done the job.

• *Select members carefully.* The skills of individual members should complement rather than duplicate the strengths of other council members. For example, one member might be a highly imaginative and creative agent who has developed unique and successful ways to promote by direct mail and trade shows. Another might be a highly organized individual who can develop practical systems for order entry and interagency communications. You have to realize, however, that incompatibilities may arise between members with different philosophies and styles of doing business. Your job should not be to keep the peace. You should be the facilitator, recognizing that in group situations there is seldom any gain without conflict. As the runners are fond of saying, "No pain, no gain."

• *Set attainable objectives.* "It's critical to meet with the members to develop a joint statement outlining the council's primary objectives," one sales manager pointed out. "It's important that there be unanimous agreement before the council undertakes any specific projects." This manager explained that he and the rep council set goals with specific dates and identify the methods by which the goals will be accomplished. "It's fine to agree on what has to be done and when it's to be done," he explained, "but unless everyone agrees on the methods that are to be used to accomplish the goals, you may be in for some surprises."

• *Establish the role members will play.* "I prefer to be the facilitator," a marketing VP explained. "However, even in this seemingly passive role, I play a strong hand. I am the guy who steps in when stalemates and conflicts result. And I also take a hand in keeping the projects moving by being in regular contact with the members. I've found that when I keep all council members aware of what the others are doing on projects on which we have agreed, things get done."

• *Develop specific procedures.* Council members will need specific procedures for group interaction and for decision making. For example, you will have to decide whether your council will be more effective through a freewheeling, brainstorming type of organization or a more formal approach.

• *Set up a reporting system.* Rep councils are only effective to the extent that their work, ideas, and suggestions are reported to others. In some cases, that reporting may be limited to you and the members. In other cases, the information may have to be relayed to top management. And in other cases, findings might be beneficial only if all the other agencies on the team are told. The important point here is that reporting systems and networks be decided on early and agreed on by all members of the council.

• *Analyze the proceedings.* A follow-up analysis of rep council activities is critical. "We have each member fill out a questionnaire regarding how well the council worked together to accomplish the goals," the president of a small manufacturing company stated. "We compile the results, distribute copies to the council members, and discuss the conclusions reached. And, of course, the members of the council are thanked publicly for the work they have done." This particular manufacturer reads the results of the council's activity and gives credit to each individual member at his annual sales meeting. "Since all agencies attend the sales meeting, this had an effect that I didn't anticipate when I first did it," he explained. "By letting all the agents know what council members had done, we set standards that new council members try to exceed. Nobody says they have to work harder than the last members, but they do."

  ➤➤➤→ ***OBSERVATION*** Rep councils have always been popular with larger manufacturers who serve their markets with a significant number of sales agencies. However, more and more smaller manufacturers are setting up rep councils. In fact, one manufacturer with five agencies has a two-agent council. We think this is a helpful way to go for everyone.

HOW TO MAKE REP COUNCILS MORE EFFECTIVE

  The usual scenario for running a rep council includes one of the agent members acting as the leader or one of the agent members sharing the leadership with you. Those who seem to get the most out of their rep councils claim that when the other members are allowed to select the leader, the rep council works much better. Group members expect more from those they select to lead, rather than from leaders who are, in a sense, imposed on them. This expectation works positively for all involved in the rep council. "I've seen elected rep council leaders take the job much more seriously than those whom we appointed in the past," a marketing VP related recently.

10

Planning and Running Productive Meetings

Most manufacturers try to run at least one sales meeting a year with their agencies. Needless to say, this can be an expensive proposition, especially if you have a large network of agencies and they are scattered all over the country. The 23-point checklist in this Chapter will not only help you improve your meetings, but it will help you run them more economically.

To be most effective, sales meetings should be planned well in advance. And this planning should include your agencies. The tips in the pages that follow will not only help you determine an effective content and structure for the meeting, but they will help you develop a follow-up system that will multiply the effectiveness of even the most productive meeting.

The most effective sales meetings are those that are actually problem-solving sessions. However, unless properly planned, these sessions can turn into very unproductive gripe sessions. In another section you have all you need to make the most of the problem-solving type of meeting.

BEING FRANK STRENGTHENS BONDS

A Midwestern agent told of an excellent device used by one of his principals that sent the agents home from a sales meeting in good spirits.

The meeting lasted two days and the second day was devoted entirely to the comments and views of the attending agents. They were told to feel free to say anything they pleased about the company and its policies.

They were cautioned that the company might not agree with them or act upon their suggestions, but they were assured that their views would be listened to by company brass and given serious consideration.

A policy of this type can go a long way toward making your representatives feel that their views are important to the company, and it's a definite boost to morale.

ARE YOUR SALES MEETINGS PRODUCTIVE?

Sales meeting questionnaires can tell you a lot. One perceptive sales manager begins his sales meetings by asking each agent to fill out a questionnaire with far-ranging questions—everything from a review of their knowledge on company policies to their familiarity with the company's newest product.

While the first session is being held, his staff quickly compiles the answers, seeking a few clues as to what subjects will be most vital for the meeting's content.

These gems are spotted easily. Any questions that are erroneously answered by more than one or two agents point up that the answers are in doubt, and it may well be that the company hasn't done a good job of agent-briefing in their communications.

This pre-meeting questionnaire helps the sales manager and his assistants concentrate on the topics that most attending agents were not clear about.

INCLUDE SERVICE PERSONNEL IN AGENTS' SALES MEETINGS

Too often, home office participants in agents' annual sales meetings consist of sales personnel and a few other executives and no representatives from other departments. For more effective meetings, try including personnel from other plant functions.

> **»»→ OBSERVATION** Almost every department, in one way or another, is involved with the customer. It may not be a direct involvement, but it's an involvement nevertheless. Having personnel from these other departments meet with your agents can help them better understand the field sales function.
>
> Have you ever noticed how much better performance becomes after a customer with a problem has gone through your plant and met the production people? The same effect can be accomplished by having production, inspection, and purchasing personnel sit in on some of the sessions with your agents. They begin to appreciate the fact that orders do not just wander into the sales department, but that a good deal of hard work is involved in selling.

Also often overlooked are the inside sales correspondents; men and women who are in daily contact with your agents and customers. Make doubly certain this valuable group is in on almost every session.

INVITE OTHERS IN YOUR AGENCIES TO ATTEND
YOUR SALES MEETINGS

Do just the heads of your sales agencies attend your sales meetings? If so, you may be missing out on some valuable input (and output). These people are undoubtedly the ones responsible for some of your present success, but things do change.

Insist that other members of the agencies are included from time to time. Feedback from the agency head to his salespeople may be good, but it's no substitute for firsthand discussions and exchanges of ideas.

Of course, if an agency has ten salespeople, attending your meeting en masse puts a financial strain on somebody—either you or the agency—depending upon who pays the travel expenses. However, having one to three extra attendees from one agency isn't too expensive and will be well worth it.

SALES MEETING TECHNIQUES THAT WORK

If you're not holding at least one sales meeting a year for your agents, you're losing out to the competition. And in this case we don't mean competitors who make the same kind of widgets you do, but rather, the sales managers of other principals your agents represent.

"Selling time" is the name of the game when it comes to manufacturers' agents. The more you can convince your agents that it's profitable to sell your line, the more selling time they'll allocate to your company. One of the methods that's being used by companies to gain this advantage is the annual sales meeting.

Warning: Simply holding a sales meeting is not enough. It has to be a productive session, and it has to provide effective tools for your agents to use in the field.

First, remember that yours is not a captive audience as is the case with direct-employee salespeople. Agents will quickly determine if their time is being profitably spent. And if it isn't, attendance at subsequent meetings will indicate this. The direct person is paid whether he's out selling or sitting in a sales meeting. The agent, however, relies on sales to make his income, and if he feels he's losing money by attending a nonproductive sales meeting instead of working in the field, you may be de-motivating him instead of motivating him.

The success of your meeting will depend upon actions you take before the actual meeting. The thoroughness of your planning and follow-through will dictate whether or not your meeting will be a success.

There are a number of important points you should keep in mind when making preparations for your meeting. Here's a checklist of the more important ones:

1. Resist the temptation to form a committee to plan the meeting. There's nothing wrong with seeking everyone's advice before setting the agenda. However, once you've gathered the collective judgment of your associates, proceed with your plans. But don't do it all yourself; appoint selected company personnel to handle that part of the meeting that best suits their capabilities.

2. Decide what results are to be achieved. Set goals that are realistic and can be met. A few well-researched topics presented in depth will be remembered by the agents. Too many presentations will tend only to confuse them.

3. Print supporting literature for every presentation and place it in a loose-leaf notebook with a copy for each agent. This helps them remember the major points discussed by each speaker.

4. Shake up the normal meeting routine once or twice during the two- or three-day event. This keeps everyone on his toes. Plan a surprise discussion of a controversial subject, such as, "Why is the new product (one on which we've spent $25,000 in promotion funds) laying an egg in the marketplace?" Bringing this in unexpectedly may bring some candid answers that can be very helpful in assessing the problem.

5. Make certain the company's speakers are in a position to deliver what they promise. For instance, don't allow the Q.C. manager to tell how effectively his department controls quality and then have the agents discover later that he can be overruled by the production manager. This destroys his credibility.

6. Get the agents involved. The longer they've been with you, the more they'll have to offer. But let those chosen to participate in the program know well in advance about their subjects and what you want them to accomplish in their presentations. For example, one agent may have brought in a big order using a technique or unusual selling point that may not have occurred to the other agents. Let him tell about it.

7. Don't hire professional motivators or sales training experts. This is a waste of money and time. Agents are self-motivated, and you can add to this motivation by promising them a quality product that sells for a competitive price.

8. Make it a working meeting. Agents like to play golf and tennis just like everyone else, but make this an optional choice. The easiest way to handle the sports portion of the get-together is to schedule it for after the meeting. Those who choose to stay and enjoy the facilities can do so; others may want to return home immediately.

9. Pay as much of the expenses as you can afford, including travel. This makes yours a first-class operation, and you'll receive first-class attention from the agents.

10. Evening sessions are usually nonproductive. This is a good time for a social gathering, mixing company personnel with the agents. It's also a good time for a low-keyed talk by the chief executive.

If you've developed a rep council in your company, you can receive invaluable aid in determining the major interests of your agents. This, in turn, can help you plan a more successful meeting for the entire agency group.

Your sales meeting will involve a fairly healthy expenditure by your company. Without good planning, the results will not justify the cost. Therefore, as suggested earlier, take full responsibility for your meeting. Consult other sources, visit the library or bookstore and read books written by experienced meeting leaders, and begin your planning at least four months in advance. With this type of preparation, you'll be able to relax and enjoy the session and assure yourself of a well-run and worthwhile sales meeting.

HAVE YOUR ACCOUNTANT TALK TO YOUR AGENTS

When was the last time a member of your accounting department talked to your agents? Five years ago? Ten years ago? Or maybe never? Under normal conditions, accounting and sales are far removed from each other—or are they?

Example: Dennis Clark, personable sales manager of a Los Angeles area metal parts firm, thinks the two departments have more in common than meets the eye, and at a recent sales meeting allocated an hour to Ed Longo, the company's controller, for a heart-to-heart talk to the firm's agents attending the annual get-together.

What did Ed talk about? What figures or numbers could he discuss that would be relevant to the group? Ed didn't spend a lot of time on figures; instead, he outlined the importance of his department's functions as they relate to the company's manufacturers' representatives. Here are some of the topics Ed covered:

Terms and Conditions: He pointed out that the sales department's understanding of terms and conditions can prevent problems from arising after the manufacture and shipment of the product. His firm, like other California firms, must charge a sales or use tax to out-of-state customers unless the customer provides a valid resale permit number. This is important for the agents to know, and they should inform the customers of this condition; otherwise, problems can arise with the customer's accounts payable department.

Overdue Accounts: Ed's company, like many others using agents, pays commissions in the month following shipment, whether or not the company has been paid by the customer. This leads agents to feel that bills are being paid promptly by the firms to which they sell. Naturally, this is not always the case, and Ed made the group aware of which customers were questionable credit risks.

Costing System: Ed noted that a job shop's pricing often seems to be inconsistent. He explained that the basis for current pricing is the experience the firm has had with production costs in the past. Certain parts, although they appear to be relatively simple, have caused excessive production costs because of certain idiosyncracies not apparent to the average agent. Ed said that the estimating personnel utilizes his department's figures on previous runs to help assess the current cost of existing parts and the estimated costs on parts that are new to the company and must be quoted from scratch.

This kind of presentation at the sales meeting can help agents understand more about the company and the reasoning behind many of its policies.

TWENTY-THREE WAYS TO PLAN AND RUN A SUCCESSFUL AGENT SALES MEETING

Some sales meetings are held at manufacturers' plants and some under the palms on Caribbean islands. But it's seldom the location that makes the difference between a good or a boring meeting; it's the preparation. Of course, everyone would prefer a pleasant place, but wherever you hold your meeting, the contents and results will be remembered long after the swimming and golf has been forgotten *if* your meeting is well planned.

It's no surprise that the cost of a sales meeting is going up along with the cost of everything else. This doesn't necessarily mean that you have to cut back or cut it out —it just means that you have to plan a little smarter. After talking with a number of people who run sales meetings, we've come up with this checklist to help you get the most for your money.

1. In addition to the people who should speak—the sales manager and some corporate officers—include some of the people who are important but who seldom, if ever, appear on the dais: your accountant, chief engineer, manufacturing manager, expediter, and so on.

2. Prepare the meeting well in advance. Nine to ten months may seem like a long time, but any less is impractical. If you had nothing else to do but plan a meeting, you could pull it off in a month. But life goes on, and meeting planning is usually done on weekends and in odd moments. Think about your last meeting!

3. Assign specific responsibilities to each member of the committee.

4. Set specific and achievable goals. Even if you have nothing spectacular—such as a new product—still set goals for the meeting. When you have set your goals, work backward to develop your program to make sure that you can accomplish those goals.

5. Most talks go in one ear and out the other. You know what psychologists say about how much and how quickly we forget. It's best to reinforce everything you say with a printed summary for every participant. You might even consider taping the sessions and having them duplicated and sent to attendees after the meeting.

6. Review each speaker's material well before the meeting. Edit for content, continuity, and interest. In other words, make sure that what is to be said will be important, that it relates to the sequence of the other material being presented, and that it will be presented in an interesting manner.

7. Don't put on a one-sided show—get your agents involved. You can do this in many ways. But before you do anything, send them a questionnaire and ask what they'd like to hear. You will probably find that the format of your meeting will be determined in large part by the responses to this survey. You should also consider putting some of your agents on the program. This takes away from the one-sided feeling and adds an important dimension.

8. Start early and end early. A seven thirty breakfast meeting followed by a fast start an hour later is always a good idea. Have a ten o'clock coffee break and then stop for an hour lunch at noon. Knock off at three. If you follow this schedule, you'll have your agents when they're most receptive, and they will still have time to enjoy themselves after the meeting. Be sure that your work and fun times meet the IRS guidelines.

9. You should pick up all the major expenses—travel and hotel. You shouldn't be responsible for incidentals, such as personal bar tabs and sightseeing trips. However, you might consider arranging some sightseeing trips for the agents' spouses during the hours of the meeting. Pay for these trips.

10. Leave plenty of time at the end of each presentation for a question-and-answer session. And leave some time at the end of the meeting day for a general open session.

11.   If you're not going to have the meeting at the plant, check the resorts for the best times, prices, and seasons. But don't buy any bargains—Florida in August will make more enemies than friends. Get the weather picture for the season, local regulations, and customs information.

12.   If at all possible, check out the meeting site in person before you commit. Many resorts that cater to business meetings will give you a few free days on the arm if they are convinced that you are serious.

13.   Choose an accessible location. Most convention centers are reasonably accessible, but it's best to think of the distance most of your agents will have to travel. After all, you're going to pick up the travel tab.

14.   It's always a good idea to invite agents' spouses. Most manufacturers will pick up the hotel room tab but expect the agents to pay for their transportation. Because many spouses are part of their agent-husband's/wife's business, they can write off the cost.

15.   Never have a meeting that lasts longer than three or four days. If you hold your meeting at a resort, have it start on a Tuesday or a Wednesday so that attendees will have a free weekend at the resort to enjoy themselves and for open consultation with you.

16.   Rehearse your meeting. We'll repeat that—rehearse your meeting! Most meetings that fail do so because no one took the time to run through the entire act. If you want egg on your face, wing it. If you want a good meeting, rehearse.

17.   Avoid being a horn blower—unless, of course, you really have something to crow about. Stick to the facts that are of interest to your agents. After all, it's their meeting, and when they're with you, they aren't selling. And when they aren't selling, they aren't making money for themselves and for you.

18.   Whenever it will help the program, use outside experts as speakers. But whatever you do, avoid the professional motivator. Your agents are charged up enough anyway, and listening to a windbag tell them how to close a sale is the last thing they want to do. If you do have such a speaker, you'll have a tough time getting the agents to your next meeting. Good experts include trade association executives, people who edit magazines in your field, and consultants with special knowledge that will benefit your agents. You might even have a few customers speak, telling what they like and don't like about the company, the products, and how they are being sold.

19.   Vary the pace. Beginning writers are told to improve their style by mixing long and short sentences. The same holds true for oral presentations. Position a couple of short presentations before and after a long one. And use a few surprises to keep up attention. We don't mean that you should use the old "now that I have your attention" line after you drop and break a glass. We mean that you should have a few surprise announcements that are not mentioned on the program. But make sure that they are upbeat, not downers.

20.   Never start cold. It's always a good idea to have a welcoming cocktail party the evening before the first day of the meeting.

21. And it's not good policy to end cold. Try to have a wrap-up party or a dinner for all after the last meeting. Be sure to circulate and listen for comments and have others from your company do the same. It's here that you will get the fresh firsthand feedback. A post mortem a few weeks later is almost valueless.

22. Be sure to leave time for individual private meetings with each agent. Most of the agents attending the meeting will have something personal that they would like to discuss with you. Be prepared to respond to their problems, questions, and comments.

23. Check local conditions. If you're going to a foreign country, be sure that your agents understand all the local customs and regulations. If you're using electrical equipment, make sure that the gear you bring will operate off local mains. Check shipping, postal, and telephone conditions. If you're shipping materials to be used during the meeting, be sure that you know they will arrive on time, even if the hotel has to store them for you for a few days. One meeting I attended in Martinique was a mini-disaster because shipped samples sat in the local post office until the second day of the meeting, long after the presentation in which they were going to be used.

All of these points are important, but there's one that is the key to running a successful agent meeting. If you don't do it, you'll never be able to devote any time to the others. The key is to plan ahead. As we said, nine to ten months is comfortable. When you plan far ahead, none of the other problems will seem as imposing.

HOW TO HAVE PRODUCTIVE MEETINGS WITH YOUR AGENTS

More time seems to be spent in meetings than doing just about anything else these days. Try to call five business associates on any given day and you're sure to find three of them tied up in meetings. "When any major principal calls to set up a meeting, I have to set aside a day for him," one agent told us. "When he arrives, we spend a day on pleasantries and solve some minor problems. But, in general, I lose a day in the territory." Such complaints are not uncommon, and they seem to be increasing, despite the cost of travel involved.

We're not talking about sales meetings. We are talking about the one-on-one and one-on-a-few meetings that occur when your principals visit with their agents. Because your time is valuable and the time of your agents is just as valuable, we have outlined the problems that most agents perceive in meetings with principals.

The following are some suggestions to help you and your agents make your meetings more productive:

• *Make sure your agenda topics are relevant to those in attendance.* This may seem obvious, but when you are trying to solve a problem, there is often a tendency to rope in everyone. If only one or two people at the meeting are concerned with the immediate status of the problem, don't waste the time of all the others by discussing it at length. Make an appointment to meet with those concerned at another time. When your agents give you their time but find that there is little that they can do to help on some problem you are discussing, you will have wasted your time and your agents will feel misused.

- *Be sure that everyone is there who should be.* Make sure that the individuals within the agency who can best contribute are there. Conversely, don't call in the entire crew when your interest relates to only a few members of the team.

- *Don't dominate the meeting.* If you called the meeting, you should run it, but don't dominate it. There has to be a leader if any meeting is to be productive. As the leader, it's your job to get the most out of each individual who participates. It's a good idea to state at the beginning of the meeting that you want to hear from individuals. If you dominate, however, you will find your listeners clamming up. Unfortunately, this withdrawal is often viewed as assent, and you will leave the meeting feeling that you have accomplished something when you really haven't.

- *State your objectives clearly.* Not only should you state the objectives of the meeting clearly, but you should communicate them in advance to those who will attend. You may have a flair for the dramatic and prefer to shake up the troops once in a while, but this will get you nowhere when you want input and participation from your agents. If you can plan the meeting well in advance and send the participants an agenda, you will give everyone the time they need to prepare for the session.

- *Set up follow-up systems.* If your meeting results in steps to be taken by you and your agents, make sure that the machinery that will monitor the progress is designed and set in place. If you want memos back from your agents, be specific about the timing and the content. If you are to report to your agents, the same rule applies.

- *Avoid personality clashes.* Even if you have severe personal differences with some of the individuals at the meeting, don't use the meeting as an arena to work them out. Stick to the agenda and the goals you want to accomplish. You should resolve personal differences in person—not in front of others.

- *Review the previous discussions.* The chances are that you meet infrequently with your agents and that the time between meetings wipes out the memory of the accomplishments of the last meeting. You shouldn't get formal and "read the minutes of the last meeting," but it's a good idea to review the discussions and the progress that has been made since the last meeting.

HOW TO GET SUPPORT FOR YOUR IDEAS IN A MEETING

Use this technique and two things will happen. First, you will know whether or not your idea is sound and will be accepted by the agencies you discuss it with; and second, you can build support for it in advance.

When you try out an idea on a few of your agencies before a meeting, you will get feedback on the idea, thoughts on how it can be improved, and support when you take it to everyone. You can get input face to face, over the phone, or in writing. But when you have taken the trouble to test an idea with a few of your agencies and the feedback is positive, the agents you talked with first will probably support you at the general presentation.

HOLD A NATIONAL SALES MEETING FOR ONLY A FEW HUNDRED DOLLARS

"A national sales meeting, with all of our agencies attending, usually costs us about eight thousand dollars. For us, this isn't an awful lot of money, but it does mean that we can talk with everyone together only once a year. That's better than no meeting, but since we discovered telephone conferencing, we get together quarterly and still have our regular face-to-face meeting." Sales managers working with manufacturers' representatives need to find ways to maintain contact, mainly because of the problems with requesting call reports. Regular call reports do jeopardize the agencies' independent contractor status and make the principal liable for withholding of social security, state, and federal taxes.

>>>→ *OBSERVATION* Research has indicated that face-to-face meetings are important but that much of the information that is passed during routine meetings can be handled very effectively without eye contact and by using telephone teleconferencing services. Content analysis of typical business meetings shows that the nub of the material frequently can be compressed into time that is one tenth the length of a typical meeting. Just to prove the point, think about how you plan your long-distance telephone calls and overseas cables, and how you tend to ramble on local calls.

Here are some thoughts on using the telephone to hold meetings with all of your agents.

There are a number of ways agencies and manufacturers can get together as a group using the phone lines. However, the most practical for most is that which uses a bridging network that can be supplied either by a commercial bridging service or by the local telephone company. When such a system is used for a national conference, everyone who is to participate must be at their designated numbers at a specified time. An operator then makes the calls and sets up the interconnecting network.

There are more sophisticated systems, such as video conferencing, facsimile, and even computer conferencing. However, in the case of computer conferencing, transmission is limited to one-at-a-time transmissions. Break-in is a problem.

Timing is often a problem, but it's nothing compared with the problem of pulling a dozen agencies out of the field for a three-day national meeting. Those who have used audioconferencing say that when national agency meetings are held regularly over the phone lines, they vary the time of each meeting so that one time zone isn't always penalized. And a one-hour meeting every few months is never a hardship on anyone.

The concept is also quite practical for manufacturers who have divided their sales territories into regional areas. With a regional manager in place, regular audio conferences with the manager and the agencies in the area become practical. And if there are more than a few regional managers, conferences among them and with the national sales manager take on interesting proportions.

For manufacturers who want to make the most of their rep councils, audioconferencing opens up some very interesting possibilities. Because fewer people are involved than are usually included in nationwide meetings, it's possible for rep councils to meet much more frequently.

Those who have used audioconferencing have one suggestion to make that makes a lot of sense, and that is to plan the meeting very carefully. In fact, you should put as much planning into these electronic meetings as you do in your face-to-face get-togethers. There should be a planned agenda, and every participant should be made aware of exactly what is to be discussed and what will be expected from him or her. Mail the agenda to everyone several weeks before the scheduled meeting. Just because you will be spending a lot less on a telephone meeting than you would for a conventional meeting doesn't mean that it should be a free-for-all.

Caution: At first glance, it may not seem possible to do the things that are ordinarily accomplished at face-to-face meetings, but with a little imagination, there are hardly any limitations to teleconferencing. For example, if your meeting involves product and application training that would normally include the use of slides, you can send pictures of the material to the participants before the conference. In fact, the medium appears to be limited only by individual imagination. You should be able to provide product and application training, introduce new products, discuss product availability, solve technical problems, review accounts, and discuss advertising and lead follow-up.

The objective of electronic conferences should not be to eliminate the face-to-face meeting; it should be to make the communications between you and your agencies more practical—and timely. And these interchanges will do a lot to tighten the ties from a morale point of view. A word of warning, though: When you run a telephone conference, you have to run a tight meeting or you can turn a relatively inexpensive way to meet with your agencies into an expense you didn't anticipate.

HOW TO HOLD PROBLEM-SOLVING MEETINGS WITH YOUR AGENCIES

It's not uncommon for sales managers to call meetings of their agencies when big problems arise. They not only seek to outline their approaches, but they want to get input from the agencies involved. Unfortunately, more good ideas are usually squelched at these meetings than are adapted. This happens because more of the ideas presented are usually off the top of the head, rather than thought through fully. And it's easier to knock an idea than it is to build it up. As you might suspect, or have already seen, these meetings are not often too productive.

Here are a few thoughts to help you make them productive:

- Don't allow criticism during the early stages. The first part of the meeting should be devoted to creating and strengthening ideas. Cut off criticism.

- Make sure that all presentations are depersonalized. When individuals become part of the discussion, personality conflicts can limit the results of the meeting.

- As the group leader, discuss the ideas with the group: Don't focus on the individual who contributed it.

- When the meeting is opened for criticism of ideas, try to rephrase it in positive ways. Ask the participants to present their thoughts in positive, rather than negative terms.

SHOULD YOU USE OUTSIDE SPEAKERS AT YOUR AGENCY SALES MEETINGS?

Yes and no. Yes, if they have something important for your agents to hear. No, if they are of the motivational type that are so often used to whip up a frenzy of vacuum cleaner salespeople. If you do use a hired gun, here are a few tips to make the presentation successful.

1. Limit the presentation of the outside speaker to no more than an hour or two at most in a one-day meeting. Even if your speaker is a VIP, it's best to limit the presentation—it's your show.
2. Provide the speaker with a detailed outline of the entire program so that he can plan his participation to dovetail with the presentations of others and with the overall goals of the meeting.
3. Leave time in the program—it can be during coffee break or lunch—for the agents to meet and talk with the speaker. When you go to the effort and expense of having an important guest, it's best to share him or her on and off the podium with your agency audience.
4. You might consider inviting your agents to submit advance questions that they would like to have the speaker address.
5. Provide your agencies with a transcript of the speaker's talk.

HOW TO MAKE THE MOST OF AGENCY SALES MEETINGS

Sales meetings can fall flat unless things get going early and unless there is more to discuss than new product features. We talked with a few sales managers who take part actively in the sales meetings run for their agencies. The following are some tips we gleaned from them:

- Play the devil's advocate. This means creating some conflict, but it should be done in a way in which everyone is stretched mentally, not bullied.
- Ask for a few more choices or opinions even when the questions seem to have been answered adequately. The results may not add much to the original question, but they will probably give you a jumping-off point for some new and inciteful ideas.
- Restate the problem if there is some confusion. In a group discussion, it's quite easy to slide into other areas without getting to the main issue. You have to pull people back once in a while, but you should do it in a positive way.
- Don't let the ramblers rule the show. Keep a tight focus at all times.

• Get the ball rolling by asking a few easily answered questions. This will not only allow everyone to participate, but it can provide the stimulus for more serious discussion.

AGENCY MEETING FOLLOW-UP LETTERS ARE IMPORTANT

Meetings with your sales agencies probably result in a lot being said and a lot being promised. However, how much of this is remembered and how much of it is ever acted on is hard to determine.

A sales VP we talked with recently claims that he spends about four months of the year on the road visiting agencies. "After every meeting," he said, "I immediately dictate a letter to the agency covering exactly what we discussed in the meeting. If I'm on the road, I dictate the letter over the phone to our company computer. My secretary transcribes the letter and within two days a letter is on the way to the agency." This man explained that he felt his meetings were important for his company and for his agencies. But he feels that they would probably be a waste of time if he didn't send confirming follow-up letters. He also claims that he expects his agencies to follow up, too. "If our meetings resulted in follow-up action on my part or on the part of the agent, letters from me and from him confirm the obligation to perform." He expects his agencies to acknowledge his letters only if there is specific action to be undertaken. As he explained, it's sort of a management-by-objectives approach. When both parties agree on something to be done, this confirmation makes it real.

WHEN YOU SHOULD CANCEL A MEETING

A marketing VP with some keen insight who is not the least bit personally insecure recently related that he was concerned about how effective his sales meetings had been. The more he dug into history, the more details he unearthed that bothered him. Finally, after sifting all the information he collected, he said: "I decided that to make our next sales meeting most effective, I would simply cancel it." As it turned out, this manufacturer had been holding national sales meetings for his agencies twice a year. From everything he could gather from talking with his agencies, each of them was rather thin. Even though this marketing executive was paying the expenses all the way, his agents resented being out of their territories twice a year for meetings that really didn't have that much new to present. "When we rescheduled our meetings to once a year, we had more pertinent information to share with the agencies, and those who attended seemed much more enthusiastic."

11

Communicating Effectively with Sales Agencies

One of the most prevalent complaints agents level against their principals is that they fail to communicate with them regularly and effectively. In fact, this lack of communication is often cited as a major factor in the dissolution of manufacturer/agency relationships.

This Chapter addresses communications problems from virtually every angle: developing and using an agency newsletter effectively; why call reports should never be required of agents; a five-point checklist to ensure that you get accurate information and that you get it on time; how feedback from the field will provide you with valuable product development information; keeping your agencies informed of your research findings; and a system that shows you how to make sure that you and your agencies are helping each other on the competitive front.

YOUR AGENTS MUST KNOW YOUR COMPANY'S PERSONNEL

Most routine visits by agents to their principals' plants seldom involve company personnel beyond the top executives and sales personnel. This is unfortunate because every opportunity should be taken to improve rapport between agents and inside personnel.

Involving more people in meetings with agents pays off surprisingly well. Without personal contact with production, engineering, and quality control personnel, the agent doesn't absorb the true personality of your organization. He needs to feel a part of the companies he represents, and by establishing a firsthand acquaintance with your people, he can represent you more confidently in the field.

This familiarity can also add to a clearer understanding of the agent's role in your firm and will create a better attitude on the part of the people in the vital departments in your organization toward your outside salesforce.

WHEN TO USE A NEWSLETTER

A solid line of communication used by a prominent gear company is its monthly newsletter. This is an internal publication edited only for the agency group, and its content is full of items of interest to every far-flung agent. Included is a listing of new accounts developed during the month—a sign business is flourishing—notices of changing lead times, a description of new plant equipment, and a host of other facts that keep its reps up to date on the progress of the company.

> ⫸➔ *OBSERVATION* What does this accomplish? By issuing an informative newsletter every month, without fail, the gear company keeps a constant communication link between its agents and home office personnel. And, through this consistent communication, the company maintains a high visibility among its representatives.

Caution: Companies that seldom keep in touch with the field forces find decreasing inquiries and orders arriving from the territories and tend to find fault with the troops instead of with their own communication systems.

Let's face it, you're in constant competition with your agents' other sales managers. Unless you discover ways to gain the agents' attention, you'll lose out in the race for their time. And the more time they spend on their other principals' lines, the less they'll have for yours.

The road to sales improvement is paved with good intentions. Many intercompany communications are started with honest intentions of continuing them, but they falter because of little positive results or because of just plain apathy. It's better not to start any type of formal communication unless you can be certain that continuity will be there. Eventually, if your letter is truly informative and helpful to its readers, you'll find your reps watching for it and complaining if it's late or lost in the mail. This won't happen overnight, but it will happen.

Once this point is reached, your messages can become more potent, with the assurance they will be read. You can use the letter as a questionnaire or as a vehicle for stimulating feedback from the field—with a separate section for this feedback feature, a necessary source of information for every sales manager.

The letter doesn't have to be fancy, just consistent and readable. It may even pay to find a budding writer among your employees who would be pleased to take over the responsibility for editing your thoughts and putting them on paper—and getting the whole thing out on time.

DO YOUR AGENTS LEVEL WITH YOU?

Agents are no different from other salespeople—in one respect. They'll often tell you what you want to hear, as long as the commissions keep coming. And this isn't all good. One electronic controls firm went for years sending out a new-customer letter that offended their agents and company salespeople alike. It asked the new customer how he had heard of the company, completely overlooking the fact that perhaps an agent or salesperson had been working on the account for years and finally brought it in.

A new agent, a particularly independent individual, vigorously objected, and the letter was changed with no hard feelings; the sales manager had simply not recognized the seriousness of the situation and the effect it was having on the morale of the salesforce.

To gain the confidence of your agents you must convince them that suggestions and complaints will not be taken personally and will be given serious consideration. If you can stimulate your agent force into leveling with you, you may find some interesting and provocative ideas that will improve results on the sales chart.

SELECTIVE FOLLOW-UP BRINGS BETTER RESULTS

Anyone selling through agents knows the difficulty of obtaining call reports or anything resembling call reports. The reason is obvious: Agents are independent salespeople and don't like any kind of control device. But the real pros are happy and willing to keep you informed on important matters.

The trick to prompting good feedback is judicious timing and common sense selectivity. Asking for a report on every visit the agent makes will bring a heap of frustration and very little response. Besides, it will put the agency and you in jeopardy with the IRS.

Those sales managers who are able to convince their agents that information is important, request only important information. "Don't bother us with routine call reports, but when something happens we should know about, drop us a line or pick up the phone." Requesting help only when it's truly needed will improve your results.

PLAIN WORDS ABOUT CALL REPORTS

At almost every seminar attended by sales managers of firms selling their wares through manufacturers' representatives one of the most discussed topics is the call report problem.

Call reports are a part of every direct-employee salesperson's obligation and are expected to detail the day's activities in glowing technicolor to justify the expense that management incurs in its effort to increase the year's sales by 20 percent. Management has every right to expect such reporting of the daily explorations and results of their paid salespeople. After all, direct salespeople are usually paid a salary and/or draw that is extracted from the company's coffers and is paid for the execution of a full day's effort designed to bring in a reasonable amount of sales.

Warning: Unfortunately, the same cannot be said about the manufacturers' representative's position; yet, in some sales managers' minds, there is little difference between the obligations of a direct person and an agent, and herein lies the difficulty.

A direct person receives regular remuneration whether or not he sells—but not for long, of course—and an agent receives remuneration only if he sells, and then the commissions are often received a considerable time after the product has been manufactured, shipped, and paid for. He feels this puts him in a slightly different position than the direct person. In fact, he's not an employee in any sense of the word, but instead a provider of services on a contract basis, much like an attorney, CPA, or consultant. He contracts with your firm to sell its products. He doesn't ask for any fringes, expenses, or promotions. His basic obligation is to solicit business for your company, and any attempt to instruct him in the carrying out of his daily routine may be considered an intrusion.

Caution: It may appear we're advocating that the agent not provide any feedback from the field. Exactly the opposite is true. Any agent worth his salt realizes that you can't perform your end of the contractual obligation—making and selling your product at a competitive price—unless you know how things are going in the field. If he's a true professional, he'll keep you informed of the very factors that can help you do your job best. If he doesn't, then he's not doing his job. The main objection he has to the call report request is the form aspect of it; that is, "Reports shall be submitted on every call on a three-part form supplied by the company. These reports shall be submitted in time for our weekly pricing meeting." This type of command is unlikely to prompt much cooperation from your agents.

Further, the sheer paper-work load this would entail for an agent with eight or nine principals would keep him from his appointed rounds. Informality, cooperation, and understanding will bring more helpful information than a weekly or monthly requirement of formal call reports.

In addition to this, the use of daily call reports is one of the tests that the IRS uses to determine how much control is exerted for tax purposes. Demanding daily call reports will tell the IRS that an employer/employee relationship exists, and they will levy taxes accordingly.

WHEN TO ACCEPT CALLS FROM YOUR AGENTS

Manufacturers' agents would like to make calls to their factories collect, and if a company allowed this sort of freedom there could be an abuse of the privilege 40 to 50 percent of the time. On the other hand, never accepting collect calls can make an agent reluctant to place a call when it may turn out to be a real emergency.

A good many representatives have a philosophy—not always agreed to by management—that they think works out very well. If the call is routine, asking about the latest shipping information, pricing on a particular job, or a question about a new lead, the call is made at the agency's expense. However, when the call is necessitated by a breakdown in one of the company's obligations, then the agents feel the company should fund the call.

For example, an order has been overdue for months and the customer has been badgering the agency unmercifully, or rejections have been claimed by the customer but nothing is being done about it and the buyer is demanding an immediate answer. The agent doesn't feel he should bear the cost of making long-distance calls under these circumstances.

The deciding factor then becomes whether or not the call would have been necessary if the principal had lived up to its obligations.

⟫⟫→ *IDEA IN ACTION* If the agent is phoning for price information on a rush basis in order to obtain an order or for some similar reason, where he stands to benefit from the call directly, then this should be part of his obligation and the expense should be his. This may be a bit difficult to monitor, but by trying to be fair you may improve communications between you and your sales agencies.

Agents and principals in major cities can reduce the cost of their long-distance calls by subscribing to one of the computer-related systems. Savings up to 30 percent are claimed by these companies.

CALL YOUR AGENTS WHEN THEY ARE MOST LIKELY TO BE BY THEIR TELEPHONES

You will most frequently find your agents in their offices on Monday mornings and Friday afternoons. Thus, you can usually get those very necessary and lengthy phone discussions handled during those times. But what about during the week?

Try calling just as early as possible on other mornings. Find out what time your agencies open their offices. If they're in town, they will probably stop by the office for a half hour or so to prepare for the day's calls. Calling them at an early hour may delay them for a few minutes, but if the message is important, don't hesitate to get on the phone.

Sunday afternoon, tough as it may be, is also a good time to catch those representatives who leave late Sunday or early Monday for out-of-town trips.

WHY MANUFACTURERS DON'T RETURN CALLS FROM AGENTS

An agent who had been in business about three years was complaining to another agent about the problems he had in obtaining answers to questions he asked his principals. "I write and phone them asking for help on shipments and quotations and nothing happens until it's too late. Why can't they follow through?" he asked.

"Don't get upset," cautioned the other agent, who had been in business for over ten years, "if three or four of your principals do a good job, you're doing better than average."

If you questioned agents about their biggest problem with their principals, their answers would undoubtedly prove that the lack of response was the most troublesome area. They don't like this failing of their principals, but it's a fact of life, and most of them do the best they can in spite of the problem.

Many purchasing agents look at agents with a jaundiced eye, and if you asked them why, they'd point out that most agents are unreliable. "They leave our office with all kinds of promises," say the knowledgeable buyers, "and that's the last we hear from them." And most agents will agree with them. It's terribly embarrassing for a professional representative to phone back to tell the buyer he simply can't get any information from his principal, so he does the next best thing—nothing.

    ⸻▶ *IDEA IN ACTION* The best training a sales manager could receive in the art of communication would be to spend a week with one of his agents. Or, better still, with someone else's agent. He could then get an impartial view of what it's like to be an agent. He'd be able to see the unanswered inquiries; the unanswered phone calls; and, sometimes, the complete disregard of the agent as an extension of the company. Many firms, in effect, tell the agent to "get out and sell and leave the details to us." But buyers are like the rest of us. When they place an order with a salesperson and have a problem or want some follow-up information, they go back to the salesperson. After all, he's the one who promised satisfaction. When the salesperson turns to his company for an answer to the problem and doesn't get it, his worth is reduced considerably in the eyes of the buyer.

Have you ever wondered why your agents don't produce as much business as you think they're capable of? Part of the reason could be because two or three of their principals are making their job easier and more rewarding—psychologically and financially—by responding promptly to their request for information. Companies that do this create a feeling of rapport with their agents and, in turn, have less difficulty obtaining return communications from their representatives. In fact, a company that sets a first-class example in communications can demand the same kind of response from its agents.

For the next month or two, try getting back to your agents with good prompt information and see if it doesn't start the juices flowing again—you may be surprised.

INCLUDE AGENTS IN YOUR SUGGESTION SYSTEM

You can learn from your agents if you'll give them the chance to contribute. However, few of them will make suggestions on their own.

One way to encourage your agents to participate is to include them in your suggestion system under exactly the same terms as those for your direct employees. Monetary or other rewards should be the same for both groups.

Naturally, you won't be receiving any ideas from your agents concerning improvements in the manufacturing process or expansion of the parking lots. Rather, the representatives' suggestions will more likely relate to communication procedures. Every company has room for improvement in this area.

Caution: Unfortunately, suggestions of this nature are harder to implement, and sometimes computing the actual savings can prove fairly nebulous. However, a good suggestion system allows for these variations by providing special standardized awards in such cases.

The agent is often your first line to the customer, putting him in a position to make some relevant and profitable suggestions that can improve your image and service, and result in increased sales.

DO YOUR AGENTS KEEP YOU INFORMED?

The inertia shown by most representatives in keeping you informed on almost any matter is in direct relationship to the amount of effort involved, particularly written effort. The easier you make it for them to provide reports on important calls or on recent quotations, the more likely you are to receive such communications.

>>>→ *IDEA IN ACTION* One sales manager overcomes this hurdle by sending out follow-up requests that include a postage-paid reply card for the agent to use.

In addition to the postage-paid card, he fills in as many blanks as he can so that the agent has a minimum of work to do in filling out the report. He inserts the customer's name and address, the date of the quotation or request for information, and other details that the agent would normally have to fill in before he even started to provide the required information.

He also uses a multiple-choice card so the agent, in most cases, can check just a few boxes, add a little detail, and drop the card in the nearest mailbox without having to find a stamp.

ACKNOWLEDGE FEEDBACK FROM YOUR AGENTS

Although agents are less than enthusiastic about call reports, good agents will keep you informed about vital information affecting your performance in their marketplaces.

A good way to stimulate this type of information and to keep it flowing regularly is to let your agents know you not only read their reports but that you utilize this information for the company's good.

It's human nature to want to be recognized for actions you deem important. To ignore information received from the field is to discourage it. Your agents will lose interest in keeping you posted.

Company newsletters, a special note to an agent, a lower price on the next quote —these are devices you can use to let your agency force know that you rely on their aid in keeping competitive.

HOW TO WRITE EFFECTIVELY WHEN COMMUNICATING WITH YOUR AGENTS

It's essential to say what you mean—in plain language—when writing to your agents.

Your agent's time, like yours, is extremely valuable. Selling hours are few, so most agents try to spend as much time as possible in the field. This means office time is held to a minimum, and the few hours there must be utilized to the maximum.

The letters and memos lying on their desks when they return compete for their attention. In order to make yours stand out from the rest, you must have that something extra.

>>>→ *HOW TO DO IT*   The best way to get their attention is to get off to a good start. If you have an important point to make in your letter or memo, make it the first sentence. Then follow up with the details.

Try to write the way you talk. You don't say *advise* in a normal conversation, yet most letters use this formal and useless word. Use *tell* or *say* for the same purpose. Be as informal as possible and avoid hard-to-understand words so your agents don't have to interpret too.

Long paragraphs are real turnoffs. Keep them short, punchy, and to the point. After writing a paragraph, go over it once again to see if you can break it into two paragraphs or shorten it.

To gain more effect from your communications don't write your agents every other day with "let's go get 'em," and "attaboy" memos. These become routine and are shuffled aside if they come in like clockwork.

Only write when the subject is important. That way when an agent sees a note from you he'll pay immediate attention to it.

If a bulletin or memo is really important, send a follow-up within a week. Even if you've followed all the rules and done a good job, communications get lost or agents come in the office for an hour and leave again for a week. Hit them just as hard the second time as the first.

One more hint: If you want an answer to your memo, specify a deadline. However, don't say "I'd like to hear from you in two weeks," because he'll forget when he received the letter. Instead say, "Please reply by September 2." You'll hear from him.

FOUR WAYS TO SUCCEED WITH A FIELD FEEDBACK SYSTEM

Field feedback is a two-way street. Factory marketing people need accurate and timely information to make sound decisions, and agents benefit from the sales strategy that results from this effort. However, when your agents are asked to handle some of the details, they occasionally find that the paper work interferes with their regular sales activity. The problem is not new, but there are ways to handle it so you and your agents will both benefit.

Today, competitors are moving faster than ever, trends are shorter and more dramatic, and marketing planning depends heavily on agent-supplied information. The solution is not to add to your agent's burden but to make it easier to get and use information. Here's how to do it:

1.   Be specific in your requests. Don't say, send us all the competitive information you can. Say specifically that you want to know why the Smith Company switched from Buna-N to Teflon O-rings.

2. Are you making the most of the competitive information you are now getting? Is someone reviewing and acting on the information that is presently being gathered by your agents? Information is of no value until someone uses it.

3. Does your system really work? Or must you kick the wheel frequently to keep it going? You may have to review the need for the material you request as well as the system you use to process it.

4. Are you turning the raw data sent by your agents into information that will be useful to them? Agents often question the usefulness of their factory-requested paper work when they are not shown how it's helping. Keep in touch. Show them how they, too, can use the data they have sent you. Regular reports help.

WHAT'S YOUR POLICY ON COLLECT CALLS FROM AGENTS?

Some principals accept all calls and others set up specific guidelines. Here are a few of the ways it can be handled:

1. Establish a monthly quota, based on previous experience.
2. Accept all calls without reservation.
3. Accept only calls relating to ongoing business.
4. Accept only calls relating to problems caused by the factory.
5. Don't accept any collect calls under any circumstances.
6. Install an 800 number for agent and customer inquiries.

SHOULD YOU ACCEPT COLLECT CALLS FROM AGENTS?

Charles Aldridge, field sales manager for Heany Industries, Scottsville, NY, suggests a way to keep communications open without spending a lot of money:

> . . . we have found that collect calls are inordinately expensive and have suggested to our representatives that they call us direct and send us the bills for the calls to us. This has worked out beautifully for both parties and we feel it offers a good alternative to collect calls.

THE POWER OF NEGATIVE THINKING

Most manufacturers seek the advice of their agents on a wide range of questions. Whether they do it through a rep council or by formal or informal surveys, they usually ask their agents what they would like in positive terms. However, there are times when the information you want from your agents may require a different approach. Agents, like everyone else, tend to tell you what they think you want to hear. It's only human. But there's a way out of this bind, and it's to ask them for the negatives.

Starting with the negatives in a search for answers not only provides interesting insights, but it also has a way of loosening up those who are expected to be helpful. Here are some of the benefits of this powerful technique:

- *You isolate problems immediately.* When you ask an agent what he doesn't want, you will very likely get some specific answers. These answers can serve to center constructive discussion later. Knowing the problems early on, you should be in a position to work on the solutions with very little wheel spinning.

- *You reduce the possibility of reaching the wrong conclusion.* Agent/manufacturer meetings usually take place on the fly. Both are anxious to get problems solved, but when the issues aren't discussed directly, there is usually a tendency to settle on a solution before all of the options have been explored.

- *You avoid wasting a lot of time.* You and your agents have pet ideas that are presented time and again at meetings. However, by starting at the other side of an issue—by presenting it as a problem—you can break this response habit and develop fresh insight.

- *You start on a fresh track.* There is often a tendency to institute a change that may appear unimportant to you but would be a major problem for your agents. It's really a matter of perspective. But when you begin by looking at the problem end with your agent, rather than mandating something right out of the barrel, you will have a better view before you launch into the how-to phase.

Example: One manufacturer we talked with said that he often got excellent insight when he asked his agents what problems they were having with the other lines they were carrying. It wasn't that he was engaged in industrial espionage, but he found that many of the problems his agencies encountered with other lines rubbed off on his line. It was just easier for the agents to talk about the other lines than it was to discuss the problems directly with the manufacturer. It's not unlike the psychologist's nondirective way of getting at problems. Incidentally, this is an excellent way to get at new product ideas. It's really the nub of the marketing concept: Discover what problems people have and solve them with a profitable product or service.

PRODUCT DEVELOPMENT—LISTEN TO WHAT YOUR AGENTS HAVE TO SAY

"All they did was change the knobs from red to blue and replace the meters with digital readout displays. And they had the gall to call it a new product." That's how one agent put it. Another, an engineer who ran the product development department at a large firm before he became an agent, said, "The best ideas usually come from those who are in daily contact with customers—whether they are agents or factory people. Listen to them. Take them seriously, and a lot of your work will be done for you."

Let's look at the entire new product picture and see how you can make the most of the information your agents either have at their finger tips or can get for you quickly.

⟫→ *WATCH THIS* First, an important point. The agents we discussed this topic with were unanimous in their feelings that a lot of new product work by their principals is aimed at copying the products of their competitors. In other words, there isn't much innovation, only attempts at one-upmanship. Remember that real gains are made with truly *new* products. Aggressive selling and the development of new products aimed at the holes left by retrenching competitors can spell success now and later when the economy gets a little steam behind it.

The systems approach to product development works nicely when you involve your agents. Here's how to do it:

- *Identify what your customers want.* The chances are that your agents have been telling you this all along. Go back over your meeting notes first and then get in touch with them for the specifics.

- *Identify the market.* Not all products you develop will be saleable in the markets you now reach. Your agents can help you identify the picture by giving you rough estimates of what their individual markets will accept.

- *Create product concepts.* These are just ideas at this point, but they should be pretty clear in your mind. If not, your agents will have difficulty helping you evaluate them. At this point your agents should be able to give you some technical input as well as economic measures so you can hit the go/no-go point with some confidence.

- *Test and recycle the concepts.* The chances are that you will get both good and bad vibes in the last step. If the balance is on the positive side, see what you can do to modify the concepts to make them workable and, in the eyes of your agents, acceptable to their customers.

- *Create a tight description of the product specifications and benefits.* This step puts you closer to the point of prototype development. It will help your engineers understand the product from the user's point of view as well as help them translate needs into product features.

- *Develop prototypes and test them.* When you use agents to help you with this work, remember that they really have nothing to sell at this point. If the product flies, they will. But you should plan to compensate them for any product and concept testing they do with their customers.

- *Modify the designs, based on agent and customer feedback.* The real world has a tendency to knock holes in some really great ideas. Be prepared to lick your wounds. And be prepared to recognize that the input you can get makes a difference between success and failure if you do get to production. After you make the changes your agents suggest, get samples back to them for further evaluation.

- *Create the marketing strategy.* Remember that your agents can be especially helpful at this point. They have been in on the development of the product and have talked with customers about it in some detail. They are the best source of advertising ideas, too. They have heard the objections and know what hot buttons your ad agency can press when they create the program. Don't ask your agents to write the copy, but do ask them to provide their personal experiences to those who will write it.

• *Take the show on the road.* You may do some further testing before the final rollout, but each product and each industry is so different that it's impossible for us to provide specifics at this point. In some fields, dry tests are the order of the day. In others, where competition is likely to land on you with both feet if they spot your good idea, you may have to jump right in.

ARE YOU REALLY LISTENING TO WHAT YOUR AGENTS HAVE TO SAY?

"Sure," you may say, "I hear every word." But do you really hear what your agents are trying to tell you? People are learning how to write better letters and memos, and they are learning how to speak more effectively. But very few people are paying any attention to the other end of the communications channel—listening. Remember, you don't have to "win" the argument every time. You need to really hear what the other person is saying and consider the topic from their point of view.

Example: One sales manager we talked with said, "I used to think that I was communicating with my agents. I wrote my letters very carefully. I had taken a course in speaking and was very conscious of the way I spoke. But when I realized that only half of my communications system was working, I was shocked." This manager later took a course in listening. He learned that listening involves much more than just receiving words.

    »»→ OBSERVATION Most people think that because they hear well they are listening and that they don't need help in the process. Not so! Because the interaction between agents and principals involves a lot of talking and listening, we have outlined some steps to take to help you make the most of the process. But first you should understand some of the problems you may encounter when you sharpen your listening skills. When you learn how to listen effectively, you become more vulnerable— you may begin to see yourself as others see you. Of course, this can be either a positive or a negative experience. But either way it will be to your benefit to become a good listener. A good listener also runs the risk of being changed, or having to change as a result of what is heard. But isn't this what personal growth is all about?

As you read the following, keep your agency relationships in mind. Think of how you can improve them by practicing the techniques we describe.

• *You must* want *to hear everything.* More often than not, conversations seem predictable. You think you know what a person is going to say. An agent calls to press for an overdue quotation, and you shift into listening neutral. What the agent may be trying to tell you is that if the quotation isn't forthcoming, you're not in the running—with the customer or the agent. This half-listening can often get you in more trouble than not listening at all.

• *Listening is a full-time activity.* The mechanics of listening mean that you don't speak when the other person is speaking. But just being silent isn't enough—

you've got to actively focus on the person who is speaking and tune out everything else. In other words, you must concentrate fully on what is being said. People can tell when you're not listening actively. When they know that you're not into what they are saying, they usually stop trying to get through to you.

• *Learn to listen with more than your ears.* Sure, the words that are spoken are very important, but the way they are spoken can often be more important. Listen for inflection. Listen for feelings. Listen for the emotions that will tell you how the other person feels about what is being said. "I ought to find another good manufacturer of fasteners," an agent jokingly told a sales manager we spoke to. At least the sales manager thought he was joking. But when the problem wasn't resolved, the agent did find another principal. Many things are said in apparent jest that are deadly serious.

• *Listen with an open mind.* Don't judge until you've heard everything. Sure, you will have opinions, but if you impose them on a person before he or she has finished speaking, you will do two things. First, you will probably miss the real essence of what is being said. Second, you will probably give away by your body language that you have already made up your mind on what is being said. You know the signals—arms crossed in front of the chest as the other person makes a point with which you don't agree. And, of course, looking as though you've heard enough and can't wait until the person stops talking is also obvious. Remember, when you prejudge, you may come to the wrong conclusions before the other person stops speaking—and miss the point completely.

• *Don't stop listening until the other person has stopped speaking completely.* Too often people begin to formulate their responses while the other person is talking and miss important points. This is not only impractical, it can be downright embarrassing when your time comes to speak.

• *Learn to analyze what the other person is saying.* The agency/principal relationship is usually one of friend to friend, as well as businessperson to businessperson. Delicate subjects are often broached from one posture when they are really coming from the other. For example, if you were concerned with a particular agent's performance, you might slip into the friend-to-friend relationship. The agent's response would probably be keyed to this situation, but would you hear the true message? In a word, make sure that you and the person with whom you are talking are on the same wavelength.

• *See yourself in the shoes of the other person when you are listening.* Show the other person that you are concerned and that you are actively listening. Maintain good eye contact and respond appropriately to the signals being sent. That is, if the other person is repeating something, you can assume that he feels that you didn't understand it or were not paying attention the first time. If you get the message, make sure that the speaker knows that you do.

• *Watch your emotions.* Whether you feel that a strong positive or negative response is required, hold it in and don't betray your feelings until the other person has finished speaking. This is how many arguments get started. People start talking before the other person finishes and resentment builds.

All that we've said presupposes that you have regular contact with your agents, and a word about this is important. Regular contact means more than hounding them for inquiry follow-up. It means more than a first-of-the-month telephone talk. It means more than an occasional thinly disguised call to see where the orders are. Regular contact with your agents means that you are interested in them personally as well as in their business success. It means that you have built a good personal and working relationship. The chemistry in a relationship really counts!

TRY A PARALLEL SYSTEM TO IMPROVE AGENCY COMMUNICATION AND MOTIVATION

Information passed from person to person usually changes a lot in the transition. People seldom intentionally distort what they hear and report—it's just a problem of perception. It can be a major problem in business, however, especially when there are several people in the information chain. "Agencies are no different from other businesses," a sales manager told us. "There are often layers of people between the owner and the guys in the field." He's right, but this can be an opportunity, rather than a problem.

The sales manager touched on a common problem. He was looking at the "layers of people" as filters and distorters, the way most people view the situation. They think this way because messages are usually passed serially—from one person to the next. If you think of these people in parallel terms, however, you change the entire picture. Rather than filters and distorters, they become amplifiers—sources of reinforcement. They add weight to your message. In a parallel communications situation, everyone gets the same message. It isn't passed from person to person.

Just to put the problem in perspective, think about the classic demonstration of communication distortion in a freshmen psychology course. A story is whispered from student to student in a classroom. The last student to get the story seldom hears anything that vaguely resembles the story that was told to the first student. The parallel situation would be the instructor telling the story to the entire class at once. Everyone hears the same message, and there's no chance for person-to-person distortion to take place.

Easier said than done, you might say. How can I get the word to the field salespeople in all my agencies without going through agency management people and running the risk of distortion? To begin with, you will have to discuss the problem with all of your agency principals and make sure that they understand you're not trying an end run—that all you want to do is make sure that everyone inside and outside the agency gets the same message. When you and the agency principals agree on which information you can transmit to everyone, you've got the ball rolling. Usually the information that is most effectively passed this way includes monthly bookings, competitive information, market data, new applications, product modifications, and so on. Obviously, this information is important to those in the field as well as to inside agency people.

How about the mechanics of communication? You're not a professor facing a roomful of students. Your agents are scattered all over the country. As simple as it may seem, it's just a matter of sending copies of your memos and communications to the list of everyone you and the agency owners agree should get your messages. You may want to clear each memo with the agency brass first, but the general distribution of information that has a direct effect on people in the field is very important. Let's look at a few situations where parallel communications will be important.

Unclear market potential. One of the main reasons salespeople neglect a line is because the manufacturer simply hasn't done a good job of convincing them that a strong market exists. And the guys in the field respond to the direction of their agency's management people. Letting everyone know exactly what the market potential is will motivate both field salespeople and the agency management. Rather than running the risk of a distorted message, you've gotten the ears of all the people who count.

Lack of product knowledge. "An agency salesperson was selling a hell of a lot of tube fittings in his area," a sales manager told us. "But he didn't get the valve business that should have gone with it." When the principal's sales manager gave the agency sales manager and the field salespeople the facts on valve purchases related to fittings sold in other territories, both turned-to. The salespeople went after the valves, and the inside people made sure that they got all the help they needed. It was a successful parallel effort.

Progress reports keep the system on course. Send your reports to everyone— owners, managers, and the field salespeople.

Caution: The few examples we have described should put the system of parallel communication into perspective. It's important to remember, however, that the system can be used on every channel. If you write to one person in an agency, carbon the others who will benefit from the information. Do the same with conversations. It's usually impossible to get everyone together on the phone, but you can send short summarizing memos to those with whom you couldn't speak. Avoid the trickle-down system of communicating with your agencies—work in parallel.

DON'T LET YOUR DISTANT AGENTS SUFFER FROM THE MAIL LAG PROBLEM

In case you're unaware of it, mail can take a week or more to cross the country once in a while. Yes, the post office is doing a much better job than they have done in the past few years. But when things get bogged down for one reason or another, the requests for quotes you get from your agencies in the hinterlands and the quotes you send to them could walk faster in some cases. There's no way to speed up the post office or to predict when the mail will be slowed down. But you can save time by processing information immediately on your end. Apart from just setting up and maintaining a good system, you can avoid problems that we've heard discussed at seminars. For example, one manufacturer stated that he read and replied to agency mail only on Mondays. That means that mail arriving on Tuesday had to wait a week for attention. Sure, this is unusual and an extreme case. But anything that gets in the way of rapid request processing reduces your chances of getting an order. Keep the mail moving.

KEEP YOUR AGENCIES POSTED WHEN YOU HAVE CHANGES IN LEAD TIME

It's probably true that more customers complain about changes in delivery schedules than just about anything else. In some cases such changes cause only minor problems. But in new construction, for example, a revised delivery on pipe could prevent construction from finishing the building. If you make products with wide demand fluctuations and you have a fixed plant capacity, make it easy for yourself, your agencies, and your customers by issuing periodic lead time schedules. This way, your agencies won't make promises you can't fulfill.

PROFESSIONAL WRITER'S TRICKS

"I'm a believer—oh, am I a believer in the power of communications," a sales manager told us the other day. "But when it comes time to write that memo, that newsletter, even a routine letter, I fall apart. What do I do? I get on the phone— that's what I do." This manager has solved his problem one way by avoiding writing. He does the job on the phone.

You may feel the same way, but even if you do a top-flight job on the phone, you still should cultivate some writing skills. The spoken word is powerful, but it is often short-lived. The written word, however, can hang around for quite a while. And from what we've seen, most agencies do keep the newsletters and memos sent by their principals. Some even have binders for the newsletters and use them to bring new people up to speed quickly. Let's take a look at some of the tricks professional writers use to get the job done.

Don't wait until the last minute to write anything. Most people who have difficulty putting words on paper—or on tape—usually let the job drag until they are forced to do it. Then, when time is short, tempers become short, and output is seldom viewed with pride. Get the job started early.

If you follow the advice in the first step, you can take advantage of a powerful professional writing technique. Forget an outline—for the moment. But do make a few notes of what is to be said, the tone of how you want to say it, and the style you will use. For example, if you're working on a newsletter, the tone should be upbeat and positive—not syrupy, but positive. What you want to say should be keyed to what your agencies want to hear: success stories, new application data, new products—not how to sell. The style will really depend on you and how close you feel to each of your agencies. We strongly suggest that you use the second person, you, rather than the first person, I.

    ⟫→ *IDEA IN ACTION*   Don't start by writing anything—start by giving yourself plenty of time and collecting everything that could possibly be important in the writing project. Don't try to sort and evaluate right away—just stuff it all in a big envelope that you keep handy. Write your ideas on a piece of paper and stuff them in the envelope. You may prefer to make large scrawly notes on 8 1/2 x 11 typing paper. Taking time to type the notes or to organize them in any way slows down the process. It's a lot easier to get the gist of the thought when it's on a large note than when it's small and fussy.

Getting ideas is easier than you might suspect. Most people who don't work with words tend to be too critical of their ideas too soon. They try to evaluate their thoughts individually, rather than to view a lot of ideas as part of a process, or a written piece. Just get them down on paper and stuff them in the envelope. Make your judgments later. Try free association with a tape recorder when you are driving to and from the office or are on a business trip. Start with the topic on which you plan to write, and then think of related subjects. But don't make any attempts to evaluate them—just get them onto the tape. At first, you may feel a little silly jabbering into a tape recorder with what seems to be meaningless banter. But when you are ready to write and play back what you have said, chances are you will have some good ideas to use. Remember, the test is not what you throw away—it's what you use. If you free associate easily, you will throw away a lot of ideas, but what you keep will be memorable.

Now you're ready to write. Get out the tape and listen to everything you said. Make notes of the good stuff—but don't erase the tape yet. You will probably find that as you write, your thoughts will turn to some of the material you weren't too impressed with at first. But the free-association process generally keeps you on the track. And even the ideas that seemed wild at the time may turn out to be useful.

Get out your envelope of notes and arrange them into categories. You will probably start out with some broad categories and find as you start sorting that an outline with subheadings will almost build itself. If it doesn't, you will have to construct an outline and get additional material if it's needed. If you need data, do the research. If you need ideas, go back to free association, or try a brainstorming session with one of your colleagues.

The next step is to review your outline critically. Check to make sure that one section leads to another in a logical way. Be certain that everything in the outline is aimed at your agent audience. See if you have too much. You probably will have more material than you need if you follow the steps outlined. The tendency is to try and use it all. But, remember, more is not necessarily better. If you are unsure, get someone else's opinion. You can be too close to your writing at times to see this. Finally, make sure that your ending reaches the conclusion supported by the material you have presented.

When you write, choose short words over long words. Avoid long sentences, and vary shorter and longer sentences throughout your writing. Think of and write to the reader. Don't preach. And be sure to read the writing of others. The chances are that the writing that impresses you will meet the standards of good writing. There's nothing wrong with copying the style of a writer you admire.

THE MEDIUM IS THE MESSAGE—OR AT LEAST PART OF IT

Every sales executive spends a good part of his or her time communicating with salespeople. However, because agencies aren't on the payroll, the time spent talking with them is frequently a lot less than the time spent talking with salaried field people. To help you to communicate effectively, we'd like to pass along two lists of words that were compiled by the University of Iowa. The first list contains words to avoid. They are words that conjure up unpleasant images, regardless of the thoughts being conveyed. Don't use these words if you can possibly find substitutes: abuse, afraid, alibi, bankrupt, blame, calamity, cheap, complaint, crisis, crooked, deadline, discredit, failure, fault, fear, flimsy, fraud, hardship, imitation, implication, impossible, improvident, in vain, liable, meager, misfortune, negligence, opinionated, poverty, prejudiced, pretentious, quota, ruin, shirk, slack, superficial, timid, unfair, unsuccessful, untimely, verbiage, waste, weak, worry, and wrong. All of these words have negative images. Many of the words that begin with the prefix *un-* should be avoided, too. For example, if you are going to use the word *uncertain,* say in its place, not certain.

>>>→ *IDEA IN ACTION* Let's look at the list of words that the same study identified as having a positive effect: ability, abundant, achieve, active, admire, advance, advantage, ambition, appreciate, approve, brave, benefit, capable, cheer, comfort, commendable, confidence, conscientious, cooperate, courage, courteous, definite, dependable, deserving, desirable, determined, efficient, energy, enthusiasm, excellence, exceptional, faith, fidelity, genuine, good, grateful, guarantee, handsome, harmonious, helpful, honesty, honor, humor, imagination, improvement, ingenuity, initiative, integrity, intelligence, judgment, justice, kind, lasting, loyal, merit, notable, opportunity, perseverance, please, positive, practical, proficient, progress, promote, reasonable, recognize, recommend, reliable, reputable, responsible, simplicity, sincerity, stability, substantial, success, superior, thorough, thoughtful, thrift, truth, useful, valuable, vigor, vital, vivid, wisdom, worthwhile, you, yours. Whenever you can use these words, whatever you're saying will have the added benefit of positive emotion. If you'd like to check this out, read good ad copy carefully and see how frequently the copywriters make use of the words in the second list and avoid those in the first.

HOW TO GET TIGHT-LIPPED AGENTS TO OPEN UP

When you have an agent who only speaks when spoken to, and then does so as briefly as possible, it's often possible to bridge the gap with a few simple techniques. However, you should remember that busy agency people seldom have the time to carry on running conversations or correspondence. But when one agent stands out by not speaking out, these approaches will help. "One of my best agents today was as quiet as a mouse during almost a year," one manufacturer told us. "But it wasn't for lack of activity or interest in us or our products, it was just his way.

We're located in a major metropolitan center where people just seem to be more talkative. The agency owner I'm referring to was from an area where people were less talkative. Once I realized this and used one simple technique, the communication lines opened and we shared ideas regularly."

Caution: It's important to note that some people are less talkative than others. And in multi-person agencies, the character of the agency is generally set by the owner. If he or she isn't especially talkative, others in the agency will probably not be too talkative either. These techniques will help you communicate.

Try asking for advice from your agency rather than for information. By phrasing your questions properly, you can get the answers you want. For example, suppose that you are concerned that a major customer may be closing a plant in the agency's territory and that a direct request for information has gotten no response. You might try approaching the agency owner with this statement: "I'm concerned about the possibility of losing business from Amalgamated, and I'd like to do some planning to cover the loss. I'd appreciate your thinking on this situation." By asking for advice, you will be putting the agency person on an equal footing with you, and in order to give you the advice, he must deal with your question.

Indirect questions are frequently more effective with tight-lipped people and with anyone else for that matter. Direct questions are often perceived in a threatening way. For example, if you feel that for some reason you might be losing business from a particular customer, rather than asking the agency directly, you might say something like this: "You know, we're running at capacity now, and in order to accommodate all the business in your territory, we should think about adding some people. What do you think?" The quiet agency is most likely to respond to this with the information you need. The lack of response is not always a sign of problems that the agency may be having. One manufacturer said: "The agency people had become good friends with us and were genuinely reluctant to tell us that we had slipped on quality. An indirect approach brought it all out in the open and we corrected it."

This isn't subterfuge, and the approaches are as appropriate with people who communicate easily as they are with others. It's important to remember that you are not seeking to get at private, privileged information—only information that will help you and help your agencies.

COLLECT PHONE CALLS WORK WHEN YOU SET GUIDELINES

One manufacturer who knows how difficult it is for agency salespeople to communicate with principals because of their tight on-the-road schedules accepts collect calls but has established some guidelines for them: They will take calls whenever they relate specifically to an immediate sales problem or when the agent needs sales or engineering help.

Another trades calls with the agencies. That is, every other call is accepted collect. They don't keep track of them—it's a matter of trust.

When the difference in time zones and the variations in rates for off-hour calls are considered, the bill for collect calls may not be too bad for the practical help it provides your communications—and the spirit of cooperation it kindles with your agencies.

HOW TO GET YOUR POINT ACROSS AND MAKE POINTS WITH YOUR AGENCIES

"I think the guy used to be a platoon leader," an agent said of one of his principals. "He'd call a meeting without giving us any idea of what he wanted to discuss and then would spend a whole morning telling us what we were going to do." The agent added that he finally had to call a halt to this one-sided relationship after the principal demanded written reports on projects that he had unilaterally dictated.

>>>→ **OBSERVATION** The job of guiding a network of agencies has been described as 60 percent educated decision-making and 40 percent putting the decisions across. However, no manager operates in a vacuum, and the decision-making and managing process benefits dramatically from extensive interaction. Research done by some of the top consultants seems to fit nicely with the input from sales managers who have been successful with their agencies.

Let's look at some of the points the practical managers and the theoretical people agree on.

Even if your plans are in the best interest of an agency and no big changes are required, there will be some resistance—it's just human nature. For the most part, new things and ideas are usually treated with suspicion. Most people can grasp the benefits inherent in well-thought-out ideas. The toughest job is convincing them to change the way they have been doing things.

If you define your objectives clearly and have all the facts gathered and presented in clear and unambiguous language, you will be off to a good start. If you stick with the facts and do everything you can to avoid emotional arguments, your agencies will be able to see where you are going and where you would like them to go.

Never assume that your plans will have the same impact on all of your agencies. Each agency is made up of individuals with different needs and different goals. Sure, there are some common elements to all, but it's the intensity of the individual feelings that are most important. Each individual is going to look at your proposal with this question in mind: "How does it affect me personally?" They will want to know what they stand to gain and to lose, and these questions must often be handled individually, agency by agency.

As in selling a product or a service, the key to success with agencies is seeing your proposal from each agent's eyes. You must be able to put yourself in each individual's shoes and try to anticipate the objections as well as the points that will be readily accepted.

Although you want to be sure to make your points, it's important to be a good listener during the process. Too often, sales managers get too caught up in the mechanics of their presentation to hear some of the objections. They may actually hear the objections, but in their zeal to give a good presentation, they fail to perceive the full impact of what is being said.

The presentation should be attractive. This may seem like a blinding glimpse of the obvious, but when salespeople are trying to convince other salespeople, they often forget that the same elements used with customers are important in their salesperson-to-salesperson meetings. Use documentation: visuals, slides, pictures, whatever will help.

Although this point is in the middle of the list, it is probably one of the most important: Make the agency an active party in the presentation and, if at all possible, get the basic material to the agency for review before you make your proposal. When you can do this, ask for agency input before you make a formal presentation. When this kind of teamwork can be mustered, plans will be strengthened, and it will be a lot easier to put them into productive action.

When you make your formal presentation, start off with points you and your agency hold in common agreement. A common ground base makes it a lot easier to move into new ideas with a minimum of resistance. If disagreement does arise, avoid defeating anyone. You can win battles but lose wars when your ego gets in the way.

This may seem too basic to repeat, but you'd be surprised at how many top salespeople forget to sell benefits when they are trying to convince someone of anything other than the virtues of their products. Spell out the benefits carefully, and make absolutely certain that those you talk with know exactly what's in the presentation for them.

At this point, you should either have agreement or you should know what problems your agencies have with your proposal. If there is agreement, there is nothing else to do. However, if there are problems, solve them and follow the same steps when you present your revised plan.

KEEP YOUR AGENCIES INFORMED ON COMPETITION

As a manufacturer, you probably get more than a few of the free circulation magazines that serve your industry. These magazines contain a wealth of solid competitive information for your agents. The chances are that your agencies don't get to see these magazines because of the controlled circulation requirements. An aggressive sales manager told us recently: "I have assigned an assistant in the marketing department to go through all of these magazines from cover to cover. She knows who our competitors are and she clips their ads and press releases. Every two weeks we make up packages that include copies of this material for each of our agencies. After all, the agencies give us good feedback on the regional and local level. This just completes the picture for everyone."

Example: Another manufacturer told us that he goes a step further. "I circle the Bingo numbers of competitors' ads and releases and have the information sent to a friend in another business. I send this material as well as the ads and releases to my agencies." Well informed is well ahead.

HOW TO USE NEWSLETTERS TO COMMUNICATE
WITH YOUR AGENCIES

We've seen some spectacular multicolor newsletters created by manufacturers to communicate with their agencies, but one of the most effective was typed on a single sheet of paper and was sent to the entire agency network—two agents! "Newsletters are the perfect tool for passing information, motivating, and building morale," we were told by the sales manager who produced this letter. "There is no reason why you can't have a newsletter with two agents if you do it right."

The key idea is to do it right. Too many manufacturers fail to take advantage of the power of an agency newsletter simply because they feel they have too small an agency team or because they will go first class or not at all. However, the definition of first class in a good agency newsletter has very little to do with pizzazz—but it has everything to do with what is said and how it's said. After talking with a number of manufacturers who produce newsletters regularly for their agencies, we have summarized the three factors that spell success.

1.   Target the purpose . . . and the audience. Before you start any agency newsletter you have to decide exactly what you want it to do. It can teach, inform, announce, motivate, entertain, persuade, and inspire. A newsletter can, of course, have more than one goal. But the goals you select should be specific and should be kept in mind when you seek material to write each issue. You're probably wondering why we stress targeting an audience when we're talking about sending the newsletter only to your agencies. Actually, within those agencies there may be several audiences for your letter: the agency owners, the agency office staff, and the agency sales staff. More than likely, the same material will be of interest to each group; but if you can, it helps to target material to individuals and identifiable groups. As important as it is for you to set these goals, it's probably more important to let everyone who is to get the letter know just what you are up to. Make them feel that you have singled them out and that you are going to talk to them in the letter directly—and do it!

2.   Determine your editorial goals. Most agents want to know about your company, its background, organizational structure, operating procedures, and business philosophy. And they want to be kept informed of new policies and how they will affect them. The agency newsletter is one of the best ways to convey this information. Also, agents like the opportunity to express themselves. Be sure to give them this chance with your newsletter. However, the guidelines for this letter, and for all company publications for that matter, should center on positive material. How-to material and helpful advice is perfect, but gripe and kvetch material should not be aired publicly. And don't forget that even a small newsletter can benefit from some feature material, such as profiles of corporate staff and agents.

3.   Get help from others to do the job. Even a small newsletter can take time to do. And if you're the one who has to do it and you get bogged down, the letter will reflect the problems in its content and probably in an irregular publication schedule. To be most effective, a newsletter should be published on an announced

schedule—and publication dates should not be missed. You'll probably find more than a few willing hands to help in doing the job if you offer a by-line. People do like to see their names in print. But make sure that you have time to review all copy before it's cast in stone.

COMMUNICATING ALONE ISN'T THE ANSWER
TO IMPROVED PERFORMANCE

Listen to the consultants who hawk communications packages and programs to businesses and you're liable to think that communications alone is all that's needed to get things moving. This just isn't true. Communications experts have recently determined that formal communications, such as a review once or twice a year, can do little to motivate and increase productivity. However, such communications are most effective when it's part of day-to-day operations. This is especially meaningful when working with agencies. Because they are not employees, many manufacturers don't keep as actively in touch as they would if they were employees. These experts have also determined that clarity is also critical for effective communications. This may seem like a restatement of the obvious, but it isn't. Clear instructions to agencies, for example, make them feel more secure in their relationship with you than they would ordinarily. And when you are consistent, your communications will be much more effective. Manufacturers who blast their agencies one day and praise them the next leave the team in a perplexed muddle that affects performance. Make it clear, make it consistent, and stay in touch regularly is the message.

HOW TO COMPENSATE FOR TIME ZONE DIFFERENCES

An agency owner on the West Coast once complained to several of his principals in the East that they had only a five-hour window with them. "When it's two o'clock in Portland, you Easterners are going home," he said. One of this man's principals took this to heart and had one person stay on in the sales department every night until eight o'clock. "The principal had other people on different flex-time arrangements, so it was no particular hardship," the agent explained. It doesn't take a three-hour coast-to-coast difference to make this work. Just keeping someone for one extra hour for one time zone can be important in some industries, especially those in which agents need price and product information instantly.

SPOTTER'S FEE BUILDS BUSINESS

More than a few manufacturers use different agency teams to sell different products. However, any agent on the move is bound to spot opportunities for the products he doesn't sell. Recently, we've heard of several manufacturers that pay agents a spotter's fee when they turn up leads for the agencies that sell the manufacturers' other products. "We give any agent a one percent commission for spotting leads for our other products," a manufacturer claimed. It should be noted that this is on top of the commission the manufacturer would pay the selling agent when a sale is made.

12

Building Business with Trade Shows

In some industries, trade shows are an effective way of promoting and selling products. They are also an effective way for agencies in the territory in which the show is held to multiply their productivity for their principals. In this chapter is a collection of reports on the techniques that manufacturers have used successfully.

Too many manufacturers participate in trade shows with only loosely articulated goals for the show. In this chapter, you'll discover how to set appropriate goals that your participating agents will support—and that you will both benefit from.

A six-point checklist shows you how to get the most from your show dollars by planning carefully with your agencies.

The in-plant show is growing in popularity. It's an especially effective tool when you can create an exhibit that can be shipped from one territory to another for agencies to use. This chapter gives you practical guidelines for making the most of this technique.

HOW TO UTILIZE YOUR AGENTS AT NATIONAL TRADE SHOWS

With more companies participating in national trade shows it becomes good sense to invite a selected group of agents to work the booth. Agents chosen for this duty will be pleased that they were selected and will likely put in as many hours as required.

The plus factor, of course, is when a current or prospective customer shows up from the agent's home territory. The agent's presence impresses the customer with the emphasis you place on your agency program. A prospective customer can be greeted by the home agent, making a follow-up visit by the agent all the more valuable.

Another advantage surfaces as the agent is able to observe experienced company personnel in the booth, answering questions about your firm's products. This increases the agent's product knowledge and is particularly helpful when a new person comes on board.

REGIONAL TRADE SHOWS—ARE THEY WORTH IT?

Firms that regularly participate in national trade shows have a yearly budget and are able to measure the results of these appearances with sophisticated data. Others realize that measurement is impossible because of the nature of their product line and use the shows as prestige-builders for their company and as morale-builders for salespeople in the field.

So much for the large companies with seemingly unlimited budgets. What about the smaller company whose promotional funds have to be spent judiciously and to whom image-building is an unaffordable luxury? How can this type of firm take advantage of trade shows?

>>>→ *IDEA IN ACTION* The regional trade show is often the answer. For smaller companies it has proven to be a good media for supplementing their other marketing efforts. But care must be taken on several fronts to make certain that a regional show can produce the desired results. A checklist is useful in determining in advance whether or not the risk is worth it. Here are some typical considerations:

What is the cost of the show in relation to a similar national show? Some small show operators charge the same fees as the larger shows but the added freight is seldom worth it.

Is the show compatible with your company's best interests? Will other companies making similar products be exhibiting? This is an interesting question because normally it is wise to exhibit only if competitors will be present, indicating that the show is ideally suited to your prospective customers. Particularly astute sales managers, however, have spotted certain shows their competitors disdain but where the audience mix makes exhibiting worthwhile.

Is the regional area you are considering overrun with similar shows? Too many shows of the same type dilute the effectiveness of the audience quality, and you may find that many of your best prospective customers won't bother to attend.

What is your true purpose in exhibiting? If you are new to an area, the regional show may be an excellent place to introduce yourself to area buyers, even though you may not be able to justify expenses based on immediate returns.

To what extent will your agents participate? Are they enthusiastic about your appearance at the show or will they be busy working at other principals' booths? Do they show a complete lack of interest in your desire to exhibit? The cooperation of your local agents is vital to the success of your exhibit.

If the show appears to be a promising one, most professional agents will be enthusiastic about your participation. They recognize the value of having your booth at their regional show. It certainly states, loud and clear, that your company is committed to selling and servicing accounts in their territory.

Your exhibit also aids them in reaching personnel of companies where they've been unable to get past the purchasing department. One agent tells of beating on a P.A.'s door for over two years with a product he knew would save the customer thousands of dollars per year. At a regional show the customer's vice-president of production walked into the principal's booth, was advised of the value of the product by the agent, and within six months had tooled up over fifteen different designs that the principal offered.

It's up to the agent to stimulate a good attendance of current and prospective customers at your booth, but you've got to help. Good promotional literature announcing your intention to exhibit can be provided to the agent along with complimentary admission tickets that he can distribute to customers. Also, try to have a good reason for exhibiting; the introduction of a new product or a dramatic improvement of an old one, for instance. This will pique customer interest and help the agent improve attendance.

> **≫→ *WATCH THIS*** Who pays for the booth? Should you shoulder the entire cost, including the exhibit, floor space, travel costs, hotel bills, as well as entertaining customers while you're in town? We don't think so.
>
> Of course, a great deal depends upon the quality of the show and who talked whom into exhibiting. If your agent was reluctant about the possibilities, you may want to absorb the entire cost so if you were wrong he won't be out several hundred dollars with no results to show for his expense.
>
> On the other hand, if he talked you into exhibiting, then some sharing is in order. Normally at a show that both parties feel is a good risk, the agent will pay for half the booth space and you pick up the rest of the costs. If the agent has his own exhibit that you can utilize, then a different proportion can be worked out.

After each show, it's important to assess the overall impact and results of the exhibit. However, the results of one show are usually not enough to decide whether or not to participate in future regional shows.

To properly evaluate results, take into consideration the following:

• Did your exhibit produce good bona fide leads? It takes several weeks, even months, to find out the quality of the leads that developed at a show. Stress to your agents that their prompt feedback on these leads is important and that their reports will go a long way toward determining the wisdom of participating in future shows.

• Did it appear that your products were good candidates for this show? Products that are made by many companies (stampings, fasteners, and so on) are frequently poor lead producers at these shows unless an innovative production process can show dramatic cost savings.

• Was the quality of attendees up to your standards? Very often the right people don't attend regional shows because the show's promoters haven't convinced them it would be worth their time. Instead, they'll send non-decision-makers in their organizations to gain a little education about various products. Certain machine tool shows, for instance, have a large registration of apprentice machinists who may prove to be potential customers but who at the present time have no power to influence buying decisions.

- Was your agent enthusiastic about the show? Did he show up on time every morning? Did he spend as much time as possible in the booth instead of wandering around seeing other people and exhibits? Did he offer to help erect and tear down the exhibit? Did he eagerly greet visitors to the booth?

- Were you or your agent able to set up definite appointments with buyers who visited your booth? If you received enough interest from visitors to be invited to their offices, you can be sure the show was worthwhile.

Trade shows are becoming more numerous every year, which is a good sign. Buyers and engineers are becoming accustomed to attending these shows with an eye toward increasing the efficiency of their individual responsibilities and to stay abreast of improvements and innovations that will help them do their jobs effectively. Exhibiting at these shows can be an excellent shortcut to new and profitable business.

HOW TO MAKE TRADE SHOWS MORE PRODUCTIVE FOR YOURSELF AND YOUR AGENTS

"Every time I spring for the money to send my agents to a trade show, they spend more time sniffing out new lines than they do working my booth." That's what one cynical sales manager told us. Fortunately, he's in the minority. Another one claims that ". . . we couldn't be any more successful at trade shows than we are without the help of our agents." Let's look at the factors that make trade shows work for you and your agents:

There's no group of businesspeople for whom the old saying, "Time is money," has more meaning than for agents. When you pull an agent out of the field and make him stand watch in your trade show booth, he isn't selling. He knows that if he's from New York and the show is in Los Angeles, not many people from his territory will be there. Much of his effort will most likely show up as commissions for the L.A. agent. However, trade shows can be productive for agents and principals.

Caution: Understand that agents have different goals from manufacturers at trade shows. You may be there because you have national distribution, but your agents are looking out mainly for people from their territories. Accept this, but make sure that your goals are understood and that your agents treat everyone with the same interest.

Set goals for agent participation well in advance of show time. And be sure to communicate these goals to everyone who will be there. Allow your agents time to respond to your memo with thoughts of their own. Then ask them to acknowledge the work that will be expected of them before, during, and after the show.

Being there is only a start. You've seen booths bustling with activity and others in which people seem to be doing nothing but waiting for closing time. The difference is strictly planning and management. Left to float by itself, even the best exhibit can look like a wake. Keep up the chatter. Keep your people on their feet. Keep things moving. If anyone needs a rest, let them take it away from the booth.

Have daily critiques of performance with everyone. Be sure to review the goals with everyone working the booth every day. Be generous with your compliments to those doing the job, and take time to point out what the others must do to hold up their end of the bargain.

Trade show success begins months before the show opens. Insist that each of your agents contacts their customers and prospects to see who will be at the show. Get times of arrival, hotels at which each will stay, and schedules for their visits to the show. With this information, you can either plan individual calls to ensure that they will stop at your booth or you can set up meetings at your hospitality suite. Do more than simply send the usual show management announcements—take the time to send a personal letter to those you want to see. Copy your agents, of course.

Leave nothing to chance. Shows are expensive, but there's no better way to see a concentration of customers and prospects at one time. Use these tips to make the most of your show dollars:

1. Tell your agents what will be shown, what will not be shown, and what you want emphasized. Be sure to hold a pre-show briefing on special programs.

2. Keep a sheet posted in your exhibit that has at least the following information: Daily booth assignments, local addresses and phone numbers of all agents and factory personnel, dates and times of arrival for all, and information to help booth attendants make the most of visits from special people. Important: Restate the goals that everyone has agreed to.

3. Try to arrange for a separate place where you and your agents can meet undisturbed by customers. It could be a specially designed section of the booth or a hotel room or local office rented just for the period of the show.

4. Designate one person as the prime contact for your agents. This person should set up meetings with factory personnel and your agents, at the request of either. You'll save a lot of time with this system.

5. If you have junior salespeople or new agents at the show, position them so they can watch and listen to the old pros in action. Some of the best training can take place in this situation. But, don't let your new people interfere with a pro in action. They should just watch and listen.

6. Plan a post-show follow-up. You will have gathered a lot of names, and your agents will have talked with many people. Keep the momentum going! Follow up with your agents to make sure that they make the most of the leads that have cost you a bundle. For best results, prescreen these names before you send them to the field.

WHEN TO HAVE ALL YOUR AGENTS ATTEND A TRADE SHOW

Some manufacturers who use agents and who participate in national trade shows feel that their agents—from all territories—should man the booth. In fact, they often play sneaky games such as having national sales meetings during the period of the show and expecting agents to take their turn on the boards. But it seems that time and the state of the economy are going to make it easier for everyone.

Regional and local shows are becoming more popular, and for many manufacturers, more practical. This means that your booth-staffing problems will be solved—the agents who cover the territories in which the shows are being held will gladly do booth duty. After all, the people they talk to will be their prospects, not those of another agent.

Even though the shows will be smaller, they will still attract the same calibre of people who would normally go to national shows. Don't skimp. Promote the show. Promote your participation. And promote the agents who will be covering the booth.

HOW TO HELP AN AGENCY WITH A LOCAL TRADE SHOW

The local trade show—the one that features regional salespeople and the agencies that cover the territory—have proliferated. This is probably due to the diminished attendance of many of the larger national shows. Whatever the reason, there seems to be more regional and local shows than ever before. Those who sponsor exhibits and the agencies that participate have discovered that it's no longer a matter of just announcing a show to ensure good attendance. It takes a bit of hustle to build a good crowd.

Example: "We used to send little announcement cards, and we'd fill the hall," a sales manager told us. "Our agencies would spread the word during their calls. This and the little mailing was all we needed. But not anymore. It takes quite a bit of effort to get people to turn out." This sales manager now has his ad agency developing hard-hitting mailings that are imprinted with the name and address of each of the agencies that will be taking part in the local show. The material is sent to the agencies for local mailing to customers and prospects. The manufacturer picks up the mailing costs and postage when the agencies submit appropriate receipts.

"We don't look for quantity attendance anymore," a marketing VP said. "We look for quality. And the only way you can be sure to get the right people—the quality factor that can spell success—is to promote the show heavily. The direct mail approach plus the agencies spreading the news by word of mouth can do a lot to make a show work for us."

"Pre-show meetings are important," an agent said when he was talking about his participation in a manufacturer's regional show. "We find that we can get some of the best application information we need to sell—not only at the show but every day at these briefings." Manufacturers that sponsor regional shows feel that they are often able to do a better job of application training before regional shows than at the bigger shows. "At the national shows," one small company president said, "we have too many other things to attend to. At the smaller local and regional shows we can concentrate on the material we know our agencies need to be successful. This doesn't mean that the bigger national shows don't work anymore," he continued. "It does mean, though, that we have learned how to concentrate emphasis where it will do the most good for us in the smaller and the bigger shows."

"When we started doing more regional shows a year," we were told by one manufacturer's advertising manager, "we began asking more questions at those shows. Actually, the increased show frequency gave us the opportunity to correct mistakes more quickly and to take action on opportunities faster than ever. When you do four or five shows a year, you should be able to make each one more productive than the previous one and end up with more growth than if you do only one or two national shows a year." This ad manager took the time to get feedback from the agencies that participated in the regional shows, and he also mailed post-show questionnaires to the customers and prospects who visited the booth. The correlation between the views of both groups was high and positive. He was able to spot problems and opportunities quickly. This same ad manager also kept each of the company's agencies informed of the results with a steady flow of brief reports.

HELP YOUR AGENCIES MAKE THE MOST OF IN-PLANT SHOWS

"Local shows have become the best way to go for us," a sales manager told us. "They are cost effective, and we get solid cooperation from the agencies in the territories in which the shows are held. However, you might want to expand on an even smaller but potentially more effective way to go the local show route—the in-plant show."

In-plant shows can be especially productive with larger companies that employ many people who are prospects for the products sold by your agencies. For example, the large engineering firms with centralized engineering and purchasing departments are prime targets for in-plant shows. Here are some tips from those who have made effective use of in-plant trade shows:

1. "I make sure to emphasize the educational aspects of our in-plant shows," an agent told us. "It is sometimes difficult for engineers to get the time off to visit an in-plant show—even when it's under their own roof—if there isn't something for them to learn."

2. "When I am planning an in-plant show, I will often shoot for an early morning or late afternoon time to make sure that I can get the people away from their work," another agent said. "Some companies don't like the idea of breaking into the day of their employees. Whenever my shows are scheduled, I make sure that notices are sent well in advance and that announcements are placed conspicuously on the plant bulletin boards."

3. Another agent had his first few in-plant shows fall flat because he got a little too dramatic. He said: "I wasn't accustomed to these little shows. I was used to working the booth in large national shows, where everyone is fighting for attention with bells and whistles. I tried to do the same things with my little in-plant show. I didn't do well at all. When I realized that I didn't have to compete with anyone else for the attention of potential customers, I got rid of the razzle-dazzle and concentrated on doing a good educational job. It worked. The glitz didn't."

4. "Believe it or not," an agent said, "I forgot to get the names of the people I talked with at my first in-plant show. I really didn't expect many people to attend, but during the day, more than fifty people came by. I knew better the next time."

Here are some additional tips:

1. Provide samples and literature, tailored for the show if possible.
2. Send invitations—you can usually get the names of the individuals in the plant who will be your prospects by contacting department heads and personnel people.
3. Send personal thank you letters to those in the plant who helped make the show possible.
4. Follow up with everyone who attended the show—send sales literature or whatever would be appropriate for your specific show.

HOW YOUR AGENTS CAN IMPROVE TRADE SHOW RESULTS

When you take part in a national trade show and have the agent in the territory in which the show is held work your booth, there are a few things you can do to make the show more productive for your company *and* for the agency. Here are a few suggestions that have been passed along to us recently:

• If you have any experience with trade shows, you will probably try to get a list of the people who will attend the show from all over the country and mail to those who are of special interest to you. Because your agent-in-the-booth will be mainly concerned with the people from his territory who attend the show, it makes sense to make a special mailing to these people. Announce that the agent in their area will be at the booth and build up the local aspects of the relationship.

• Help your agent develop a targeted presentation if conditions are different in different territories. For example, those selling process instrumentation will have different approaches for shows in Texas oil fields than they will have in another part of the country where their products might be used in pharmaceutical processing. When you can key this presentation to the agent in the territory, you give that agent strong tools to use.

• Have an extra quantity of your sales literature preprinted with the local agent's name and address. This literature should be handed only to those who have been identified as coming from the local territory.

• Keep a stock of your local agent's business cards in the booth to hand out to visitors from the territory. Have everyone in the booth—not just the local agent—give out cards to those who come from the territory.

Even though a trade show may be billed as a national show, most of the people who attend will come from rather close to home. This means that the local agency should get a lot of play.

HELP YOUR AGENCIES DO PRE-TRADE SHOW ADVERTISING

Even when a trade show is billed as a national event, most of the attendees come from relatively close-by areas. It makes sense for you to promote the show if you are participating. And it makes excellent sense for you to earmark a good portion of your show promotion budget to helping the agent or agents in the area who will be most affected by the show. "We always launch a heavy direct mail campaign before a show," a marketing VP explained recently. "Most of the direct mail money is spent to promote the participation of the agencies in the primary coverage area of the show." This executive explained that he sends letters to key accounts and prospects to invite them to attend the show and clearly identifies that he would like these people to meet with his agent, who will be manning the booth. "I always follow up on the phone with the most important of these people," he said. The results are worthwhile, according to this executive and to the agency he has promoted at show time.

HOW TO AVOID TRADE SHOW OVERKILL

We probably shouldn't complain when a manufacturer spends a lot of money on designing and building a trade show exhibit that will be used mainly by sales agents in their territories. But we think it's worth passing along this comment from a midwestern agent: "When _____ told us that he had budgeted for a new trade show exhibit specifically for agents to use in their territories, I was very pleased. When he told us how much he was spending, I thought it was terrific. But when we saw the exhibit, we all knew it was a dog. Not that it had been done by a tasteless designer or built by a shoemaker, but it was a razzle-dazzle that completely overpowered the product—and the product benefits. The manufacturer had not only tried to cram every product into the exhibit, but he had insisted on overdesign. It was pure show biz; not practical at all." Although the agent was too modest to suggest it, we think that if you're building a trade show exhibit that will be used by your sales agents, they should be given the opportunity to make some constructive suggestions.

13

Creating Effective Advertising, Publicity, and Contests

In the industrial sector, much of the average manufacturer's advertising dollars are spent to develop leads for their sales agencies. In this Chapter, we provide guidance in not only developing effective promotion, but in merchandising this promotion with sales agencies.

The question of sales lead qualification is explored from virtually every perspective. You are guided in how to do it effectively, in determining who should do the qualifying, and when the qualification work should be done.

A seven-point checklist shows you how to get the most out of the inquiries your agencies may tend to ignore. We also discuss the tight-focus technique of direct mail. You will have enough guidance to not only create effective direct mail, but to make use of all the subsystems such as list acquisition and follow-up.

We also detail exactly how you can use public relations techniques effectively to promote yourself, your products, and your agencies. You will be shown why sales contests are seldom very effective with agencies and what you can use in their place.

BUSINESS CARDS—WHO SUPPLIES THEM?

You do. Leaving this up to your agents can result in some pretty sorry cards. Although they may be whizzes at selling, most agents have a lot to learn about graphics and promotional techniques.

If you've designed a good card for your home office personnel, why not take advantage of the money spent and pass along this benefit to your agents. With a little modification, your card can be revised to include the agent's name, address, and phone number. It's done all the time.

By providing cards, you avoid having your agent visit a prospective customer using his own card, which usually tells little about the products he's selling. A golden opportunity is sometimes lost because the buyer is unaware of the product being sold and so refuses to see the rep.

When you supply your agents with a good-looking prestigious business card, you are assuring yourself that he's putting your best foot forward.

A word of caution though—when providing your agents with company cards bearing their name, be sure to use the title "Sales Agent" or "Sales Representative." "Sales" is the key word that limits that agent's authority and responsibility to his contracted territory.

USING DIRECT MAIL ADVERTISING? SEND YOUR AGENTS A COPY

Believe it or not, some firms conducting imaginative direct mail campaigns neglect to put their agencies on the mailing list. They figure the agents know all about the company anyhow, so why waste postage.

What they forget is that a direct mail piece gives an agent a good reason to make a call on current or potential customers—he can discuss the features outlined in the mailing and occasionally discover a customer who has been inadvertently omitted from the list.

Keeping your mailing list current is essential. We'll discuss later how to get your reps to help you keep your names up to date.

HOW ABOUT AN AGENCY BROCHURE?

When interviewing prospective agents, you'll find it worthwhile to have a brochure outlining the features and facilities of your company and its philosophy toward its agencies. It doesn't have to be a four-color creation—just an offset-type folder or sheet detailing the essentials.

Agents like to know that a prospective principal is committed to the agency way of selling. And if you can convince them of your company's stability and longstanding relationships with current agencies, you'll have a better chance of attracting the top agents.

Features to include in your brochure include names of your current agents, length of their service, how long you've had an agent program, a description of your advertising and sales promotion backup, and names of inside personnel and their functions. Even a few references from current agents would be helpful.

Anyone can sign up agencies, but attracting the top professionals takes a little extra effort and sophistication.

FIRST INQUIRIES ARE PURE GOLD

When your agent mails you an inquiry from a company you've never dealt with before, give it the red carpet treatment. That inquiry may have cost hundreds of dollars of the agent's time and expenses, so don't let it slip away with a "sorry, not compatible with our equipment," reply.

Caution: Inquiries cost money; orders cost even more. If you don't treat that first inquiry with tender loving care, all the groundwork your agent performed with that prospective customer may go down the drain.

Even if you can't make what the customer wants, stretch a little. And if you still can't make it, write him a considerate letter outlining why you can't meet his requirements and then go on to explain how you might help him in the future. Getting a buyer to think about changing sources is costly, so go all out in keeping him on the line.

FIRST ORDERITIS—TRY TO OVERCOME IT

That first order from a new customer may have cost the agent (and you) a bundle. He may have vigorously pursued an elusive account for months or even years; and now he has an order. Praise be!

> ⫸ *WATCH OUT FOR THIS* If you treat it as a routine order, you're doing the agent and yourself a disfavor. All the customer knows about your company is what the agent has told him, and any slip-up on quality or delivery can eliminate the agent's hard work.

Red-tag that first order. Watch its progress like a mother hen. Make sure everyone remotely connected with its processing is aware that this is for a new customer. Tell the production manager, the quality control manager, and even the shipping department head. Drop the buyer a thank you note. Tell him you're happy to have him with you, and then make sure the order receives a No. 1 priority from the troops in the plant.

Good "first order" performance will keep your agents out scouting up new potential customers; poor performance will dampen their enthusiasm.

UPDATING YOUR CHRISTMAS LIST?
ASK YOUR AGENTS TO HELP

Companies sending presents to customers often wait too long to update their lists, and retired or departed purchasing agents receive unexpected gifts whereas current buyers are left out in the cold.

Make sure your agents get in on the act as early as September, since reps are notoriously slow about responding. One way to make sure they get their list back to you promptly is to put their name at the head of the list. They won't want to miss their turkey or bottle of spirits and will get about their task quickly.

> ⫸ *IDEA IN ACTION* A much more effective way of giving gifts to favored customers is to send them a "Choose Your Own Gift" booklet late in the spring—just before they start thinking about vacations. This makes your generosity stand out in vivid contrast to a gift at Christmastime when other vendors are pressing good things on them.

$250,000 A YEAR FROM THE YELLOW PAGES
FOR A DALLAS AGENCY

Sounds like an ad for the Bell Systems, but it's not. The Dallas agent involved has documented his case to us.

One of his seven principals co-ops with him in the phone advertising directory, but he went ahead and entered small insertions for his other principals at his own expense—the tab runs about $70 a month.

He admits he's been lucky and often receives calls for one principal and winds up selling the customer a product of one of his other lines; so all principals benefit.

>>> *OBSERVATION* Cooperative advertising in the Yellow Pages may not pay off this year or next, but eventually a contact is made and the possibility of a sale becomes a reality. It only costs a few dollars to divide this expense with your reps, and it could bring surprising results. Most agents aren't as entrepreneurial as the Dallas man, so unless you stimulate them by co-oping, no ads will appear. Why not try it for at least three years—but make certain you receive feedback from the agents as part of the condition for financially participating.

SEND A COPY OF NEW INQUIRIES TO
YOUR REPRESENTATIVES

Agents are accustomed to receiving copies of quotations, whether or not they initiated the original inquiry. But often when they didn't initiate the inquiry, the first thing they know about it is when they see the quote. This may be right after they made a call on the customer in a town 200 miles from their office.

More and more companies are making a copy of an inquiry they receive and sending it off to their agents the same day it is received. Why? It makes for a more efficient operation by the field force. Since it takes up to three weeks for some companies to quote, the agent may have been in a customer's office completely unaware that the customer had a large inquiry pending with the agent's principal. Without this knowledge, he's missed an excellent opportunity to review the customer's requirements and pass along vital information to his principal. For instance, he may find out that several quotes may have already been received by the customer and he's about to place the order. Or perhaps he'll discover that no one else is quoting and a conventional markup will be sufficient to get the job.

Also, when a representative knows there's a big job brewing at one of his distant customers, he may be able to alter his travel plans so that he'll arrive at the customer's plant a day or two after your quote is received.

USE YOUR BUSINESS CARDS TO YOUR BEST ADVANTAGE

Only three out of seven principals supply their agents with business cards. There are a variety of reasons for this omission: Some sales managers don't understand the importance of supplying cards, managements object to the cost, and others simply don't want the hassle.

Business cards are as important as the receptionist who greets customers and answers the phone—they both give an impression, good or bad, of the company.

When your agent walks in to see Mr. Customer and hands him a card that reads, "James Haskins, manufacturers' representative," it doesn't mean a thing to the person receiving it. He doesn't know if the man is selling diesel engines or children's toys. But that's what the average agent does if you don't supply him with your cards. Very few go to the bother and expense of making up a special card that indicates they represent your company.

>>>→ *IDEA IN ACTION*   If you're not supplying cards now, check with your printer and find out how much it costs to run your standard card with each agent's name and address on several hundred cards. By running a volume of cards at one time, you'll find the cost surprisingly low.

Ask each agent how many cards he'll need for a year. Then send each of them their cards and plan for another run when the year is up. Also have the printer make up an extra thousand or two with only the company name and address on them. If you add an agent (or direct company person) during the interim between printings, you'll have these cards ready, and the printer can insert the new agent's name and address at a very nominal cost.

When providing your agents with company cards bearing their name, be sure to use the title "Sales Agent" or "Sales Representative."

"Sales" is the key word that limits that agent's authority and responsibility to his contracted territory.

MAKE THE MOST OF YOUR DIRECTORY ADVERTISING

Companies that advertise in the *Thomas Register* and other trade directories often don't take full advantage of their listings. They show their name and address under the correct product heading but neglect to do the same for the agents, and that's a mistake.

A close inspection of these directories will show that many firms list each of their agents and their addresses and even phone numbers.

If there's anything a buyer likes, it's to be able to pick up the phone and have a salesperson trot over to his office the same day to help him out of a bind. To go to a far-off city for help is a natural deterrent, yet many firms ignore this opportunity to include agents in their listings.

Example: Yes, it probably will cost a little more. Space costs money. But the chance to pick up an order that otherwise would have gone to the competition is worth the risk. A southwestern agent picked up a $100,000-a-year account because an electronic firm's buyer wanted a local contact and found the agent's name in his industrial directory.

This is a rare occurrence, but if you do advertise in directories, increase that budget just a little and help your agents latch on to prospects that want a local contact. It'll help you, too.

TELEPHONE SELLING VERSUS PERSONAL SELLING

The rising cost of travel over the past few years has spawned a tremendous interest on the part of sales managements to emphasize the use of the telephone in selling the products of their companies. With sales costs now averaging over $100 per call, it's no wonder that alternatives such as the phone and direct mail are becoming increasingly attractive as methods to cut down on overall sales expense.

But the question always arises: Can the phone and direct mail be as effective as a direct personal call, an in-person visit? And the answer, on balance, has to be no.

Of course, the effectiveness of the phone depends somewhat upon the product being sold. Standard off-the-shelf items can be sold much more successfully by phone than can products involving technical expertise. For instance, stock fasteners, office supplies, and many maintenance items, where price and delivery usually decide who gets the order, can be handled by phone in 90 percent of the cases, with an occasional personal call made to retain the relationship. However, when a product's major selling point is the fact that it can be substituted for a product made from higher priced material or a design feature can eliminate excess machining, then a phone call simply won't do.

Naturally, the phone can be used to interest the prospective buyer in the cost-saving features of the product being sold, enabling the salesperson to make an appointment for a personal call; but often, without a skilled person on the selling end of the wire the message simply doesn't get across well enough to impress the buyer.

The phone will continue to be used for qualifications of sales prospects, following up leads, making appointments, and for many other sales-related purposes, as pointed out in the latest issue of *Agency Sales* magazine. However, the company that can find a way to make personal calls will continue to get the lion's share of the business, which brings us to our point.

Although manufacturers' agents' costs have increased along with everyone else's, and they have had to judiciously utilize the phone and direct mail more than in the past, they also can continue to make those important sales calls in person because they are not selling for just one company. By selling the products of two or more principals to the same customer, the agent can justify higher selling costs. Since he can realize more volume from a customer than can a direct salesperson, the ratio of the cost versus the income allows more personal calls per week than the single-product salesperson.

For those of you using manufacturers' agents, there will be few agonizing decisions necessary about whether to hire a telephone selling consultant and concentrate on a phone selling campaign. Your agents have solved the problem for you.

HOW TO GET THE MOST OUT OF THE ADVERTISING INQUIRIES YOUR AGENTS TEND TO IGNORE

"My agents pushed me to increase my advertising budget so that they would get a lot of inquiries. Last year I spent $60,000 that produced over 3,000 inquiries. Do you know that those agents only followed up on 20 percent of them!" That's what one unhappy manufacturer told us. He's not alone. Many manufacturers have had similar experiences. Now let's listen to the agent's side of the story:

"You wouldn't believe the garbage they (the manufacturers) send me that they call 'sales leads.' They tell me how much it costs to produce these leads and expect me to spend my time bird-dogging every job shop in the territory where the owner is building up a literature file."

Who is right? In truth, both are right. But each has a lot to learn about leads produced by magazine advertising and product publicity.

>>>→ *OBSERVATION* Every year American manufacturers spend millions of dollars on advertising to turn up leads. However, very little is spent on screening these leads to ensure that agent's calls are most productive. When properly screened, inquiries can be called sales leads, but not until then! Remember, readers are selective in the information they request, they do buy the products you sell, and they use other sources when seeking product information.

Many of those who respond to advertising have no current purchase in mind, but those who do will buy from a competitor unless you get to them first. The trick is to sort the prospects from the catalog collectors and to keep after them until a buying decision is made.

About one third of all inquiries are for immediate needs, another third are six months to a year away from a sale, and the balance represents some indefinable future market. This is what most trade magazine publishers have found, but the trick is to sort the inquiries and treat them accordingly.

It's best to begin with tight internal screening, say those who have been most successful with advertising inquiries. Today, most magazines not only provide the name and address of the inquirer, they also give a lot of helpful information. Many ask the respondent to indicate the urgency of the interest, the application, the anticipated time of purchase, and the possible volume or unit of sale. If you start with this information, you will have a good first sorting.

If the inquiry doesn't have much information, you or someone in the sales department should look up every lead in one or more of the standard directories, such as *Thomas Register,* or one of the D & B guides. At least you will then know the size of the company, and you should be able to get an idea of the nature of their business and how your product might be used.

Don't neglect your own records and the information stored in the heads of your marketing people. You may already be selling to the company, but the lead may be from another division. Your people may have personal knowledge of the company or the individual who inquired from previous experience or with those for whom they may have worked in the past. Circulate the inquiries to all and ask for comments.

Try to come up with hard facts, such as estimated sales potential, where and how the product might be used, and what the competitive picture is.

Get on the phone once you have done your preliminary screening. The first review usually eliminates about one third of the inquiries. Now you want to find out who's in a hurry to buy and who can wait for a few months. This is the toughest and most critical part of the screening process. But when you tell your agents that the leads you have just sent are prescreened and that all have an immediate need, you will get fast cooperation.

Now it's up to your agents. If you do a good job of screening, the number of leads sent to the agents will be less than they have been accustomed to. However, be sure to tell them exactly what you are doing. If you send fewer leads than you have in the past, even though they may have complained, your agents may think you have cut back on advertising. Tell them that you have done the screening and that the leads you have sent are all good.

Ask the agents to tell you what they intend to do with each lead. Don't ask for a long-winded report—a simple check-box form will do nicely. If you ask your agents to tell you of their intentions on each lead, rather than just asking for a follow-up report, you will get better results. You have asked for a commitment, and few will be willing to renege.

Be sure to get follow-up information. Again, a simple form will do. Don't burden your agents with detailed reports. However, if you want more information on any individual leads, it's best to get it verbally during one of your regular calls, to avoid burdening your agents with paper work.

Don't get annoyed with an agent's low opinion of advertising and product publicity inquiries. Most have been bugged by zealous marketing people who spend a lot of time figuring the cost of each lead and want to make sure they get their money's worth. They will get their money's worth when the leads are culled and everyone can operate more productively. But don't let the screening process drag on and on. A recent survey showed that almost half of the literature requested by advertising inquiries arrived too late to be of any value.

We talked with a number of manufacturers, agents, and people who respond to advertising, and here's a summary of the thoughts they had that will help you get the most out of your advertising inquiries:

1. Don't assume that all inquiries are good or bad based on the source. Whether you get the inquiry on a company letterhead or on a magazine card, treat each with equal respect until you know which will pay off and which will not.

2. Don't assume that an inquiry from a company with whom you are already doing business is of little or no value. This is especially true of large multi-division companies, but it's just as important to follow up on leads from small companies with whom you may already be doing business. People come and go, and it's foolish to think that everybody knows about your company and your products.

3. Don't rule out a person just because his or her title doesn't match the job description of the people with whom you have been doing business in the past. Many new markets have been opened up through people who, on the surface, seem to have no interest in your product.

4. Do send everything a prospect might need, including price information. This is the biggest single complaint most people have when they are asked to evaluate inquiry follow-up.

5.   Do send the material as quickly as possible.

6.   Be sure that the material you send is clear and not likely to be misunderstood.

7.   Be sure to tell the inquirer the name and address of your local agent.

HOW TO CREATE THE KIND OF VISUAL AIDS YOUR AGENTS NEED AND USE

"Sales aids or an ego trip—who knows?" That's what one agent said of the long-heralded visual extravaganza that had just arrived from one of his principals. "Many visual aids are so clever that the product as well as its benefits and features get lost in the shuffle," he continued.

However, there's no doubt that well-planned and carefully executed visual aids can do a lot for selling.

Most agents welcome sales aids that are designed with them in mind. However, many visual aids are a tour de force of the designer. We talked with a number of agents and these are the points they feel should be considered when visual aids are planned for their use:

1.   The visual aid should be small, easy to carry, easy to use, and—above all—it should not intimidate the prospect. Nothing makes a prospect more nervous than the sight of a movie projector and screen being rolled into his or her office for a cinematic tour of the plant.

2.   Stress the benefits. You may be proud of your plant, but the buyer wants to know what your product, not your building, will do for him.

3.   Include applications that relate to your prospects. If your product can be used in many ways in several fields, design the presentation so that it can be easily field-modified to tell the appropriate story.

4.   Avoid a totally canned program. Asking your agent to simply turn on a slide show while he and the prospect sit and watch is a turnoff for both.

5.   Design the presentation to ensure that there will be active participation by the agent as well as the prospect. The agent should be the focus and the visual aid should serve as a supporting tool. When this is done, the agent can tailor his presentation to suit the needs he perceives in the prospect without having to follow a rigorously planned program.

6.   If possible, include samples of the products, show case histories, and try to show how the products will have specific application for the audience.

What kind of visual aids are most popular with agents? The answer to this question is not easy. There is a big difference between what agents prefer and what manufacturers think they need. However, of those agents we polled, most seemed to think less of elaborate presentations involving visual aid equipment such as tape equipment or projectors. They tend to favor such things as cutaways of the product that might be backed up by a small easel display. However, being the pragmatic, down-to-earth people they are, agents seem to sense what prospects will respond to, and that seems to be reality-oriented material, rather than a company history complete with pictures of the president and his family.

Example: A company in the valve business once supplied agents with kits of parts for one of their needle valves. There were only about a half-dozen parts, but the agents handed them to the prospects and talked them through a step-by-step assembly. As the prospect assembled the valve, the agent highlighted the features and benefits of the components and the reasons the valve was designed and assembled the way it was. This short presentation was accompanied by an easel display of pictures of manufacturing and assembling as it was handled at the plant.

The prospect not only had a hands-on experience, he also got a plant tour that was directly related to something that was dynamic and interesting—the valve that was being assembled by hand at the time. After the presentation, which took less than ten minutes, the prospect was told that he could keep the valve. He could either final assemble it with tools for test use or he could pass it around loosely assembled for others to take apart, assemble, and examine. The presentation met all the agent requirements: It was small, easy to carry, easy to use, and it presented the product benefits in real terms.

CO-OP ADVERTISING HELPS AGENTS PROMOTE YOUR LINE

In many fields there are local and regional magazines published. Some are technical, such as those published by local chapters of the Instrument Society of America. Others are business oriented, such as those produced by local purchasing associations. You may not think it worth the few hundred dollars it costs for a one-year schedule when your national advertising budget is in the hundreds of thousands of dollars. But an ad for your products with the name and address of the local agent will not only stimulate business, it shows your agents that you are willing to help them.

Your advertising budget should include funds for local agent advertising. Include a specific budgetary category; don't just draw from a general fund or nothing will ever be done. Here are some points to consider:

1. Have your advertising agency design the ads so that you can use the same material for all of your agents in different territories by only substituting the name and address of the local agent.

2. Local publications seldom grant the 15 percent commission to advertising agencies—the rates are just too low to make it practical. Under these circumstances, most agencies will bill you for the creative work necessary to produce the ads plus a fee for the media research and placement of the insertions. Normally the charge is 17.65 percent of the ad rate. But because the costs are so small, many agencies charge a flat fee for the research and placement that has no relationship to the cost of the space. This is fair because they are just charging for the time and work done.

3. If you can afford it, pick up the entire tab. If you have many agents and the rates are high, you might consider splitting the tab.

4. If you go the co-op route and only pay part of the freight, don't get into tricky accounting by deducting the cost of ads from commissions. Make each transaction individually.

How big should the ads be and how often should you run? If you must choose between size and frequency, it's best to use smaller space but run in as many issues as possible. Frequent exposure in these publications is important. However, if you've got the money, run larger space and give your agents greater total exposure.

What should the ads try to do? Ads in local publications should be directed at building the image of your agent. This doesn't mean that you have to downplay your product. It simply means that the thrust of the copy and layout should try to get local prospects to think of your agent when they have a need for the products you make. Stress service, local stock if one is available, and the reputation of your agent.

Caution: Watch out for legal and tax problems. Be sure that your ad states clearly that the company named in your ad is an independent agent. If the ad gives the impression that you are doing business in the state in which the publication appears, you may be stuck for a tax bill. Have your agent check this with a local attorney before you stick your neck out.

Get tear sheets of all the ads you run. Next time you need an agent, you can dazzle the prospects with a showing of your advertising assistance program. Many manufacturers talk about it, but when someone does set up a good co-op program, the news spreads and you should have little difficulty locating interested agents.

A CO-OP DIRECT MAIL PROGRAM THAT WORKS

Let's take a look at how you and your agents can build sales with direct mail.

Your product bulletins, catalogs, house organs, and other printed pieces can be used effectively by your agents, but you are going to have to help them with the project. Because few agents will be willing to give you their mailing lists, this program depends on you sending them the material for their own mailings. Here's how it works:

1. Just mailing manufacturers' literature is not very effective; it has to be personalized and carry a message from each agent. Have your ad agency write a strong sales letter to accompany each piece, and have the letters printed on each agent's letterhead. Have business reply cards printed, too.

2. Set specific dates for each mailing. This is very important. If dates aren't set, mailing schedules will slip, and you'll find half a dozen mailings going out at one time at the end of the year.

3. Offer to share some of the agents' expenses. You have already spent a bundle creating the sales literature, but you should still offer to help each agent with his or her mailing expenses. The expense you can share most easily is postage.

If your agents have small mailing lists, you might want to pick up all the postal costs. If the lists are large, you can negotiate a figure that will be acceptable to both of you. You should pay for the writing and printing of the personalized letters.

4. Since your agents will be mailing the material themselves, ask them to get postal receipts to verify the costs and mailing dates.

5. Ask your agents to keep records of the responses. This information will be helpful when you plan future mailings. Be sure to tell your agents of the successes.

6. If any of your agents have poor results, see if their lists are at fault. Lists must be updated regularly. It's estimated that mailing lists go bad at the rate of 2 percent a month—almost 25 percent a year! This means that a fourth of your list can be out of date in a year. One of the best ways to keep your list current is to get the help of your agents. Sure, it's paper work, and agents hate paper work. But there should be a lot of good information in your list that will be valuable for your agents. Just don't ask them to do it overnight. Given enough time, most agents can handle the job and benefit from the names you have that they don't have on their own lists.

MAKE THE MOST OF NATIONAL DIRECTORY ADVERTISING

Most national business directories allow advertisers to list their agents' addresses and phone numbers. Do you take advantage of this important benefit? There are too many directories for us to list here, but we strongly urge you to have your advertising agency review your directory advertising to make sure that all your agents are listed correctly. And be sure to let your agents know that you are doing this. You will want them to question those out-of-the-blue calls they get to determine how they originated. If any directories turn up frequently, you may want to consider expanding your advertising in them as well as merchandising your participation.

HOW TO USE THE PHONE TO QUALIFY SALES LEADS FOR YOUR AGENTS

As you know, it costs a bundle to develop leads from your advertising, publicity, and trade show programs. And, as you should also know, personal calls are very expensive. This means two things: First, the days of smokestack chasing are over; second, the days of following up unqualified inquiries are drawing to a close. We've talked about this problem before, but now it's reached critical proportions.

>>>→ *OBSERVATION* Few manufacturers can use the phone to actually sell products. But most can use it to save a lot of time and money for themselves and their agents. We strongly suggest that you consider using the phone to qualify your advertising leads so that the names you forward to your agents will not only be prequalified, they will be expecting a personal call. If you can work it out with your agents, you might even try to set times for them to follow up on the receptive people you contact. Your agents can then call to set up a meeting.

There's a real science to telephone selling. You've been using the telephone for years, and you think that you know how to use it to turn up good prospects for your agents. Don't be too sure! Unless you've had special training in this modern prospector's tool, it's just not going to work well. It's like setting out to write a novel because you've had experience writing memos. What we're saying is that you should make a commitment to learn to do it right.

You can use the phone to do many things. Many manufacturers have found it invaluable for reactivating old accounts as well as for following through on sales that were started face to face. The phone is also a good tool to use to introduce a new product. Be sure that the people you talk with who show interest are followed up with sales literature and then another phone call seeking to set up a sales call. And, of course, the phone is an ideal instrument to use to remind customers of overdue accounts. But, let's talk about prospecting, the most important way phone use will benefit your agents.

How do you get to Carnegie Hall? The answer is, of course, practice. And the same goes for success in telephone marketing. You have to be well prepared. Set a goal and plan your pitch to reach the goal. If your goal is to set up an appointment, avoid selling the product too hard. If you get a turndown on a product sales pitch, your pitch for an appointment will fall on deaf ears. Plan your pitch carefully, but don't use it as a canned spiel. Use your material in outline form and be prepared to roll with the responses you get from your prospects. Here's how to do it:

- *Have a backup pitch ready.* If you find that you can't get prospects to agree to an appointment, you can often get them to agree to your sending sales literature. They usually figure that this gets them off the hook, but it does allow you the chance to get back on the phone a few days later to see if they've received the material and have given any thought to your proposal. Like a good direct mail program, you want to work over your list carefully and often.

- *Learn to speak at a controlled rate.* Psychological studies show that the average person speaks at the rate of 125 words per minute but can listen at a rate of 500 words per minute. This doesn't mean that you should talk like an auctioneer with two hot bidders. You should keep your delivery to the rate at which most people are accustomed to listening—125 words per minute.

- *Make sure that you're talking to the right person.* It's tempting to launch right into your pitch without qualifying the listener. It's no different from personal selling; find out who makes the decisions and be sure that you are talking to that person.

- *Have a hook.* That is, decide what will be most important to the people you plan to call and tailor your presentation to that interest. If you're selling paint and the prospects you're calling are near an industrial area, you can stress the corrosion-resistant capabilities of your paint.

- *What am I going to get out of all of this?* That's the question prospects ask themselves during any phone presentation. When you're working a prospect face to face, you have more time to get the answer than you do on the phone. It's a lot easier to hang up the phone than it is to shake free of a salesperson face to face. If you remember that you've got to tell the prospects what's in it for them within the first fifteen seconds of your call, you will have a good chance of being successful on the telephone.

- *Involve the prospect in a controlled way.* People don't like to be talked *at*, they want to be part of a conversation. But if you want to retain control, you must plan your approach to allow the prospect to feel that he or she is part of the process. Usually the best way to do this is to phrase an occasional question during your presentation that can be answered easily and positively by the prospect. Usually a question with an implied yes answer works best.

- *Get to the close quickly and make it strong.* Your phone close should not be open ended. That is, don't allow the prospect to dope out his or her own response but present a few limited alternatives, all of which benefit you. Don't say, "When would be a good time to see you with the samples?" Rather, say, "Would next Wednesday at eleven o'clock be OK to come around with the samples?"

- *Timing is very important.* Every industry lives on a different time schedule. If you're trying to get hold of building contractors, for example, you'll have to do your calling before nine or after five. At any other time they are most likely to be on site. Know the habits of your prospects and you'll save a lot of time and phone bills.

- *Practice first.* You may want to try your pitch on an associate as you both sit in your office. Instead, leave the room and call your associate from another extension out of sight and out of earshot. Face to face, you will read physical responses. But when you do your phone work, you won't have these cues to keep you on the track. You'll have to learn to read voices, to listen for telltale inflections that tell you you're making it or striking out.

>>>→ *WATCH THIS*   What's WATS? If you're going to do the calling for your agents, you might consider installing a Wide Area Telecommunications Service at your office to cover the areas you want to work. Depending on your anticipated use of the WATS line and the areas to be covered, you may be able to save a lot on your phoning. But before you take the plunge, have the phone company do an analysis of your needs. They'll give you an economic analysis of the program. Although 800 numbers are similar, they are reserved for incoming calls and aren't practical for prospecting unless you train your phone people to cross-sell when the 800 number is used for order taking.

PUBLIC RELATIONS PROGRAMS THAT BUILD AGENT SALES

An agent we know never misses a chance to talk at a local technical society's meetings. "Where else can I see so many of my prospects under one roof at the same time and have them sit still and not say a word while I tell them my story?" he asked. Others we know have found unique ways to use the tools of public relations to build sales. We will highlight some of the more successful techniques and how you can help your agents use them.

Without rehashing the litany of rising selling costs and all the other economic factors that seem to be stacked against us, let's say that well-planned and executed P/R can do more for less money than just about any other promotional approach. However, there is effort involved—effort on your part and effort on the part of your agents. Let's look at some of the ways your agents can develop a successful P/R program.

Participate in Local Societies and Associations

Virtually every industry has an association. These groups usually meet regularly and are hungry for good presentations. Many agents join these groups and participate. When we asked a number of agents what was most helpful in their P/R efforts as society members, many claimed strong support and the resources of their principals. For example, some principals supplied prepared talks that can be delivered at local meetings. The materials often include a script, slides, and samples of the product for demonstration. Some principals send headquarters' staff to aid in the presentation when they feel the audience warrants it. If you can't afford to send your people across the country to be luncheon speakers, you certainly can afford to send your enterprising agents the material they need to put on a good show themselves.

Get Your Customer Relations Department Into the Act

Normally, customer relations people stick to the routine aspects of handling the business your agents work to build. That is, they expedite orders, handle technical questions, and solve problems. But note that all of these activities are reactions to something someone else has started. Sharp companies use customer relations people to get the message out because they are in regular contact with customers. If you feed your customer relations people with information they can play back to customers about agents in their territories, you can help your agents a lot. Supply your customer relations people with periodical fact sheets about each agent. When they are talking with customers, it's a simple matter to mention the seminar that Agent Smith is giving in the territory, or the new person who was just added to the sales staff. The possibilities are endless, but be sure to keep the program rolling with updated fact sheets.

Get the Local Press on the Side of Your Agents

Even the big city papers are interested in what small business people, such as most agents, are doing. The chances are that most of your P/R is confined to product releases to the trade magazines that your customers read. With a slight twist and a local angle, your new product release will be good copy for local newspapers and society publications as well. Regular mailings are the backbone of such a program, but you should encourage your agents to contact personally the appropriate editors of the publications. Also include the business editors of the local papers, the technical editors of regional society publications, and association newsletter editors who will have an interest in the application of your products. Not only will your agents be able to build their own local P/R, but friendship with an editor can often be a good source of information. Remember, a good editor will never breach a confidence, but you just may be able to get helpful information before it appears in print.

Develop a Local Community Relations Program

So far we have been talking about working with people who are directly related to the businesses your agents work with. But you should also plan for a community relations program as well. Many high schools have career days for their seniors. Apart from the real satisfaction of helping some students decide on their life's work, you can often make solid contacts at the programs. Many businesspeople in a variety of fields give a day or two a year to programs such as these, and they are very serious about them. Meeting such people can be helpful to the career of your agents as well as the students. Of course, you should do everything you can to help make these programs successful. Help with talks, displays, and even sending company people if it's possible will benefit your agent's cause.

Help Your Agents Become Teachers

One agent we know has been teaching an evening graduate school course in marketing at a local university for a number of years. His faculty salary and rank are not very high, but the graduate students in his class are excellent contacts for him. Some turn out to become customers and others become candidates for sales jobs with his organization. Most part-time business faculty people draw upon the working professionals they know to provide practical material for their students. An agent who treats a prospect or a customer with the honor of being a guest expert goes a long way to build solid relationships.

If you have an agent who doesn't want to commit the time to teaching a course, you might encourage him or her to volunteer as a guest lecturer for others who teach regularly. Even this limited exposure can be quite valuable.

Sponsor an In-plant Training Course

Many companies sponsor basic training programs for their new employees, as well as advanced classes for senior people. More often than not, the training director will welcome the offer to teach a topic that relates to the products your agent sells and the company buys. However, coach your agents to keep the sell to a minimum during the actual program. The contacts made during the program should be followed up quickly—and with sell!

Coordinate with Your Own P/R Department

Most company public relations or outside counselors seldom include agents in their plans. Their main concern is the placement of product releases, feature stories, and the like with the appropriate media. However, they should include the publications in the areas covered by your agents. Normally, an editor of a local newspaper who gets a new product release on your titanium bellows valve will think your P/R department has gone 'round the bend. But when the release is covered with a short note describing the local angle, they will consider using it. The local angle is, of course, that Agent Smith, a local businessperson, is selling these products. Local business is news—as long as you point it out to the editor.

LET THE WORLD KNOW WHEN YOU APPOINT A NEW AGENT

Well, maybe not the whole world, but at least that part of it that will be covered by your agent. When a new agent signs on, be sure to have your ad agency prepare a press release and send it to the following:

- The business editors of the local newspapers in the new agent's territory.
- Secretaries of local trade and professional associations.
- All your present customers and prospects in the territory.
- All the names on your new agent's list that will be important to you.
- Editors of regional business magazines and newsletters.
- Distributors in the territory, if the new agent will be calling on them.

BUSINESS CARDS—MAKE SURE THAT THE CARDS YOUR AGENTS USE TELL YOUR STORY

At a recent trade show, the cards we saw that were produced by agents were a sorry sight. Few of them said anything about the products sold, but those that did were book length and could only be read with the aid of a magnifying glass—or two. Help yourself to better exposure by providing your agents with business cards at a nominal cost. It's a simple matter to have your corporate cards modified slightly to be usable by your agents. However, you should make absolutely sure that the card specifies very clearly a sales agent/principal relationship. Anything on the card that implies more than this is likely to bring up all sorts of tax and liability problems. To keep out of the clutches of the courts and the IRS, we suggest that you get a copy of MANA Bulletin #507 "Company Name—Employee Titles Can Mean Various Liabilities."

PRODUCT SAMPLES—SHOULD YOU CHARGE FOR THEM OR GIVE THEM AWAY?

"A sample of one of my flowmeters costs a couple of grand. And if I make a cutaway—which is really necessary to explain the operation—I've invested a lot of money. Think of the cost when I have nine agents to supply." That's how one manufacturer feels about the problem, but he really doesn't charge outright. He just issues a memo bill. If he and an agent part company, the cutaway sample must be returned in working order or the cost is deducted from residual commissions.

If your product is small and inexpensive, there should be no question about supplying free samples. In fact, many companies we discussed this problem with say that they encourage their agents to use their samples as giveaways. Some have even had small plastic boxes made for them that include specs and some selling copy.

    ⋙→ *HOW TO DO IT* Whether or not you charge for samples, there are some guidelines you should follow to make their use by your agents most effective. Make sure that the samples are perfect, even if each has to be hand inspected and individually tested. Package them attractively. Be sure to include sales and technical literature with each sample that is to be given away. Ask your agents to supply the name of every person who is given a free sample. Use this registration list for regular mailing follow-up from the plant. If you have design changes, send out new samples to those who have been given the originals. This approach can give you a good promotional peg to use for aggressive follow-up.

CATALOGS—THEY DON'T DO MUCH GOOD ON YOUR SHELF

"Charlie uses more catalogs than any of my other agents, and he's got one of the smallest territories. I ought to put him on a ration. Those multicolor babies cost me over a half a buck each." So spoke a manufacturer the other day about one of his agents. When we asked him how effective Charlie was relative to some of his other agents, we were told that he was one of the top three.

The top three with a small territory? Obviously, old Charlie was doing something right. It might be that he gets a lot of catalogs into the right hands. Or it might be that he's a better salesperson than the others in the larger territories. But the point is this: Before you come down on an agent for going through your stash of catalogs, find out what he's doing with them and how effective his use of them is. Too many manufacturers take the short view. They produce a catalog and then become too careful about its distribution. Sure, you have to keep tabs on the stock. But if you set arbitrary limits, you will surely limit your agencies' effectiveness. Remember that catalogs don't do you a bit of good collecting dust on your warehouse shelves. Rather than playing cop in the storeroom, why not see how you can help your agencies make good use of your sales literature?

USE 800 NUMBERS TO PROMOTE YOUR AGENTS

You may not feel it's worth the expense of installing your own 800 number. But there are a number of companies who will handle the 800-number chores for you —for less than the cost of your own line. The most obvious use of such a line is to handle direct inquiries from advertising and sales promotion. But have you ever considered using one of these services to promote your agents? Think about engaging one of the 800-number services, using their number in your ad, and then equipping the company with a short pitch and the names and addresses of all your agents. Such a direct and immediate approach, followed by a direct call from the local agent, can do a lot to give you a fast edge over a competitor. This can be especially practical if you have a relatively small internal phone force. Since most of the calls will be routine, the 800-number service companies can do the qualifying and then pass the information directly to your agents.

CO-OP ADVERTISING—HAVE YOU EVER THOUGHT OF USING RADIO?

Outside of metropolitan areas, radio advertising time can be quite inexpensive. Obviously, you aren't going to buy time on a day-time soap opera. But when you share the cost with local agents, you can get your message on morning and evening news shows during prime "drive" time. That is, you can hit businesspeople in a regional area with your story and your agent's story through a medium that probably offers little or no competition. Sure, the audience is going to be limited, but it will be limited to those you most want to reach. Spot radio buys can be handled easily by your advertising agency. Radio advertising can do a lot to position your company and your local agents effectively in the minds of the driving-to-work businesspeople. However, don't jump in until your ad agency can demonstrate that your market is listening. Ask for demographics.

HOW TO QUALIFY ADVERTISING LEADS

The problem used to be that of sorting through a mass of inquiries sent by principals and picking the most likely prospects. Related to this was the problem of trying to tell the manufacturers why it was impossible to chase down every lead personally. Now, however, the number of leads generated by industrial advertising is declining, on the average. Sure, it's going to be a lot easier to process fewer inquiries, but this is not the way you and your agents wanted to solve the problem. There is always the feeling that fewer inquiries will result in fewer sales. Not so, according to Rich Amelar, president of ACI Advertising, a Leonia, New Jersey, agency specializing in industrial and high-technology accounts. "The inquiries our clients are getting are stronger and more promising than when they arrived by the bushel," Amelar said. "Those who respond to ads seem to feel less like collecting catalogs, because they know their present limits of growth. Therefore, they screen ads more critically and respond to ads for those products or services that truly interest them."

> **⋙→ OBSERVATION** Magazine advertising in a recession tends to be less valuable for short-range objectives, but so is just about every other form of promotion. However, once the climb out of the economic doldrums begins, those who have continued to advertise will fare much better than those who did not, or those who have cut back drastically. Make sure that your agencies are aware of your advertising—and the important fact that you are spending money now when it's in short supply.

Here are a few tips to help you make the most of your advertising dollars when you use agents:

- *Respond to inquiries immediately.* It usually takes a few weeks for the publisher to process inquiries; don't add to the problem. Be sure that the leads are sent to your agencies as quickly as possible—after you have prequalified them.

- *Develop a measure of inquiry effectiveness.* You do want feedback from your agencies, but don't make them take part in a tedious program. If you can develop a form based on a checklist—a system that requires no writing unless the agent feels it's important to make a statement—you will have a good system. Incidentally, the same caveat applies as those we've stated for call reports in the past. Don't put your agencies in such a position that the IRS could consider them employees.

- *Create your own data base of inquiries.* When you do a follow-up, be sure that your agencies are aware of it. They can pick up on your activity to make the program even more effective.

MAKE THE MOST OF YOUR AD BUDGET— QUALIFY SALES LEADS

Most trade magazine publishers are looking for higher levels of spending on industrial advertising. But the increases in many cases will be roughly equivalent to inflation and the higher rates being charged for advertising space. This, of course, means that you should be squeezing everything you can out of the responses you get from trade advertising. We've said it before but it bears repeating: Qualify those leads before you send them to your agencies. Check them out to see who the hot prospects are and which are the catalog collectors. If you're spending less on advertising this year, it's especially important to do a good job of qualification. Some companies spend a lot of money developing inquiries but do only a lukewarm job of lead follow-up. When you consider all the steps that have to be taken before the average industrial product is specified and finally bought, you know that the warm leads of today could very well be the hot leads of tomorrow. Work those inquiries and work them hard!

NARROW YOUR AD FOCUS TO IMPROVE LEAD QUALITY

Agents who once complained that they were getting too many unqualified sales leads are now saying that they get too few leads of any kind—qualified or unqualified. Dollar for dollar, co-op mailings will usually pull more inquiries than advertising. And a well-planned and well-placed product publicity program will also pull more leads. As important as sales leads are, neither of these approaches will do very much for your company image and the image the prospects have of your products. Here are some ideas that will produce leads and help you build a corporate image.

Cooperate with your agent in his territory by providing material and postage for a mailing to his customers—and his prospects. This is shooting with a rifle.

⋙➤ *IDEA IN ACTION* Narrow your media focus. If you're running a six-page schedule in four magazines, decide which two of these are most important and run a twelve-times schedule in the two best magazines. The chances are that you won't dilute your inquiry production but you will certainly enhance your image with the readers of the better magazines.

Use a few of the co-op post card mailers that serve your markets. These programs are out of sight, out of mind, and don't do anything to build an image. But for the dollars spent, they will often outpull the magazines. Crank up your product publicity program. Sure you can get releases published on other than new products. Have you noticed what has happened to product development in the past few years? And have you spotted your competitor's 20-year-old product on the "new" product pages? Sure you have. And the reason is simple. Magazine publishers realize that not every reader sees, much less reads, every issue of his magazine. So running releases on products that have been around is being done. But, don't abuse the privilege. Editors do want to reserve their pages for news and new products, but an old product with a new wrinkle or an unusual application can be just as newsworthy.

And remember, qualify those leads before you send them to your agencies.

SHOULD AGENTS BE EXPECTED TO PAY FOR YOUR SALES LITERATURE?

It seems that at just about every seminar an agent tells us that one of his principals expects him to pay for the sales literature that has been produced. And at the manufacturers' session someone usually asks if it's OK to charge. The question seldom creates a big flap with the other attendees, but it's asked often enough for us to address it here.

»→ *WATCH THIS*   It really is not in your best interest to charge for literature. In most cases, there is high positive correlation between the number of catalogs you get into prospects' hands and sales. Any bottleneck that impedes the flow will affect sales.

However, there are occasions when asking an agency to share a promotion cost is valid. When you create expensive packages that are designed for limited distribution, sharing is reasonable. For example, many companies with extensive lines will create a special binder for all of their individual product bulletins. It's not uncommon for these binders in limited quantities to cost the manufacturer $10 or more apiece. Remember, although these binders are not for general distribution, they are for individual distribution to customers and prospects with potential. As such, many manufacturers do ask their agencies to share some of the cost.

Caution: Agencies should never be asked to share the development cost of such a project. And their share should be limited only to impress them of the value of the piece—not to recover the cost. And when you do ask them to share, make sure that you share the billing—imprint the agency name on the pieces you supply.

BUSINESS STATIONERY FOR YOUR AGENTS? BE CAREFUL

Manufacturers who offer to have stationery printed for their agencies have their hearts in the right place, but unless it's done right, there could be problems for both of you from the IRS! If the stationery is plainly identified as that of the agency and states that the agency represents the sale of your products—in much smaller type— there should be no problems. But anything that shows your company as dominant just might give the IRS the idea that you have a branch office. If you're called in, your records and the complete lack of call reports will prove your case. But you could go through a lot of hassle.

AGENTS IDENTIFY THE ELEMENTS IN SALES LITERATURE THAT HELP THEM SELL EFFECTIVELY

"The catalog is a mess! Nothing hangs together, and most of the items in it are the low profit, low need items of the line." This is a common complaint we hear when talking with agents at seminars and in the field. To help you prepare sales literature that not only showcases your products but encourages agency use, we have summarized the suggestions we have heard over the years from agents in all fields.

>>→ *OBSERVATION* Catalogs should show some consistency from page to page. However, every page should have a product or a few products shown in an unusual way. This not only breaks up the monotony but encourages the readers to browse for items other than those they might be looking for. This is a tough assignment—building a consistent format, yet adding enough variation to stimulate interest—but it can be done. You can do it with larger or more dramatic illustrations than those on previous pages or it can be done by using larger or bolder type to highlight one product.

Here's a case where the 80–20 rule can be used in your favor. In sales, it's not uncommon for 80 percent of the business to come from 20 percent of the customers. However, when this rule is applied to the selection of products to be included in a catalog, the result is always positive. When you emphasize the 20 percent of the products in your line that produce 80 percent of the business, you will have a powerful working tool. This doesn't mean you should not include the other products, but you should design your catalog so that the products you want most to sell will stand out. Agents stress that they make active use of catalogs in sales calls when the important products are stressed in terms of features—and benefits.

The catalog should give a strong impression of your company as well as your product line. This is seldom a problem for larger manufacturers with extensive lines. However, even smaller manufacturers with limited lines can make a big impression when they approach the design of their catalogs in a creative way. Even though the 8 ½ × 11 format is preferred, a smaller size format with more pages can often create the impression of a line that is more extensive than it really is. Larger illustrations, greater use of white space, larger text type, and headlines can make a smaller line loom larger when an agent is using your catalog with a prospect.

⨠⟶ ***IDEA IN ACTION***   The catalog is more than a listing of your products—it's a working tool. Agents stress that customers use the catalogs that are most convenient. Think about the buyer's habits when you design your catalog. Put yourself in their shoes and try to create a format that makes it easy for people to find what they are looking for and to be exposed to products you want them to see. Tabbed pages are frequently mentioned as being very helpful. But the section that agents say is most frequently ignored is the index or contents page. Even if yours is a small catalog, make it easy for your agents and your prospects to find the products in which they are interested. And, if at all possible, create a strong cross-indexing system. For example, if you makes valves, you would obviously have a *Valves* heading. Under this you would list all the types—needle, ball, solenoid, and so on. Then, cross index by type—needle, ball, solenoid, and so on.

Your catalog should push for some action. Don't be pushy, but make sure you tell the prospect how the products are sold and where they are sold. Be sure to leave space for agency imprints or have the catalogs imprinted with each agency's name, address, and phone number. If you use an 800 number, include it on the catalog as well.

Producing a good catalog is the first step. Once you have a first-rate in-print sales piece, help your agencies make the most of them. Run releases in the new literature section of the magazines that serve your industry and get the inquiries out to your agencies as quickly as possible. Encourage your agents to use the catalogs during a sales call. When the agents use the catalog and point out the appropriate products as well as the best way to use the catalog, it will be better received and more easily used by prospects.

Caution: If your catalog is large and quite expensive, the distribution has to be carefully controlled. However, remember that catalogs on your shelf are not selling for you. You might consider registering all catalogs. That is, have each numbered and have your agencies give you the names and addresses of those to whom the catalogs have been given. This list serves as an up-date list when new products and product changes are announced. It also tells the person who receives the catalog that it's important.

MAKE YOUR PUBLICITY WORK HARD FOR YOU

Trade magazine editors always know when a company is growing: Their press releases pay less attention to the products and more attention to top corporate executives.

If you're going public and need to put over an image of capable corporate people, by all means do it. But don't do it at the expense of your product publicity. A steady stream of information to the editors who count in your industry is critical for the success of your agencies. Press exposure, along with advertising, is the best way to keep a steady stream of inquiries flowing to your agencies.

Warning: Ad agencies that push corporate exposure when there is no real reason for it are usually looking to add to their income—and make the client execs happy by seeing their pictures in newspapers and magazines. When there is a solid reason for corporate exposure, do it. But make sure that your ad agency has real reasons for it when they propose corporate P/R for you.

INQUIRIES FROM DIRECTORIES ARE SELF-QUALIFIED

When a person responds to an ad in a trade magazine, a safe assumption is that he or she is in the field covered by the magazine and is interested professionally in the product. That interest may be competitive, but it's still field related. However, when a person responds to an ad in a directory, it's a safe bet that the interest is keener than the interest of those responding to an ad in a periodical. People simply don't thumb through directories as they do magazines. They go to the directory with the intention of finding something specific. And when they find your ad and respond to it, the chances are that there is some very strong interest. Several manufacturers have told us that they red-flag the directory inquiries they send to their agencies. Of course, all advertising inquiries should be screened before they are sent to your agencies, but it does seem appropriate to make a special effort to get the directory inquiries out as quickly as possible, and to identify them clearly.

POST-SALES FOLLOW-UP CAN DEVELOP ADDITIONAL ORDERS

"One of our agencies did so much better than some of the others, even in what we felt was a thin territory, that we asked them for their secret." The manufacturer was pleased to learn that this productive agency had been trading on the old notion that it's easier to sell someone to whom you have already sold something than to beat a lot of unproductive bushes.

It's called cross-selling when other products are added to the order at the time the original sale is made. However, combining a genuine interest in their customers' welfare with a desire to sell more products gave this agency downstream sales power.

Example: The agency recognized that the valves they sold to the new construction market could lead to the sale of analytical instruments they handled. By showing genuine interest in the installation as it was under construction, they were able to meet others in the company who had the responsibility for buying the instruments that were to be used in the new lab. In fact, the agency was able to work closely with the principal's advertising department to do a story on the valve installation in their house organ. Once the lab was ready to be fitted, they had their contacts and their orders.

Another agency does routine follow-up on how the OEM products he sells are working out with his customer's product. This approach not only allows the agency to present an image of caring, it gives them the opportunity to look for other opportunities during their visits.

And another agency reported that it developed questionnaires that are sent to new customers requesting information on how the products were performing. Part of the questionnaire was worded to elicit information on additional applications for the product and other products that the agent represented.

Still another agency brought the regional manager from one of his principals to review the product in use. No attempt was made to sell at this meeting, but every attempt was made to leave the customer with the impression of a manufacturer and agency that cared.

It may take more effort, but whenever you can do it, make the time to work closely with your agencies in after-sale activities. How many times has someone called you a month after you bought a product to see how satisfactorily it was performing? We don't imagine too often. But think of how impressed you'd be if someone did this.

HOW TO USE AGENCY INCENTIVE PROGRAMS

Incentive programs for manufacturers' agencies are seldom practical when the approach taken is the same as that used to motivate a salaried sales staff. Merchandise, trips, and similar traditional prizes just don't have the same effect on most agencies. However, there are ways to make sure that an incentive program will have more than a fighting chance, as follows:

• Make sure that the goals that have to be attained are realistic. And make sure that they are specific. If the program is aimed at opening new accounts, key the rewards specifically to the number of new accounts brought in, not to overall sales. One agency might bring in ten new accounts, all with small but potentially growth-oriented billing. Another agency might bring in one new account that bills more than the ten of the other agency. If your goal is new accounts, that's what should be rewarded.

• Make sure that all agencies are fully involved, that they take the program seriously, and encourage their salespeople to participate.

• Keep the program visible regularly. Send out regular memos to everyone, bring them up to date on current achievements, and continue to remind everyone of the benefits of winning.

• Keep the rules simple, make sure that more than a few individuals share in the awards, make the objectives obtainable, leave plenty of time for everyone to try, and make sure that the winners get more than the awards that were promised. Make sure that they get personal recognition from your management as well as the agency management if they are agency employees.

USE YOUR AGENCIES TO BUILD A CORPORATE IMAGE

You can spend a bundle on a professional public relations program, but the battle is really won or lost in the field. "Our P/R counselor wrote and placed articles for us in all the magazines that mattered," a manufacturer said. "But for some reason, we neglected to tie in the campaign with our agency team and the whole program was a lot less effective than it could have been."

Public relations is a powerful tool, but it is only effective when everyone is in on the act. Ray Dreyfack, co-author of the Dartnell manual *Customers: How to Get Them, How to Serve Them, How to Keep Them,* points out:

It's important to develop a field staff of image-builders. Corporations spend billions of advertising and P/R dollars each year trying to build and maintain an image that will make customers and prospects feel that your company might be a good one to do business with. It's no secret that companies with a poor image lose out in many ways. Yet far too many companies fail to take advantage of the prime image—building opportunities that exist with their network of manufacturers' agencies. In the final analysis, customers' goodwill depends most directly on the people in the field selling for you. And if you are selling through manufacturers' agencies, you have an opportunity that others simply don't have. Each agency is owned by an entrepreneur, a person who is as interested in seeing his or her business grow as the manufacturer is in seeing his company grow. When a manufacturer spends money on public relations that will increase public exposure to his product—and to his agencies—those agencies do their best to make it work.

Many individual factory people see the opportunity to help them build sales, and they do everything they can to build the corporate image in the field. However, remember that agency owners are building their business at the same time they are building the manufacturer's business. They have more at stake—a personal and a financial investment.

Get the agencies into the act early. Ask for their input on topics that should appear as articles in the magazines read by their customers. Ask them what problems your competitors may be having so that your stories can be salted appropriately. Don't knock your competitors, but make sure that you present a strong image where your competitor may be failing. And when the campaign is ready, review it in detail with your agencies before giving your public relations people the go-ahead. Once the campaign is rolling, keep in touch with the agencies, ask them for input on their experience with it, and share that with all the agencies.

Remember that a good public relations campaign is usually based on one or a small number of strong points. The company that delivers on time doesn't let anyone forget. The company that sells for less plays that tune. It's critical for sales agencies to know this story cold and to use the theme at every opportunity. This reinforcement is worth ten times the price you pay a P/R firm for the program.

SALES LEAD SHELF LIFE

Agents who value sales leads generally hold on to them for about a year and review them regularly to tie in any activity they may have heard about the company. "Sales leads often foretell events within a company," an agent said. "When the lead seems cold today, but indicates that something is going on, I hold onto it and check it out regularly. New products and OEM component interest starts early, but the business is usually quite a way downstream. It's worth keeping an inquiry tickler file."

GETTING TO SMALLER PROSPECTS WITH GOOD POTENTIAL

Traditionally, manufacturers have turned to agencies to build business for them with smaller customers that were difficult and expensive to reach with factory salespeople. However, there is now an even better reason to use agencies when you want to reach a field of low-volume prospects. The reason is agency telemarketing. Hardly an agency today isn't involved in some form of telemarketing. Whether it takes the form of simply qualifying prospects and setting up appointments or runs to an elaborate operation that is geared to actually getting orders on the phone, the chances are that the job can be done by agencies.

Example: "If the product is going to be sold by the telephone," a manufacturer's sales manager said, "we might as well do it from headquarters with a WATS line. Why pay commissions?" The answer is direct but not obvious to some who have tried it and failed. The simple fact that the person calling is from the territory—not from a few thousand miles away, gives the agency a major advantage. There may never be a personal call in some cases, and service may be only a minor consideration, but think of the buying decision you have made. Don't you feel more comfortable buying from someone nearby, rather than someone on the other side of the country?

We were quite surprised to learn just how many agencies are taking their telemarketing skills well beyond the traditional applications. Think about the possibilities of market-testing with agencies that have telemarketing capabilities. And think about the possibilities of contracting with them to use their telemarketing equipment and personnel to help with some of your market research projects. Traditional ways of selling are rapidly giving way to new technology, and selling costs are making life difficult for everyone. The pioneers in local telemarketing are manufacturers' agencies. See what they can do for you.

AGENTS TAKE SALES LEADS ONLY AS SERIOUSLY AS YOU DO

"We get the sales leads about two months after they get them from the magazines," an agent told us. "If they don't think enough of them to send them out to us right away, I guess they aren't worth very much."

It shouldn't come as a surprise to some manufacturers when they survey the results of a lead-building advertising program that the longer they hold them, the less their value is perceived by agencies. Here are some suggestions agents have made to ensure that advertising dollars work hard for everyone:

1. Process all inquiries within 48 hours.
2. Weed out the garbage.
3. Identify the strong prospects.
4. Keep a set yourself for follow-up and send a set to your agencies.
5. Be sure to let everyone know when leads turn into sales—and how the sale was made.

SELECT YOUR ADVERTISING MEDIA WITH
YOUR AGENCIES IN MIND

Frequency, reach, demographics—these are all important points to consider when you pick publications for your advertising. But you should also consider the selection with your agencies in mind. Make sure that at least some of the magazines reach the people the agencies call on. You may want to impress a process design engineer with a very technical magazine in the chemical processing field. But you also want to make sure that the people who buy your products see your ads. In the case of the process design project, you might have to cover the consulting firms, purchasing people, and even operating and maintenance people. It's the inquiries from these people that open doors.

PUT YOUR AGENCIES ON YOUR PUBLICITY LIST

"We got calls from customers asking about a pump that one of our principals was supposed to be making. When the callers started talking specs, I was lost. As far as I knew, the pumps my manufacturer made handled flow up to ten GPM. I never heard of the model they were talking about, but they claimed that they had read about it in a magazine." Sure enough, the manufacturer had run a press release and never notified the agencies. The manufacturer claimed that they were testing media before placing advertising and would have notified the agencies of the advertising schedule. In the meantime, the manufacturer and the agency had a lot of egg on their faces. Put your agencies on your publicity list. In fact, it's a good idea to send each agency a few copies of your releases. There might be a local publicity opportunity that the agency can help with. The business section of a local paper; the publication of a branch of a professional association—there are a lot of opportunities.

WHO PAYS FOR SPECIAL PROMOTIONAL MATERIAL?

Recently an agent asked us about policies on sharing the cost of special promotional material. The promotion in question was a large-capacity three-ring binder in which all of the various catalogs of the manufacturer were filed. In general, we feel that the cost of all product literature should be borne by the manufacturer—unless the material is tailored for each individual agency. In this case, there was to be no special treatment. The agency's name was not to be printed on the binder, but it was to be controlled carefully. The binders were numbered and were to be given only to those people considered to be top prospects. The manufacturer wanted to control distribution—and cost. If the agencies are going to be expected to share the cost, then there should be some personalization.

Quite a few companies have created premiums such as specialized slide rules for their agencies to use. Again, if the agency names are imprinted on the items, it's fair to ask the agencies to share some of the cost. But without the personalization, it isn't.

SALES CONTESTS: SOME PRACTICAL POINTERS TO MAKE
THEM WORK WITH AGENCIES

"It went on forever. By the time it came to an end every one of my salespeople had forgotten there was even a sales contest going on," said an agent recently. A sales manager we talked with claimed that sales contests don't work with agents—only with factory salaried salespeople. In short, there's a lot of folklore around on the subject of sales contests. The truth is that sales contests do work with agencies as well as with factory people—you just have to plan and run them differently.

>>→ *OBSERVATION* According to the people we talked with, just about everything that works with factory people will work with agents—but under different circumstances. Agency people are just as interested in winning something as others, but they look at contests from a different point of view. The factory salesperson has one product or line to be concerned with—the agent has many. This basic factor dramatically alters how agency people perceive sales contests and the way they react to them.

GOALS—All sales contests must have well-defined and attainable goals. These goals must be related to the territory potential. For goals to be meaningful for agents, they should not only be based on reasonable territorial expectations but on the amount of time that the agent can spend on the line while still selling the lines of the other principals. We realize that most sales contests are designed to get more of the agencies' time. This is reasonable, but don't make it impossible for the agent to sell his or her other products if you want your contest to succeed.

TIMING—All the usual timing ideas apply, but the critical point for agency sales contests is to make absolutely certain that your contest period doesn't interfere with events the agencies' other principals have planned. Another sales contest, a trade show, sales meetings—all of these activities can wreck an otherwise well-planned sales contest. We've heard of manufacturers who have had to plan their contests as much as a year in advance to avoid all the possible conflicts.

TIME PERIOD—Depending on the product, the market, and the contest goals, sales contests should be run in as short a period as possible. There are, of course, circumstances that will prevent some contests from running for less than a year. If you find yourself facing a long, drawn-out contest period, it might be better to drop the idea in favor of some other sales development plan. Short contests greatly reduce the factor of boredom. The goals can be kept in sight and valued better over a short period. It's easier to capitalize on the burst of enthusiasm that shows up in a sales contest if it runs for a short period, rather than if it goes on and on. Remember, short has to be thought of as a relative term.

Plan your agency sales contests to generate the highest level of interest and participation based on the fact that each agency is selling more than just your products. You will get better interest and participation if you plan the contests with your agencies. Don't just drop the idea on them.

USING DIRECT MAIL TO PROMOTE YOUR AGENCIES

It goes without saying that travel costs make it prohibitive for the average manufacturer sales manager to do the kind of territory traveling that should be done to back up agencies. However, there is a lot you can do with direct mail to help your agencies sell. Here are some suggestions from direct mail pros:

- *Make sure that you have the right offer.* Every direct mail piece should have an offer. This doesn't mean that you are going to try to sell your products by mail. But it does mean that you are going to offer something, and that offer should be appropriate. Offer a catalog, a sample, a test report, a phone call. The list is endless —but it must be appropriate for your product, your target customers, and your agencies in the field.

- *Demonstrate the product in print.* Simply sending a product specification sheet in the mail is next to useless. People want to see how your product works and how others have used it. This is one reason why case histories are so effective as direct mail pieces.

- *Give the envelope a job to do.* An envelope is more than a wrapper for your direct mail piece. It should contain a message that makes the prospect want to open it and see more. But don't be too cute.

- *Have a well-defined strategy.* Relate your promise to your product in a direct way so that your prospects get the point immediately. If you talk in terms of your prospects' needs—and not your own—you'll have no trouble with this approach.

- *Don't let your reader off the hook.* Simply put, this means that your direct mail should be targeted to a specific response. It isn't enough just to mail information. For direct mail to pay its way, it should get the reader to do something, even if it's only to return a card for additional information.

- *Repeat your successes.* If your direct mail piece works, you can space it out and do it again—and again. Since so few people actually read everything they get in the mail, this repetition works to your advantage. Those who have already responded will just ignore your mailer.

WHY NOT ADOPT A SCHOOL?

Some manufacturers are developing sources of employees and making a contribution to society by running intern programs for college students. Some companies have taken this concept a major step further. These businesses are committing to specific programs for at least one school year. They provide personal as well as corporate resources to the school. Many send company personnel to lecture and to act as resources to the faculty. Those who are doing it claim that they have not only had a great reception from the schools and the faculty, but that they finally feel that they have some control over the process that provides the workers of the future. It's just as practical for manufacturers as it is for agencies. Since this is a relatively new concept, there's a lot of room for innovation—and there are very few restricting guidelines.

A SIMPLE BUT EFFECTIVE CONTEST FOR YOUR AGENCIES

It won't work with all agencies, but where referrals can become a source of new business, some manufacturers pay bonuses for all referrals for business outside their territories and special bonuses when referrals turn into customers. This can be for agents who refer business to agents in other territories. This not only adds to your sales figures, but it builds a strong network for your agencies. Remember, full commissions should be paid in addition to the bonus.

HOW TO SELECT SALES INCENTIVE PREMIUMS

As we've mentioned before, the traditional sales contests that can motivate salaried salespeople just aren't that effective with sales agency people. They would rather see the incentive tied to an enhanced commission. However, if you do run a contest in which you offer merchandise as prizes, make sure that the merchandise is a recognized brand. A sales manager recently reported on a sales contest flop in which the prizes seemed impressive until the contestants realized that they were off-brand merchandise. The difference in cost between the top of the line and an also-ran is seldom worth the savings when the agencies don't respond to your efforts. You could be stuck with a lot of premiums for a long time.

INVOLVE YOUR AGENCIES IN YOUR TOTAL MARKETING EFFORT

Building a strong and productive agency salesforce depends on a number of factors, none of which is more important than involving every agency in your total marketing effort. The ability of an agency salesforce to help achieve corporate goals is greatly improved when the agency people fully understand corporate marketing strategies behind the selling responsibilities they have, as follows:

• Integrating agency sales activities into the corporate marketing plan can have these direct effects on your profitability: (1) Focus agency sales efforts on the most profitable products, customers, and areas; (2) Build stronger positions in new as well as existing markets; (3) Generate feedback on customer reactions, changes in the marketplace, and competition; (4) Provide better synchronization between agency sales efforts and company profit goals; (5) Compensate the agencies in proportion to the results they achieve.

• It's not enough just to pay lip service to the concept. If it's to work effectively, the agency salesforce must be given regular access to corporate marketing data that will help them gear their efforts for maximum corporate profitability. However, many manufacturers are reluctant to share this information or to involve their sales agencies in their market planning. Some feel that commissions alone should be sufficient for motivating the agencies to make a major contribution to profits. However, these manufacturers miss an important point. Commissions do motivate agencies to achieve profit objectives, but they are best used as a reinforcement tool, not as a communication tool.

• There are some manufacturers who feel that it might be risky to release classified marketing information to their agencies, especially in the light of high turnover statistics in some industries. Others find it difficult and even impossible to generate the kind of information that will be helpful on a timely or a cost-effective basis. Remember, without good marketing information, you are cutting your agencies off from productive sales tools.

• From all the evidence we have been able to gather, it does appear that agencies make better sales decisions and are more effective when they see how their efforts contribute to company profitability.

• Merely going through the motions of involving your agencies directly in your marketing planning is a waste of everyone's time. The involvement should be direct and real. And one of the best ways to make this work is to present your agencies with a clear sales mission.

Sales Mission Strategies

The sales mission that is presented to your agencies should clearly reflect your company's marketing strategy in that it provides specific objectives and guidelines for markets, customers, products, and agency sales activity. Your sales mission will include specific sales figures. However, remember that setting quotas for agencies just isn't appropriate. Goals that include specific objectives such as opening new accounts, reviving old accounts, and the like are, of course, appropriate. Your sales mission statement should be quite specific in that it provides a clear direction for your agency team.

Here are some of the topics that are especially important to include in a sales mission statement:

(1) Inform your agencies which products to emphasize;
(2) Establish prospecting priorities to make the most of time;
(3) Define your sales approach, such as consultative selling or building presentations on demonstrations.

All your sales mission statements must be compatible with your company's short- and long-term plans. As you might imagine, this puts a heavy burden on your company's management to set the purpose and goals. And the ultimate success of the agency sales team will depend heavily on just how well each agent understands and supports the statements.

Your agencies will be better able to sell your products if they are fully aware of your corporate goals. Since you are dealing with independent contractors and can't exercise the same control you would over a salaried salesforce, your approach to implementing your sales mission strategies will have to rely on different techniques. For example, most manufacturers seem to feel that if they could get more of each of their agent's time, more of their products would be sold. The task with agents is to see that they all have the support they need to make the most of the time they spend on your products. Rather than fighting for time, fight with corporate management to see that sales literature is available, that advertising inquiries are qualified before they are sent to the agencies, and that the support people at the plant know what the agents are doing and are ready to help them when the need arises. All of this will help the agent give you *quality* time. The key word being *quality*.

TRY SOME NONTRADITIONAL ADVERTISING TO BOOST YOUR AGENCIES

Outside of the major metropolitan areas, most businesspeople still drive to work and listen to their automobile radio. And many of these regions have business shows for these drive-time listeners. Rates are low and exposure is high. You might consider buying some air time to sell your products, featuring your local agent as the source. If you're a large company and work with one of the larger advertising agencies, you will probably not be taken too seriously by them simply because the air time rates are low, which means that the commissions to the ad agency will be low. However, we think it's worth it to try this medium. Many are already using it with surprising results.

BOUNCE-BACKS: A CONSUMER MARKETING STRATEGY WITH INDUSTRIAL POSSIBILITIES

The bounce-back is a consumer marketing technique that is usually used to increase sales by offering a discount on a future purchase. It's a technique that would probably work well in the sales of quantity parts that are sold on an irregular but ongoing basis. So far, we haven't heard of any manufacturers doing this, but we think the idea has possibilities. In fact, it seems that it would be especially practical where agents can carry the message.

TURNING SMALL CUSTOMERS INTO BIG CUSTOMERS

An agent we talked with recently claimed that he spends about as much time trying to upgrade small customers as he does looking for new customers. As he put it:"It's a lot easier to sell to someone who is already a customer than to turn a tough prospect into a customer. However, the trick lies in being able to determine which customers have the potential to buy more and going about the development of these customers in an economical way." Here are some ways to do it:

• *Use special promotions.* One agent said that one of his principals had developed a special direct mail campaign that was aimed specifically at getting small customers to buy more of the product. The mailing was made by the factory, but all responses were keyed to the local sales agencies. In this case, the products were bought on a volume basis. The greater the volume, the larger the discount. The manufacturer offered for a limited time to sell at a higher discount to those smaller buyers who were willing to single-source their buying in the future. It worked.

• *Revise your credit terms.* Several agents claimed that some of their small-volume customers were not buying much because they had been put on a cash basis by the manufacturer. Try for larger orders by offering to revise your credit terms if you feel that it's economically safe.

• *Help your small customers.* Many agents said that when they and their principals built a relationship in which the customers rely on them both for things that are not directly related to the products, the smaller customers get bigger quickly. Just offering good advice on a problem the small customer may have can often do the job. Another manufacturer told us that he had helped a small customer locate a key executive and in appreciation, the small customer began ordering exclusively from the manufacturer and thus became a big customer. There are probably hundreds of ways to help your small customers, but only you can spot the opportunities when they are ready to be seized.

GIVING AWARDS TO AGENTS? DO IT WITH CLASS

There is hardly a manufacturer that doesn't have some kind of an award program for its agency team. From Agent of the Year to bonuses and plaques, the alternatives are almost endless. However, we recently heard from two agents who were named Agent of the Year by their principals. One agent said: "We were given the award at a very impressive ceremony that was held in conjunction with the annual agency sales meeting. I have to tell you that the plaque and the presentation made me feel very proud. The company president and the sales manager both made speeches and they meant every word of what they said. It was great!"

The other agent who had been elevated to his principal's agency hall of fame said this: "We were just notified by letter that we had been selected Agency of the Year. I'm not sure how they made their choice because we certainly weren't the big producer for them. A few days after we got the letter, we got our copy of the newsletter the company mails to all the agencies. There was no mention of the award in the newsletter. And the annual sales meeting was last month, so I know that we won't get to feel good about this publicly."

»→ *OBSERVATION:* The second manufacturer would probably have been better off if he had never made an award. The first manufacturer made the most of it from his point of view and from the point of view of the winning agency. Can you guess which agency was most motivated?

NEXT TIME YOU REVISE YOUR CATALOG, START FROM SCRATCH

A product catalog with lots of product listings that is revised regularly can often become much more effective when it's fully revised, rather than just updated. According to some advertising experts, even customers who have been dealing with you for years will buy more. It's worth a try!

HOW TO GET A MILLION DOLLARS' WORTH OF ADVERTISING FREE

We don't have to tell you that the price of advertising lineage in the major trade publications was, for the most part, higher this year than it was last year. And, in many cases, it will be even higher next year. However, the power of word-of-mouth advertising can be one of your most effective and cost-effective promotional tools without spending a penny. Since your agencies are calling on regular customers as well as new prospects, it makes a lot of sense to get testimonials from satisfied customers. When an agency is calling on a satisfied customer and pitching a non-competitive prospect, why not encourage the agency to get the two together, even if it's only on the telephone. The cost of a lunch for the two has got to be a lot less than the cost of even some of the smallest advertising space in even the small circulation magazines.

HELP YOUR AGENCIES SELL BY SUPPORTING TAILORED PRESENTATION MATERIAL

If you're a large company selling through sales agencies and you have established an extensive computer data bank of product applications and competitive information, the chances are that you are in a good position to develop tailored presentations for your agencies. The first of these presentations we saw were done by insurance companies for their agencies. These companies had enormous banks of data to draw on. When their agents called for material, the companies were able to select material and print out presentations that appeared to be the result of considerable research. Much research went into compiling the data bank, but it didn't take much effort to select and print out the presentations. Think about this as a sales tool for your agencies. Think about the effect a personalized presentation can have on capturing business. If you have the computer and the data base, this is a good way to use it.

14

Providing Special Help to Sales Agencies

Manufacturers' agents and salaried salespeople work under different rules and require different types of factory support. In this Chapter, we reveal the techniques used by many of the country's leading manufacturers to provide the special assistance that not only builds business, but that builds strong manufacturer/agency relationships.

Many manufacturers provide annual subscriptions for their agencies to the trade journals that cover their field. And many have assigned one or more people other than the sales manager to be responsible for dealing with the agency contract. In this Chapter, we provide the guidelines you need to determine, first, if any special assistance is needed and, second, how to go about providing that assistance.

Hardly a manufacturer or an agency is without a computer today. In this Chapter, we explain from several perspectives how to make the most of computers.

Also in this Chapter the topic of pricing and quoting is explored, and a number of suggestions are provided to help agencies do pricing on the spot, especially when deadlines are short and competition is hot. Finally, we reveal the training techniques that result in effective customer service personnel.

TRADE JOURNAL SUBSCRIPTIONS FOR AGENTS MAKE GOOD SENSE

Help your agents keep up on your industry trends by giving them subscriptions to trade journals serving your product line. Agents spend waiting time in reception rooms reading old cast-off magazines that bear no relation to the lines they handle. With a pertinent journal or two in their attaché case, they'll put this time to good use.

Why don't agents get their own subscriptions? An agent carrying nine lines would need fifteen or twenty subscriptions to keep up with all the products he handles, and that's costly.

Also, agents are not entitled to free subscriptions from publishers (as company execs are for some journals) and therefore have to pay a high rate for journals.

If your firm advertises extensively in trade journals, then by all means make sure your agencies have a subscription to the journals you use so they can make the most of your promotional efforts.

ALERT YOUR AGENTS WHEN MAKING FIELD TRIPS

In addition to regularly scheduled field trips to the territories, it occasionally becomes necessary to make a quick emergency visit to a customer to put out a fire or personally handle some other important development such as a price increase. Most sales managers plan regular visits with their agents, but some fail to notify agents when making emergency trips.

In all cases when visiting an agent's territory, let him know as soon as possible, even if only one day's notice is practical. Often you can help him close a sale at a nearby customer's plant, or he can warn you of other developments at the very plant you're going to visit.

Caution: Failure to post the agent on your emergency travel plans can cause strained relations if he finds out after the fact. In many instances the agent may be unable to change his plans in time to travel with you on short notice, but he can make a phone call to apologize for his absence. If you appear in front of the customer without the agent (and without a phone call from him) you've decreased his importance in the eyes of the customer, which could hurt his effectiveness for you with that customer later on.

USE YOUR INFLUENCE WITH YOUR PURCHASING PERSONNEL

Encourage them to establish reasonable calling hours for visiting agents.

As a sales manager you're well aware there's an increasing trend toward extremely limited calling hours. Some firms now allow visitors only between certain hours once or twice a week.

What if your agents were restricted to making calls at these hours? If they were, your purchasing people would have little to purchase, since with fewer calls by your agents there would be fewer sales and no need for well-paid experts to purchase raw material.

Agents understand, as you do, the need for some limitation on calling hours—Tuesdays through Thursdays, for instance, are legitimate calling days. Mondays and Fridays are often reserved by purchasing people for paper work and special appointments, and understandably so. But don't forget, quite often it's a salesperson who introduces your company to new and innovative ideas and procedures that make everyone's job a lot more secure.

SALES CORRESPONDENTS HELP AGENCIES SUCCEED

Every company selling through agents needs a solid citizen at the home office that the agents can count on. In most companies that person is the sales correspondent. He or she may also be called the inside sales manager or customer relations manager. Whatever the title, the person is an absolute necessity if communications are going to flow smoothly and problems are going to be ironed out fast.

In smaller companies this function is often handled by the sales manager or even the president. But usually the sales manager is out in the field and the president is out scouting up new financing sources, so the letters and phone calls go unanswered for days, leading to unhappy customers and dissatisfied reps.

In larger companies, however—and not necessarily the giants of industry—it's imperative to employ a full-time sales correspondent who's in the office all the time and who's skilled in the art of personal diplomacy. He must also possess the necessary intelligence to be completely knowledgeable about your entire product line and perceptive enough to be familiar with the whims and fancies of your customers.

> ⫸→ *WATCH THIS* Unfortunately, most calls and letters received by your sales correspondent are about some problem, ranging from a minor delay in delivery to rejection of an entire carload of your goods. To meet this constant negative flow of communications, your person must have a strong constitution and a talent for soothing ruffled feathers.

Not every personality can survive this daily onslaught, and therefore those who are capable of handling the challenge are scarce and higher priced when you do find them. And this is where most firms fall down. Their pay scale for inside personnel is usually insufficient to attract the right person able to perform the job of sales correspondent, so they settle for second best and performance usually suffers.

One of those suffering the most is your agent. He's called by his customers when all else has failed. He then phones the office and talks initially with the same person who's handled the irate customer, usually with very little improvement in results. Ultimately, he has to talk to you or to some other executive about a minor problem that has been blown into a major one, a situation that could have been avoided with more adroit handling.

So, the next time you're looking for a good sales correspondent, ask the controller if he can relax the purse strings a bit and increase the salary. And if you have a good person now, an attractive raise will keep his morale high and his performance consistent.

PURCHASING AGENTS ARE BECOMING MORE ACTIVE IN AGENCY APPOINTMENTS

On several occasions the purchasing agent of a large oil tool company has cautioned agents he considers to be professionals against signing up with certain vendors. This is not a vendetta against selected companies but rather is prompted by his concern that the prospective agents are not aware of the reputation of companies soliciting their sales assistance.

This is good news for reputable companies and bad news for disreputable firms. It also injects a new factor into the rep/principal relationship. If this is a trend, it means that no longer can firms change agencies every year or two in order to reap the benefit of the contacts each new agent possesses.

Also, if purchasing personnel are becoming more selective in the choice of firms and agents they wish to do business with, it would pay to contact purchasing people of your acquaintance when planning a new appointment in one of your territories.

PHONE MANNERS BUILD BONDS WITH AGENTS

When an agent phones his favorite principal and is asked, "What company are you with, sir?" he knows that the company hired a new switchboard operator.

This happens to every company eventually, but the way in which it is handled has a lot to do with the impact it has on the agent salesforce, to say nothing of the customers.

Normally this question doesn't bother the agents; they identify themselves and are transferred to the sales manager or sales correspondent.

This can have a negative effect, however, when the agent has been wooing a particular customer and has regaled him with tales of his rapport with his principal. If the buyer decides that now is the time to place an order and asks the agent to phone the plant to get a delivery promise, an explanation to the new switchboard operator about who he is can really deflate him in a hurry—and may drop him a notch in the eyes of the buyer.

> ⬚➤ *IDEA IN ACTION*   One of the best plans we've seen is for a list of
> the people in the field with their addresses, as well as the names of the
> prominent purchasing people around the country who could be calling in,
> to be placed with the new switchboard personnel, and the old ones for that
> matter, so that the phone greeting is warm, recognizing, and cordial. Lit-
> tle things like this make an agent—and a buyer—feel a part of the team.

PRICING AND QUOTING FOR THE TERRITORIES

A veteran agent with two principals having a slight overlap in product lines received an inquiry for a component that could be made by both companies. Since both principals were aware that this overlap existed and had not objected to it, the agent sent the inquiry to both companies.

He was astounded at the results of the experiment. Company A quoted the part within two weeks and its price was very competitive; Company B took five weeks to quote and was priced out of the competition. Both firms had indicated their interest in the type of part the agency submitted.

Fortunately, in this case, the agent had a company that could compete for the business he had uncovered, but he was disappointed in his second principal and its performance.

> ⬚➤ *OBSERVATION*   Although this is an unusual circumstance, it may
> point out in vivid detail why agents often seem to devote a major portion
> of their selling time to one or two of their principals and spend less time
> on the balance of the companies they represent.

The previous occurrence caused the agent to review the performance of Company B, and he discovered that the firm was habitually late in quoting and was usually not in the running, competitively, for the business. His selling efforts for Company B diminished considerably thereafter.

Late quotes, high pricing, and slow delivery are three of the most frustrating burdens that agents have to bear, and laxity in these areas is the leading cause of disenchantment with a principal.

Since many companies' primary method for obtaining business is through quoting competitive prices on time, why do so many firms neglect these important sales tools? Most of the time it's not intentional, but the reasons are often complex and the solutions hard to come by.

Let's examine some of the reasons for late quotes:

• The estimating job is performed by someone who has other responsibilities and estimating chores have a low priority.

• The sales manager doesn't place enough emphasis on fast processing from receipt of inquiry to mailing of quotes.

• The product requires prices from other firms or subcontractors for a portion of the manufacturing process. The later these quotes are received, the later the quote is mailed to the customer.

• The sales manager lacks authority to insist on receiving estimates within a given number of days after an inquiry is received.

And here are a few reasons for high prices:

• The estimator is "protecting" himself. He figures it's better to estimate a little high than a little low, in case he miscalculates. If the sales manager follows the same line of reasoning when adding profit to the estimate, the order is lost before the quote is mailed.

• The estimator or sales manager, whenever an agent is involved with a potential order, adds the agent's commission to the cost, which may already have a generous GS & A allocation, thus making the price too high.

• The sales manager may have other priority orders he wants, and on inquiries from certain territories he puts an exceptionally high markup on costs to guarantee that if an order is received there is an extra profit margin.

What Can Be Done About Poor Pricing and Late Quotes

Although there are no quick solutions because of the different departments and personnel involved, it is important that top management realizes how essential it is to produce fast quotes at competitive prices. It's the lifeblood of the company's future business.

After realizing the importance of the quoting function, the chief executive should, together with his sales manager, formulate a program that emphasizes speed in quoting and competitiveness in pricing.

A program designed to correct these faults would include some of the following procedures:

A short "quote meeting" could be held daily to bring together all personnel responsible for getting out a proposal promptly at competitive prices. This would include the estimator, sales manager, production manager, and representatives from the engineering and purchasing departments.

A definite time limit should be set for the processing of each inquiry; for instance, seven to ten days. If a quotation has not been mailed within ten days after receipt of the inquiry, the reasons should be discussed at the "quote meeting" on the eleventh day.

At the meeting, all personnel should be charged with the responsibility for suggesting possible methods to make the product at the least possible cost. The engineering representative may find that a small design change not affecting the use of the part can reduce the raw material needed; the production manager in turn may then discover that the part can be made on a smaller machine with a lower burden rate.

Efforts should be made to deal only with subcontractors who can respond to the company's requirements for prices within a very short time.

After a cost has been developed by the estimator, it should be discussed at the meeting to make certain no excessive costs have been figured in. And the estimator should be allowed the luxury of being wrong occasionally. Without some freedom from criticism, he will tend to estimate costs on the high side.

An estimate should not linger on the sales manager's desk until he returns from a business trip. There should be one or two other sales personnel with the authority to price the product. This requires them to be knowledgeable about the competition, the agent involved, and the company's pricing philosophies at any given time.

After establishing a policy of prompt quoting and competitive pricing, let your agents know about it. Whether or not you realize it, this specialized attention to your customers' inquiries is a real selling advantage. Your agents will be delighted to be able to tell your customers that they'll receive a quotation within ten days after you receive their inquiry.

Many an order has been lost because a quotation was received by the customer after he had already placed the business; a discouraging result for your agent and a waste of time for your estimator. Armed with a new outlook on your response to your customers, your agents will be out digging up many more new inquiries.

STREAMLINE YOUR AGENT SALES OPERATION BY MAKING THE MOST OF YOUR CUSTOMER SERVICE DEPARTMENT

"When I saw my valves as well as those of a competitor on the same fermentor, I thought that either I had done a poor sales job or that my competitor had done a great job." The sales manager who told us this went on to say that he called his agent who sold to the fermentor manufacturer and was told that the customer had difficulties expediting their order and couldn't afford a slowdown if the valves weren't delivered. "It's just a safety precaution," the buyer had said. But it was lost business to the agent and manufacturer, no matter how you looked at it.

Caution: The agent had done his job—he had gotten the order. But because of internal factory problems, neither the agent nor the manufacturer realized the full profit from the account. When it costs many times more to get a new account than it does to keep an existing one satisfied, it's time to examine ways to ensure that your agents are in a position to do what they do best—sell—and to see that every penny is realized from existing accounts. The secret lies in making the most of your customer service department.

When an agent has to act as your trouble-shooter, he isn't making money for you or for himself. Of course it depends on the kinds of products you make and the degree of technical sophistication required to sell them, but you can get the most out of an agent organization by relegating routine questions, complaints, and even order taking to in-house customer service people. It's just a matter of efficiency. The more routine nonselling work an agent is expected to do, the fewer sales calls he can make. And the fewer the calls, the fewer the orders. After all, most manufacturers go the agent route because it's most cost effective. Why turn a good situation into a bad one!

You have to change your view of customer service. Most manufacturers look at their customer service department as nonproductive operations. This may be true from an accounting point of view, but if you view your customer service department as a group of people who enable your agents to sell more, you will have taken a very positive step. When agents have strong backup and are not asked to handle a lot of nonselling jobs, everybody benefits.

Warning: There is a fast way to lose agents. When an agent is required to do customer service work, he is, as we've already mentioned, taken away from his most productive work. If this happens enough, he isn't going to hang around. Remember that agents are paid commissions, and even though you may pay special fees for nonselling work, a good agent knows that the only way to make money is through commissions. Without an adequate customer service organization, you could lose your best agents.

How to make the most of your customer service people. Too often, the people who man the phones at the plant know the product line cold but don't know how to handle a customer call in a positive way. We're not talking about the usual complaints or expediting calls but the calls for product and delivery information. Smart marketing managers train their customer service people as thoroughly as they do their independent agents. Here are some ways you can handle this:

1. *Train your customer service people to cross sell.* When they get a call for a dozen couplings, make sure that they ask if any pullies are needed. Remember that the person who called is ready to buy and is most receptive to suggestions that he buy more than he had originally thought he would.

2. *Train your customer service people to sell up.* If you make three grades of oil and someone has just asked for grade C, it's the job of the customer service person to make sure that grade A is sold.

3. *Train your customer service people to anticipate needs.* After a person has been on the job for awhile, he should begin to recognize order frequencies. If he can anticipate a customer's need with a phone call, he might prevent the order from going to a competitor.

An investment in customer service work is an investment in productivity. Considering what it costs to contact and train an agent, the investment in customer service is small. But don't be mislead into thinking that even the most productive customer service people can do the entire job. They're part of the team. They're like the flight crew on an airplane—they make it possible for the captain to get the plane in the air and to its destination.

HOW YOU AND YOUR AGENTS CAN USE CREDIT AS A MARKETING TOOL

Let's face it—a lot of companies are paying more slowly than they did before. Some are even being refused credit after years of enjoying a first-class reputation. Despite the reluctance of most marketing people to get involved with company accountants, now is the time to get their input. No matter how you look at it, credit policy is part of marketing. Even a marketing manager who can't balance a checkbook must understand that Return on Investment is more important than just increasing sales.

>>> *OBSERVATION* In the past, many companies got their agents involved in the credit picture to collect information before credit was offered and to collect money when bills were overdue. In both cases, it was an imposition on the agent and a bad use of time that should have been used for selling. Now, however, with the emphasis on short-range goals, you and your agents are going to have to help each other in ways that you may never have thought about. You may be surprised at some of our suggestions, but times are changing, and so are agent/manufacturer relationships.

Credit is a marketing tool. When you know who is paying on time, you generally know where the better sources of sales will be. Credit can be used to expand sales volume as well as to maximize profit. And, of course, different market segments will have different credit needs. At this point, your agents will be in a better position to give you practical information than any of the expensive professional credit reporting services.

Your agents know the local credit situation. Agents haunt their territories. Even though they may not have sought the information directly, they get the bits and pieces from their customers and other agents that can be put together to provide the picture that is needed to make sound credit decisions:

1. *The nature of the business seeking credit.* It's difficult to tell anything about a company from its name, but your agents can often tell you what the company does, how they do it, and what their prospects are for success, all based on calls they've made for other principals.

2. *Managerial competence.* If you're going to give credit to a company, you'd better know how competent management is. Think about it. Credit is like making a loan. Make sure you're lending money to someone who will use it wisely. Most agents can spot four-flushers in a hurry.

3. *Appearance of the business.* This may sound like a relatively unimportant point, but most major credit reporting services lean heavily on this factor. Because your agents are calling on a lot of similar businesses, they are in a good position to make comparisons and relative evaluations. Always ask them to qualify the report by having a base line for comparison.

4. *Personnel.* You will want to know if the company is up to staff. Just counting the cars in the company parking lot will give you an idea of how many are employed and how honest management is. If the credit application states that 100 are employed and your agent spots 20 cars in the lot, you must ask the obvious question.

5. *Customers.* You will want to know what the credit applicant's customers think of them. Quality of product? Delivery? Service?

6. *Competition.* Who is winning the competitive race and why? Is the competitive picture serious enough to warrant the restriction of credit? Most agents can answer these questions without doing any research. The agent grapevine is robust and reliable.

As you can see, sound credit decisions must include answers to these nonfinancial questions. Most credit reporting services either gloss over the details or don't provide the answers at all. Yet it's the kind of information that many agents have at their finger tips or they can get it quickly and easily. If time and effort are involved on the part of your agents, you should expect to pay for it. Now let's look at how your agents can help clarify the credit picture without slowing down on what they do best—selling.

• Don't ask your agents to gather specific credit information. That is, don't expect them to provide you with the same financial information that you would get from a D & B report, for example. Rather, ask them to help by gathering information that can be used to infer the financial health of the company as well as validate the credit information you get from professional financial sources. Use the points mentioned earlier as a guide. The chances are that your agents already have much of this information and will not have to do much digging. The information they will get for you will be as important in making credit decisions as will be the actual financial figure you get elsewhere.

• Don't press your agents for information unless it's absolutely needed. What we're saying is that you should limit your requests to situations where the decision to offer credit will bear directly on the efforts of the agent. In a sense, you will be asking your agent to be a partner to a decision that will affect both of you. Agents don't get paid unless the manufacturer gets paid. So both of you should share in the decision.

• Don't use agents to collect past due bills. Some agents may do this on their own initiative, but the agents' job is to bring in sales—not overdue money. If you must use your agents to collect past due bills, they should be paid for their effort. How you pay is up to you and your agents. Most agents can tell you what their time is worth on an hourly basis, and with this figure a fair charge can be set.

• Never send a dunning letter without notifying your agent first. Your agent may be working on the past due account and a letter from you could turn a softened account back into a closed wallet. Consult with your agent before you write or call, if you know that your agent is working on the problem, too.

THE TIME TO SOLVE CREDIT PROBLEMS IS BEFORE THEY EVER GET STARTED

Let's take a look at the ways your agents can be most helpful:

1. Consult with your agents on credit terms on the initial sale to a new customer. You and your agent should review the size of the initial sale, the terms of the credit, and even contingency plans if the customer finds himself strapped when the payments come due.

2. Think ahead to future orders. You may tend to play your future credit policies by ear, depending on how the initial sale goes, but we strongly urge you to discuss future credit terms right up front. If you and your agent make the customer aware that you are just prudent and not hard-headed bottom-liners, you will build a strong relationship early in the game. And you can tailor your credit to fit the anticipated growth of sales to the new customer. It's the old stick-and-carrot routine, but it works wonders these days when everyone is so nervous about money.

3. Decide your limits in advance. Despite the best plans and the most noble of intentions, things can go wrong. You, your agent, and the customer should know exactly what will constitute a breach of the credit agreement, how much latitude can be tolerated, and how much authority your agent has to set things right. It's just a matter of planning so that there will be no surprises when you least need them.

4. Keep your agents aware of credit problems. Even though you may not expect them to do anything about credit problems, your agents should be aware of what is happening in the territories. They may have information that can help put the problem in perspective, and they may want to slow down their selling efforts on slow-paying accounts in favor of those who pay on time. As we said, credit is very much a marketing tool, and you and your agents should use it for all it's worth, literally and figuratively!

HOW TO HELP YOUR AGENCIES HANDLE COMPETITION

"One of my principals thought they were being very helpful when they sent me a competitor's catalog and price list. I already had that. What I really needed was for someone at the plant to compare their products, point for point, with those made by the competitor." We hear this frequently from agents. And we also hear from manufacturers how difficult it is to get reliable competitive information for their agencies.

>>>→ *OBSERVATION* We've never seen a product sold by agencies that didn't have a few competitors. Some products compete head-on; others compete on the basis of differences that are the result of promotional hype—advertising and product publicity. It's not enough to recognize that there are differences. It's important to help your agencies neutralize real competitive disadvantages in another's products and to help them to put minor differences into perspective for their customers. Remember, any salespeople—salaried or independent contractor—can get discouraged when competition keeps heading them off at the pass. Here are some of the better ways to help your agencies handle competition. And be honest with yourself and with your agencies. The following tells how to do it.

• Begin by creating specific product-for-product comparison sheets. Don't leave out any products or any information. The chances are that you already have a lot of this information available if yours is a relatively new product. You should have gathered all the information during product development stages. This sheet should contain all the facts, and it should be organized so that your agency people can get the information they need with as little effort as possible. In fact, you should plan this sheet so that anyone talking with a customer on the phone can get right at the information needed with almost no effort. Specifications change—keep the sheets up to date.

• In addition to the product-by-product comparison sheet, you should also include—on a separate sheet—text in which you describe your products, your competitor's products, and the strengths and weaknesses of both. Whenever possible, try to point out to your agencies how their salespeople can counter strong competitive claims. For example, if your product has limited ratings compared with that of a competitor, make sure that your agencies know when expanded ratings do nothing for the customer. A competitor's flowmeter may be rated at .001 percent error full scale. But you will probably find out that such a factor is not very important to many people, especially at a higher price than yours at a lower error figure.

• Show your agencies how to meet competitive claims, especially those used in advertising. It's not too difficult to make a product seem like the greatest thing since sliced bread in an ad, and the effects of such claims often remain in the minds of buyers as they review other products. If your agency people face a buyer who has seen nothing but the advertising puff of a competitor, they can be in for trouble. In addition to the spec-for-spec sheet we suggested, it's also a good idea to create a claim-for-claim sheet for your agencies to use to compare advertising copy. Some manufacturers who go this route also key the advertising claims back to the specification comparison sheets. This can be a powerful tool to use when facing a buyer who is relying on what he or she has seen in a competitor's advertising.

• Help your agencies to fend off competitive attacks. If you make it a point to know your competition well, you will know where you are weak as well as where you are strong. It's just as important to prepare your agencies to fight a defensive action as it is to be aggressive about the positive points of your products. And one of the best ways to do this is to give them examples they can use along with the unvarnished facts. Let's say that your strip chart recorder has all the connectors on the back panel and your competitor has put his on the front. Your competitor shouts in his advertising about how easy it is to hook up his recorder, implying that because the connectors on yours are on the back, it's difficult to use. When you tell your agencies that your connectors are on the rear panel for an important reason—to prevent the recorder from being dragged off the bench by front-access cables—you have provided your agencies with the ammunition they need.

• Give your agencies the material they need to dislodge a competitive product that has been satisfying customers. It's tough enough to compete for an original sale, but trying to get a buyer to switch once a product has been accepted is very difficult. However, when your agencies can make a strong pitch for future purchases based on solid competitive information, you will have helped a lot. It's easier to do this with a consumable product, such as bulk chemicals, and OEM components. Often just supplying samples and the competitive facts will do the job. But it isn't that easy with equipment. Showing how your product could be interchanged with a product already in use and supplying a demo model is frequently the best way to handle this.

> **⫸➤ OBSERVATION**   Gathering and using competitive information is an ongoing process. Products, specifications, and customer needs are changing constantly. Be sure that the information you supply to your agencies is current. Frequently, your agencies can help you keep the records up to date by submitting material that they have gathered in the field. The manufacturers who do the best job of handling competitive problems not only get information to their agencies, they get material back from them. It's a team effort that pays the biggest dividends.

NEW PRODUCTS? DON'T NEGLECT EXISTING MONEYMAKERS . . . AND PLAN WITH YOUR AGENCIES

"One of my principals spent a bundle developing a new product—new to them but not to the market—and while they did that they allowed production to slip on the bread-and-butter line," an agent said. "Sure, they asked for my input, and they took some of my advice. I warned them that they must continue to be able to deliver on the standard products, but they didn't pay any attention." This is not an unfamiliar story.

> **⫸➤ OBSERVATION**   Seed money is easier to come by—markets are expanding and enthusiasm is up. These are all the elements of new product fertility, and many manufacturers are taking the steps they had put off taking during the last few down years. However, in the rush to

make up for lost time, some manufacturers have a tendency to neglect the lines that made them successful. Inventory of established products slip, and customers then go elsewhere to fulfill their needs.

Here are a few thoughts on the subject:

Watch the timing very closely. Know when to begin on new product development as well as when to introduce new products. More often than not, your agencies can give you considerable input on timing. They are close to the needs of their customers and to the thrust of your competitors. No matter how closely a new product secret is kept, some word usually leaks out. There are times when being first is critical, and there are times when it's wise to let someone else make the market before you bring out your product.

Make sure that you can project the sales and profits of existing products accurately before you take the new product plunge. If you are working with limited capital and physical resources, you should anticipate worst-case scenarios early in the plan. "The new product was a proven prototype when demand suddenly doubled for the old product," a sales manager related. "If we didn't fill the demand, the customers would have gone elsewhere and we would have lost our standard business and would have had to move fast in order to introduce the new product in time to sustain business. Luckily the agency in our prime territory had alerted us to this possibility before we were locked in and we could respond with production."

"Most of their new products are just modifications of the standard line," an agent said of one of his principals. However, this agent is perceptive enough to see where changes can be made in existing products that won't adversely affect the production of the pieces that are bread and butter. "It's basically a screw machine operation," the agent said. "With some simple secondary operations on the fitting, they have a new product. It's as simple as that, and it doesn't affect production of the standard line."

Watch your raw material inventories carefully. If the new and old products are made from the same material, as is often the case in industrial components, the preliminary production of new products can siphon off material that should be used to fill orders for standard products. This is a problem that agencies are especially sensitive to. "I sent orders for standard products, and shipment slipped from the usual 30 days to 60 and 90 days simply because they were working in stock that could be moved anywhere in the factory," an agent said. When agencies get orders and shipments fall behind, they often turn their attention elsewhere. They are paid for orders filled, not orders that never get billed. Most agencies will let you know what's happening quickly, but don't take them to task when you don't ship.

    ⫸→ *WATCH THIS* In many cases the new products being developed today will not augment existing products, they will replace them. When this is the case and you must clear the inventory of the old product, make sure that your agencies are fully aware of exactly what you are doing. And make sure that they are kept up to date on stock levels so they don't sell products that you can't deliver.

Identify what your customers want; identify the market; create product concepts; test and recycle the concepts; create a tight description of product specifications and benefits; develop prototypes and test them; modify the designs based on agent and customer feedback; create the marketing strategy; take the show on the road.

HOW TO TRACK COMPETITORS

There's no question about it, agency feedback is one of the best ways to keep tabs on the doings of your competitors in the field. They have to see what's happening every day in the field, and they're in the best position to make on-the-spot evaluations of the importance of what they see. However, as effective as agencies are in gathering intelligence, they need your help in the same area. They need information on the competition that you can gather but that is seldom around for them to spot in their regular field calls. Here are some sources you can tap for your own information and to guide your agencies.

Industry Specialists. There are the "in" people in every field who know what is going on and what is about to be going on. These people are sources of information that your agencies can use in combination with the facts they dig up in the field. Such industry specialists can be consultants, the editors of the trade magazines that cover your field, and even salespeople from noncompeting companies. The important thing to remember when you seek information from these people is that you are not out to compromise them. Each has a personal and a professional reputation to uphold, but each has general information and usually an overview that is difficult for any single individual in the plant to have.

Association Executives. The executives who direct and operate the trade and professional associations to which you may belong are usually excellent sources of general and confirming information. Don't expect them to give you any secrets—they can best serve you by giving you the details of your industry against which you can evaluate the information you gather directly and from field sources.

Magazine Advertising Salespeople. No magazine advertising salesperson is going to spill the beans on you or your competitor, but you can get some interesting insight by listening between the lines of a media presentation. Ad salespeople like to let you know how much advertising your competitor is planning—you know the effect this can have on a tight ad budget. Even if you can't get the numbers, you can get a feel for what is happening with a competitor by evaluating what you hear in terms of other information that you have.

Competitive information is critical for success when selling with sales agencies. This is the kind of information that most agencies feel is critical for their principals to supply to them: (1) The geographical coverage of each competitor—essential for territorial planning and salesperson deployment; (2) The products sold most effectively by the competitors—you don't want your agencies wasting time selling against products that don't amount to much competition, considering the overall strength of the competitive line; (3) The industries in which your competitors are most active, for the same reason as item 2; (4) The competitors' capabilities—it helps to know where you will face a tough front and where you can make inroads quickly and inexpensively; (5) The ability of the competitors to maintain the customers they have—many are great at getting business but drop the ball when they have the first order; insight on this can ease market penetration; (6) The image of the competitors in the marketplace—it's never worth the effort to bad-mouth anyone, but it's just good selling to stress your good points when you know that they tell a story about the problems your competitors have.

15

Building Business with Practical Research

Some manufacturers have full-fledged research departments and can usually supply their agencies with considerable research information. However, agencies usually don't have these facilities. The tips in the pages that follow are mainly for those who do not have an active research department but who do want to provide their agencies with up-to-date information.

Agents should not be held responsible for the credit capabilities of their customers. However, by using the tips provided in this Chapter, your agents can provide some of the information that will help you make sound credit decisions.

One of the best sources of competitive information is your agency team. The four guidelines detailed in this Chapter will help your agencies discover the competitive facts you need, without putting a burden on the agents' selling time.

We have also included a seven-step checklist you can use to help your agents make more effective use of the market research data you provide them.

INFORMAL CHECKS BY AGENTS CAN HELP REDUCE CREDIT RISKS

Dun and Bradstreet and other credit-checking services can offer numerous advantages to firms trying to pin down the financial health of potential new customers in far-off territories. Often, however, information is sketchy due to company management's reluctance to provide up-to-date and accurate financial information.

Agents can help. Veterans who have served the territory for years are often more acquainted with the financial status of companies in their areas than are the credit pros.

Your agents may already have experienced credit difficulties with certain firms through sales made on behalf of their other principals. They can also check out other tip-offs to the stability of a company, such as the number of cars in the parking lot and the condition of the premises.

Caution: Don't rely on their information exclusively—they're agents, not credit managers. However, by asking their cooperation and coupling their feedback with that of your banker and credit sources, you'll have less chance of getting stuck by poor credit risks.

ASK YOUR AGENTS FOR FORECASTS

No company, no matter how small, should go into the new year without some projection of the sales volume it can expect. Ask your agents for forecasts of the business you can expect from their territories for the coming year.

Most agents have had experience at forecasting, either as former direct-employee salespeople or as a result of their other principals' requests for this information.

An added bonus is the opportunity for the agents to make contact with your current and prospective customers in the interest of gathering information for their forecasts. A meaningful contact with a customer is always worthwhile.

EARLY ECONOMIC WARNING SIGNALS AVAILABLE
FROM YOUR AGENTS

Many companies rely on conversations with people in their own business to keep tabs on the economy. As a result, they are unable to recognize or forecast a slowdown or pickup in business until it's too late.

There's a much more reliable barometer available as near as your phone—your agent. He can tell almost immediately when a change in the economic climate has occurred.

> **⫸➔ IDEA IN ACTION** How can he do this? He may represent companies in as many as seven or eight different industries. If he's competent, he keeps a running backlog of orders on a monthly basis. He has to know how his business is doing, just as you do. While your industry may be booming you may find that you're an exception and merely two or three months behind the industrial trend.

Keep in touch with your representative. Ask him what kind of a month he's having in incoming orders. How are his other principals doing? Are blanket orders being placed? Is there more pressure, or less, on pricing?

Agencies are also in constant contact not only with your customers but with many others. This gives a much broader and comprehensive feedback than that available from your customers only.

YOUR AGENTS KNOW THE COMPETITION

Few of us really have sufficient knowledge of our competition's capabilities. If we did, we'd do a better job of marketing our own products. Pricing could be adjusted to allow higher profits; the salesforce could emphasize our products' strengths versus the competitors' weaknesses; packaging, credit terms, and many other selling strategies could be utilized.

Too frequently, we fail to take advantage of our best source of competitive information—our own representative salesforce. They're on the spot. They know the competitions' products and customers.

Presently, most manufacturers are receiving feedback on competitors' new products from only about 15 percent of their salesforce. These guidelines will help you obtain this vital information.

1. Specify the kind of information you need to get the edge on competition.
2. Set up a channel for reporting that makes it easy to relay the information. To get around salespeople's distaste for paper work, as well as to speed up the flow of information, many companies are using telephoned reports or even tape cassettes.
3. Assign one person in the home office to receive and process market information from the field and prepare a weekly summary for management.
4. Set up a system for feedback informing salespeople how their input was used.

- Modify the above points to fit your specific needs.
- Don't expect reams of information. You simply won't get it. But, insist on vital information—information that's important regarding your major competitors.
- Handle most communications by phone. Set up the last Friday of each month for reporting, and you initiate the call.
- Each time you make a field trip, stress how important this information is to you and your agents.

Implementing this program will take effort on your part, but it can only mean increased profits for your company.

HOW TO LAUNCH A NEW PRODUCT WITH AGENTS BEFORE YOU GO INTO PRODUCTION

There's no such thing as a free lunch. Every agent knows this, but there are still some manufacturers who aren't sure. They expect their agents to gather market information "in their spare time" and to help test-market new products before they go into production—activities that keep them from selling and making money for themselves and you!

If you feel your agents can handle these marketing assignments and you would normally pay someone else to do the work, why not pay your agent? It's true that some agents can only peddle products, but most of the people in the business today have solid marketing savvy. They know how to conduct an interview, introduce new products in the development stage, and can handle many other marketing assignments. After all, most of them came from the corporate marketing and sales side where they did this kind of work regularly.

We talked with a number of agents, sales managers, and consultants and here's what they feel most agents can do to help plan and launch a new product.

1. Determine the potential in their territories.
2. Identify prospects who will adopt the product early.
3. Locate and evaluate information on competitive products.
4. Evaluate specifications as they relate to applications.
5. Help develop a pricing structure.
6. Assist in test-marketing the product before it's given a national send-off.

You may want to get help from your agents at each step of the way, or you may want to use them in special situations. We feel that the manufacturer/agent partnership calls for close cooperation if both are to profit, but we feel that agents, being marketing professionals, should be paid for their work. But how can you tell whether your agents can handle the work, and how do you pay them to do the job? The people we talked with had some very specific thoughts. Here are the highlights.

➤➤➤ *EXAMPLE Agent*—We charge a consulting fee if the work takes us away from our regular selling routine. If the work can be done while we are making our regular calls, we can often work it in without charging the principal.

➤➤➤ *EXAMPLE Sales Manager*—Not all of our agents are capable of doing the type of research and new product introduction work we need. But we can often base our plans on the work of the few who are.

➤➤➤ *EXAMPLE Consultant*—Agents who are capable of doing the work and willing to commit the time should charge their principals for the time they spend on the project. Every agent should know what his hourly time is worth. This amount should be billed for any nonselling marketing work done for a principal.

When you want to test a product before you commit to full-scale production, you can use your agents, but you should get clear answers to these questions before you give out the assignment.

1. Do you and the people in your organization have the skills and the time needed to do the job?
2. Will you give us a written proposal, stating how the project will be handled? Or will you agree to follow the plan we will supply?
3. If the job is to be done apart from regular sales calls, will you guarantee that the time will be allocated?
4. How much will you charge per hour, and how long will it take to complete the assignment?

5. Will you be able to supply raw data, summary information, and conclusions?

If you get positive answers to these questions, you should be able to use your agents in ways that will help both of you. After all, even though the agent is conducting research, he can return to the people he talked with to sell them the product when it is on the market.

HOW TO USE MARKET RESEARCH TO HELP YOUR AGENTS BE MORE PRODUCTIVE

Whether you have your own research department and produce all the information you need, use outside consultants, or depend on the research done by trade publications or associations, the data you have can be used to enhance your agent sales program.

There are several ways that the results of marketing research can be used to strengthen your agent network. First, share with your agents not only your raw data but also the conclusions you draw from it. Your conclusions will be based on the total picture, but your agents, working in smaller isolated territories, will have personal interpretations that will be especially important for them. Here are just a few ways to use the results of your research to strengthen your agent salesforce.

1. You can use research data to plan effective distribution of your advertising and promotion by territories. Depending on territory potential, competitive activity, and other marketing elements, you can maximize your promotional investment.

2. Your research can show you how to maximize various product and sales approaches by territory. Regional differences in some products can make it difficult for some agents to make a go of it.

3. Your research should be able to forecast trends—up and down in individual territories—that you can use to help your agents be most efficient.

4. Your research should pinpoint weak spots in a territory's competitive positions, inventory levels, stock-out situations, prices, profits, and so on. This approach to individual territory management is becoming especially important today, considering the significant variations in regional economies.

5. Your research should help you to establish individual territory goals. Without such information, you will never be able to differentiate between good territories with poor sales and poor territories with strong sales by effective agents.

6. Your research should be able to provide you with a profile of the territories best suited for test-marketing specific products. Without knowing the strengths and weaknesses of each territory, you are much more likely to make poor decisions.

7. Your research should give you a picture of customer good will in each territory. This, of course, can serve as a rough index of the kind of job each agent has been doing.

HOW TO USE YOUR AGENTS TO GATHER
MARKET INFORMATION

For some reason, many people who use agents seem to feel that they have a right to expect the agents' help with research at any time and that the tasks they assign can be lengthy. There's a lot wrong with this notion, but there are ways your agents can help you gather information that you need. Remember that agents don't make money until a sale is made. How ever you decide to solicit their help, be prepared to pay for it. If you can convince your agents to do the research without actual payment, you will pay for it in lost sales and in agent resentment. The approach we are going to describe doesn't take any time away from selling and it eliminates the personal bias that usually accompanies work done by agents who are untrained in interviewing techniques—and who usually have a personal interest in the outcome of the study.

- *Caution:* The premise used by most principals when they ask their agents to conduct research for them is that they are making calls anyway and they might as well ask a few questions. There's a lot wrong with this. Most agents simply don't have the training to probe for answers. Instead, they tend to guide the interview in the direction they would like to see it go. When they do this, the answers are biased, and usually the agent has spent a lot of time that could have been used to sell your products.

- Even if you provide your agents with a carefully structured questionnaire, there is still a problem of bias—and, of course, the loss of selling time.

- However, there is one fast and effective way to get the answers to your marketing questions. Before we describe the system, you should know that surveys done by mail are usually the most unbiased when the respondents are given only a few questions to answer and when they are told not to identify themselves personally. However, a major problem with direct mail market research is that few people return the questionnaires, and of those who do, it's very difficult to tell how much influence those people actually have over the problems addressed by the questions.

Now consider this:

- You can reach every decision-maker with your questionnaire, and you can assure respondents complete anonymity. What this means is that you can get the answers from the people who count. And you will know that they count because you can select them carefully. In other words, your agents can get your questionnaires to key people, and they can do it on a sales call. The only thing they have to do is request that the individual fill out the questionnaire on his or her own time— without signing his or her name—and mail it back to you in a post-paid envelope.

- When you use agents to do this research, you should provide them with careful instructions. They should be told to explain the nature of the survey, the facts that respondent anonymity is critical, that the information they provide will help the principal provide better products and service, and that both you and the agent value their opinions highly. All this can be done in a few minutes. After the questionnaire and the post-paid envelope have been given to the customer, the selling can continue.

• What kind of information can be gathered effectively this way? The information that's most important to growth: (a) production information, (b) market conditions, (c) competitive developments, (d) the effectiveness of sales and promotion programs.

• Here are a few hints to help you with questionnaire design. Don't make the questions open-ended. That is, don't expect your respondents to write out lengthy answers. Rather, use questions to which the individuals can respond by checking off various choices. Keep the questions and the choices short. And keep the entire questionnaire short. Although you can often get people to answer long questionnaires when they are hand delivered, it's still best to limit your survey to no more than ten short questions. When you have the questionnaire typed, leave plenty of white space around and between the questions and choices. A lot of type will intimidate the respondent. Be sure to indicate clearly on the questionnaire that the respondents are not to sign their names. You will reduce the bias factor considerably without signatures.

• You can help increase returns if you have your agents tell the respondents that, if they like, they will be sent a copy of the tabulated results. This device is a very powerful motivator.

SET CLEAR GOALS WHEN YOU ASK YOUR AGENCIES TO HELP WITH MARKET RESEARCH

To make the most of your agencies' valuable time, it's critical that you set specific goals for the project. Just giving agencies a list of questions to ask their customers is not exactly the most productive way to go. You should make it clear to your agencies just what decisions you are planning to make based on the information they will be gathering. And when the agency people interview their customers, it helps if they can explain why the information is needed. Of course, there are times when information is needed for new products and tipping that hand could give competitors a lead. But whenever possible, make the reasons clear to the customers. Unless you need a specific stratified sample, a random sampling is usually called for. This decision is usually dictated automatically by the nature of the project and the specific informational need. And, finally, make sure that your agency people record the information carefully. If at all possible, design the questionnaire so that the agency people can record their answers on a preprinted form.

Caution: Always remember that do-it-yourself market research is risky. You are working with people who are not specifically trained to dig for information and who, because of their selling skills, can frequently lead a person to make statements that are not valid. If you keep the questions to a factual level and don't dig for meaning or interpretations, you're on very safe ground.

SOME OF THE BEST MARKET RESEARCH IN THE WORLD IS AVAILABLE FREE

Sure, you will probably have to spend some money if you are introducing some major new products. But the best ongoing advice about your products and your customer service is available without charge. Listen to this marketing manager from a medium-size manufacturer of retail hardware: "Every six months I mail a short questionnaire to a random sample of our customers. I ask them for their opinions on just about every subject that could affect sales. And I make it easy for them to complain about everything from the product to the service provided by our sales agencies. Although I usually ask between six and ten questions in each survey, I make it easy for them to answer by providing check-off categories. No one has to write a word—unless they really want to." This may seem like nothing new, but the wrinkle is that this manufacturer gets input for the questionnaires from all of his agencies—and he shares the results with all of them. "This is a team effort," he said, "and we can't function as a team unless everyone knows what's going on."

Appendix

WHEN A MANUFACTURER DECIDES TO USE SALES AGENCIES

Harry Small was a sharp sales manager. He had a good education, lots of practical experience in selling as well as managing other salespeople. One day his employer acquired a small company that manufactured products that could not be sold to his company's present customers. Being up on these things, Harry decided that the best way to get this acquisition moving was to use agents. After all, he reasoned, agents provide lower and more predictable sales costs and require little administrative overhead. He could handle this new company with one arm tied behind his back. The agents would give him immediate access to a new market, and he wouldn't have to train new employees and go through all the hassle he had gone through when he built the direct sales team for the parent company. In fact, with the recent trend to multi-person agencies, Harry would have more than one person in many territories, unlike the one-person, one-territory he'd have if he hired a direct sales employee.

Harry gets an A + for his reasoning. And we'll even give Harry top marks for his ability to make decisions decisively.

Harry did everything right. He got leads on good agencies from the company's present customers and from other manufacturers selling related but noncompetitive products. He prescreened them by telephone and set up meetings in their territories. He asked them about the other products they sold, the markets they covered, the customers they had, competitive products, and even discussed tentative working relationships—a textbook case so far. It took Harry about six months to talk to over sixty agents in nine territories, but he did the job well.

When he finished, he had the nine territories covered, and covered well. Each agent had the experience Harry needed. And each had the individual flexibility to provide the different services that were dictated by specific territory conditions. His boss was pleased. In fact, he was so pleased that he told Harry to take a week off.

Harry took the week off. But he never came back, at least not to the job he had started so well. Sure, he returned to the plant and he continued to work. But when he had decided to use agents and had gotten them all on board, he also decided he could turn all his attention, all of it, to other matters. After all, he reasoned, he had picked the best, and the commissions he was paying were among the highest in the industry. Nothing else was needed.

Initially there was good activity. A sufficient quantity of orders came in to make it seem as though the sales chart on his wall could be left up even when the president visited his office. But things turned sour in a hurry.

Why? Not because Harry made the wrong decision, but because he simply didn't go far enough with it. A network of sales agencies must be nurtured and tended with care. Yes, a lot has been written on this subject, but too often people discover the writing when it's too late—when they are faced with problems. The whole point of this is to move this thinking back to the decision stage—to the point where commitments are made. Committing to the use of independent agents is one thing, but committing to active participation in the management of them, the support of their activities, and the encouragement they need is another. If you make a firm commitment to support your agency network, your chances for success will be excellent.

Selling Your Agents

The word *sell* has many meanings. We use it when we talk of any business transaction in which one person convinces another to part with money for a product or service. But the word is also used when we talk about trying to convince people. "You've got to sell him on your ideas" is a common expression and one that doesn't mean that a person is going to pay money for someone else's thoughts.

Let's think about the word sell in this sense. You've got to "sell" agents in many ways. If you think of agents as customers, you will get a clearer picture of what we mean. It's simply a matter of mental imagery, but this simple shift of a frame of reference can make a lot of difference.

Those who sell through distributors—companies that buy, stock, and resell the product—think of the distributors as their customers. Even though agents don't buy from you, you've got to sell them. And I don't mean sell them a bill of goods.

Agents have already bought the idea that they can sell the product; they have already bought the idea that being an agent is a better way for them to make a living than by working for someone else. And they have invested not only money in their decision but large chunks of their lives. What you have to sell them on is your product, your service, and the fact that the two of you are going to make a lot of money together. Remember that this selling is not a snow job—it's a matter of showing the agent how the partnership is going to be a profitable one because you and the agent are going to do a lot of good things together. And you've got to decide right up front that you're going to work very hard at it.

How to Get the Ball Rolling

Set ground rules, right up front, and include your agents in the process. Unfortunately, most manufacturer/agency relationships that go sour early in the game do so simply because both parties assume things and never discuss them with each other. This is especially true for the sales manager who has worked with a salaried salesforce and never had any experience with independent agencies. Direct salespeople are paid regardless of what they do. And this may include spending weeks on a pet market research project for you while the territory goes to pot. If you expect an agent, an independent businessperson who doesn't make money until a sale is made, to do all of the things a salaried salesperson will do, you're in for a big surprise.

However, given time and the appropriate compensation, you can often get better nonselling help from an agent than from a salaried salesperson. Let's look at some of the work that agents can do in addition to selling. Remember that these are topics to be discussed when you've first decided to use agents and are talking to prospects.

Collections

Although the best agent/principal contracts state that the responsibility for collections lies with the manufacturer, there is quite a bit an agent can do to help the cash flow situation short of becoming a collection agent. When an agent does try to help, it's important for you to keep the legal picture in mind. Since you are responsible for the approval of credit, orders, and contracts, any help the agent offers should clearly limit any possibility of liability. After sounding this legal warning, we can tell you that agents are just as interested in seeing you get your money as you are. Even though agents are normally paid either on acceptance or delivery of the order, they want to be able to sell the customer more products. If the customer doesn't pay, either you or he may put a freeze on future orders until the balance is cleared up.

When a collection problem does arise, agents can be most helpful if they approach the customer in a friendly, offhanded way. Any formal attempts at collecting money should not be part of an agent's work. In fact, most good agents ask their principals to let them know when bills are slightly overdue. They feel that's the time when they can be most helpful with a little reminder. For best results, let your agents know when invoices begin to age, but don't make them responsible for collections.

Forecasting

Depending on how demanding you are, your agent can be an excellent source of planning information. However, if you expect him or her to take time out to do specific research, you should pay for it. Most agents who have been selling one market in the same territory for a while can give you off-the-top-of-their-head estimates that will come pretty close to reality. If a few points of precision are important to you and you want more than this, make sure that the agent knows what is expected up front and well before you want your forecasts.

Market Research

Unfortunately, most people don't recognize good market research when they see it. They think in terms of carefully planned studies, statistically validated and presented on a computer printout. But when you listen between the lines in your conversations with agents, you will probably pick up more good information than when you ask for quantified and qualified data. If quantified and qualified data are what you need, your agency people should know this before you and they sign any papers. Again, if the work takes time from selling, be prepared to pay for it.

Sales Policy

Every company has a different style, different requirements, and a unique way of promoting and selling. If you work trade shows heavily, for example, and you expect your agent to do this for you, be sure to spell out the details.

Reports

Agents love to talk about the things they do to make sales. And it's important for you to listen carefully to what they have to say. But you shouldn't expect them to file formal call reports. In the first place, writing reports takes them away from what they do best—selling. In the second place, requesting formal reports is contrary to the agent's independent contractor status. The tax and legal implications of this can be staggering to you, the manufacturer.

This isn't a one-way street. When you sign up an agent, he's got an agenda, too. There are things he will expect from you as well.

Clear, Up-Front Communications

Again, much has been written about the value of communications, but it's still a major problem in agent/manufacturer relations. There are two parts of the problem: (1) what you say and (2) how you say it. What you say is a plea for truth. We can't tell you how many sour agents and principals there are just because one felt that the other wasn't able to handle something. This runs the gamut from simple exaggeration about territory potential to out-and-out lies. How you say it is something else, and the subject of many books and articles and seminars. If you remember that the simplest words are best and the shortest sentences communicate most clearly, you've had more than half the course.

Attainable Goals

Apart from hard and fast quotas that are difficult to set and even more difficult to administer, you should both agree on general goals. In its simplest form, this is management by objectives. When you and your agents agree on the things each is to accomplish or provide, you will have a basis for good management and motivation.

Training

Agents do want training, but they want specific help in learning your products, markets, and their applications. Don't make the mistake of sending a trainer around to your agents with basic training. After all, you went the agency route because you wanted professional salespeople on your team right away.

Start Out on the Right Foot

Few decisions are made on the basis of 100 percent certainty. Choosing to go with agents is no exception. However, once you've made up your mind, don't agonize over the other possibilities. Move out, and get that agent team built and going. Let's look at the major reasons that most people go the agent route. The chances are that most of your reasons are in this list:

1. *Selling skills.* Although most manufacturers' agents have considerable education and experience in specific fields (engineering, for example), they are first and foremost professional salespeople. More often than not, they started out in a specialized field, moved into the company sales department, and then out on their own when they realized that they were good, very good, at selling. Because of this combination, the agent knows his customers' needs and problems intimately. And he knows the buying influences in his territory well. Customers tend to seek advice from agents more than from factory people. The agent, carrying several lines, appears to be more impartial. On the other hand, the factory person has only one product or line of products to sell. Because of this, he has to make more of a sales call than the agent, who can sell other products at the same time. Often sales managers see this as a benefit, but when a pushy factory person breaks his pick with a stubborn buyer, he's not likely to get back in very easily.

2. *Training.* As I mentioned in the last point, when you appoint the agent, you have a selling pro on the team from the day the contract is signed. No training is required other than to go over the product, its applications, and markets. Sure, this can be extensive in some cases, but at least you don't have to teach the person how to sell and wonder how long he will take to be productive. You can also hire an experienced salesperson for direct selling, but the costs can be out of sight.

3. *Time.* You can argue that the factory person will spend all of his time with your line, and you have a valid point. But, it's often an expensive buy. The agent is going to devote only part of his time to your line. But you should remember that if you choose the right agent, his other lines are going to provide an entree for your products that a factory person would find difficult to compete with. For example, if your line consists of products that range from inexpensive to expensive, it's often difficult to get the factory person to do justice to the low-end items. However, a good agent will cross-sell all of his products and move those nickel-and-dime products at the same time he's selling big-ticket items.

4. *Territory penetration.* Without doubt, an established agent can open and cover a territory for you much quicker and for a lot less money than a factory person. Even an experienced factory person has to poke around the territory before he can make it work. And this costs money, but it doesn't when you use agents. And don't forget that many agencies are multi-person operations, giving you far better coverage than one factory person could ever provide.

5. *Cost.* For most people, this is the most important reason for using manufacturers' agents, especially in these days of spiraling inflation, expanding territories, and ridiculous travel and living costs. The manufacturers' agent is paid for the sales made. If there are no sales, there are no commissions. Yes, it's possible to pay a factory person an incentive that can often be as motivating as full commission, but there are other considerations. For example, it's seldom possible for the factory to keep a direct salesperson in a territory with limited potential. Yet there is business to be obtained. And it's best gotten by an agent who can afford to make the calls because he's spreading his selling cost over a number of lines.

Today, many manufacturers that use direct salespeople spread the cost by expanding the territory covered. But how far can you go with this policy? Sooner or later, the factory person is going to be spread too thin building the new areas assigned to him and trying to hold his own in those he has already established. Don't forget the problem of fringes. An independent agent pays all of his expenses—including fringes such as insurance, pension, and so on—that have become so costly.

6. *Supervision.* For those of you who feel control is important, agents can be a problem. But for those who believe that good people should be left alone to do what they do best, agents are the best choice.

Think about your own business relationship. How much more productive could you be if others would just let you do your job without constant interruptions and hassles? If you think that this is too big a chance to take, that agents are going to take advantage of you because they are not under your direct control, think about your ultimate power. If the agent doesn't perform, you can replace him without the need to pay unemployment and go through all of the severance procedures you must with a salaried person. This may seem a bit crass, but you will find very few agents who abuse their privilege of personal freedom. Face it, they just can't if they're going to make money.

Perspective

As stated earlier, perspective is important when you make the decision to use manufacturers' agencies to sell your products. And it's important as you review your progress with them. Sure, the system isn't perfect. And there are times when agents just aren't the best answer. However, this wasn't written to convince you. It was written to put the process in perspective, to help you when you make the decision based on your best instincts but still aren't sure that you have gone the right way.

A few years ago psychologists found that when people bought a particular make of automobile, they did so with some reluctance. There were enough positive factors to push the decision in favor of the car bought, but the buyers were still not absolutely sure that they had made the right decision. This leads to an uncomfortable feeling, and when it does, most people stop reading the advertisements for the competitive cars and for reinforcement, concentrate on the ads placed by the manufacturer of the car they bought. It does reduce tension and make you feel comfortable.

You should be comfortable when you make the decision to use agents, but you shouldn't stick your head in the sand. To do yourself the most good and to help your agents do the best possible job for you, you should continue to read, ask questions, and examine all methods of selling. However, do it this way. Since your decision has already been made, you want to make it work and work well. Whatever you read or discover about other ways of selling should be applied to your decision to use agents. In other words, don't continue to evaluate the process. Seek out the winning techniques used by others, regardless of which way they sell their products, and try to help your agents do a better job by applying them when practical.

The topic of this section is perspective, and one of the most difficult areas of agent/principal perspective is the understanding of money. Looking at a territory you may see an agent being paid $60,000 or $80,000 in commissions. Over a martini you may let your mind wander and envision that the same agent is getting similar commissions from the other principals he represents. Telephone numbers, you say. The agent is getting rich, you think. You could put a salaried man in the field for much less.

But can you? Remember, that money you pay your agent isn't net. Out of the money, the agent must pay all of his expenses: travel, entertainment, automobile, office, clerical, insurance, plus all the other costs of doing business.

Now think about the salary you would pay a direct person. This is only the beginning. Consider his expenses and fringes. They are going to be high, no matter how short a leash you put on him. And don't forget that the fixed costs go on and on with a direct person—even when no sales are made. The only expense you have with an agency is when its salespeople sell something for you. The more money the agency makes, the more money you make.

Working with agents, as Harry Small found out, is not an automatic procedure simply because they are personally motivated and have their necks on the line daily. It's a program that requires support, counsel, understanding, and careful teamwork. When you take the time to fine-tune an agent organization, your life will be a lot easier—and a lot more profitable.

TEN ADVANTAGES OF THE AGENCY METHOD OF MARKETING

Manufacturers are worrying more and more about the impact that inflation is having on profits. In most cases their options for remedial action are few and filled with drawbacks. They can continue to raise product prices until they become uncompetitive; they can make the product for less by cutting quality and take a chance on losing their position in the market; they can buy new equipment that will produce the product for less, which usually requires a high capital outlay; they can stay competitive by cutting selling costs and administrative overhead.

Given today's economy and the outlook ahead, the latter option seems the most viable to many, and an increasing number of manufacturers are looking at it seriously. For the most part, they are cutting selling costs and attendant expenses by switching from direct salespeople to manufacturers' agencies or using agents to build volume by expanding their markets beyond its present boundaries. Here are some of the major reasons why agency sales are more attractive today than ever before:

1. *Provides predictable sales costs.* The manufacturer and agent agree in advance on a set commission. Good times and bad, it remains the same for the life of the agreement; with the direct sales method, costs may go sky high just when sales are floundering. Knowing the costs of sales up front—a percentage of the unit price—obviously eliminates many planning and pricing headaches.

2. *Lowers sales costs.* Current estimates are that the average direct salesperson costs the company $70,000 to $80,000 per year. To a base pay of $40,000, add automobile, travel expenses, insurance benefits, stock and profit-sharing plans, sick leave, vacation and holiday pay, and per diem expenses such as food, lodging, and customer entertainment. Covering these expenses currently requires a minimum of $30,000 to $40,000 per year.

If this is disturbing, take a look at still another sales expense: payroll taxes, workers' compensation insurance premiums, bonding fees, liability insurance protection, and so on. They will run between $25,000 and $30,000 over and above the salesperson's base salary and maintenance costs.

3. *Reduces administrative overhead.* Internal costs of administrating the sales payroll and furnishing various backup services for direct salespeople is reduced when the switch is made to sales agencies—and, of course, costs of administrative personnel will continue to rise.

4. *Eliminates the costs of training and turnover in sales personnel.* The training period for the agent will be minimal and largely related to learning about your product. Whenever you hire a new direct salesperson, you can estimate that he will, in the first six months, miss thousands of dollars in sales that an established agency would have brought in. There is no way to recover these sales once they are lost. And the manufacturer must pay his direct person a salary plus expenses long before he is able to produce.

5. *Gives immediate access to the market.* With the agency, manufacturers have an experienced sales team in the territory immediately. The agency people will be familiar with the area and have a number of good prospects ready to consider the new line.

6. *Provides a highly experienced, more aggressive salesforce.* Surveys show that today's agent is highly educated and trained and was a sales manager or a senior salesperson for a number of years before going on his/her own to establish or work for an agency. Since there is no base salary to rely on, agents can't afford to slack off at any time; they must sell to live, and therefore must make sales time count—for both the principal and the agency.

7. *Provides sales forecasting equal or superior to those of a direct salesforce.* The volume of future sales is no less predictable with agents than with direct salespeople; in fact, it may be better since so many of today's agents use sales analysis and forecasting methods that are often more sophisticated than those of the manufacturers they represent.

8. *Provides a broader sales context for your product.* Because he sells several related items (none of them competitive with yours, of course) the agent calls on a wider variety of prospects and customers and, in so doing, often finds applications for products denied the single-line salesperson.

9. *Adds marketing flexibility at less cost.* Sales agents can increase your volume by selling outside your present marketing territory—and you'll pay them only when they produce, by commission. Agents can also sell a new line without conflicting with your present sales organization. There are numerous ways that manufacturers' agents can fit into your marketing picture. Many companies use both direct salespeople and agents and find that the two salesforces are completely compatible.

10. *Increases sales.* Many manufacturers have switched from direct salespeople to agents and enjoyed increased sales. Further, it has been estimated that the individual agent sells approximately 70 percent more than the average company salesperson—due in large part, no doubt, to his independent status and a greater need to succeed.

Selling through agencies is not for every manufacturer. But it is the most efficient method of moving goods and services known, and it currently produces an estimated $250 billion of the nation's gross national product. It may well be the method—used in whole or in part—to give your company the cost effectiveness and added sales impetus it needs in these difficult times.

GUIDELINES FOR WORKING WITH MANUFACTURERS' AGENTS

Independent Sales Agents and You

1. Know your own sales and marketing goals.
2. Analyze each territory individually as to your marketing needs.
3. Examine your selling costs.
4. Determine the actual amount of control needed.
5. Decide how fast you must penetrate the market.
6. Decide whether you know your product and market well enough to provide the agency with leadership and guidance.
7. Know the trade practices affecting your marketing through a sales agency.

Selecting the Agency That Is Right for You

1. Establish standards for the selection of your agency's salesforce.
2. Plan the marketing functions that your agency must perform.
3. Develop a plan for hiring the proper agency.
4. Qualify and screen the agency by interview.

5. Make one person responsible for contracting with the agency.
6. Thoroughly investigate the agency's background.
7. Be sure that you and your agency are compatible.

Planning Your Work with a Professional Sales Agency

1. Thoroughly understand the functions of a professional sales agency and be certain that your employees understand them.
2. Establish a set of priorities for your sales agency. Make a list of the things that you want the sales agency to do first, discuss it with the agent, and agree on these priorities.
3. Devise a checklist of the professional qualities that you expect your agency to have.
4. Develop a plan for finding out how the prospective agency meets your professional standards.
5. Provide a program that will assure the maintenance of high standards of professionalism for both agency and principal by stressing cooperation and communication between your employees and the agency's employees.

Communications for a Mutually Profitable Relationship

1. Effective communications with your representatives is the result of a well-thought-out program.
2. Establish a clear-cut executive responsibility for your communications program.
3. Review your program frequently.
4. Consult with your key representatives and establish a representative council, and use it!
5. Look at the message, the emphasis, and the motivation when analyzing your communications.
6. Communicate with your agencies in the same way you do with full-time factory people.
7. Create an environment for good communications.
8. Make frequent phone calls to each agency.
9. Evaluate the rapport you have with your representative in light of the rapport he shares with his other manufacturers.
10. Balance your communications with memo, letter, newsletter, and phone call.
11. Encourage your representatives to complete the communications cycle by making it easy for them to respond to you.
12. Publish a list of the personnel your agencies can contact.

13. Talk over the effectiveness of your communications with your representatives.

Agreements

1. List all of the points that you want the contract with your sales agency to cover.
2. Discuss the contents of the contract with the agency, making sure that both parties agree.
3. Clearly indicate the products that you expect the agency to sell.
4. Stipulate the categories of trades to be covered.
5. Clearly spell out the territory to be covered.
6. Make sure that the commission rates are clearly stipulated.
7. A clear statement of the duration of the arrangement is legally necessary.
8. List the exclusive covenants that your agreement covers.
9. Indicate the dates on which the commission will be paid and any special arrangements, such as split commissions.
10. Indicate that the agency is an independent organization.
11. Include a complete termination clause.
12. Determine how disputes will be arbitrated.
13. A valid agreement must cover five points:
    a. Duration, defining length of contract
    b. Territory, exclusivity, house accounts responsibility
    c. Commissions, defining proper commission for activity and product
    d. Duties, defining activities of agreeing parties
    e. Termination, terminal commissions, length of tenure, extraordinary circumstances
14. Make sure that you have a lawyer who understands the relationship between a manufacturer and sales agency.

What to Expect from an Agency

1. Develop a policy manual.
2. Devise a workable marketing program with the assistance of your agents.
3. Set realistic goals that your agencies can meet.
4. Periodically review with your agencies what it is that you expect from them.
5. Make an exact list of what you expect from your agencies, other than selling.
6. Adjust your expectations to each territory's requirements and review them frequently.

What Agencies Expect from You

1. Seek a team relationship, rather than an I-am-boss philosophy.
2. Inform all principals and personnel of the nature of the principal/agency agreement.
3. Give the new agent a complete history of your company.
4. Tell the agent all you know about his territory before he takes over the selling responsibilities there.
5. Keep your agent informed about what is happening back at the plant.
6. Make the agent a partner when setting your goals.
7. Make every effort to understand what motivates each of your agents.
8. Make your relationship honest and open, as one professional to another.

Training Agency Personnel

1. Recognize that your personnel know more about the features of your product than anyone else.
2. Know exactly what you want the training to consist of.
3. Decide who will do the training.
4. Publish a specific training program.
5. Develop a separate plan for retraining your established agencies.
6. Decide how the training program will be financed.
7. Determine what tools you will need for the training program.
8. Plan a follow-up program.

Sales Tools

1. Plan useable, efficient marketing tools.
2. Establish follow-up to assure that they are used properly.
3. Assign responsibility for the development of sales tools.
4. Update existing sales tools to reflect your current programs and products.
5. Ask your representative council for assistance in developing sales tools.
6. Develop a proper method of distribution for sales tools and see that it is maintained.

Motivating Sales Agencies

1. Motivate your agencies by prompt and accurate communication.
2. Give prompt attention to requests, quotations, samples, and so on.
3. Consider your agency personnel as pros. Ask their opinions, and listen.

4. Schedule factory sales meetings with agency personnel at least once a year.
5. Schedule working visits with customers and agency personnel in their territory.
6. Establish the feeling of a joint venture for profit with your agency.
7. Recognize that your representative is an independent businessperson and is entitled to make a profit.
8. Make sure contests and incentives have clear-cut objectives.

Measuring Performance of an Agency

1. Establish reasonable goals with agency personnel.
2. Recognize what elements are measurable.
3. Recognize that sales quotas are not the only assessment of productivity of an agency.
4. Determine the agency program for new long-range business prospects.
5. Monitor the agency program for continuing personnel education and professionalism.

How to Unmotivate Sales Agencies and Lose Your Sales Volume

1. Be consistently late in quoting.
2. Set aside communications with the territory until a convenient time comes up.
3. Pay commissions late.
4. Call on or communicate with customers without informing the agency.
5. Spend excessive, unproductive time on territory visits.
6. Fail to recognize that your agent is your image in the territory.
7. Allow your inside people to feel competitive with your manufacturers' agents.

Index